Liz Jobey was Deputy Editor of *Granta* from 1998 to 2002 and Associate Editor of *Granta* from 2002 to 2009. Before that she was Literary Editor of the *Guardian* and Editor of the *Independent on Sunday Review*. She previously edited *Are We Related?: The New Granta Book of the Family*, and is Associate Editor of the *Financial Times Weekend Magazine*.

Jonathan Raban's writing has won many prizes including the National Book Critics Circle Award, the Heinemann Award, and the Thomas Cook Award. He is the author, most recently, of *Driving Home: An American Scrapbook* (2010). He lives in Seattle.

Also from Granta Books, edited by Liz Jobey

Are We Related?: The New Granta Book of the Family

THE NEW GRANTA
BOOK OF TRAVEL

Edited by
Liz Jobey

With an introduction by
Jonathan Raban

GRANTA

Granta Publications, 12 Addison Avenue, London W11 4QR

First published in Great Britain by Granta Books, 2011
This paperback edition published by Granta Books, 2012

1 3 5 7 9 10 8 6 4 2

ISBN 978 1 84708 330 2

Typeset by M Rules

Printed and bound by CPI Group (UK) Ltd, Croydon, CR0 4YY

MIX
Paper from
responsible sources
FSC
www.fsc.org FSC® C020471

Contents

INTRODUCTION

Jonathan Raban

Travel narratives are a loose and mongrel form, generally better liked by readers than they are admired by critics. Most are trite and forgettable – but one can say the same of most novels. Those that have survived to be recognized as classics (such as Darwin's *The Voyage of the Beagle*, Kinglake's *Eothen*, Dickens's *American Notes*, Twain's *The Innocents Abroad*, Apsley Cherry-Garrard's *The Worst Journey in the World*, T. E. Lawrence's *Seven Pillars of Wisdom*, Orwell's *Homage to Catalonia*, and Robert Byron's *The Road to Oxiana*) have little in common beyond their shared use of the first-person pronoun.

When, in 1983, Bill Buford put together the first 'Travel Writing' issue of *Granta*, he wrote an editorial in which he claimed that the Second World War 'marked the end of the great age of travel', but that the 1980s had seen a 'sudden' renaissance of the travel book. This seemed untrue to me at the time, and seems more untrue now. It was Evelyn Waugh who put it about (in the preface to his 1946 digest of his own 1930s travel books, *When the Going Was Good*) that real travel, as he and his contemporaries had known it, died in September 1939, and this second-hand idea was the thesis of Paul Fussell's nostalgic study of prewar travel writing, *Abroad* (1980). Yet even as Waugh was writing his slyly self-serving elegy on the travel book, publishers were already bringing out new examples of the genre that reflected the changed dimensions of postwar life.

First were the stories of audacious escapes from German prisoner-of-war camps, and hazardous journeys back to England, of which Eric Williams's *The Wooden Horse* (1949) is probably the most memorable example. Then came a flood of well-written escapes from Britain in the age of austerity under the Atlee government, with its ration books and severe currency regulations – escapes that were often undertaken in old, small, leaky boats, sailed by ex-servicemen who couldn't adjust to the constraints of civilian life at home. After *Maquis* (1945), a bestseller about his experience as an Englishman in the French Resistance, George Millar wrote *Isabel and the Sea* (1948) and *A White Boat from England* (1952) about his waterborne travels around southern Europe with his second wife. It was then so difficult legally to take sufficient money out of the country to pay for a trip abroad that an eager audience of British armchair travellers fell on such books as Lawrence Durrell's *Prospero's Cell* (1945) and Norman Lewis's *A Dragon Apparent* (1951), and lavishly contributed to Thor Heyerdahl's royalties on his international blockbuster *The Kon-Tiki Expedition* (1950).

Between the 1950s and the 1970s, a very various assortment of authors – including Freya Stark, Wilfred Thesiger, Patrick Leigh Fermor, James (later Jan) Morris, Dervla Murphy, Eric Newby, Peter Matthiessen, John McPhee, V. S. Naipaul, Ryszard Kapuściński, Colin Thubron, Bruce Chatwin, and Paul Theroux – published travel books that continue to be read today. But the named writers belong to no 'school', let alone to a developing literary tradition. One could see how the travel writing of those who were also novelists (Matthiessen, Naipaul, Thubron, Theroux) was tightly connected to their own fiction, but beyond that every travel book was so bereft of close relations that it had to make its way through the world as an orphan.

The interest of Buford's first travel issue of *Granta* lay not in his discovery of a non-existent renaissance but in his gathering together of seventeen disparate pieces, by writers from Gabriel García Márquez and Norman Lewis to Saul Bellow, Jan Morris, and Redmond O'Hanlon, and his invitation to read them alongside each other as examples of a distinct literary genre. More than twenty years later, Buford said of that issue, 'Finally I fucking did it': he'd taken an under-regarded form of writing and promoted it as the spanking-new cutting edge of contemporary literature. Editors need to be good hucksters, and Bill Buford was ferociously talented in that department. Today, rereading *Granta 10* (the magazine's most frequently reprinted issue), I'm struck by how well the pieces cohere, and, when read together, work as a plausible manifesto, as Buford meant them to do. He created an extended family of travelling stories and made them look as if they belonged to a tradition.

The 'I' of each story was not an eyewitness-reporter but a participant and character in the events described – the writer travelling as a private person, an amateur abroad. The stories were crammed with contingent details of the kind more usually found in novels than in newspaper reports – the weather, the smells, the behaviour of the dog at the edge of the picture – and they showed no respect for the usual journalistic priorities. 'A Coup' by Bruce Chatwin described how he'd been briefly imprisoned during a coup in Benin, but it's impossible to tell which coup this was (Benin went through a succession of them during the 1960s and 1970s). A 'head of State' is heard broadcasting over the radio, but he is not named, no date is given, we don't know what provoked the coup, and we don't learn whether or not it succeeded or was put down. Everything newsworthy is excluded from the story, which is about how a traveller becomes ignorantly entangled in the unexplained violence of someone else's country. Chatwin's piece, like others in the issue, is rich in total-recall conversations – a fictioneer's dialogue rather than the transcribed interview of the reporter. It's a memoir of an event that took place many months or years before, on which the memory and imagination of the writer have played at leisure. It also aims to satisfy the reader's hunger for reality with that sometimes unreliable guarantee of truthfulness, *I am the man; I suffered; I was there.*

All but three of the pieces in *The New Granta Book of Travel* were first published after Buford left the magazine in 1995, but his editorial spirit and his insistence that travel writing can be a vital literary form suffuse this book. The journeys here are impressively diverse. At one extreme, Redmond O'Hanlon mounts a Victorian-style imperial expedition, complete with a retinue of 'natives', into the heart of the undernourished and sickly Republic of Congo in search of an apocryphal dinosaur, but reconceives it as a self-mocking, and painfully self-aware, post-modern, post-colonial comedy. At the other, Kathleen Jamie takes a walk on a stretch of boggy moorland in her native East Ayrshire, where she has a chat with a farmer. Her journey lasts an hour or so, and covers perhaps a mile, but one need not travel far or for long to travel deep, and Jamie, as she interrogates the now inscrutable landscape of Airds Moss, where her ancestors once worked in coal pits long since filled and lived in 'rows' long since demolished, comes away with a lovely piece of psychogeography, exploring both how the people shaped the character of the land and how the land shaped the character of its human in-habitants.

Psychogeography, a word older than I thought (I just looked it up in the *OED*, and see that its earliest entry goes back to 1905), is one of the haunting preoccupations of this book. Intent reading of the landscape is both the traveller's primary means of personal navigation and his or her best tool for discovering the mindset of the strangers who live there. When the asylum-seeker, Albino Ochero-Okello ('Arrival'), is escorted by the immigration officer to the rail station at Gatwick Airport, where he catches a train to Victoria, it is the quiet orderliness of his carriage, the absence of pigs and chickens as fellow passengers, that first astonishes him, then triggers his initiation into the dauntingly strange new labyrinthine world of England. Situations like this turn us all into avid psychogeographers, as we scramble to decode what we can see and smell in order to establish our own place in a new world – which is partly why the merely contingent details of the traveller's experience loom so importantly in these stories. Everything, from the bucket on that step to that bird, glimpsed as a passing flicker of yellow, is a potential clue.

As often as not, we misread. Paul Theroux, revisiting his spell as a Peace Corps teacher in Malawi from a forty-year distance in 'Trespass', finds that he got every detail wrong when he embarked on what seemed to him at the time as a bold sexual adventure. The cockily assured traveller wasn't bold; he was weak, the dupe of the story, the vulnerable, ignorant American among people who were a lot wilier than he was himself. The encounter turns into a parable about late-twentieth-century American power: Theroux in Malawi, Rumsfeld in Iraq, McNamara in Vietnam – fearless Americans abroad who each emerged from his adventure as a gullible loser (a pity the others didn't gain from their travels Theroux's rueful self-knowledge).

Like Theroux's, several of these journeys are so private that they tremble on the edge of being metaphor or fiction. When James Hamilton-Paterson descends in a high-tech submersible to the bottom of the Atlantic Ocean in 'When I Was Lost', it's not the sea floor, or the two Russians who are also aboard the craft and whose language he can't speak, that command his and our attention, but the condition of lostness itself, of becoming temporarily detached from all communication with the outside world. Because his immediate surroundings are relatively exotic – somewhere off the West African coast, the windowed egg in which he's travelling, a little over three miles below the surface of the water – they serve to give a memorable shape to a mental state that one might as easily experience in the safety of one's own home. Or there's Robert Macfarlane's frigid, moonlit hike in 'Nightwalking', where the location is not named (though it seems to be the Lake District), and the solitary journey through the snow becomes a deeply private excursion into both lyrical rapture and optical science. Or there's Ian Jack's 'The Serampur Scotch', in which a homesick dream and a nimble memory stitch together a run-down industrial city in West Bengal and the landscape of Jack's Scottish childhood, fusing them into one.

When Ryszard Kapuściński drives through the tropical forest in Cameroon ('The Lazy River'), he travels in the company of one Polish Catholic missionary to meet another, and we're as much in the landscape of Polish expatriation as we are in equatorial Africa. Inside the car, as in the sorry rectories of the priests who guard their ramshackle churches, we're in the hum and buzz of Polish thoughts and preoccupations, while Cameroon – a religiose and superstitious land, where Catholicism has lost most of its adherents to rival belief-systems – jerks and slides past the window, a dark maze of vast mahogany trees. We're on a kind of Pilgrim's Progress, deep in Cameroon's equivalent to the Slough of Despond.

Just how much this story tells you about the reality of modern Cameroon is open to question: Kapuściński has been attacked for his factual errors and his mythmaking, most notably by the anthropologist John Ryle in a review of *The Shadow of the Sun* in the *TLS* in 2001. A posthumous biography, published in Polish and written by a critic who'd once been a protégé of the writer, was sneeringly titled *Kapuściński Non-Fiction*. It's clearly true that Kapuściński's Africa is not the ethnologist's Africa, or the Africanist's Africa, and that many of his accounts might find little favour with people who were born and live on the continent. Kapuściński's writing offers an explicitly partial, personal, often profoundly observant, and eloquent view of the world as it is seen by one travelling stranger from Poland. In being true to that vision, he failed to conform to the rules of 'objective' reporting, but that doesn't turn his work into 'fiction'. He was, rather, a consistently brilliant memoir-ist who readily acknowledged (as he does in the first paragraph of 'The Lazy River') the inherent unreliability of memory, even as he used that capricious faculty to shape and make sense of the remembered past.

W. G. Sebald's books were published as 'novels', though the word fits them poorly. Their journeys can be precisely mapped, and most of their characters are, or were, verifiably real people, as is their neurasthenic, history-burdened narrator. Sebald once said that he did not have the mind of a novelist and preferred to think of himself simply as a prose writer. His 'Going Abroad' shimmers with characteristically Sebaldian ambiguities. One would need his diary to check whether he 'really' went on leave in October 1980 from the University of East Anglia in Norwich, where he was a lecturer, in order to travel to Vienna, Venice, and Verona. Quite possibly he did, and he may well have made a daytrip from Vienna in the company of the schizophrenic poet Ernst Herbeck, who died in 1991, aged seventy. Casanova certainly existed. But what does one make of 'a Venetian by the name of Malachio, who had studied astrophysics at Cambridge', with whom Sebald falls into conversation at a bar? And so on. Travelling with Sebald is an arduous experience, in which one frequently becomes lost, mistaken, touched by paranoia, beset by sudden phantasmagoric visions, and assailed by seemingly haphazard memories and mental associations. His grave and formal prose conveys the turmoil of a mind in constant, troubled motion, and he returns 'travel' to its roots in 'travail' and to its ultimate Latin source, the trepalium, a three-staked instrument of Roman torture.

Why do we continue to need and read travel narratives? In part, obviously, because they can take us to places that we think of as being too dangerous, too difficult, or too expensive to visit for ourselves, and the intimate, novel-like form of travel writing allows us to vicariously experience parts of the world to which we've never been. So Wendell Steavenson, befriending a Sunni insurgent in Baghdad ('Osama's War'), Andrew Hussey, visiting the angry immigrant banlieues that ring Paris ('The Paris Intifada'), and Basharat Peer, returning to his homeland in 'Kashmir's Forever War', bring us close to the heart of conflicts that we've read about, but haven't seen or felt in such arresting and personal terms. These pieces fulfil travel literature's traditional function of escorting home-bound readers on journeys to strange and interesting worlds, and we read them in much the same spirit as our eighteenth-century counterparts kept up with the voyages of explorers like Anson and Captain Cook.

Yet remote people – to borrow the phrase with which Evelyn Waugh titled his 1931 travel book about Abyssinia and Kenya – are remote no more, but run the restaurant down the street, or the dry cleaner's, or the newsagent's; their children go to university; their churches are loud with music on a Sunday; they are part of the human swirl and diversity of the twenty-first-century city, as are we. Fewer and fewer of us live within cycling or even driving distance of where we were born. We're chronic travellers. We show up at airports as tourists, asylum-seekers, job hunters, transplants, conventioneers, college-goers, fugitives from bad marriages ... the list goes on and on. To live among strangers, in a culture not – or not quite – one's own, is so common a fate that deracination is a normal state of being in this migratory age. Meanwhile, people who remain attached to their roots, who persist in living in their ancestral villages, doing what their parents and grandparents did before them, have become objects of sentimental curiosity, the subject of nostalgic TV documentaries and rose-tinted travel books whose writers have quartered the globe in search of those rare folk who've stayed home.

So the travelling 'I', negotiating his or her way through unfamiliar territory – however close to where he or she lives – holds up a mirror to the life of the equally transient reader. We've grown painfully intimate with the traveller's afflictions, and we need the traveller's skills. I think one reason for the immediate international success of Sebald's *The Rings of Saturn* (1998), an account of a long, pensive hike around the East Anglian coast, was that readers instinctively recognized how Sebald, meditating on his twenty-year expatriation in England, was speaking directly to their own condition. They could share his sense of estrangement from the past and from his adopted country, as they could share his attempts to recover his identity by means of prodigious feats of memory and dreamlike leaps, connections, and coincidences. Sebald's intellectual pyrotechnics pleased the critics, but for the reader there was a more basic comfort to be had from a book that seemed to whisper on every page, *We are all exiles now*.

The travel narrative is not in decline, though it may have lost some of its prominence in bookshop window displays. Over the last few years, the first of this century, I've read haphazardly and for my own pleasure a bunch of new travel books. Some were by old acquaintances and contemporaries – Theroux, Thubron, O'Hanlon. Others were by writers who were new to me – Sara Wheeler, Rory Stewart (represented here by 'Dervishes'), William Dalrymple, William Fiennes. None are tales of amusing foreigners, told with resistible self-effacing humour by someone out on a lark, nor are they memoirs of escape into the exotic. All are serious (which in no way means they're short of wit) journeys through a mobile and disjunctive world. They explore the defiant survival and resurgence of belief in magic and religion, the fate of people crushed in the collision between one culture and another, the lives of civilians in countries that have been torn apart in our new wars. Each renders the writer's first-hand experience of the way we live now with intimacy and directness, and with a blessed freedom from the colonialist assumptions that scarred much travel writing of a generation or two ago. 'I' can be the most annoying pronoun, especially when used for self-mythologizing, but, handled well, it can carry with it both the glisten of authenticity and the sense of private communion between reader and writer.

Because the travel narrative has so often been treated with critical condescension, there's a need for an anthology like this one to remind us of the form's elastic range and literary potential. But be warned: anyone in search of magic-carpet rides to idyllic, far-flung destinations should put this book back on the shelf. There are no idylls here.

ARRIVAL

Albino Ochero-Okello

As I stood in front of the immigration officer, I was already worrying about my answers to the questions he might ask. What would I say if – when – he asked, 'Why are you coming here?' And what would I do if they didn't let me in? I tried to be calm and to compose myself.

I was asked for my passport which I had ready in my hands. I handed it to the immigration officer. The immigration officer took it and looked in it. He then asked me one of the questions that had been burning in my mind, 'What have you come here to do?'

I answered, 'I am a refugee. I have fled my country to seek political asylum here.' The immigration officer told me, 'Please could you go and wait inside that office over there. Somebody will come and attend to you soon.'

I went to the waiting room that he had pointed out. It was next to the interview rooms. When I went in, I saw two women sitting on the chairs, holding their children on their laps. They too were asylum-seekers, waiting to be interviewed.

In the same room there was also another woman sitting on a chair. She did not have a child. She was sitting by herself at the corner of the waiting room. From the look on her face, I could tell she was not at all happy and was worried about something. She looked very, very depressed. She was probably fearing the consequences of her fate.

In the same waiting room there was a young man sitting by himself on a chair. His face, also, showed no joy at all. The atmosphere was very tense. The young man's face looked familiar to me. I remembered that I had seen somebody looking like him before somewhere. 'Where have I seen this person?' I asked myself. I could not immediately recall. But then I suddenly remembered. It was in the aeroplane. He had been on the same plane that I had flown in on. We never talked to each other in the plane.

So when I saw him in the waiting room I smiled at him and went over. I smiled again and then greeted him. 'My name is Okello. I come from Uganda.' I told him, 'I have come here to seek political asylum.'

'How about you?' I asked him.

The young man introduced himself to me saying, 'My name is Frederick.' He went on, 'I, too, am from Uganda and have come here to seek political asylum.'

From Frederick's accent, I immediately knew that we were both from Northern Uganda where the civil war was raging on like wild bushfire. Frederick is an Acholi and I am a Langi, the two tribes that were being persecuted since the change of regime in Uganda. Although we were from different tribes, we spoke similar native languages. We could understand one another. Meeting Frederick was a great relief for me.

From the moment that we introduced ourselves and realized that we were in the same boat – fleeing from our country for our lives – we became friends. For me, to find a fellow Ugandan in the same situation as myself gave me a bit of confidence. But the confidence was not strong enough to prepare me for the interview with the immigration officer. I was still feeling very traumatized from the experiences that I had had at home.

After everyone else had been interviewed and cleared by the immigration officer, our turn came. The immigration officer called us to the side interview room. He was a young white gentleman. He was helpful and understanding. He was human in his work. It did not take him very long to realize that I was traumatized and he seemed sympathetic. I was unable to tell the immigration officer much about what had forced me to flee my country. The feelings and the pains of what I'd experienced at home were too much for me to bear.

Another thing that hindered me from telling all my problems to the immigration officer was that I felt he might be the eye of the government. Because of this, I felt withdrawn and insecure, anxious lest I emptied my heart to somebody who would betray me. Such mixed feelings are felt by many refugees when they first arrive abroad seeking political asylum. Not even afterwards, when I was given leave to remain, did I feel comfortable talking about it.

During the interview, the immigration officer asked me for my personal details. I gave them to him. He then asked for the details of my immediate family members, my wife and children. Again I gave them to him. Then he asked for details of my other relatives, my father, mother, brothers and/or sisters or of any other dependants. Again I gave them to him.

When this was done, the immigration officer asked me, 'Why have you come to the UK?' I replied, 'To seek political asylum.' Then I explained to him in brief why I had fled my country, Uganda.

I told him about the vicious problem of the political situation in Uganda whenever there is a change of regime. I explained, 'In Uganda, when the leader comes from your tribe, it may sound like a good thing. But in reality, you are in serious trouble when he is kicked out of power. It has become customary in Uganda that, when a ruler is kicked out, all the people who belong to his tribe and those of other tribes who were associated with his regime are held liable for the sufferings that other Ugandans are alleged to have experienced during his time in power. The vicious cycle of punishing the tribe-mates of deposed rulers for the sins committed under their ruler's regimes started when Idi Amin burst on to the arena of politics on 25 January 1971. Milton Obote, the president he overthrew in a bloody military coup – his tribe-mates suffered a lot. When Idi Amin's turn came and he too was deposed, his tribe-mates suffered the same fate, and the same happened after Obote's second presidency in May 1985 and General Tito Okello's military junta on 25 January 1986.'

When I told the immigration officer this, he sighed. 'Oh, I see. Is that how politics works in your country?'

'Yes. But I think similar things are probably happening in other parts of Africa too,' I answered.

'It sounds terrifying,' the immigration officer said. He then asked me, 'Can you tell me precisely why your life is in danger? Be more specific.' So I told the immigration officer my role in the politics of Uganda. I told him that I had been branch chairman of the political party of the civilian government that was overthrown by the military junta in May 1985. I told him that being in such a position at that time had put my life under constant threat. As I started to tell the immigration officer my story, tears began to roll from my eyes. The memory of what had happened to me and to my parents at home triggered this. The whole episode of what had happened at home started to come alive in my mind. I felt a big lump come into my throat but I swallowed it.

The worst memory was reliving the way my elderly, partially blind father was stripped naked by the so-called Karamojong cattle-raiders. They stripped my half-sister Maria too, and then shot her dead in front of him, before driving off with his 400 head of cattle. The thought of the fate of my family, the wife and three children that I had left behind, increased my grief. I thought about my daughter Gloria, who had been very unwell when I left, and whom I did not expect to live for very long.

With all these memories flooding back into my mind during the interview, I found it too much to say anything any more. I just sat there, my face looking down at the table and the tears rolling down my cheeks like a river.

It was impossible to continue with my story. I could not do it because of the lump in my throat. I felt like a dead person.

The interview had taken about twenty minutes. Although I did not tell the immigration officer who interviewed me everything, he seemed sympathetic and understanding.

When the interview had finished, I was asked by the immigration officer to go and wait in the waiting room. Inside the waiting room I saw my friend Frederick sitting on a chair. I asked Frederick if he had been interviewed. Frederick said he had. We stayed in the waiting room for about ten minutes and then the immigration officer came in. He told us to wait there for a few minutes more and he would be back soon.

The time was nine p.m. There were hardly any asylum-seekers left in the waiting room. The two women with their children had been cleared and had left. The third woman, the unhappy one, was still there. Now she did not just look unhappy, but she was crying. I could see the tears rolling continuously down her cheeks. 'What is the matter?' we asked her.

'I have been told that they are going to deport me back home,' the poor woman replied.

'Where do you come from?' Frederick asked.

'I come from Nigeria,' she replied.

'What have you come to do? I mean, why have you come here?' I asked.

'To seek political asylum,' the woman answered.

Before we could find out more from the woman about the circumstances that had led her to flee her country, another immigration officer came in. It was not the one that had interviewed me. This one was a woman. She smiled very broadly at us. Her smile restored some calm and a sense of hope in us. She came over and addressed us by our names, 'Okello' and 'Frederick'. 'Follow me,' she said. We picked up our small bags and followed her. Our bags had hardly anything in them. Mine contained two shirts, two pairs of trousers, and a towel. I had also brought a Bible.

We followed the immigration lady not knowing where we were being led to. My heart started to beat rapidly. I was thinking that this is it. We are being led back to the plane to be deported back to Uganda.

I whispered to Frederick in our own language, 'Hey, Frederick. Where do you think we are being taken to?'

'I don't know. Let us keep on praying to God,' Frederick answered. The immigration lady led us through the maze of the huge immigration building. We went through many doors and eventually ended up outside the building. There was a van waiting with two security guards. The immigration lady handed us over to the two immigration security officers. She told us that they were taking us somewhere to sleep. Then she said goodnight to us before going back into the huge building.

One of the immigration security officers opened the door of the van for us with his keys. The keys were chained to his waist. He told us to get in. We got in and sat down. The immigration security officer locked the door behind us and went and sat in front next to the driver. Then they drove off.

I asked myself, 'Why did they have to lock the door of the van?' I did not understand why. I didn't immediately realize that we were being locked up because we were detainees. The immigration security officer was just doing his job. Maybe he'd had past experiences where people who were being led away had jumped out of the van and escaped. They didn't want to take chances that might engage them in chasing about after runaway asylum-seekers.

After about ten minutes' drive, we arrived at the Beehive, as we later found out it was nicknamed. It was a detention centre. The van stopped in front of the gate. The security officer got out and unlocked the gate, and then came and unlocked the door of the van. He asked us to get out and follow him. We followed him inside and he handed us over to the duty officer.

We saw many people of various nationalities inside the Beehive. We later found out that the majority of them were political asylum-seekers. Some of the detainees were sitting in the living room watching the TV. Others were making telephone calls. Some were relaxing in their rooms with the doors open. Others were walking up and down the corridor.

I could not tell what the exact reasons for the other people being in the Beehive detention centre were. I didn't really want to know about other people's problems. I had my own problems to think about. So I minded my own business and did not bother to ask any of the detainees why they were there.

After a short wait, we were registered by the immigration officer on duty. He showed us to our room. It was a double bedroom, which we were to share. Nothing about the atmosphere of the Beehive made us feel we were being imprisoned or detained. It was quite clean and nice. After we had been shown our room we went and had hot showers. Then I sat on my bed and rested for a while. My bed was well made. I put my bag next to a small chest of drawers. I lay back on my bed for about twenty minutes feeling relaxed after the long, long journey from Uganda. I took out my Bible and read a chapter or two, thanking God for helping me over the first hurdles in my endeavour to gain political asylum. I felt lucky that I hadn't been thrown back on to the plane instantly and deported back to Uganda.

Later we went and ate some dinner. We had tinned fish, beef, potatoes, rice and an assortment of other dishes. I think the woman who served us the food probably guessed that we were new arrivals, exhausted and hungry. The strain showing on our faces was not solely from exhaustion and jet lag, but was also caused by worry about the future. We did not yet know what the future held for us.

Although the food was nice, my appetite had vanished. It had been wiped out by the fear of what would happen to me in the morning. The anxiety kept the adrenaline dripping inside me all the time. I was feeling hungry, but I could not eat.

When we had finished our dinner we went to the living room. We sat down to watch the TV. I watched the TV with my friend Frederick until about eleven p.m. We then decided to go and sleep. The weather seemed very cold that night. The detention centre veterans said it was warm compared with other times of the year, but we found it very cold. I had come from a country which has hot weather almost all year round. When the central heating went off at ten-thirty p.m. the centre seemed freezing to me.

Frederick and I said our prayers and then got into bed. But it took me a long time to fall asleep. Thoughts about my future here and the fate of my family back at home in Uganda kept me awake. I tried to forget all about it, but it was impossible. The thoughts kept on coming back again and again every time I closed my eyes. I struggled to make myself fall asleep. But it was all in vain. It was a long time before I eventually fell asleep.

The following morning we woke up, had a shower, said our morning prayers and then went and had breakfast. A short while later the immigration security men arrived. One of them came inside and asked, 'Where are Okello and Frederick?'

We answered, 'Here we are, sir.' The immigration security officer greeted us and then said, 'Please take your belongings and then follow me.'

We followed him outside, into the van. He locked the doors and drove us back to Gatwick Airport immigration office.

When we arrived at Gatwick Airport we had another interview. This time I was interviewed by a woman. She was a very kind woman, at once charming and good-looking. She said, 'So you are here to seek political asylum?'

I answered, 'Yes madam.'

'Do you have any family?'

'Yes madam.'

'Where are they?'

'I left them in Uganda.'

'Do you have any children?'

'Yes. I do have some children.'

'Do you have any intention of bringing them here to join you in the future?'

I paused for a moment and looked into her face. She smiled at me. She looked very positive and welcoming. I answered, 'Yes madam. If possible.'

The immigration lady then asked me about my family. I felt a big lump come into my throat and was choked by it. I could hardly speak a word. I immediately started to think about my little daughter Gloria, who had been ill when I left, Henry, Ronnie and their mother. Then I thought of my poor old father and wondered how he was coping with the loss of his daughter.

These thoughts brought tears flooding into my eyes. I wondered what could be happening to my family. Given the volatile security situation in Uganda when I fled, it could be anything. There was a ferocious civil war going on in the East, and in the North, where my family lived. Although the tears flooded into my eyes, my eyes were closed. My mind was far away back in Uganda thinking about the fate of my family.

When I opened my eyes, the immigration officer was looking at me. She asked me if I was all right.

'Yes madam. I think I am all right.'

She paused for a moment to allow me to compose myself. Then she asked me, 'Would you like to bring your family over to the UK?' I felt my hopes rise at her words. I thought that at least then they will not be left to suffer for long by themselves. I answered her, 'Yes madam, if it is possible.'

At that moment, the moment when the immigration lady asked me if I wanted to bring my family, I felt hopeful for the first time since arriving in Britain. 'Would you be able to help me?' I asked.

The immigration lady looked at me sympathetically. She smiled and then she said, 'Well. If you win your case, and after you have settled, if you would like to do it you may get in touch with me and I will give you contacts for some organizations that are set up to help refugees with their cases.' I then asked her, 'But madam. How will I contact you? I don't know your name and I don't have your telephone number.'

'Don't worry,' she said. 'Here.' She wrote her name and her office telephone number down and gave them to me. But unfortunately I later lost the piece of paper when the bed and breakfast hostel where I went to stay was attacked by an arsonist. Because we had to vacate our rooms in a hurry, I left it inside. I will never be able to thank that immigration lady enough, though. I would like to thank her again but I can't. Whoever she was and wherever she may be working now, all my best wishes for her.

After a brief interview, the immigration lady told me that my case would be passed on to a higher authority who would notify me in due course of the result of my application. But it may be some time before you hear from the Home Office, she told me. 'In the meantime, you have been given temporary admission into the country. This is a letter with some rules and regulations about your stay.

'Take it,' she said. 'Read it well when you reach the bed and breakfast hostel. And remember to keep it in a safe place. You will need to refer to it whenever you wish to contact us.' The immigration lady put the letter in an envelope and gave it to me. I took it and said, 'Thank you. Thank you very much.'

'You're welcome,' the immigration lady replied with a smile. Her smile was not only warm and welcoming, but also reassuring. The letter I had been given was a standard temporary admission pass. The same type of letter is normally given to every political asylum-seeker entering Britain.

After she had given me the letter, the immigration lady made a few telephone calls. She was calling various bed and breakfast landlords, trying to find a free room. After making a few calls, she found one who had spare rooms for us. I listened to her talking on the phone: 'Yes. Yes. That's fine,' she said. 'Yes, two of them. That's OK. I'll send them over right away.'

I could hear the voice of the other person at the end of the line. It was a man with an Asian accent. He asked the immigration lady, 'Do the two lads speak a little English?' The immigration lady reassured him, 'Don't worry about that. That's not a problem. They both speak very good English.'

'Did you say they're coming today?' asked the voice on the phone.

'Yes, they'll be coming today. They should be there in a few hours' time.'

'Good! I'll be waiting for them, then,' the landlord said.

But the few hours that the lady had said it would take us to get to the bed and breakfast hostel turned out to be a rather optimistic estimate.

Smiling at me with that reassuring smile, the immigration lady said to me, 'You will soon be OK. I have found a place for you to live.'

'Oh. That is very kind of you,' I replied wearily. Although it was very difficult for me, I managed to splash out a little smile. But inside I still felt traumatized, and worried about my future.

The immigration lady told me to wait for a few minutes. She then went to another room to interview Frederick. When she came out, she said, 'Okello, please follow me.' She took me to where Frederick was waiting. She said, 'OK. I have found a place for the two of you. It's a bed and breakfast hostel in west London.'

We thanked her and she gave us a photocopied map showing the location of the hostel. We hadn't realized that it would be up to us to navigate our way to the bed and breakfast hostel by ourselves. After giving us the map, she gave us some train tickets. She said, 'And here are your travel tickets for the train. They are one-day Travelcards. If you want to travel for the whole day with them, you can. You can use them up until twelve midnight.'

'Thank you,' we said.

She said we could travel with the tickets up to twelve midnight. But even if we had wanted to use our one-day Travelcards to travel for the whole day, where would we have gone? We were new to the country. We hardly knew anybody. Let alone where the bed and breakfast was that we were booked to go and live in. We did not know where it was or how long it would take us to reach it from Gatwick Airport.

Anyway, at this stage we did not plan to travel anywhere until midnight with our Travelcards. What we felt instead was a feeling of relief. It became apparent that we were not going to be thrown back into the frying pan after all. The lump which had been stuck in my throat since the day before when I arrived in the country slowly began to ease and melt away.

The immigration lady explained to us how to get to the bed and breakfast. 'I will put you on the train from here and you will have to go up to London Victoria station. When you arrive at London Victoria, you may change either to the Victoria underground line, then to the Piccadilly Line, and get off at Hammersmith. Or you may take the District Line from Victoria up to Hammersmith, if you prefer.

'Whichever line you choose to travel on, take it up to Hammersmith station and then get off. When you come out of the station take the number 266 bus. It will take you near to where the bed and breakfast hostel is.

'Alternatively,' she said, 'you may take the Victoria Line and change to the Central Line, then go up to Shepherd's Bush station. When you arrive there, get out and take the number 207 bus. The number 207 bus will also take you up near to the bed and breakfast hostel where you are supposed to go and stay.'

The explanation given by the immigration lady was difficult to master. However, we listened to it all very carefully. Imagine all those details given to be mastered by the newly arrived asylum-seekers. People who haven't been in the country before. People who have not come under any normal circumstances and therefore are far from relaxed, people who may be thinking that they're being followed or who're filled with uncertainty about their future. We decided that the immigration lady must have taken it for granted that, because we were highly educated, we would experience no difficulties in finding our way through the meandering maze of the city to the bed and breakfast hostel in west London. But the maze to the bed and breakfast hostel was too complicated for us to follow. It was a very big challenge for us to undertake.

The immigration lady finished her briefing about the location of the bed and breakfast hostel and took us down to the trains. At the platform there was already a train waiting to leave in a few minutes' time.

The immigration lady saw us on to the train and then she wished us good luck. She waved goodbye to us for a few seconds, smiling, and then she went back to her office. When she left, I asked Frederick, 'Do you think we will make it?'

Frederick answered, 'I don't know. Anyway, we will try.'

We sat in the train for a few minutes waiting for it to leave. I closed my eyes and started to contrast the trains back at home in Uganda to the British train that we were currently sitting in.

When I'd heard the immigration lady talk to us about taking the train, I'd said to myself, 'By the train?' I thought I had said it to myself. But it seemed I'd said it aloud and the immigration lady heard me. She answered, 'Yes. By the train. You will have to travel by the train.'

I must've looked downcast. But she reassured us that it was OK. She said, 'It is faster by train than by bus. It is the easiest and quickest means of transportation here in the UK.'

'Is it?' I asked.

'Oh yes, it is.'

I exclaimed at the idea of travelling by train because back at home in Uganda people hardly travel that way. I started to think of the hazards, the inconveniences and the difficulties that people who use the train there always face. Travelling by train in Uganda means travelling in the company of an assortment of livestock including cattle, goats, pigs and chickens – just to mention a few – and not forgetting a range of agricultural produce. So I thought that travelling by train here would also be full of such hazards. Fortunately it didn't seem to be the same case here in the British train.

The first impression was marvellous. The seats were smart. There was no overcrowding. There were no domestic livestock nor agricultural produce being ferried inside it alongside the passengers. The condition of the Gatwick Express train did not turn out to be as we had feared.

We quickly realized that we were in a new world, Great Britain. We were in a developed world, much more developed than our country, Uganda, which had been ravaged by brutal civil wars. It was inevitable for us to make such comparisons and contrasts. Without them it would have been difficult for us to understand the full meaning of development when people spoke of it.

THE CONGO DINOSAUR

Redmond O'Hanlon

The boy lay stretched out on a low wooden platform under an orange tree. His father sat on a stool beside him, bending forward, chanting at the top of his voice, over and over again, 'I've lost my child. My poor son. My son is dead.' Twenty or so women, sitting on mats behind him, rocked back and forth, wailing in chorus.

I squatted nearby on the roots of a mango tree. I was with the principal companion of my journey through the forests of the northern Congo, Doctor Marcellin Agnagna, the Cuban-educated head of the Ministry for the Conservation of Fauna and Flora, and two of his young nephews: Nzé, our cook, whose left eye, in moments of relaxation, pointed to the sky while his right one was focused on the ground, and Manou, too weakened by attacks of malaria to be much more than my quiet informant. Djéké was by far the largest, best-ordered, most advanced village I had seen in three months of travel: you could walk for almost two kilometres through its plantations of manioc and bananas, cacao and plantains; it even had a little shop. And having bought coffee and sugar for the mourners, a goat for the father and a winding-sheet for the corpse, I felt I had a right to ask a question.

'What happened?'

Doctor Marcellin put a finger to his lips and shook his head at me.

Mourners continued to arrive. I spotted Léonard Bongou-Lami, Commandant of the People's Militia of Djéké (and my temporary translator from Bomitaba into French).

'This is the right way to do things,' I said lamely. 'It's wonderful to share your grief with everyone. We don't deal with death like this in England.'

The Commandant turned on me. 'But the father,' he said, pausing to spit, 'killed his own children. He did it himself.'

'What do you mean?'

'He killed his wife, *and then all five children*. He's a sorcerer. We're all frightened of him.'

Without looking back, the Commandant walked off and joined another crowd of onlookers.

Around dusk, a group of men pushed past, bearing an eight-foot-high drum. They were followed by a gaggle of boys carrying chopped wood who made small fires round the centre of the enclosure. Bats as big as blackbirds appeared, their wings creaking as they laboured over us. The fire burst into life and the men picked up the drum and held it with its top towards the flames to warm its skin. Night fell with equatorial abruptness.

Doctor Marcellin, whom I'd sought out in Brazzaville and persuaded to come with me because he was the one man who swore he'd seen the Congo dinosaur, Mokele-mbembe – three hundred yards out in Lac Télé, with a hippo-sized body and a long neck, a brown face and black back (on which the sun glinted) – took the pipe I'd given him out of his trouser pocket, filled it from our last remaining tin of tobacco, lit up and inhaled deeply. His mistress of two nights, young, eager and beautiful, came and sat between us. She gazed at him in the firelight.

An old man appeared, put his head back, held out his arms and shouted into the darkness towards the forest.

'Who's he calling?' Marcellin asked the girl to translate.

'He says that his grandson Kotéla loved to dance,' she whispered, 'so we must show how much we miss him by dancing. And he calls to the ghosts in the forest: "If god took young Kotéla, then god took him; but if young Kotéla died because of sorcery, then, spirits, search out the sorcerer and kill him now."'

Men formed one half of a circle, women the other. The drum, judged to be ready, was set up in the centre and a platform brought for the drummer. He produced a massive sound; another man beat the trunk of the drum with two short sticks, and the dance began. The two nephews, Nzé and Manou, drifted back to our guest-hut, and Marcellin, his mistress and I joined the dance: five steps forward, a half turn to the left, a half turn to the right, five steps back and on round the circle. After two or three hours, during which we danced the *mozambique*, the *mobenga* and the *ekogo*, Marcellin said goodbye to the girl and then we, too, made our way back to where we were staying.

Children ran past us, carrying lemons to their parents at the dance, up late with the licence of the fiesta, wide-eyed and quick with excitement. I felt, walking under this moon and these unfamiliar stars, beneath the tiny orange glow of the Russian observation satellite hanging stationary in space above the Marxist People's Republic of the Congo, that Djéké itself was a village in an idyll, a place where nothing bad could happen.

In the guest-hut Doctor Marcellin lit a candle, and I took out the gourd of palm wine I had bought that afternoon. Nzé and Manou were waiting for us.

'Redmon,' said Nzé, pleased with himself, skew-eyed and sweaty in the Cuban Army fatigues and peaked cloth cap of the People's Militia of Dongou, 'I need 500 CFAs.'

'Not yet, you don't,' said Doctor Marcellin. 'You'll make our supper first.'

I got the 500 francs (the equivalent of one pound) from my bergen pack. A pound a night was the going rate.

'But Nzé,' I said, 'I've only just cured the gonorrhoea you got in Enyellé. That was the last twelve Amoxil.'

'Your Western medicine didn't help at all,' said Nzé, picking up the pot of our leftover monkey stew and taking it outside to place on the fire. 'I was discharging for three days afterwards.' He turned round for greater emphasis, flicking his free hand down his crotch to mime a stream of falling pus. 'And then when I drank the bottle of bark-water my brother gave me, it went at once. He made it in the way our grandfather taught him. That's what did it. That's why I'm cured.' He squatted down, arranging the fire. 'My grandfather was the greatest sorcerer in Dongou, Redmon. Even more powerful than the Chief of Dongou. The Chief of Dongou visited my grandfather once, in the spirit way, but my grandfather won the battle and took away the Chief of Dongou's clothes – and in the morning he made the Chief of Dongou walk in his sleep from one end of Dongou to the other and back again, in the nude, with his dick standing up. *That* taught him a lesson.'

'It's not as funny as you think,' said Manou. 'Take that poor father. They say he killed his son, but that's not so. He did only one thing wrong. Long ago, he arrived at his uncle's wedding without a present of drink or money. His uncle was a sorcerer, so he said: "Right, when you get married and have children of your own, I'll kill them all. I'll wait until they're fourteen or fifteen years old, each one, and then, when you love them more than anything on earth, they'll die slowly in front of you."'

'That's not what I heard,' said Doctor Marcellin. 'I heard that the father *did* kill his own children, but he didn't mean to do it. He visited a *féticheur* to get a fetish for his own protection. That was all right. But then he asked for a fetish that would make him a great fisherman. And that was his mistake. "Put so-and-so in a bottle," said the *féticheur*, "something that you really value, and then throw it in the river." And that's what he did. But then his child died so he went to a second *féticheur*, who said "Yes, well what did you expect? When you cut those locks of hair from all your children's heads and put them in that bottle and threw it in the river you threw away their futures. It's simple. All you have to do is get your bottle back at once, or all your children will die." But it wasn't simple. The river here is a blackwater river, and you can't see into it, and he spent three months trailing the mud with his nets and found nothing. And now his last child is dead.'

'So what do you think it is really?' I said. 'Hereditary leukaemia? Haemophilia? Something like that?'

'You and your white man's questions,' said Doctor Marcellin. 'That's not what really *matters*.'

Nzé doled out the monkey stew and a piece of *fufu* (manioc stodge) into our mess tins.

'So, Marcellin, why don't you want to go to Boha and Lac Télé? Is that a matter of sorcery too?'

'You don't understand, Redmond. You don't understand the risk I'm taking. They'll murder me. Boha is a village unlike anywhere else. They hunt the gorilla and the chimpanzee, in preference to all other meat. They use special spears that are twelve feet long. The young men provoke the male gorilla, until he charges on to their points.' He jumped to his feet, yelled and impaled me in the chest with an imaginary spear – with excessive enthusiasm, I thought, for the head of conservation. Calming himself, he sat down again. 'There are all kinds of problems. The young men loyal to the traditional chief kill the men loyal to the Party. Almost all the men of Boha have been put in prison at Epéna and locked up for five days – the punishment for a murder that is domestic or a matter of sorcery. The Political Commissar of the People's District of Epéna put a policeman at Boha once, but he ran away. We also will run away.'

'Why?'

'Because they think I put their *Chief* in prison. And that's a terrible insult to them. They've taken a blood-oath to kill me if I ever set foot in Boha again. I have one friend there – the mother of a young man who works for me in the department in Brazzaville. She sent a warning to my mother in Impfondo.'

'How come you put the Chief in prison?'

'I didn't. After my last expedition, the all-Congolese expedition, when we saw the dinosaur, I wrote in my report that the Chief made us pay 75,000 CFAs to enter his forests. I had to, Redmond; I had to account for the money I spent to our minister in Brazzaville. And when the Political Commissar of the People's District of Epéna saw the report he said that the Chief of Boha must be taught that he does not run an independent state. So he called in the army and they went downriver with big outboards and forty soldiers and captured the Chief at dawn when he was still asleep with his wives and they took him back to Epéna and locked him in the People's Prison for three whole days.'

'But it's ridiculous,' I said, suddenly inspired. 'You're the head of conservation for all of the People's Republic of the Congo. You're a very important chief in your own right. You can't pretend to be in charge and then have areas you're too frightened to visit. We've got to see your dinosaur. We'll leave in the morning.'

'I've had enough,' said Marcellin, jumping to his feet. He was rigid with anger; for a moment I thought he was going to hit me. 'I'm leaving,' he said. 'I'm going to see my girl.'

Nzé drew the door aside, but Marcellin, even in his rage, remembered to return to his pack, reach into its side-pocket, and pull out the bottle of aftershave I'd given him in Brazzaville. He sprayed himself inside the front of his shirt, replaced the bottle, and, in a cloud of scent, disappeared into the night.

Nzé peered round the door. Satisfied that Marcellin had really gone, he lunged at the pack, snatched the magic bottle, sprayed himself so hard he sneezed, tucked it back, mimed a few practice thrusts up against the wall, announced that 'He's not the only one who has a woman!' and followed Doctor Marcellin into the darkness.

Manou sat with his head in his hands, his palm wine untouched.

'What's the matter?' I said. 'You don't believe it, do you? You don't think there's any danger?'

'Of course it's dangerous,' said Manou, unusually quiet, even for him. 'They'll kill you, too.'

'Why me? It's nothing to do with me.'

'It's everything to do with you,' said Manou. 'It's a white man's problem. It's white people like you who cause all the trouble.'

'I don't understand.'

'It's simple. Marcellin wants white people to come here to see Lac Télé. He says his minister will set up a national park and make him rich. He told the men of Boha that if they didn't like it he'd call in the army and have the village moved somewhere else. But the men of Boha can't move. The lake is three days' walk away in the forest, it's true, but that is where the spirits of their ancestors live. If the villagers are moved any further, everyone will die. The ancestors will no longer protect them.'

Manou stopped and said nothing. Seeing that he was starting to fall asleep, I decided that it was probably the right time to go to bed myself. I blew out the candle, unzipped my tent, climbed through the opening, strapped on my head-torch, caught a couple of mosquitoes which had followed me in, put fresh Savlon and plasters on the tsetse-fly bites that had ulcerated on my swollen legs and ankles, and, from a plastic bag in the document wallet in the lid of my pack, drew out a sheaf of photocopies I had made in Oxford. They were chapters from Roy Mackal's *A Living Dinosaur? In Search of Mokele-Mbembe* (1987). Mackal himself had never reached Lac Télé, but Doctor Marcellin Agnagna, with an all-Congolese expedition, later made another attempt. And that one had been successful.

2

At first light, our tethered cockerel crowed five feet from my head, his challenge at once answered by the local champion with a burst of outrage from the other side of the door. I put on my boots and binoculars, unzipped the tent, stole a few spoonfuls of last night's (already left-over) male-monkey stew (still tasting of unwashed crotch), clattered back to the door, eased the cockerel aside with my foot and took a deep breath of the morning mist. Some mad woman laughed at me.

Confused, I traced the hysterical chuckle to the top of a straggly tree. It was a kingfisher. A small blaze of iridescent azure in the grey dawn. He must be the Congo blue-breasted, I decided, the freak kingfisher who never fishes, lives in the forest, makes his home in termite nests in high trees and eats only frogs, scorpions, crabs, whip-scorpions, cockroaches, beetles, mantises, toads, spiders and millipedes. Deciding, in his turn, that I was too big to be interesting, he gave a final descending laugh of disappointment, dropped sharply out of the tree and flew off fast and low.

Crouching behind a bush by the manioc plantation, I looked up from a spasm of diarrhoea in time to spot another misfit curving overhead towards the river, the vulturine fish eagle, the only (mainly) vegetarian bird of prey in the world (it has a passion for palm-nuts). And walking back, I disrupted the sex-life of the pin-tailed whidah, a sparrow-sized bird with a white stomach, a blue back and bright red beak – and a tail of two long black plumes, which he held beneath him while jerking rapidly to and fro, fluttering his wings, a little bundle of feathers in the last stages of ejaculatory passion. Three dull brown females pecked about on the ground beneath him, unimpressed by the frantic adulation a yard above their heads.

Back in the hut, Manou was listlessly packing the cooking pot and mess tins into an old manioc sack.

Our paddlers arrived along with my translator, the Commandant, and I handed out paracetamol, plasters and fifteen glossy white quinine pills to everyone. Together we carried our baggage down to the creek that led on to the main stream of the Likouala-aux-Herbes River.

The Commandant stowed our packs in the middle of his dugout; Manou gently placed the wicker cage containing our cock and two hens in the bow; and we settled down on the short scuffed grass of the bank to wait for Nzé and Doctor Marcellin.

Marcellin was not his usual self. He came down the path, barking questions like a Nazi. Why had we left the hut so early? Where was his breakfast? And why, he wanted to know, stepping into the dugout, was his pack at the bottom of the pile? Why were there no duckboards? What if his shirts got wet? Who had done this to him?

Marcellin, I thought, does not want to leave his young girl. But then it gradually dawned on me, as I watched him yank his pack to the top of the pile, scrabble at a pocket, pull out his Walkman, ferociously snap in a Bob Marley tape, cover his ears with the headphones, sink back against the baggage and close his eyes: Marcellin was afraid. He really did think there would be trouble at Boha.

The north Congo floodplain of the Likouala-aux-Herbes is a narrow savannah; the high forest began again a mile or so to either side of us. At first we were all as silent as Marcellin, but then the three boys began their paddling songs, the rhythm in time with the long blades cutting down and thrusting back in the water.

We passed a long beach of white sand, almost too bright to look at in the sunlight – perhaps part of the friable white sandstone that formed beneath the great lake which filled the Congo basin some 225 million years ago, when you could see dinosaurs every day of the week. And upriver we came to a low overhang of dark grey soil and a stretch of scrubby trees.

Small blue-green birds, blue-cheeked bee-eaters, were perched on the branches, fussing over their long tail feathers. They flew out fast like swallows, low across the water, and then up and above our heads towards the rough grass of the savannah, their undersides glowing orange in the reflected light.

We passed a small village hidden behind its oil palms on a piece of high ground, which the Commandant said was called Ipongui. Whenever there was the slightest hint of another human being in the landscape – the splash of a paddle up a creek, smoke from the roof of one of the lone huts on the bank – the Commandant shouted a greeting in Bomitaba, and news was exchanged for a good hundred yards or more at an ever-increasing volume.

In a stretch of comparative quiet, by a shore of white sand, I recognized a bird wading carefully in the shallows. It was brown all over, rook-size, but its head was remarkable: a big, broad bill balanced by a triangular crest at the back gave its head the shape of an anvil – a hammerkop. It walked slowly, concentrating on the water surface as it shuffled its feet, stirring up the sand to flush out small fish, molluscs and beetles, letting us come very close before it rose jerkily into the air on surprisingly broad wings, its head stretched out, light and silent as an owl. The hammerkop was impossible to classify. It was thought to be related to the herons, or possibly the flamingos, or even the shoebill; but recent egg-white protein analysis put it closest to the storks, while the parasites on its skin related it to the plovers, snipes and sandpipers. And its behaviour was all its own: the bird was known to throw some spectacularly open-minded parties. Eight to ten hammerkops would be invited, some unattached, some married, some divorced. They would turn up near the nest, everyone would pair off and they then ran in circles side by side until an orgy of (technically speaking) false mounting took place. No actual rubbing together of his everting and her receiving opposable vent was allowed in public, but you couldn't complain. The soliciting bird crouched down, the other mounted and balanced on top with open wings; and then, both of them shivering with the erotic charge of it all, they would press their tails together, the whole party accompanied by loud duets known as *yip-purring*. Males mounted females, females mounted males, males mounted males, and only lesbians were disadvantaged.

Just as I was thinking about all this sex, and wondering why, as far as I could remember, so few birds actually had a penis (only the ostrich, the rhea, the emu, the cassowary, the tinamou, the duck and the screamer), the Commandant swung the bow of the dugout into a small tributary, and I realized that we had arrived at Boha.

3

'Quick!' said Marcellin, as we put in to a landing stage, grabbing the gun from the bottom of the dugout and bounding past me, 'get up into the village and in among some women and children. And don't get separated.' His white basketball boots sprayed pebbles off the sandstone path. 'Nzé! Manou!' he shouted over his shoulder. 'Stay right by me! Commandant! You and the paddlers. You follow with the packs. You must stay for one hour. Just one hour. Redmond will pay you in one hour.'

Nzé, Manou and I ran hard and caught up with Marcellin at the top of the path. He had his arm round an old man, outside the open lean-to of a cooking hut. 'Bobé!' he shouted, not letting go, 'Bobé, my old friend!'

Bobé, bemused but happy, smiled, showing his gums. Barefoot, he wore torn, dirty white cotton trousers rolled up his shins and a red-and-white-striped pyjama top opened to his bony chest and wizened stomach.

A group of children, attracted by the noise, appeared in the space between the huts.

'*Mondelé!*' they shouted, '*Mondelé! Mondelé!*' (White man! White man!)

The children pressed around us, and the boldest, a boy of five or six, held up a grasshopper for my inspection. He was pinching it by its back legs, between his index finger and thumb, and as I bent down to admire it – noting the light green of its rear end, the yellow on its back beneath a slight all-over froth, the white spots on its red, black and yellow head – he jammed it up into my nostril. I leaped backwards, my sinuses full of acrid musk like the pong of a dead stoat. Warning colours, I thought ruefully, in between sneezes; this must be one of those forest grasshoppers that makes such a stink of itself that no sensible predator goes near it. The children jumped up and down with delight, the boy turned away with one of those half-private smiles that only personal triumph produces – and suddenly they all scattered away between the huts.

Four broad-shouldered young men were swaggering towards us down the right-hand path. I walked up to shake their hands but they brushed past me and surrounded Marcellin. Nzé, who had seized the gun, pointed the barrel at their feet. He patted the stock. Marcellin did not look reassured.

'You will come with us,' said the leader in French. 'We will talk at the table of the Vice-President of the People's Village Committee.'

In the silence, while Marcellin apparently considered the offer, I found myself staring at their T-shirts. The leader, heavy-faced, wore a plea from the World Wildlife Fund across his massive chest, '*Ne tuez pas les gorilles et les chimpanzes*'; a string round his cotton trousers held a dagger at his side, about fifteen inches long. One of his lieutenants sported a blue vest with 'Woods Hole Oceanographie Institution' emblazoned on the front; another had 'Harley-Davidson' on a green background; and the third displayed a cartoon of a man eating popcorn, ogling a big-breasted woman flopped beside a swimming-pool with her husband approaching stage left.

The legend read, 'IT'S A NICE AFTERNOON FOR BILL, BUT BE CAREFUL, FIGHT MAYBE COME.'

Disappointed that Boha was obviously so visited, I started matching up the intruders to their T-shirts: the first three would have been left here by the American Philip Lobel of Woods Hole who, according to Marcellin, claimed to have discovered forty-five new species of fish in Lac Télé; and the last came perhaps from the Japanese dinosaur-hunting expedition of 1988. The Commandant and his nephews appeared, laden with baggage. Marcellin gave a nod, and we followed Doubla into the village.

The village was much smaller than Djéké, with winding paths leading away from one short broad street. There were fewer gardens and only the occasional hut of clay bricks among the mud and thatch.

I paused to watch a middle-aged man, his head shaved, working at his kiln. He was building a new house in his enclosure and, sweating, barefoot, in only a pair of ragged shorts, was feeding logs into a clay block furnace that had been plastered with mud to retain the heat. He looked round and gave me a friendly flash of gappy white teeth. Simultaneously I felt a little hand creep into mine.

The bold boy, now without his grasshopper, beamed up at me. He looked new, ready for life, as yet untouched by disease of any kind, and he talked fast in Bomitaba about something so special and pressing that my inability to reply seemed not to matter. Marcellin and the others had disappeared, so I allowed my new guide to pull me along a path branching off to the right. His gang, now swollen to a band of twenty or so, followed at a respectful distance, still chanting 'Mondelé! Mondelé!' and pointing at me as proof.

A little further on, we came to the object of our quest. The boy tugged at my hand, and we all processed into a small enclosure and up to the entrance of a hut where, suspended beneath the shelter of the overhanging thatch, a green fruit-pigeon sat bedraggled in a cage.

The boy talked to it, and the pigeon cocked its head and listened. One of the children eased a piece of papaya through the bars. The pigeon was green all over except for a purple patch on its shoulder, the black on its wings and a blue tail. Quiet, mating for life, it is so sensitive that it is reputed to die of shock at the sound of a gun. I was just beginning to feel sorry for it when the boy yanked at my hand again and we were off round the corner and down a little incline to another hut. Five young children and two women sat on a raffia mat. They smiled. Behind them stood Marcellin, Nzé, Manou, the Commandant and his paddlers.

'Where the hell have you been?' said Marcellin.

The boy let go of my hand.

Marcellin moved forward and stood over me. 'I thought I told you not to get separated,' he hissed into my ear. 'Just do what I say, will you? You do not understand. *You are now out of your depth.*'

And you are out of your mind, I thought crossly, until a piece of genuine fear moved in my stomach like the first warning of oncoming dysentery. Four young men in torn camouflage fatigues stood motionless under a safou tree twenty paces away. They held outrageously long spears, the beaten-iron blades tilted at the ground, the shafts stretching way up and back over their shoulders.

'Where did they get those uniforms?'

'From the Japanese,' said Marcellin without looking round, 'on my last expedition. But please, Redmond, *no more questions.*'

A thin, nervous, middle-aged man stepped out of the hut.

'Are you ready?' he said.

'Yes, *Monsieur le Vice-President,*' said Marcellin. 'Now we can talk.'

Nzé, looking uncharacteristically serious, stood guard by the door with the gun. The Commandant and the paddlers sat down in the shade and Marcellin, Manou and I filed into the hut behind the Vice-President.

I took the chair by the door, the sunlight bright and hard on the baked ground outside. Marcellin sat beside me, and the men in the exotic T-shirts entered. Their leader, the giant wearing the plea for gorillas and chimpanzees, placed himself at the head of the table. The Vice-President sat at the other end. The giant demanded to see our papers. Marcellin unzipped his money and document pouch and produced our *Ordre de Service* from the Secretariat General de L'Economie Forestière and our *laissez-passer* from the Ministère de la Recherche Scientifique et de L'Environnement. They were passed from hand to hand around the table.

The giant turned his heavily lidded eyes on me. 'Your papers are in order,' he said, as if nothing else was.

'It's an honour to be here,' I said.

There was a scuffling noise in the passage and an old woman rushed into the room and seized Marcellin's arm. He followed her outside. When he returned moments later, he had a wild look in his eyes.

'It's all your fault,' he said to me in English. 'That's the mother of my friend in Brazzaville. They are going to murder me. She says we must run away. I should have brought my Kalashnikov. I didn't know we were coming here. You said we need not go to Boha. You lied to me. What about my little daughter? What about her? You should have brought me a pistol.'

'Marcellin,' said the Vice-President, returning the papers, 'the People's Village Committee demand to know one thing. Why did you put our Chief in prison? It is a great disgrace. Because you have come again to our village the Chief has taken his wives and hidden himself in the forest.'

'Why? What for?' said Marcellin, looking startled, his words rising to a high shout. 'What's he going to gain by that?'

Manou slid down the wall, slumped to a sitting position and put his head between his knees.

'Why did you put our Chief in prison?' said the giant in his preternaturally deep voice.

'It wasn't me,' said Marcellin, turning, bizarrely, to look at me, his eyes blankly searching my face.

'Marcellin Agnagna,' said the giant, 'when you reply to the questions of the People's Village Committee you will address yourself to the Vice-President of the People's Village Committee, and not to a white man.'

'It wasn't me,' repeated Marcellin. 'I am not a soldier. I am not a politician. I am under the power of the Political Commissar of the District of Epéna. I am a man of science.'

'You are a man of science,' said the giant, pointing a calloused finger at Marcellin's head, 'and that is why you came here with a bomb to kill the fish in our lake and to starve us to death.'

'That was not a bomb. That was a sonar. That was a machine to measure the depth of the water.'

'That's your story,' said the giant.

'There are men in the Party here who are jealous of me,' said Marcellin, his eyes flicking from one committee member to the next. 'They make a great noise and accuse me unjustly. The truth is we have different mentalities, you and I. I do not belong to your world. And that is why you are jealous of me.'

'You killed a gorilla,' said the giant. 'You tell us not to hunt the chimpanzees and the gorillas that belong to us and our ancestors, and then you kill a gorilla.'

'It was an old male. He was in a tree above our canoe. He was going to attack us.' Marcellin had become very excited. 'He was going to jump into our boat. So I fired.' Marcellin raised an imaginary gun.

'I don't believe you,' said the giant. 'We found dead turtles in the lake when you came with the small yellow men. We found dead antelope in the forest. The antelope and the turtles, they belong to us.'

'I have brought three expeditions here,' said Marcellin, raising his voice again. 'I have given many presents to the Chief. I have given many presents to the People's Village Committee. You should thank me. I bring fame to your village. They know your name in distant lands. And I ask you, can I help it – *is it my fault if the men with me transform themselves into animals in the night and go hunting where I cannot see them*? Eh? Am I responsible for that?'

'That is possible,' said the giant, seeming to contract in his chair, as if the argument had suddenly swung against him. 'But our Chief hides in the forest. He has nothing to say.'

'The white man has presents for him,' said Marcellin. 'He has a pipe from England, a knife, cloth for his wives and two pairs of shoes.'

There was a pause. 'You will stay where you are,' said the giant at last. 'We will decide what to do with you.' He picked up his chair and carried it outside. The others followed.

'Get up, Manou,' said Marcellin, 'we share a mother. You must be a man.'

'I've got malaria,' said Manou, rising unsteadily to his feet. 'I'm shaking all over.'

'You shake because you are afraid,' said Marcellin, staring at the table top in front of him. 'I promised our mother I'd make a man of you.' And then, without shifting his gaze, 'You've failed me, Redmond,' he said. 'I should have come with soldiers. These are not educated men. They kill gorillas and chimps and each other and tonight they will probably kill us too. Lac Télé is too precious to be left to such people. We should move these murderers to another village and bring in tourists and make money and protect the animals.'

A little boy peered round the door behind us, holding a yellow plastic football. He wiped his nose with one hand and lobbed the ball at me with the other. I patted it back.

'Don't talk to him,' said Marcellin. 'He's a spy.'

The giant leaned through the other door. 'We have decided,' he boomed. 'We will talk to the Chief. He will know what to do. The Vice-President will take you to the schoolmaster's house.'

We picked up our packs and followed the Vice-President down past the safou tree to the school playground, bounded on one side by a row of clay-brick schoolrooms roofed with thatch. The schoolmaster's hut was to our right.

'So, Marcellin,' I asked, 'where shall we pitch the tents?'

'No, Redmond, I'm not going to be axed through the canvas in the night. Not even for you. Tonight we sleep in a brick hut with only one door. Nzé and Manou will sleep across the door.'

'Remember Djéké, my friend,' said the Commandant, twisting his shoulders sideways to shed one of our bergens against the hut wall. 'Remember the place where you were happy, Redmon, because – you mark my words well – one way or another, the men of Boha will make you wish you'd never come to the Likouala.' He put his hand on my arm and looked anxiously into my eyes. 'You'll wish you'd never heard the name of our river, my friend.'

I paid him his 12,000 francs. He and the paddlers turned and left. They did not look back. The hut was very isolated, and ominously quiet.

Marcellin ordered Nzé to sleep by the door. 'And Redmond,' he said, 'is going to sleep with me.' He gave the bed a tremendous kick. There was a small rustling noise, like the movement of dry leaves. 'Bugs,' he said.

I dropped to my knees and inspected the dry mud floor under the planks. Dark brown insects about a fifth of an inch long, thin and flat, were scuttling towards two long cracks in the ground. Marcellin kicked the bed again, and another brittle dusting fell to the floor. 'Bedbugs,' he said. 'Their bites don't bother me.'

So this is it, I thought, my own secret fear, much more real than the idea of a Boha dagger in a kidney, and I tried to remember just where

I had read that bedbugs carry the HIV virus for exactly one hour in their blood-sacs: it explains how three-year-olds and grandmothers pick it up. The bugs, sick with disappointment when their host gets out of bed, exude a drop of blood from their proboscidean hypodermic needle on the end of their noses, and then, sick with excitement, they throw up another drop as they reinsert their bloodsuckers into whoever is left between the sheets. The words of the consultant in tropical medicine at the Radcliffe Hospital in Oxford came back to me: 'The Congo is very interesting,' he had said, with a dreamy look in his eyes. 'Very interesting indeed. It's the HIV1 and HIV2 overlap zone. If only you could send me some fresh blood samples. I'd be most grateful. I really would.'

'Marcellin,' I said, unsteadily, wondering how many women he had slept with in his hyperactive life – five hundred? a thousand? – 'why don't you sleep in here? I'll sleep in the back room. And Manou and Nzé can sleep together as usual.'

Marcellin shouted, as if I were fifty yards away. 'They'll push a spear through the window in the night. I don't want to die alone! Only a coward would let me die alone! And besides,' he added, starting to calm down, 'it's all your fault. But for you I would never have returned to Boha. Never.'

'You'll thank me,' I said, momentarily hating the sight of him, and wondering why his weeping leg ulcers never quite healed despite my treating him with two courses of Floxapen. 'This is the expedition when we find your dinosaur. We'll take its portrait.'

Marcellin sat down on the edge of the bed and held his knees. 'Sleeping with you is my protection. Everyone knows there's terrible trouble when you kill a white man. With you, I'm safe. It's not right, but there it is.' He shrugged his shoulders and looked up at me with a helpless smile.

'Of course I'll sleep next to you,' I said, ashamed of myself. 'I'll sleep nearest the window.'

Well, I thought, bedbugs feed just before dawn. I'll get up at four in the morning.

There was a bang at the door. Marcellin jumped to his feet.

'Fuck off!' sang Nzé and Manou in unison.

The Vice-President appeared in the doorway, very self-effacing. 'My sister has malaria,' he said.

I counted fifteen quinine pills into his palm. 'Now,' he said, 'the Chief is waiting. He will see you now. You will follow me.'

We walked up the wide main street and stopped at a rough square on the right. In front of us was a long, windowless hut of wattle-and-daub and palm-thatch. In its doorway, on a three-legged stool, sat the Chief of Boha.

He was much younger than I had expected, perhaps in his late thirties, a handsome man of strong features, with a neatly cut moustache. He wore a thick band of red paint across his forehead, a baggy ochre loincloth with embroidered flowers over his genitals and a pair of Adidas running shoes. He held a spear upright against his right thigh, and from his shoulder hung a large twine bag full, I presumed, of the royal fetishes. He looked at us solemnly, without moving. A yellow dog lay asleep at his feet.

Twelve spearmen stood in a circle around him and three chairs, towards which an old man in red plastic sandals tilted his spear, indicating that we were to be seated. He then pointed his spear at Nzé, motioning him away to a group of women and children who stood watching at the far side of the square. We took our places, and the circle of spearmen closed in behind us.

The Chief inclined his head to the old man, his *porte-parole*, his word-carrier, and spoke softly. The old man then straightened his back, strode into the centre of the circle, and sang out a speech in Bomitaba. At the end of the pronouncement, there were shouts from some of the spearmen and the people around the square. When the old man wanted one of them to speak he tipped his spear; and when he wanted them to stop he held it horizontally, to bar their words. The debate concluded, he returned to the Chief's side, took his instructions and returned to the centre.

'The white man will pay 75,000 francs to the Chief of Boha,' he shouted in French, 'and 20,000 francs to the Vice-President of the People's Committee. Then if the government come with soldiers to take our Chief to prison in Epéna the soldiers will have to take their own Vice-President away, too. The white men will keep faith with our customary rights.'

'It's far too much!' I said.

The old man nodded. The warrior at my back pricked me gently between the shoulder blades with his spear.

'It's a bargain!' I said.

The old man smiled, bowed his head and waved two spearmen forward to collect the presents. The Chief, without ceremony, bent forward and put the knife, the pipe and the tobacco into his shoulder bag. He stooped down to gather up the shoes and the bolt of cloth and disappeared through the dark doorway. The old man picked up the stool and followed him inside. The royal dog lay undisturbed, his tail twitching.

4

By the time I returned to the hut, it was already full of candlelight and laughter, women and food. 'Uncle!' shouted Nzé to me, happy and sweating, standing by the table. 'Palm wine!' He passed me a mug. '*Saka-saka!*' He nodded imperiously at an old woman who was ladling mashed manioc leaves and scraps of fish from her cooking pot. 'Pineapples!' Four were on the table, with two ripe papayas 'Women!' He put his arm round an enormous girl sitting on his right. She looked up at me and giggled, her bright yellow-and-green wraparound barely restraining her breasts, her buttocks overflowing the chair.

'She's rich!' he yelled, overexcited, his wink a chaotic crush of his right eyebrow. 'Her father's a boatman! He goes to Epéna! She's well fed, Uncle!' – he squeezed the flesh of her upper arm. 'When I take her, I'll have two women at once!

'Manou!' shouted Nzé with redoubled force. 'Manou! I almost forgot. I found you a woman. Look!' He pointed into the far corner, where a young girl sat clutching a mug of palm wine, staring at her knees. She glanced at Manou, smiled and looked away. Manou sat down by the door, embarrassed. Everybody laughed.

Marcellin took me aside. 'Come on, Redmond,' he said. 'Let's leave them. Let's go and see Old Bobé. You always want to talk to old men. He knows the history of Boha. And it was he who sent us the food tonight.'

Bobé, still wearing his red-and-white-striped pyjama top, a lantern at his feet, was waiting for us in his lean-to, beneath his hunting-nets, wicker fish-traps, carrying-baskets and bundles of gourd water-containers slung from the beams.

'Welcome!' he said, jumping to his feet and shaking hands. 'You are welcome to my house.'

His wife put three empty cans labelled NORWEGIAN MACKEREL on the table, handed Bobé a gourd of palm wine and withdrew. Bobé filled the cans in silence. We picked the insects out of the white froth on top, dabbed them on to the floor and drank.

'Me, I like to be old,' said Bobé, sitting back in his chair, 'I used to be the greatest hunter in all Boha. I knew the best places to sink my fish-traps, too. But now I am old and wise. I am proud that I understand the history of my people. I know all our stories. My grandchildren and all the boys in Boha come to see me, and I tell them how it used to be. I tell them about the *colons*, the French people, and how the Communists helped us to build our school. I tell them where to hunt. They like old Bobé.'

'Perhaps you could tell us about the history of your people.'

'You may talk properly,' said Marcellin to Bobé. 'He is a white man, but he respects the old ways. He has agreed to pay the traditional dues in full.'

'So I have heard,' said Bobé, turning to me, 'and you have entrusted yourself to my son Doubla, who will be your guide tomorrow. Well, we have a long history.'

He refocused his eyes to a point somewhere on the floor just behind the drum, and the hesitant old man's voice became a low incantation. He told us how the first people of Boha came from the village of Bongoye, near the plain of Sakoua, and of the path that connects the village to Lac Télé. He told us how the people moved to make the village of Bombolo, and later the village of Ngouamounkale, which also became known as Old Boha. He told us of the first chiefs and of the sorcerers and their dreams.

'So where do we all come from?' I said, pleased with myself. 'That's what I want to know. What's the origin of life?'

'That's very simple,' he said, leaning forward, refilling our ex-mackerel cans, handing me the gourd of palm wine and relaxing back into his chair, 'I can put your mind at rest. The origin of life reposes in a symbol whose name is Bolo. Bolo incarnates all creative power. It is a unique symbol. This symbol embodies all the spirits, good or bad. The origin of sorcery comes from the symbol Bolo. This symbol endows certain people with a power, a power which is generally transmitted through dreams.'

Bobé drained his second can of palm wine, refilled it – and with the can in his right hand, halfway to his lips, stopped, apparently mesmerized by something just behind the drum.

'Bobé, my old friend,' said Marcellin softly, 'we're here. Are you all right?'

'Yes, Marcellin,' he said slowly, confused. He put his can down unsteadily on the edge of the table. 'I am all right. I was listening. There is something I must tell you.

'We have come to know,' announced Bobé, intoning again, his eyes glazed over, 'that an animal of mystery lives in the forest of Boha. This animal, which is called Yombé, resembles the chimpanzee and the gorilla but its upper limbs are very elongated. It is vegetarian, and above all else it eats two species of plants which are present in our forest. This animal has already been seen on many occasions, but its mystery lies in this: you must never look into its eyes. Ten years ago, two hunters from the village shot at one of these animals, not with an arrow but with a gun. The animal, which was sitting in a tree, fell, and it disappeared, leaving not the slightest trace. The two men returned to tell their story, but as they finished speaking they were struck down. The men died.

'I, the Bobé who sits before you, affirm, now, that I too have seen this animal. I, also, met it when it was sitting in a tree. The animal began to turn its head. But the spirits of the two hunters saved my life. They called to me gently, inside my skull, and I remembered how they told their story and died. I lowered my eyes to the path. I returned to my wife and my children. So I, Bobé, I am still alive. And now I have warned you in my own house, Mister Redmond, because you are said to respect our traditions, and also because you are well known to my friend Doctor Marcellin. I warn you, on pain of death, do not meet the eye of this animal when you come across it in the forest.'

He pressed the palms of his loose-skinned old hands into his eyes, as if to shut something from view, and then looked at us with his slow smile again. 'I am tired,' he said. 'It takes courage to talk of such things. And now I am very tired. We will speak again. Perhaps you will visit me again.'

I was surprised to see that I was still holding the gourd.

'What did you make of that?' I said, as we walked back to our hut.

'I think you ought to know,' said Marcellin, 'that in Lingala, *Bolo* means "vagina".'

I laughed.

'So why is that funny?' he said, rounding on me.

'I'm sorry,' I said, shocked at the venom in his voice. The happy pace of my walk involuntarily slowed to a shuffle. 'I thought you meant that Old Bobé was making a fool of me.'

'Oh no you didn't,' snapped Marcellin, slowing his stride to match mine, 'that's not why you laughed. Why the hell should Old Bobé want to make a fool of you? Didn't you see how tired it made him? *It's dangerous for him to talk like that*. Didn't you see how afraid he was? And then you laugh. How dare you laugh at Old Bobé!

'And anyway,' he shouted, kicking a lump of mud off the path, 'it makes as much sense as your white man's superstitions! Tell me: do you or do you not eat and drink the body and blood of the big white chief of your tribe once every seven days? Oh no – you've no right to laugh at us, at Old Bobé, at Africans.'

'I apologize. And anyway, I've told you, I'm not a Christian. I don't believe it.'

'Believe it or not, my friend, it's in your head. You think it's normal. You call it part of your culture. You think you're a people of reason and science, that the daylight belongs to the white man and the night to the African. And I agree, you make motor cars and outboards and airplanes, and we don't. But what about your three gods in one, your big holy ghost that can go anywhere? Tell me, why sneer at the African? And what about your other god who became a man and let himself be stuck on a piece of wood and speared so that he could save you all? What could it possibly mean? Where's the sense in it?'

'There is no sense in it. It's a matter of faith. Faith means saying goodbye to reason and science, that's what faith is. When you get faith you throw the switches, blow a gasket, go deliberately soft in the head. It's more comfortable.'

Marcellin ignored me.

'No wonder we were frightened of the white man when he came here with his guns and killed us and talked about eating his god all day long. We thought you were cannibals. And there's another thing – your god who never had a woman. Look' – he shone the torch on his arm – 'I'm the blackest African I know, with a strong need for sex. It's genetic; it's in the skin. I think about it all the time. If I don't have a woman every night I get ill. I'm ill now. You should pay me double for making me risk my life in these forests with these people. And then you should pay me double again for making me sleep in a tent without a woman at night. And for months on end! You white men, we don't know how you breed. You have a god born without any sex! And then he never had a woman! And what about the god's mother – a woman who never had a man? If that's not plain silly, I don't know what is.'

A fierce drumming began suddenly, from the far end of the village.

Marcellin was silent. Then: 'Love your neighbour as yourself,' he said, his torch beam waving wildly off the path and into the cactus hedges.

'Love your neighbour as yourself! What hypocrites!' His voice rose to its highest pitch, a falsetto shriek of indignation, of real temper. The dog turned and bolted.

We entered the hut, in silence. Cigarette butts were strewn over the mud floor. Nzé and Manou had hung tarpaulins flat across the doorways of the two small bedrooms.

'Oh I can't stand it here,' said Marcellin, spinning round where he stood. 'I am angry with you and your kind. I'm going to sleep at Bobé's hut.' And he picked up his pack and went.

'Psst!' said Nzé, from behind his curtain. 'Has he gone?'

'Yes, he has. He's not happy with me.'

'Well, I'm *very* happy with you,' came the whisper. 'That was the best 500 francs you ever spent on me.'

'How's that?'

'Put your head round the new bedroom door, Uncle. Just take a look at this.'

I put my head round the curtain.

'Isn't she wonderful?' said Nzé, full of pride, beaming, his towel over his genitals. 'I tell you, Uncle, she's as juicy as a ripe papaya. *She's better than a whole bottle of whisky.*'

The girl was asleep on the bed beneath the tarpaulin, her head on a pillow of Nzé's T-shirts, her yellow-and-green wraparound discarded on the floor.

'There's no end of her,' he said, gently drawing back the tarpaulin.

'I had her first in the school,' said Nzé. 'We had to go to get away from the others. She got so excited! "Calm yourself!" I had to say, "Calm yourself!"'

'Then what?'

'I brought her back here and I had her on the bed. And I'll tell you something – she says I'm the best! It's the gift my grandfather gave me! She's exhausted. I *am* the best. I tire them all out. There's nothing like it, Uncle.'

'I'm sure there isn't.'

'I'm going to wake her up in a minute. We're going to the dance. And then I'll have her again! Are you coming Uncle? Are you coming to the dance?'

'No, I'm not. Not tonight. I'm going for a swim, and then I'm going to bed.'

I went to the back room and found my mould-covered towel and the remains of a bar of soap, and walked down to the river by the nearest path.

Frogs quacked along the bank, and I found the washing place, took off my boots, placed my glasses gently in the left boot and my torch in the right, stripped, laid my clothes on top of the boots and waded in. To see a dinosaur suddenly seemed such a sensible Western

achievement: how scientific it would be to record a small sauropod
from the Cretaceous. And there must be *something* odd about the lake,
I thought, as I smeared myself with the towel, dressed and walked
slowly back to the hut in the warm night, the drumming reaching me
as a soft reverberation through the river water in my ears. It is clear
that Roy Mackal in his book *A Living Dinosaur?* really did think that
the lake was home to a dinosaur, partly because he supposed this to
be the oldest undisturbed jungle on earth, and partly because he was
sure the dinosaur was the subject of pygmy reports – and pygmy
reports (unless designed to frighten the Bantu) are reliable. It was
persistent Bambuti pygmy descriptions, after all, that set the English
colonial officer and naturalist Sir Harry Johnston on to the search that
became the greatest triumph of his career, the eventual discovery of
the forest giraffe, the okapi.

As I entered the hut Mackal's other conviction seemed sensible
enough – that this was the oldest undisturbed jungle on earth. Even
a hundred yards from the little school, the presence of the surrounding forest felt immensely ancient, rich in evolved life. It was easy to
believe that this land had remained stable for sixty-five million years,
or even (pushing it a bit) to agree with Mackal that 'in a region known
as the Likouala, just north of the equator, lie some of the most
formidable jungle swamps on the face of the globe ... 140,000 square
kilometres of mostly unexplored swamp and rain forest.'

Nzé and his girl had gone to the dance, and Manou and his shy love
had disappeared, too. I was alone in the hut. Too tired to take off my
boots, I spread a tarpaulin on the planks and tried to sleep. It was no
use. The voice of the Commandant echoed in my head, telling us
again to stay clear of the lake, not just because we might see Mokele-
mbembe but because we would certainly hear his cry, a long-drawn-
out, high-pitched, echoing cry, a sound which, once heard, would
deprive you of your mental balance for ever.

I lay on the planks and tried to think of something peaceful: of the little bedroom in the Wiltshire vicarage of my childhood; of the blackbird which used to perch each summer evening on the roof of the bicycle shed below my window and sing me to sleep; of the wood-pigeons in the conker tree. But it didn't work. Nothing held for long enough; my brain was too disturbed to be directed in its dreams; my imagination obstinately filled with thoughts of Bruce Chatwin, the only person I knew who had died of Aids.

'Redders!' would come a familiar voice down the phone far too early in the morning. 'Not even Bunin was interesting yesterday. I can't stand it a moment longer.

'I'm sick of writing. I'm tired! Tired! Tired!' (said with enough energy to crack your ear-drum). 'And when a man is sick of writing he must walk.' (*Oh god.*) 'I'm coming to get you.' (*Panic.*) 'What are you doing?'

'I'm in bed.'

'Up you get! Two glasses of green tea. See you in half an hour.'

I wondered who or what Bunin was. With Bruce you could never be sure. The new Stravinsky from Albania? The nickname of the last slave in Central Mali? A lighthouse keeper from Patagonia? Scroll 238B from a cave in the Negev? Or just the *émigré* king of Tomsk who'd dropped in for tea? Still vaguely wondering, I lurched out of the house.

A white 2CV puttered into the drive. There was a sailboard strapped to the roof. Chatwin got out, his wife Elizabeth's two dogs wagging at his feet.

'Come on! It's almost dawn! I'm taking these brutes to a hill-farm in Wales. We'll look at the tree of life on the south door of St Mary and St David at Kilpeck; we'll deliver the dogs; we'll call in on my old friend Lady Betjeman; and then I'll walk you over the Black Hill.'

'So what's the sailboard for?' I said, suspicious.

'Oh that. That's my new hobby. You bring your car and make your own way back tonight, and I'll go sailing in the Bristol Channel in the morning.'

And you'll probably be in Dublin for supper, I thought.

Beneath the first ridge of the Black Mountains we parked by a track and got out our boots: mine, black Wellingtons; his, a pair of such fine leather that Hermès would have done a swap. I put on my bergen (a loaf of bread and two bottles of wine) and he put on his small haversack of dark maroon calfskin (a Montblanc pen, a black oilcloth-bound *vrai* moleskin notebook, a copy of Alymer Maude's translation of *War and Peace*, Strindberg's *By the Open Sea* and the most elegant pair of binoculars I have seen).

'Werner Herzog gave them to me,' said Bruce, his eyes blue and bright and eager. 'He wants to film *The Viceroy of Ouidah*. And Jean-Louis Barrault had this pack designed just for me. But you *could* get some decent boots, Redders. The Canadian Moccasin Company. Just say you're a friend of mine.'

He took off up the hill with a strong, loping stride through the heather and the whinberries, a nomad's pace. In a few minutes I fell behind, trying not to pant like an engine shed.

'The twins I wrote about lived there,' he said, turning without slackening and pointing to a long slate-roofed farmhouse set back from the road in the diminishing valley below us.

'And ... that's ... where!!!' His words whipped past me, split up and lost to sense in the wind. The speed of ascent was effort enough, replying to the wild and ceaseless monologue an impossibility – which was just as well, because it was far too late in our friendship to admit that, much as I admired *In Patagonia*, what with one siesta and another I had just not quite read *On the Black Hill*.

'There's a hippie camp down there,' he called, nodding north-west. He shouted with laughter. 'All the locals are terrified of them. They think they'll be strangled in their beds! When I was staying with the

King of Afghanistan he had an old English colonel about the court. "Your Royal Highness," said the colonel, "You must let me remove all the hips from your country. You must let me put all the hips in trucks and take them to the border."'

Down on the Llanthony road, we walked through the hail, and Bruce talked about a female albatross that had wandered into the wrong hemisphere and built a nest in Shetland, waiting for the mate that never came, and about the train he caught from King's Cross on his way to see her, and how the only other passenger in his sleeper compartment was a Tierra del Fuegan ('On his way to the North Sea oil rigs – they're the only men who can throw a boat's painter through a ring on a buoy') whose settlement Bruce had visited on the journey that became *In Patagonia*. He talked about his love for the herd-people of the Sudan; about smuggling Roman coins out of Turkey; about the design of a prehistoric wheel which linked the Irish to an ethnic sub-group in the Caucasus (I think); and about his real dream, the Russian novel he would write one day.

There was the noise of an engine shaking itself to bits, three violent backfires, and a rust-holed van lurched up the road towards us. I jumped on to the bank at the base of the hedge, but Bruce, engrossed, was still walking in the road. Surprisingly slowly, it seemed, the van nudged the Jean-Louis Barrault haversack and, equally slowly, Bruce, still talking ('Just tell the story straight as Tolstoy. No tricks!'), turned a full somersault in the air.

'You stupid bastards!' shouted Bruce, getting to his feet. 'That was unnecessary.'

A young boy, his hair in a ponytail, jumped down from the cab. 'Sorry, squire,' he said, 'I'm sorry. Honest. What more can I say? It's like this – my wheels hasn't got no brakes '

'I say,' said Bruce. 'How exciting. Can we have a lift?'

Just back from months in the jungle between the Orinoco and the

Amazon, I thought I'd celebrate with warm scallops in a London restaurant and got a six-month dose of hepatitis A. Half-asleep, eyes shut in the isolation wing of the Churchill Hospital in Oxford, I heard a familiar voice.

'Shush,' it said, 'don't tell anyone. I'm not here.'

I opened one eye. So it was true. Hepatitis A-induced delirium. You saw visions on it.

'Shush, I'm in France. Bill Buford's after me. I'm meant to be writing a piece for *Granta*. I'm not here. But with you here too I might just as well phone Reuters and be done with it.

'I've brought you some liver pills. They're from Elizabeth's guru in India. I'm having aboriginal warts removed from my face. I'm in the room next door. Look, will you be my literary executor? I'll do the same for you if you die first.'

'I'll do anything you say. I want to go to sleep.'

'You know, there's something else I want you to know. When I first came in here they told me I was mortally ill. They said I had a fungus of the bone marrow which I must have picked up in a cave in China. It's exclusive! It's so rare that I'm only the tenth recorded case in the medical literature! And they also let me know why I got it, Redders. I got it because I have Aids. They told me I had six months or a year to live. So I thought, right, Bruce is a dog's name and I'm not going to stand for this. I can't get on with my big nomad book as it is. I can't see how I can pull material out of my notebooks and on to the page. And I'm not going to waste away and go feeble in the head and defecate all over the place.

'So I went to Geneva – there's a place in the Alps that haunts me, a ravishing cliff near Jungfrau – and I wanted to jump off it. Or, failing that, I thought I'd go to Niger and simply take off my clothes, put on my loincloth, walk out into the desert and let the sun bleach me away.

'But the bone marrow got me first. I fainted on the pavement; someone took me to hospital in a taxi; and Elizabeth came and rescued me and brought me back here. I was so weak I couldn't whisper. I came in on a Friday and they thought I'd be dead by Monday. Then Juel-Jensen put me on his anti-fungal drip, and Elizabeth nursed me night and day, and I pulled through: I owe it all to them.

'I've almost finished my big book – there's a terrible old character with a twisted gut called Hanlon – and now I have a whole novel growing in the notebooks, too. I can see almost all of it. It's set in Prague and I shall call it "Utz" – "Utz"! Anyway, one day you must tell people, Redders, but not now. It's a fable. It's all there, ready-made. And the moral is simple: never kill yourself. Not under any circumstances. Not even when you're told you have Aids.'

I last saw Bruce in Elizabeth's light-filled house which looks south down an Oxfordshire valley; he was in his second bedroom, books on the counterpane, the manuscript of a young novelist he had befriended and encouraged stacked in a box by the bed, cassettes of young musicians he had supported piled on the bedside table, his newly bought Russian icons on the walls. Though he was very weak and so thin you could see the white bones in his arms, his telephone was still plugged into its socket. He was making and receiving calls, talking to his friends all over the world.

'Just for now, Redders, I can't hold a pen. It would be ridiculous to start yet, and I hate dictation. But the moment I'm better I'll begin that Russian novel. It's going to work. I can see almost all of it. No tricks!'

His grin gave out in a burst of coughing. As I left, the sun bright on the walls, I took his hands in both of mine. A thought struck him, and he gave a snort of laughter.

'Redders! Your hands – they're so soft I don't believe you ever go anywhere. You just lie in bed and make it all up.'

They were his last words to me. And quite right, too, I thought. I must read Bunin. And get a sailboard.

But it won't be the same.

5

I woke well after dawn, covered in small red bites, and went for a swim to calm the all-over itch. When I returned Manou was up, moving at twice his normal speed, his eyes bright.

'She likes me,' he said.

'Of course she does. She knows how strong you are, how fast you're going to walk in the forest.'

'It wasn't like that,' said Manou with a proud little smile, 'she said she loved my body. And my hat.'

Nzé emerged from behind his curtain; he held on to the edge of the table, as though he had just suffered a mild blow to the back of the head. 'She's gone to her mother,' he mumbled. 'She's gone to sleep at her mother's house. She kept screaming, Uncle. Every time. She begged me to stop. She said, Nzé, that was the best night of my life, and I said, Yes, you big bag of happiness, for me that was the best time I've ever had at a school desk.'

Marcellin, looking grim, arrived with our new guides, Doubla (because of his double character) and Vicky (the Chief's favourite son). 'What are you doing?' Marcellin shouted at Manou and Nzé. 'Why aren't you ready? Why aren't the loads outside the hut? The bearers are here.'

We pushed everything into the bergens and lined them up against the hut wall. Doubla and Vicky, I noticed, had come barefoot. 'Shoes are precious here,' said Marcellin. 'No one wears them in the forest.'

Nzé fired his gun into the air to mark our departure. The African grey parrots shrieked and swore somewhere off to our right.

We were on the move again, beneath the familiar trees, away from the insistent press of village life. For me, every time we entered the jungle, it seemed like an escape; Marcellin felt it very differently. For him, as he wrote and underlined in his diary which I was secretly reading whenever I got the chance, '*Setting out into the forest is like a soldier going to war, the return is never certain.*'

What was he so afraid of – a leopard? disease? snakebite? breaking a leg? Or was there, underneath all that Cuban Marxist education in Havana, all that French pharmacy and biology at Montpellier, just a trace of suppressed terror? Did he half share his sorcerer-grandfather's belief in the power of fetish? Was he so tense simply because he thought this particularly malign stretch of forest was haunted by spirit animals? Or maybe, I thought, Marcellin just suspects that Doubla and the brothers have secret instructions to murder us in the forest.

Vicky led the way and I followed, trying to match his stride: his bare feet slapped easily over the ground with fast, small steps – the only way to walk at speed, I now knew, without sliding across the dank scatter of leaves on the wet mud. Getting vaguely into the rhythm, the sweat oozing down my face in the humid, unmoving air, I fell into a trance. It was only really possible to be alone in Africa, it occurred to me, when walking like this, or when awake on a tarpaulin in the middle of the night: anyone on his own was in danger, an isolated man was an easy prey for wandering spirits, friends must keep together always, and talk.

The great trees towered above us, their sixty-foot-high trunks not even tapering until they reached the canopy, where their massive branches spread out horizontally. Lianas looped and sagged in spirals along their branches; ferns and epiphytic orchids grew whenever plant debris had lodged in their high forks; and every surface was patched with lichens. But it was not a dense forest. We passed many gaps in the high canopy and some of the smaller trees had prop roots. But there were very few bushes and herbs in the understory, and even the broad-leaved grasses were sparse. We were well on our way towards swamp jungle.

Vicky suddenly stopped, leaned his spear against a sapling, eased himself out of the bergen and bent down to pick up yellow, cooking-apple-sized fruits which were scattered over the path.

'Gorillas and chimpanzees like them,' he said, grinning at me, a super-signal of white teeth across his wide, brown, sweaty, happy face. 'You try one.'

He took his machete, cut the top off the fruit like an egg, gave it to me, and selected another for himself; under the wrinkled yellow skin a cup of orange flesh enclosed a ball of white fluff. Vicky scooped it out, discarding a cluster of big brown seeds, and I copied him, gathering a mouthful of sweetish floss.

'Mokele-mbembe,' said Vicky, mysteriously, and winked.

'Malombo,' said Marcellin, coming up behind me. The others arrived and everyone began to eat.

Malombo, according to Roy Mackal, is the main food plant of Mokele-mbembe, and I half expected a brown, skin-flappy sauropod head on its giraffe-length neck to come slithering over my shoulder and muzzle up my fruit. (Would its lips be cold, I wondered, or were the dinosaurs really warm-blooded?) Or at the very least we might hear the high-pitched ululating cry that would drive us all berserk.

The forest grew wetter, prop-rooted trees more common, and we heard the alarm calls of greater white-nosed monkeys. The men of Boha were gossiping loudly in Bomitaba; Nzé was shouting tales of Dongou in Lingala to Marcellin; and Manou was too busy conserving his strength to say anything at all. We saw little: the occasional pile of fibrous grey lowland-gorilla turds, clumps of wild ginger and strands of some kind of arrowroot, a herb with gigantic leaves borne on single stems six to eight feet high. We stopped, finally, to examine a line of fresh, elongated rat-like droppings.

Doubla said they were mongoose turds, so I got Haltenorth and Diller's guide from the side pocket of the bergen. Doubla inspected all the possible snouts, feet, thick coats and long furry tails of the twenty-seven mongooses illustrated on plates thirty-three to thirty-seven and chose the marsh mongoose.

The marsh mongoose was plainly an emotional mongoose ('VOICE: purrs when content; in threat or defence, growls, nasal snorting and spitting; in excitement, a staccato rising bark; with fluffing up of fur expressing rage'), but the details of its breeding and development were not known. This was promising. And what's more (apart from the lack of a light yellow rim to its ears) it looked exactly like the *extremely* rare long-nosed mongoose, also reported from the northern Congo swamp forest – a mongoose whose 'teats, glands and penis bone' were *still* undescribed, and of whom 'only 30 specimens known . . . No details of habits.'

'So why not this one?' I said, getting excited, pointing at the illustration. 'Look – *only thirty specimens known*.'

'Why not?' said Doubla, shrugging his shoulders. 'If that's what you want.'

'But, Redmond,' said Marcellin, bristling, picking up the turd between two fingers. 'I am a scientist and I tell you – it's not likely is it? *All we have here is a piece of shit!*'

OK, I was on the verge of saying, as I put the book back in its pocket, as far as your Mokele-mbembe is concerned you don't even have a piece of shit, do you? And, come to that, I'll bet a decent dinosaur turd is something we could really feast our eyes on. In fact I'd settle for one-eighth of a dingleberry hanging off its bum. Or an absolutely genuine sauropod snot. Or a toe-nail clipping. Or even a discarded fag-butt. If it's not too much to ask.

I thought of the hard time that Mokele-mbembe must have had in the last sixty-seven million years.

In his book, Roy Mackal tells us:

One of the most exciting things about Africa is that, at least since the end of the Cretaceous period, 65 million years ago, the Congo basin has not undergone further climatic and geophysical changes . . . When conditions remain stable for extended periods, some well-adapted species continue to survive and even flourish with very little physical and behavioural alteration. And that is what we find in the central West African jungle-swamps where, for example, crocodiles have persisted unchanged over the past 65 million years. What other ancient creatures might still lurk in this vast expanse of seemingly changeless, ageless, largely unexplored primeval forest?

In fact if we go back to the beginning, from Mokele-mbembe's point of view, I thought, getting excited, taking a sleepwalker's swig from my water bottle and almost running into the back of Vicky's spear, then Mackal's case – resting on the assumption that the jungle here has not been disturbed – becomes even more convincing. The sauropods evolved 225 million years ago, and if Mokele-mbembe's ancestors were in Lac Télé or thereabouts for the next few million years, then, apart from that very bad moment sixty-seven million years ago when an incoming meteorite six miles across blasted pulverized rock into the atmosphere and greenhoused all other large dinosaurs to oblivion, they might have had the odd minor, nasty surprise over their breakfast as the sea came rolling in, once or twice. We can picture them in the late Cretaceous, seventy-two million years ago, basking with their Loch Ness necks and little heads and humpbacks out of the water, surrounded by recognizable plants and recognizable birds: gulls, ducks, waders and herons. There were snakes about, as well as frogs, salamanders and of course freshwater crocodiles. And for Mokele-mbembe, life went peacefully by until about six million years ago, when the Congo basin filled into a giant lake. The relics of that vast lake were all about us: the swamp forest, the Oubangui and Congo Rivers, the shallow lakes and, perhaps, Lac Télé itself, just one day's walk away.

There was a swish of wings like a quetzacoatlus overhead, a call like the braying of dinosaurs – and a pair of black-casqued hornbills returned me to the present. As big as cormorants, they were perched high up on a branch to our right, their great bills swaying from side to side, peering down at us.

We made camp in a tiny clearing off the path, beside the black patch of an old cooking fire whose ashes glinted with mother-of-pearl – scales from the undersides of the forest crocodile. Hundreds of bees and four species of butterflies were feeding round its edge.

Doubla and Vicky cut poles from saplings and set up a shelter with our tarpaulins on one side of the clearing. And as Marcellin and I pitched our tents on the other, the feeding bees transferred their attentions to us. They settled on our sweat-soaked shirts and crawled down our chests and necks; they clustered in our armpits. They were joined by clouds of black bees, who buzzed around our faces and made their way into our hair, sucking at the corners of our eyes and mouths and at the mucus in our noses and the wax in our ears. We took off our shirts and hung them near the fire, cut switches and then tried not to let our arms touch our sides (stings in the armpit are almost as painful as stings in the crotch).

Doubla and Vicky sharpened two heavy saplings into stakes, enlarged the muddy pit of a waterhole and filled Nzé's cooking-pot. The light failed and the bees left, and Nzé slopped sour manioc stodge and two sardines apiece into our mess tins. We sat on our different tree roots round the fire and ate in silence.

'Cheer up!' said Nzé finally, pulling a small gourd of palm wine from his food-sack. 'Let's have a last drink, because in a day or two, when we get to Lac Télé, anything may happen. I'll tell you what I'm going to do – I'm going to shoot myself a Mokele-mbembe. In fact,' he paused, and inclined his head to one side, as if in deep deliberation, 'maybe I'll shoot more than one!'

'You shouldn't talk about it,' said Manou quietly. 'You don't know anything about it.'

'Oh yes I do,' said Nzé, 'and what's more I can make you laugh whenever I want to. I've got the power – so you can't help yourselves.'

He put his mug down, stood up and, turning to me with a flourish, fixed me with his good eye. 'I'm teaching Redmon to speak like a man,' he said. 'I'm teaching him Lingala.' He leaned forward and wagged a finger in my face, as though I were a child. 'I WANT SOME FOOD,' he shouted, '*MAKATA ELLOKO MOLOMOU.*'

'*Makata,*' I repeated dutifully, '*elloko molomou.*' Everyone howled with laughter. Even Doubla laughed, a bark of horrible energy.

'Nzé, that's enough,' said Marcellin, regaining his dignity. 'What if he said that in a village? Eh? What would people think of me?'

'Redmond,' said Marcellin, 'if you really want to learn, I'll teach you Lingala myself. You can trust me. I am a scientist. "I want some food" is *Na liki ko liya biliya. Makata elloko molomou* on the other hand is what Nzé tells all the girls in all the villages. It means "MY COCK IS BEAUTIFUL."'

I stretched out luxuriously on the tarpaulin in the safety of the little tent, moved my strained ankle joints this way and that, wiggled my bruised toes, flexed my aching calf muscles and decided that, having lost at least three stone since coming to the Congo, I was probably fitter than I'd ever been in my life. I shifted my position to avoid the roots under my shoulder blade and was injected in the back with two small syringes of boiling water.

Cursing myself for forgetting the insect-check routine, I switched on the torch, found my glasses and squashed the two bees in the bed with Haltenorth and Diller's *Mammals of Africa.* I killed another one crawling across the sweaty webbing of my bergen and three more resting, surfeited, on the socks in my boot. I eased off my shirt and picked about with my Swiss Army knife tweezers, trying to remove the barbs; I rubbed Anthisan into the swellings, put a fresh dressing over the main ulcer on my right foot, which the day's march had re-opened, and, still waiting for the immediate pain in my back to subside, retrieved the document wallet from my pack and drew out my photocopies. Yes, here it was: Marcellin on record, as plain as could be, in the appendix to Roy Mackal's *A Living Dinosaur? In Search of Mokele-Mbembe*: in 1983, Doctor Marcellin Agnagna writes, he stayed for a week at Boha, 'the inhabitants of which "own" Lac Télé, one of the reported habitats of Mokele-mbembe.' And on 26 April

the expedition then set out on foot, accompanied by seven villagers from Boha who were to act as guides in the forest. The trail through the forest proved to be quite difficult and it was usually necessary to cut through the foliage to allow passage. It being the dry season, water was scarce, and it became necessary to drink from muddy pools.

The 60-kilometre trek to Lake Télé was completed in 2 days, and it was with some emotion that we finally looked across this little sea, located right in the heart of the equatorial forest of Central Africa. The lake is oval in shape, about 5 kilometres by 4 kilometres. A base camp was established at the water's edge, and one of the Boha villagers caught a large turtle which served as dinner that first night. Two days of intensive observing of the lake produced no sightings of the supposed Mokele-mbembe, although there were frequent obser-vations of a large turtle, with a shell reaching 2 metres in length.

On 1 May 1983, the author decided to film the fauna in the low-canopy forest surrounding the lake. This forest is a habitat for many mammalian and bird species. The author and two Boha villagers, Jean Charles Dinkoumbou and Issac Manzamoyi, set out early in the morning. At approximately 2.30 p.m., the author was filming a troop of monkeys. One of the villagers, Dinkoumbou, fell into a pool of muddy water, and went to the edge of the lake to wash himself. About 5 minutes later, we heard his shouts to come quickly. We joined him by the lake, and he pointed to what he was observing, which was at first obscured by the heavy foliage. We were then able to observe a strange animal, with a wide back, a long neck, and a small head. The emotion and alarm at this sudden, unexpected event disrupted the author's attempt to film the animal with a Minolta XL-42 movie camera. The film had been almost totally exposed already, and the author unfortunately began filming in the macro position. By the time this was realised, the film had been totally exposed, as determined by subsequent processing in a French laboratory.

The animal was located at about 300 metres from the edge of the lake, and we were able to advance about 60 metres in the shallow water, placing us at a distance of about 240 metres from the animal, which had become aware of our presence and was looking around as if to determine the source of the noise. Dinkoumbou continued to shout with fear. The frontal part of the animal was brown, while the back part of the neck appeared black and shone in the sunlight. The animal partly submerged, and remained visible for 20 minutes with only the neck and head above the water. It then submerged completely, at which point we trekked rapidly through the forest back to the base camp, located 2 kilometres away. We then went out on the lake in a small dugout with video equipment to the spot where we had observed the animal. However, no further sighting of the animal took place.

It can be said with certainty that the animal we saw was Mokele-mbembe, that it was quite alive, and, furthermore, that it is known to many inhabitants of the Likouala region. Its total length from head to back visible above the waterline was estimated at 5 metres.

A soft but persistent rain began to patter on the canvas. I turned off the precious batteries, lay on my side with two mould-rotted shirts under my hip and a pair of pants for a pillow and half-dreamed about Darwin's cousin, Francis Galton, pioneer geneticist and statistician, father of the anti-cyclone and fingerprinting. It was one of Galton's ostensibly more trivial experiments that filled my mind as I fell asleep. Fascinated by the so-called worship of idols, he decided to investigate its mechanism and cast around for an entirely inappropriate image. He settled on Mr Punch. He pinned a cover of the journal up in his study and forced himself to make obeisance every morning, detailing his fears, whispering his hopes, until the experiment began to work so well he had to stop. Each time he entered his club and caught a glimpse of Mr Punch lying in state on the periodicals table his mouth went dry, his legs became unsteady and a sweat broke out across his shoulders.

Here in the forest, I thought, there seemed no mystery at all about the power of Mr Punch.

6

To avoid the bees we broke camp at four-thirty and left at first light. The rain had stopped, and the forest seemed subdued. We heard little: the odd troop of mangabeys chatter-grunting; the electric swarm of bees passing overhead, late for some appointment; and the usual background calls – the prolonged, mournful *hoo-hoo-hoo* of the grey wood-pigeon, from high up in the canopy of the tallest trees, and the spectral laugh of the redbilled dwarf hornbill.

Around midday, we came upon a small clearing that had been made by machete. Everyone stopped and slid off their loads.

'What's this?' I said.

'It's nothing,' said Marcellin. 'It's a piece of superstition. You stay here with us.'

Doubla stuck his spear upright in the soft ground and he and Vicky moved off in single file beyond it, up a path to our right. They stopped by an old safou tree and bowed their heads. I took off my hat, bowed my head likewise and held my hands behind my back. Vicky shouted into the bushes, the umbrella trees, pausing occasionally as he listened to the short replies of the dead.

The conversation completed, he took me by the arm. 'We can go now,' he said, with a smile. 'It is good you were here. We are pleased. I told them that we have come here to take a white man to Lac Télé and asked them to give us food and to protect us from seeing something.'

'Mokele-mbembe?'

He laughed.

'No,' said Doubla, giving the air in front of him a rabbitchop, as if to break the neck of the question, 'you might think it was a chimpanzee or a gorilla, this something, but it's dangerous. It is not good to name names.'

'Was this your old village?'

'Yes, but they became frightened. They were frightened of strange things in this forest. There are strange sounds in this forest.'

'No more questions,' said Doubla. 'That's enough. We must not disturb them any longer.'

Marcellin was sitting on one of the surface-roots of a forest giant. 'Redmond!' he said, 'I have been thinking. If we ever get out of here alive – if the Chief of Boha really has forgiven us – then you owe me a great deal.' He began to swing his feet, kicking his heels against the side of the root. 'This is the longest expedition I have made in the forest but I have also made eight others. I have conducted a survey of the forest elephant populations in this country and I am well known in England and North America for my work on Mokele-mbembe. I am a scientist. I do not belong here. What future is there? And how about my daughter? How will she get an education? Eh? You Redmond – you must pay me back. You must get me a job in Oxford. I want to be an Oxford Professor.'

'But that's not how it works,' I said, taken aback. Perhaps *this* was Marcellin's sustaining fantasy. 'I don't have the slightest influence in Oxford,' I said. 'And even if I did, it's not as easy as you think. There aren't any jobs in England. There are two million people looking for jobs.'

'I don't believe you,' he snapped. 'I don't believe you, Redmond. You just say that. You say it because I am a black man. I understand you, my friend. Two million people! That's, that's more than the entire population of the Congo! I don't believe a word you say.'

He stopped drumming his heels on the side of the root; he stared out beyond me, over my head, at some point in the dark tangle of shade on the far side of the clearing; he looked wistful. His shoulders seemed to collapse in on themselves, shrinking his chest; his hands hung limp over his knees. 'You could try,' he said, in a voice so small it was almost a whisper.

'There are bound to be scholarships,' I said, without conviction. 'You could probably get a grant. You could finish your doctorate.'

Marcellin looked at his feet. 'I am not a student!' he shouted, swinging off the root and drawing his machete. With one blow he severed the loop of the thick liana a foot above his head. An initial gush of water adjusted itself to an even flow as wide as a finger; he pulled the liana over his upturned mouth and drank. When he had finished Doubla followed suit, splashing the water over his head and neck, and we each took a turn.

'You see,' said Marcellin gently, 'I know about little things, too. I know which vines to drink from, and which vines will kill you.'

We set off again, with Marcellin in the lead. A little snakebite of shame spread up from the path and into my skull with the rising sweat and rhythm of his absurdly fast pace. 'You're bloated, aren't you?' went the usual refrain in my head. 'You're fat with all the unearned privilege that has come your way, with all the gross advantages that were yours for the taking just because of the country you were born in.' And I thought of the light on the ochre stone of the Bodleian quadrangle in Oxford on a summer morning, the tall mullioned windows, the books – every book a man could possibly need, ascending row after row to the high ceilings, or standing in the stacks underground, beneath the ancient paving stones and the manicured gravel, shelf-mile on mile. And I thought of Marcellin's hut of an office in Brazzaville with nothing in it but two issues of the *Journal of Cryptozoology*.

I thought of the young Marcellin and his father, who deserted his mother upriver in Impfondo and moved to the capital, living in the poorest part of the poorest quarter of the city with an open drain outside their shack; and I imagined the boy walking uptown every evening to do his homework under a street lamp, intent on winning the scholarship that would take him to Cuba. And then the path plunged waist-deep into black water, and I rapidly ceased to think of anything except the invisible submerged roots which trapped my feet and cracked my shins.

Marcellin was flailing ahead of me, hardly slackening his pace, and I was spitting out another mouthful of leaf-rot, retrieving my hat, when suddenly there were bright flashes as if someone were holding mirrors up among the trees ahead. The flashes grew together and turned into a consistent layer of light, head-high between the trunks ahead. And there in front of us was a stretch of water, three or four kilometres across. It was open water, a real horizon for the first time in months. We had reached Lac Télé.

Nzé, bedraggled, ran straight for the low bank as if to hurl himself into the water, but Doubla, with fearsome energy, lunged out and gripped his arm – so hard that Nzé yelped like a hit dog. 'Wait!' said Doubla. 'You'll harm us all. You'll kill our children.'

Vicky took a step forward, bowed his head and shouted towards the far shore. 'The spirits of the lake,' he said, turning to us, 'tell me we are welcome here.' Nzé, released, laid his gun down, lurched forward, stretched himself full-length on the low bank, cupped his hands in the water and drank like a bushpig.

We walked a little way along the shore, behind the palms and trees and lianas to a promontory where a space had been cleared: Marcellin's old camp. A tree had been felled as a makeshift jetty, and two small fishing canoes lay wedged against it, half-submerged.

'I made these here,' said Doubla, suddenly friendly. 'I made them myself.'

'Doubla! You take the gun!' shouted Marcellin, imperiously, as if he had never suspected he might be murdered. 'We need meat.'

Doubla gave a half-smile, slapped me on the back and slipped away into the jungle behind us.

He returned, triumphant, with a blue duiker, a forest antelope about the size of a roe deer, grey-brown with a whitish belly, large black eyes and two tiny horns.

'There you are,' he said, dumping it down in front of Nzé, 'one cartridge! One *mboloko*!'

'So what?' said Nzé, hurt. 'My grandfather didn't need cartridges. He used to change himself into a leopard at night – and in the morning we'd have bushpig to eat, whenever we wanted.'

To my surprise, nobody laughed.

After supper I went to my tent to get my head-torch and was amazed to discover that the canvas roof of the tent had turned white: thousands of small translucent moths were crowding over it, their eyes glowing red in the torch beam like tiny cigarette-ends. As I watched, looking to see what they were doing – feeding? mating? migrating? – and wondering why you'd want to be white and visible at night if you were a moth, and why I was so ignorant about everything, Manou, in his silent way, appeared at my elbow.

'I have something important to tell you,' he whispered. 'Let's sit by the water. No one must hear us.'

'What is it?' I said with excessive eagerness.

'Last night, there was a snake,' he said quietly. 'Right beside us. Just where Nzé and I were sleeping.'

'But what was it?'

'We don't know. It was asleep under the leaves. Doubla and Vicky were making so much noise that we couldn't question it. You can only ask its name at night, in the silence.'

'So what happened?'

'We felt it after that, later on, right under the tarpaulins you gave us. It kept moving in the dark.' He straightened his shoulders and arched his spine. 'Nzé prayed to his grandfather. But his grandfather said he couldn't help us.'

'A burrowing python! That's what it was! They live underground in the Congo forest.'

'Whatever it was, real or not, it was sent to warn us.'

'Warn us?'

'Not to come here. Not to come to this place. And have you seen the waves?'

'Waves?'

'They come from the centre of the lake. Everyone has noticed. Marcellin saw it. There's something at the centre of the lake which lifts the water from below. Those waves, my friend, they have nothing to do with the wind.'

I was silent.

'Nzé and I – we are frightened. It's a great honour to be here, Redmon. No one in my family except Marcellin has ever been to this holy place. I will tell my children that I went to Lac Télé, and they will tell their children and their children's children. But this is enough. We must leave tomorrow.'

'I had a dream,' I lied, pleased with myself, feeling that I was getting the hang of things. 'We saw Mokele-mbembe and he made our fortunes.'

Manou stood up. 'You must be serious with me,' he said, disgusted. 'You can fool Marcellin, my friend, but not me. I can see the spirits in your face.' And he walked sharply back towards the fire.

I crawled into my tent, tied the flap securely, took off my boots, torch and glasses, lay down and wrapped myself in a tarpaulin. There were no roots or burrowing pythons beneath me; the ground squelched as I turned over; for the first time in months it was as soft as a mattress. The talk from the fire reached me as a murmur, the lake lapped gently at its bank and from among the chorus of frogs I picked out a note that was new to me: a double call like the bark of a vixen on a November night in Wiltshire. Someone began to snore, but with a resonance of such depth and volume that not even the giant of Boha could have produced it. It's Mokele-mbembe, I thought, and he must be hung with testicles as big as beer-barrels – when the reverberation signed itself off with a deep hoot, followed by three more, shorter and higher, and I realized it was just a pair of Pel's fishing owls (huge and brown with great round heads), hidden in the canopy somewhere nearby, agreeing that it was time to stop their marital cuddling on a high branch (they mate for life and sleep together), proclaim their territory, and go fishing (they watch for ripples on the surface in shallow water). As the male called again (he is said to be audible for a mile and a half) I wondered if I would live long enough to hear a Congo bay owl, which is known from only one specimen collected in 1951, told myself it was statistically improbable, blew a fuse in my brain and fell asleep.

In the half-light just before dawn, after a breakfast of boiled duiker bits and rice, Marcellin, Doubla and I bailed out the fishing canoe with our mess tins. A thick mist hung over the lake, unmoving.

'So where did you see the dinosaur?' I said.

Marcellin paused, as if I had been impolite. 'Over there,' he said, pointing off to the left. 'Three hundred yards out. But who knows? Perhaps it was a manifestation ...' His voice trailed off. He looked intently at the now emptied bottom of the dugout as if the pattern of adze marks in the wood might hold some meaning. 'And anyway,' he said, 'I'm not coming with you. *I hate this place*. I don't feel well. I've had enough. I have malaria. I'm going to stay in my tent. I'm going to stay in my tent all day long.'

He lowered himself to the ground like an old man, dropped his mess tin in the mud, crawled into his tent and closed the flap behind him.

Doubla winked at me, touched the side of his nose with his forefinger and smiled broadly. His teeth, I noticed, were all in place. If anyone gets punched in the mouth round here, I thought, it isn't Doubla.

'Our Chief is a powerful man,' he said, shaking his head with admiration. 'He is making Marcellin suffer. He'll take his revenge – you watch. Marcellin sent our Chief to prison at Epéna. Our Chief is now sending Marcellin to prison in his own tent. And the prison at Epéna is much bigger and cooler than Marcellin's tent. Our Chief oversees everything that happens at this lake. This is our lake. It belongs to us, the *paysans*.'

I collected my hat, binoculars and water bottle belt from my bergen and joined Doubla and Vicky at the jetty. Nzé and Manou came to watch.

Doubla pulled two long-handled paddles from their hiding place in a bush at the edge of the promontory, laid his spear down the right-hand side of the dugout, and climbed in after it with such ease and agility that I followed at once, without thinking: the narrow little craft yawed badly at the slightest uneducated movement; or, in other words, it suffered an attack of classical hysteria the moment I touched it, hurling itself left to right and back again, dementedly trying to fling me into the lake. 'Sit down!' yelled Doubla.

I managed to perch my buttocks on a log, my knees up to my ears.

'But I want to paddle!'

'Paddle! You don't know your arse from your tit!'

When the canoe calmed down enough for me to concentrate on a wider horizon, I became aware that Nzé, braying with laughter, had snapped to attention and was saluting. Manou, however, having had no idea that such incompetence was possible, merely smiled, bemused. He looked concerned; I was touched. 'Keep still!' he shouted, as we pushed off. 'You fall over all the time! There's something wrong with your legs!'

No sound came from Marcellin's tent. He's slit his throat in there, I thought, as the promontory fell behind us in the mist.

As the sun rose, the mist grew whiter, thinned, dispersed and evaporated; three tsetse flies arrived over the canoe, buzzed Doubla's legs in a series of fast zig-zags and landed in the open spaces between the clumps of hairs on his right calf. Brown, with big heads and about half an inch long, they folded their wings like the blades of scissors and bit him. His leg twitched; he detached a hand from his paddle as it swung past, and, without interrupting his rhythm, slapped at them, hard, killing two. Inspecting my own legs I counted six on my trousers – I was anaesthetized from the waist down by my position on the log, I realized; I couldn't feel their probosces piercing my skin. In an hour or two I'd start to swell. It was extraordinary, I thought, that an insect with a reproduction rate slower than that of a rabbit could be Africa's most successful conservationist: it has been the sleeping-sickness-trypanosome-carrying tsetse fly (with a little help from the malaria mosquito and the Congo rapids) that has preserved this vast jungle for so long. If there had been none of the terrible fevers, the population of the Congo might be a great deal more than two million, and if it weren't for nagana, the sleeping sickness that kills cattle, both the Bantu and the white colonials might have begun to clear the forest in earnest.

And yes, I said to myself, momentarily glad I couldn't feel their bites, in the long term you have a lot to thank these flies for. But, a little voice said, you'll change your view of things, won't you, if you actually get the disease? And then, come to that, how do you know you haven't caught it already? After all, the symptoms listed in Elaine Jong's *The Travel and Tropical Medicine Manual* fit you rather well, don't they? The western form of trypanosomiasis, endemic here in the forest, starts with a tender papula within five to ten days of the tsetse bite and then ulcerates and disappears over two or three weeks (*and you've had plenty of those*). Next come intermittent fever, headaches and tachycardia (*often*); then a transient skin rash (*not so transient round here*). Which is superseded by increasing indifference, somnolence and a reversal of the sleep cycle (*somnolent for years*). Which is in turn succeeded by incoordination, rigidity and Parkinsonian effect (*every night in Oxford, when drinking with the poet Craig Raine*), followed by irritability and periods of mania (*ditto, but then he always starts it*), stupor and indifference (*most mornings*) and finally death (*any minute now*).

'Quiet!' hissed Doubla, as I began to clap at my legs.

He crouched low, slid his paddle to the floor and reached for his spear. A brown hump, like the roundel of a shield, lay on the flat surface of the lake ahead. In one unbroken movement Doubla rose to his full height, leaned back slightly and, pitching forward, threw the spear with a force which would have been impressive even if his feet had been planted on the ground.

Two small waves collided where the turtle had just been, and spread out in concentric ripples. The shaft of the spear, sticking out of the water a yard off-centre, vibrated slightly. About seven feet of it was visible. So, I thought: let's assume that the point of the spear is buried one foot deep in the mud; that makes the lake, 100 yards out from the shore, around four feet deep. So maybe there are deeper pools in the middle. Or perhaps Mokele-mbembe is a very small dinosaur. Or maybe he is just a very flat dinosaur.

Doubla ran the canoe into a clump of arrow-plants, lopped a big green seed-pod from its stalk, cut it in half, cleaned out its seeds and handed one to me. 'You bail with them,' he said, pushing off again, keeping the canoe close in to the shore and rounding every little promontory.

Scooping out the water slopping round my ankles, I disturbed a tiger bittern in a reed-bed beside me. He rose into the air, a rustle of dark brown and reds like autumn leaves, and banked into the forest, his long yellow legs dangling behind him.

The tiger bittern, I thought, is very rare indeed (the great James P. Chapin only saw two on all his travels up the Congo River and explorations to the east) and if you heard its call for the first time, a deep single or double boom repeated for several minutes at dusk or in the middle of the night, a fog-horn of a note, it would be much more reasonable to think of monsters than of a shy brown bird. But then Doubla and Vicky, being local fishermen, would have heard it all the time. I'll show them its picture in Serie and Morel, I told myself pedantically, and see if they can imitate its call.

I counted five fish eagles at various points in the air above us, and I decided that I was almost happy, that I would forget about my numb bum and lost legs and the tsetse flies that I couldn't swat when, rounding the tangle of a fallen tree, Doubla saw something. He shot the canoe in under a clump of arrow-plants and we crept ashore.

Nothing moved; and then there was the sound of breaking vegetation in a patch of wild ginger. 'Look! Look!' yelled Doubla, pointing into the branches above us. 'It's one of his wives! The husband – he runs away! But look! One of his wives!'

The female gorilla sat in a high fork of the tree, plainly visible, and, through the binoculars, I looked straight into her shiny black face – at her averted eyes beneath the big protruding brow, her squat nose, the two linked horseshoes of her nostrils, her wide thin lips. She seemed extraordinarily human. I was seized with an absurd desire to hold her hand.

She appeared unsure what to do; she stood up, one hand grasping the branch above her, and sat down again. She was carrying something; there were two small black arms tight around her chest; she was carrying an infant.

'We need a gun,' said Doubla in my ear. 'Poof!'

'She's got a child,' I said, lowering my binoculars, afraid they might be a threat signal, an enlarged stare. 'We must leave her alone.'

'They're good to eat,' said Doubla, gesturing with his spear, 'they make you strong.'

'You shouldn't eat them,' I said, over-emotional, taking his arm, pulling him back towards the canoe. 'They're protected.'

'Protected! You white men. The ideas you have! Don't you eat gorillas in England? I bet you do. You're rich. Your forests must be *full* of gorillas.'

'There are no gorillas in England or anywhere else. They live only here and to the east. You should protect them.'

'Huh!' said Doubla, twisting his tendon-hard arm out of my grasp.

A big sitatunga, a swamp antelope, kicked up arcs of water as it made for the bank and safety. Eight long-tailed cormorants straggled past us and disappeared into the haze, a dancing migraine of heat. It was hot, sweaty, skin-crackling, painful.

We landed beside a raffia palm and walked a few yards through the bushes into a small clearing. A tree had been felled. 'This place belongs to my ancestors,' said Doubla. 'They come here to go fishing.'

He ran a hand across his stubbled chin and short moustache, pulled at his scraggy sideboards, reset his eyes and mouth into a mask even more implacable than his usual expression. He then shouted, listened, replied, listened, shook his head enigmatically and sat down on a log.

I took my water bottle out of its belt-pouch and passed it to him.

'Look,' I said finally, feeling like some nineteenth-century ethnographer, 'I'm sure you can tell me the truth in this holy place. There's something I'd really like to know – have you seen Mokele-mbembe?'

'What a stupid question,' said Doubla, looking genuinely surprised. 'Mokele-mbembe is not an animal like a gorilla or a python. And Mokele-mbembe is not a sacred animal. It doesn't appear to people. It is an animal of mystery. It exists because we imagine it. But to see it – never. You don't see it.'

Half an hour later we put in to the bank beside two crossed sticks driven into the mud. 'Crocodile eggs,' Doubla said. 'She will have finished laying by now.'

We struggled up a narrow flattened trail to a pile of leaves and twigs and loose soil about a yard high and six feet across. But something had got there before us. The nest-mound was open and fragments of brittle white shell lay scattered everywhere. Judging by the bigger pieces, the eggs must have been around three inches long and oval, perhaps those of the African slender-snouted crocodile. Doubla dug down with his hands. Nothing.

'The *zoko*'s had our supper,' he said.

'What's that? A marsh mongoose?' I said, excited. Or better still: perhaps the eggs were eaten by that long-nosed mongoose. ('Up to now only thirty specimens known ... lives entirely in rain forests. No details of habits.')

Doubla shook his head.

'A servaline genet?' (Cat-sized, low-slung, black spots on ochre, long bushy black-ringed tail – 'HABITAT: dense woodlands and primeval forests, HABITS: details not known.')

Doubla inflated his chest and cheeks like a bullfrog.

'A Congo clawless otter?' ('HABITS: little known.')

He put his right arm behind his buttocks and lashed it from side to side; he opened his mouth, displayed his thirty-two teeth and came at me with his fingers crooked rigid like claws. At this point I realized that he was trying to tell me something.

'Mokele-mbembe?'

'Much worse than Mokele-mbembe,' said Doubla with one of his short dry laughs, like the first warning bark of a dog that intends to take your leg off. 'The *zoko* is a real monster. He's bigger and faster than a man. And if you annoy him he attacks.'

He held his arms bent inwards at the elbow-joint and imitated something heavy trundling across the forest floor. He flicked out his tongue.

'A monitor lizard!' I yelled to myself. 'It's a Nile monitor!' (Six feet long, first appearing in the fossil record 130 million years ago: and having the good sense to lay its own eggs somewhere safe – by digging a hole in the side of a self-sealing termite's nest.)

A faint hooting call reached us: *woow-ooow-woow*.

Doubla hissed like a monitor: 'Chimpanzees!'

We followed the intermittent calls into a creek; an inlet sheltered from the lake, secluded and still, its surface covered in water lilies.

We floundered ashore in silence; the bursts of chimpanzee conversation increasing in volume and coming from straight ahead. I scooped up handfuls of black mud and plastered my shirt and face with it.

We crossed two swampy streams, crawled on all fours across a patch of firmer ground and slithered on our stomachs to the base of a tree where an old male sat, halfway up on a big bough, slowly pulling twigs towards his surprisingly mobile lips, fastidiously biting selected leaves. Munching, he was deep in thought. He was almost bald, with big ears, deep-set brown eyes and a black face. Doubla put a finger in each nostril and made a high-pitched nasal grunting, the love-call of the male duiker. The old chimpanzee stopped munching, bent forward to look down, swung his head from side to side to get a view through the branches, saw us and took a huge piss. He put his elbow against the tree-trunk and ran a hand over his bald head and face and thought a bit, looking away.

'Waaaa!' he said.

Other chimpanzees immediately began to appear around us, all of them, as far as I could see from my position in the mud, with black ears, faces and palms and black skin on the soles of their feet – adult tschegos, I thought reassuringly, giving them a name. They're the western lowland rain forest variety in which only the very young have faces like white men.

They swung lower, crowding down towards us, until one was about thirty feet away and another above us. Two more, I noticed, were behind us.

The old male stood up on his bough, opened his mouth wide – transforming his peaceful face into a shocking display of Dracula canines – and screamed short, fast, ear-drum-cracking screams. He stamped on the bough and slapped the trunk of the tree. He gripped a small branch in each hand and shook them with appalling purpose.

The others joined in, their throat sacs distended with air and indignation, their hair erect with rage. They whooped together, a *whoo-whooo-whooo* which increased in volume, a frenzy of screaming and branch-shaking. The male above us let fly an explosion of small round turds on our heads, a shotgun-blast of shit. It was unnerving to be the object of such concentrated dislike; no wonder even socially insensitive leopards turned and ran.

This is a very effective display, I thought, patronizingly. Then, I thought (less patronizingly), these apes are big. And then I remembered Jane Goodall's account of the chimpanzee's idea of maximum excitement, a really good day out: you grab a young baboon or colobus by the foot, bash its brains out on a tree, rip it to bits and eat it. I had a sudden twinge of fear, and in the maelstrom of whirling sound waves it was not amenable to reason. There was a stamping on the ground behind us. Doubla, obviously sharing my thoughts, jumped to his feet, shouted and banged the flat of his machete-blade as hard as he could against the tree trunk.

The chimpanzees dropped to the ground and fled.

We reached camp well after dark. Nzé and Manou and the brothers came to greet us but Marcellin remained sitting in silence by the fire.

'Did you hear it?' whispered Manou, taking me by the arm the moment I stepped ashore, staring into my face, as anxious as I had ever seen him.

'Hear what? What's the matter?'

'It called this afternoon. We all heard it.' He made a thin, high-pitched cry, *ooo-ooo-oooo*. 'Nzé is frightened, too. Maybe things will not go well

with us. Maybe we will not live to buy our bicycles with the money
you will give us. If you hear Mokele-mbembe – you die.'

'It's the chimpanzees!' I shouted like a Bantu, feeling I had made a
great discovery, my one contribution to science to date. 'It's the sound
of chimpanzees! You're just not used to sound carrying across open
spaces! You can't be. This is the biggest stretch of open water for
hundreds of miles!'

'We heard Mokele-mbembe,' said Manou, completely unaffected by
my logic. 'We're going to die.'

After supper, the Southern Cross bright above the lake, Doubla and I
happened to be alone together, washing our mess tins by the dugout.

'So, Doubla,' I said softly, 'why did Marcellin swear he saw the
dinosaur?'

'Don't you know?' said Doubla, giving me his first real smile, 'it's
to bring idiots like you here. And make a lot of money.'

Pel's fishing owl began to call.

THE ROAD TO OUIDAH

Bruce Chatwin

*Bruce Chatwin died on 18 January 1989 at the age of forty-eight. He left
behind more than fifty pocket-sized moleskin notebooks and exercise books.
The books are not so much diaries as a reference library of on-the-spot
observation, the literary equivalent of a painter's sketchbook, written for later
use and for the author's eyes only. The selection that follows describes the
journey Chatwin made from Niger through the country of Dahomey and on
to the city of Ouidah on the West African coast.*

2 January 1971, Hotel du Sahel, Niamey, Niger. The usual horror of air
travel. Packaged and processed on a death cart, let down at an African
airport that one might mistake for the moon, swindled by the taxi-
driver and porter and installed in one of those anonymous hotels
with white tiles, angular leatherette-covered furniture, gleaming
chromium. From the window, a terrace with limp, feathery acacias
and the Niger valley rising beyond.

Wandered in the town, to the museum and zoo. These capitals of
Africa are quite formless, isolated concrete villas in acacia plantations
and jacaranda trees. The African smile – slow, stupid, full of good
nature. The procession of women moving up and down with their

baskets. The sense of balance is amazing. Tiny little woman with shrivelled breasts carrying a pair of calabashes full of millet flour. The degree to which an African mother is a self-contained unit – feeder, etc. Thin legs walking on dusty pavements. All the cars save for taxis are driven by Europeans. Europe wealth glittering. No excitement, merely a dull lethargy.

Sore feet. The basketball boots bought at great expense in London pinch the toes. I believe I have curiously deformed feet.

Don't admire this culture very much. Pure asceticism of the desert appeals to my arid sense far more.

Huge blackened cauldrons. The booths – one a reddish contraption of flattened tin cans and wood painted maroon. Scrawled across it in white painted lettering *lait frais et lait caidé Amadou Adina No 1*.

The barkers seem to be a caste of Hausas from Nigeria. Their booths are plastered with posters of the country's 'National Rulers'. Very preoccupied with unity. 'Unity is Strength.'

The French always export the very worst of their culture to the colonies. Yet the combination is not displeasing.

Meat-sellers with hurricane lamps. Umbilical hernias protrude from the bellies of children like some strange tropical fruit.

A restaurant in a garden. I drank a beer on a red spotted cloth-covered table. Mosquitoes bit the hard parts of my fingers. Cool, even quite cold. My backache has completely disappeared. For such small mercies one can be thankful. *Il n'y a personne*. Sometimes there are people, sometimes none at all, says the boy. Yet the menu has fresh caviar, blinis, *terrine de faisan* etc. A tart came up to the next table and began slapping a Frenchman in a yellow shirt patterned with Tahiti-style Pacific fronds.

The sunset left an afterglow. Bands in the sky dark indigo to grey to soft rose. Hills on the other side of the river two shades of grey. The light of the sky reflected in the river.

The smell of Africa.

The American party at the next table. He announced himself very grandly as the Deputy Director of the Peace Corps, so signifying I had no right to address more than a few words to such a person. Their conversation was banal to the point of fascination. It centred on the merits of this or that Jewish comedian on American TV. Both women are tough and pointless, the men are ineffectual. Very straight and square and they want to know Vice-President Agnew and help the blacks. Poor blacks.

Where can a man go to be free of this chit-chat?

I am going home to the hotel.

7 January. Bus journey to N'konni. Niger olive green. Peuls in hats hacking up the road. Piles of peanuts arranged in conical heaps. Rocks in the river. Green islands of vegetation floating downstream. Land the greenish ochre colour of a lion. Villages like mushrooms. Skeletal trees in the heat haze.

A pair of Moorish marabouts travelling. They come from Néma in Mauretania and seem pleased to have been there. They travel for six months of the year. Their next stay is in Néma. One (*'Un grand marabout,'* he confides) will go to the sheikhdoms of the Cameroons. His companion has the startling physiognomy I have noticed among the Moors. High cheeks, long, well-formed jaw and sharp pointed chin emphasized by a goatee. Elegance of the Moors. Clean ascetic quality of Islam. The smell of course is less than anything one might expect on a European bus.

The driver, tough, wearing a leather jacket and a red-and-white checked turban over most of his face. Dark glasses give him total protection.

The women tugging at strips of sugar cane, peeling great strips off like the sound of sticking paper. Heat cannot suppress the female conversation. Child with huge gold earrings. What age do they pierce the ears?

Passed huge Ali-Baba-jar granaries raised on stilts like giant ostriches. Green powder-puffs of trees. Horses feeding on bleached grass. Red roads of Africa. The advertisement for Bière Nigérienne carries a photo of a blonde. Someone with a powerful sweet smell has come into the bus. Voyages bring out the best in people – this voyage brought out the worst in me.

Birnin N'konni. Arrived here in the dark and dined in a pea-green painted restaurant called Le Lotus Bleu. *La Patronne* was a Vietnamese-Negro half-caste who kept a few Vietnamese dishes on her menu as a tribute to her oriental past. Then taken by a charming self-deprecating Martiniquais who wore a bright scarlet shirt and had been a student in Nanterre in 1968 at the time of the *événements*. His friend spent the whole night buried in my book by the light of a spirit lamp.

Chez Vietnam. Concrete balustrade and black women coming up the ochre landscape with half-moon calabashes, light-blue wraps covering the ends of their breasts hanging down like envelopes flattened. The Hausas have scarifications like cat-whiskers. Scarifications make the face into an artificial landscape, intersecting the natural contours. Peuls have little blue triangles low down the cheeks. Rich men in lavender-blue cotton *boubous,* caps in orange, bright colours, chequered bright. Kites and feathery foliage. Mud walls. The red dust whipped up in the wind gets in the eyes and hair. It makes the hair wire-stiff. The boy who looked as if he had red hair till I saw it was the dust all over it.

Gutted cars like carcasses of animals. Dogs look as though they're dead – bleached out. The *patronne's* dust-coloured poodle. Straight bristly hair. Her tiny little feet and bow legs that go in at the kneecaps like hourglasses.

Football the boys were playing. When one kicked the ball, the other would go flying round in a circle pirouette.

Bearded Frenchman and a friend entered. Delighted, the woman screamed with joy and said she had a sausage specially for him. He didn't want a sausage but he wanted *café au lait* and she promised him *un bon bifteck bordelais* but he still said he wanted a *café au lait*. Beard parted in the middle almost like the wings of a butterfly.

Face came over the wall – a Peul, sharp featured in a straw hat that looked like an old-fashioned beehive, and a mouth filled with teeth chewing pinkish cola nuts which came away in little pieces in the wind as he spoke.

Touareg boy with a regular brown handsome face and close cropped hair. He stayed still, silent, grave like a sculpture until he smiled – flashed friendly quick smile – then went silent again and grave. Walked round the edge of the room for fear of disturbing anything in the middle. His boss the Martiniquais played a flute during the night. He wasn't very good at it.

Tomorrow in search of Peuls to a market called Tamaské.

Tamaské. My travelling companion is a charming girl student at the École des Hautes Études at Zinder. She is naturally on strike against the greed of President Pompidou who will leave today on his round to shore up the mineral reserves of France. Niger is the world's third-largest exporter of uranium. Ten per cent for Niger, eighty per cent for France.

Open-air markets under trees. Goatskin sacks, some adorned with green leather clips. Village idiots lying in the dust in heaps with their shirts pulled over their heads to protect them from the sun, their buttocks uppermost. Trousers patched with little patches, doodling threads. Old man erects a stall with a canopy painted with guinea fowl. Pottery not unlike that of ancient Egypt – gourds, origins of pots and pottery.

Village – round huts, granaries, sandy streets lined with wattle fences and weeds, all shades of ochre and green. The fact that several thousand people can congregate from the hinterland and market. Piles of batteries and soapcakes, tins of tomato puree, Nescafé, safety matches, Sloan's Liniment Kills Pain.

The calabash, orange or yellow or dun coloured, is the symbol of fertility of the mother. Upright, globular, it suggests the form of the womb. The Hausa and Peul women with their plaited hair and cicatrized faces ladle milk from spoons made of smaller calabashes. And you gather from the air of condescension they present it with that you are getting the teat of the Great Mother to suck, not the sourish milk of their goats and cows.

Women wrapped in indigo with coral beads. Arms bangled and gleaming with bead and yellow bone bracelets – rings in pierced ears like curtain rings. Next to the milk-sellers was a broken woman, legs spindled and scabbed, her hair matted not tied with plaits like her companions, when she crouched on the ground not covering her sex. Breasts withered into leathery pouches that never nursed a child. A woman broken in pieces. On her head arranged in a pile broken calabashes, all fragmented like her life yet neatly piled in a pyramid on her head.

Tahoua. Returned early with the hope of sleep, but the noise coming from the bar increased in crescendo, increased and increased. Thumping of fists on the table and songs and more songs which increased in volume and incoherence as the whisky increased. Finally at one-thirty I thought a shot of alcohol might assist sleep, put on my trousers and bought a whisky. The *patronne*, her name is Annie, was surrounded by men, six Negroes and two French. One of the French said, '*Vous n'êtes pas la police?*' and I said I was not and he went on singing and banging. Annie in a long tartan skirt, her auburn hair brushed up and lacquered in a pomade, her eyes reduced to bleary slits, more double-chinned than ever, squealed with false pleasure and her gold teeth glittered in her mouth. '*C'est pour moi, ce chanson.* Zey are zinging zis zong for me. *Ecoute, mon cher,'* and she held me by the ribs and said she was sorry they'd woken me.

> *Quand on vient á Tahoua*
> *Viens*
> *Voir Annie*
> *Et son whisky*
> *Annie et*
> *Son whisky*

– repeated and repeated.

Next morning there was a solemn-faced gentleman with a briefcase, and from the looks of Annie's companion who raised her eyebrows that were hardly raisable any more I guessed the gentleman was the law.

10 January. Lay sweating in the sleeping bag with the hot/cold sweat around my balls, dodging, waiting for the mosquitoes that lunged around. Cockroach in the room. Husband of Annie left her. Now she hates all white people. She likes Negroes. Only Negroes. White Annie getting laid by the groom. Good for old Annie.

Waited by the same bedraggled tree and waited and they said the truck would come and it didn't. The negro boy with jeans and plastic sandals said it would come, *Je crois, Je crois, Je crois,* he said, but it didn't come because it had gone long ago, or wasn't going to go. Sat by the fenced compound planted with pink oleanders that lay right by the barracks, that might have been a barracks but was a school. Reminded me of Afghanistan with the round silver grey leaves all covered with dust, plants poisonous with mauve and white flowers that were more like boils or pustules than flowers and their fruit green like sagging squashy testicles.

Speckled shade, grass that crackled underfoot, flowers that defy the heat, shrivelled patches of oil. *Mus, mus, mus* – tiny grey kitten howling viciously in a pile of rocks.

Beautiful Hausas in water-blue on black horses, their black faces reflecting the blue of their clothes and the blue of the sky so that they turned the colour of a night sky without a hint of brown in it.

13 January. Half-past six. Half-past six in the market – one empty lorry, and next to it a couple of Hausas with a smattering of English. Donkey grazing by and a cold, cold wind as the sky turns from indigo to grey. The sound of guinea fowl and cockerels and the thumping of mortars. Light by the petrol pump and the muffled intonation of morning prayer. Morning flight of the vultures till they come to rest on the office of the Compagnie Africaine Française. Figures come out of the shadows, a boy in an orange cap and another veiled and turbanned man, and the lorry begins to fill as if of its own accord.

Pathological wandering has its place among the Peuls. In one of the great nineteenth-century droughts the herdsmen went mad and wandered about the bush chasing phantom cattle.

Kites casting their shadows on the courtyard. A military installation of the French saluted by an old man with colonel's moustache and his head covered by a dishcloth.

They say the Touareg boys are always the most intelligent in the first two years of school, but the novelty of learning rapidly wears off and, conscious of their racial inferiority, they refuse to work. This refusal is of course tantamount to racial suicide. They are gradually being squeezed out and out and further out.

The Bouzous are blackened up Touaregs who live in villages, grow things but speak Tamashek and wear the veil. Rather disquieting.

Peuls are virtually useless when it comes to crafts of any kind. Hausas are energetic businessmen.

Very comfortably installed in the corner of the lorry. Less cold now.

16 January. Will not hire another truck in a hurry. Less uncomfortable last night on the mattress, but a pin stuck into my behind when I moved into one position. Arrived as dawn was breaking and could see the amazing outline of the mosque's minaret, bristling with wooden spires like the vertebra of some defunct fauna. Agadès in the morning light. Another world, the world of the desert. Golden sun hitting the ragged red mud walls, magpies around the mosque and the awful blue of the sky.

The desert men at once recognizable for their white toothy smiles.

The Hausa wrestling match – drugged, gleaming boys, incredibly tough and lean, flexing muscles in animal skins with eyes in the buttocks and tail for nose.

A Hausa house – mud-coloured and on the outside the texture of a good-natured bath towel. Inside, a pillar supporting a vault of thornbush logs. Gummy smell. Door made from the gate of a crate of canned pineapples from the Côte d'Ivoire. Stepped on an old champagne bottle. And a plate that could have been made by a maiden of the Neolithic age. And an old French military camp-bed recovered lovingly with camel leather. It is home. I am happy with it.

Shopping with El Hadj Dilalé. Made to carry everything – sacks, couscous, dirty rice, pinkish rock salt, dried tomatoes, sugar, green tea, etc. Rice from a merchant – 'You will find everything else there.' One merchant, very sophisticated and superior with gold teeth and a pink *boubou*, made out measures of couscous in plastic bags. The other a sweet man who kept trying not to ask me too much. Corrected my *boubou* by announcing it was a Bouzou style and therefore inferior.

The trots. Shat in my underpants in the sleeping-bag. Horrible dawn. Decided not to go.

En marche (have lost all track of date). Crested larks and flocks of black parakeets whisking around as they part in flight. Silence but for creaking of the saddles. Camel docile and amenable. Sound of women's laughter like water bubbling from a spring.

The camel has the most elegant arsehole of any beast I know, none of the flushing flesh pink of the rectum which shows in a horse. And it produces the most exquisite turd – a neat elliptical shape which rapidly hardens in the sun. The shape and texture of a pecan nut.

Tahoua, 30 January. Mme Annie held her *soirée musicale* during the night and looked rather the worse for wear this morning.

'*Equipe Zaza-Bam-Bam et les Supremes Togolaises.*' The Togolese band was of excessive black elegance with expensive electronic equipment in plastic cases that had been patterned in tortoiseshell. The noise of the electric guitars was frightful, full of rhythm but without basic musical taste.

Mme Annie sang:

Si j'étais une cigarette
Entre tes doigts tu me tiendras
Et sous le feu d'une allumette
Je me consumeras pour toi.

The schoolmaster said that the life of the Peuls was unique. That the death of a cow which had borne six calves was of infinitely more account than the death of a parent – a cause for wailing and mournful vigils. In order to get the children to school they (the authorities) have to beseech a chief (resident in Tahoua) for his active participation. Otherwise they disappear into the bush – to Mali or Tchad – and are never heard of again.

Visited a local village stretched out on the flank of a hill with one solitary white house. Then returned to town to watch the break up of a political meeting at the Maison du Parti. A single-roomed mud structure just below the abattoir where the morning's subject was the sexual freedom of teenagers.

Birnin N'konni, 5 February. Have been in Africa for a month only and it seems an age. Nothing particular to record except the extraordinary silhouette in profile of the Vietnamienne. How I wish I could penetrate her thoughts. She has a slight cold this morning. The dust-coloured poodle still ever present.

Slept in the Martiniquais's house in a proper bed this time, not on the floor. He complained that the alphabetization programme is synonymous with the learning of French. No suggestion that Hausa or Djima or Tamashek might even be put into letters. The effect is supposed to make the whole nation speak French and intensify its ties to France. I wonder. I believe the French speakers develop a sense of frustration, inadequacy and loathing for France. The President maintained the view – not an unacceptable view – that it was better to be neocolonialized by people one had partly got rid of than to let down the floodgates to unknown ideologies tinged with oriental fanaticism.

Le Lotus Bleu. Small Vietnamese crêpes submerged in a sauce to which one adds another sauce which cancels out the taste of the first sauce. The crêpe is then ready to be enfolded in a lettuce leaf and a sprig of fresh mint. The taste of the fresh mint cancels out the taste of the second sauce.

Houses like aquariums. Concrete walls. Baby-blue gates. Children playing roundy-roundy in a blue-and-white mosaic podium like an inverted swimming-pool.

The bus. God, what have I let myself in for? I am the last passenger, the ultimate miracle in overstuffing an African bus. First Class in the train after this. To Abomey. To the place charmingly called Dassa Zoumé.

A lady with her hair tied up in three-inch spikes like classical personifications of the dawn, the illusion intensified by the cloud of dawn-pink gauze wrapped about it. Her baby's mouth never leaves her breast, its hand never leaves her mouth.

*

Dahomey. This country – about which I know absolutely nothing – will forever remain fixed in my mind as the land of the decent train. I was – as I said – the ultimate passenger in the overstuffed bus and only succeeded in browbeating my way into it by sheer force of personality – that is, white bloody-mindedness. The last passenger at the edge of the town was an enormous Negress in blue-and-white print who heaved herself in as well. Feeling remorse for my behaviour I let her pass – as a lady – a thing no African would dream of doing. This was a bad thing. She monopolized my precious extra three inches of leg room. Worse, she brought two infant children. One she treated as a headscarf, the other as a handbag. She also had a large enamel basin full of millet balls, chicken, pineapple, papaya and hard-boiled eggs – none of which she shared out to anyone. I was forced to sit on the edge – hard edge – of a tin trunk in between a dreamy long individual's legs. The journey lasted fourteen hours. Arrived in Parakou to the hotel where the staff of the Routier's I shall always remember with gratitude. May even send them a postcard. They provided *café-au-lait*, butter, *confiture fraise*, hot fresh bread in two minutes flat. Then got me a taxi and on to the train with two minutes to spare.

Abomey. Vegetation. Total change. It will take me some time to get used to it. Depressing effects of slack and lava. Dead black skeletons. Big black phallus-like pods in the trees which have no flower. Same family as jacaranda and acacia.

If we have moved into a new vegetational world, we have certainly moved into a new gastronomic one. Consider lunch. Aperitif – coconut milk. Followed by grilled agouti, yams, pineapple. The meat of the agouti was rich and gamey and not a bit tough. The locals hunt it with bows and arrows.

The palace of the Kings of Dahomey. Architecturally unimportant but not at all displeasing. Long low thatched halls with polychromed plaques – now of course refurbished – which served to instruct the kings in their own history and prowess. The series of thrones, dating back to 1600, perfectly preserved, was particularly interesting – also the ceremonial standards of beaten bronze which didn't change in style over three hundred years. Cutlery presented by English in return for trade concessions.

Cotonou, 9 February. Have made a bad start with the Hotel de Port, imagining some sort of old-style joint where the poor whites congregate for a Ricard and whore. Instead the most elaborate motel with *piscine* and thatched beach cottages. The outside looked not unpromising but concealed the deadly Tropical-Americanization of the interior. It is rather pathetic the degree to which the ex-colons will go to preserve their gastronomic links with France. I am eating a *Bresse Bleu* which has blushed a sort of apricot pink in the tropics.

Hard still to take it in. The sheds of corrugated iron, armadillo-ish in appearance, rusting and covered with a rust-coloured dust. The stations where the women sell custard apples. The smells. Sweat, fruit, dust. The stunted goats. On the beach the straight line of white breakers, a pale blue sea, the colour almost of the sky. The bleached hulls of the pirogues. The blown coconut palms.

Leaving Cotonou for Ouidah with high rain clouds building up, perhaps for a storm.

MISSISSIPPI WATER

Jonathan Raban

Flying to Minneapolis from the West, you see it as a theological problem.

The great flat farms of Minnesota are laid out in a ruled grid, as empty of surprises as a sheet of graph paper. Every gravelled path, every ditch has been projected along the latitude and longitude lines of the township-and-range-survey system. The farms are square, the fields are square, the houses are square; if you could pluck their roofs off from over people's heads, you'd see families sitting at square tables in the dead centre of square rooms. Nature has been stripped, shaven, drilled, punished and repressed in this right-angled, right-thinking Lutheran country. It makes you ache for the sight of a rebellious curve or the irregular, dappled colour of a field where a careless farmer has allowed corn and soybeans to cohabit.

But there are no careless farmers on this flight path. The landscape is open to your inspection – as to God's – as an enormous advertisement for the awful rectitude of the people. There are no funny goings-on down here, it says; we are plain upright folk, fit candidates for heaven.

Then the river enters the picture – a broad serpentine shadow that sprawls unconformably across the checkerboard. Deviously winding, riddled with black sloughs and green cigar-shaped islands, the Mississippi looks as if it had been put here to teach the god-fearing Midwest a lesson about stubborn and unregenerate nature. Like John Calvin's bad temper, it presents itself as the wild beast in the heart of the heartland.

When people who live on the river attribute a gender to the Mississippi, they do so without whimsy, and nearly always they give it their own sex. 'You better respect the river, or he'll do you in,' growls the lockmaster. 'She's mean – she's had a lot of people from round here,' says the waitress at the lunch counter. When Eliot wrote that the river is within us (as the sea is all about us), he was nailing something true in an everyday way about the Mississippi. People do see its muddy turmoil as a bodying forth of their own turbulent inner selves. When they boast to strangers about their river's wantonness, its appetite for trouble and destruction, its floods and drownings, there's a note in their voices that says, *I have it in me to do that ... I know how it feels.*

I went down the Mississippi in a small boat in 1979 and met a woman, born in 1880, who'd grown up in the town of Milliken's Bend, a name I couldn't place.

'Nothing left of the town now,' Miss Lily said. 'The River took it.'

She spoke as if it were common knowledge that you had to feed whole towns to the Mississippi every so often to placate it. Within her memory, the river had sluiced many places clean off the map, as it had taken chunks of Illinois and moved them over to Missouri and left busy grain ports high and dry in the cornfields. It had drowned a score of Miss Lily's friends and relations. She began to tick them off on her fingers for me, but lost count. She grinned new teeth in an old alligator face. 'In a boat, huh? Well just *you* take care,' she said.

When the Mississippi climbed out of its banks last summer, I felt a surge of vicarious pride as it spread like a stain over Iowa and Illinois and tangled with the swollen Missouri River in the suburbs of St Charles and St Louis. The television pictures showed a power of darkness on the loose as the Mississippi rolled a trailer home over, squashed a summer cottage flat against the hull of a moored barge, liberated caskets from a graveyard, filled a restaurant kitchen with a moving tide of sludge, got up streets and inside marriages.

Ignoring the calls of hypocrite television reporters for 'gawkers' to stay home and not get in the way of the troops and the sandbaggers, I flew to Minneapolis, rented a car and followed the river downstream for a thousand miles.

Up in Minnesota the flood was in its infancy, the river only just out of its banks; yet even this far north the Mississippi had grown enormously since I'd last seen it, and it was hard to get my bearings. There should have been sandbars – there were none. All that was left of the islands I remembered were some sprigs of green shivering in the current. There should have been a towboat coming round the bend, pushing a fleet of shovel-fronted barges, but the river was empty of boats of any kind. The sunlit water was a yellowy purple, the colour of a ripe bruise, and it sounded like fire as it crackled through a nearby wood.

Out in the channel, the river wrestled a navigation buoy under-water – a big red can, about five feet in diameter, and no easy pushover. Inch by inch, this barrel full of air sank into the Mississippi and disappeared for a full minute. Then it splashed back. The struggles of the buoy, as it weaved and shuddered on its chain, gave a fair idea of what this current might do to something altogether less resilient, like a grain elevator, or a house.

The upper Mississippi is supposed to be a staircase of artificial lakes, with only a trickle of current between them. From St Paul, Minnesota, to Alton, Illinois (just upstream of St Louis), there are twenty-six locks-and-dams, built by the US Army Corps of Engineers in the late 1930s and early '40s. In normal times, these enormous military installations, each with a lock chamber big enough to hold a multi-storey apartment block, lord it over the river like castles. Every twenty-five or thirty miles, you see them looming in the distance, blocky and turreted. This river has been conquered, they assert; it's under army control.

Not any more. At Lock and Dam 7, near La Crosse, Wisconsin, the great roller-gates of the dam had been cranked up, to hang clear of the water, and the Mississippi was pouring through unhindered. 'It's just cruising right on by,' the lockmaster said. 'It's what we call open river right now. The gates are as high as they can go. It's been like that since March.'

Below where the dam should have been, the river seethed, a noisy shambles of steep pyramidical waves and quaking scud. One had to shout to make oneself heard over its hiss and rumble.

'How fast is the river moving?'

'Normally this time of year you'd expect anything between twenty thousand and thirty thousand cubic feet a second. Latest figure we have, it's coming through here at about a hundred and thirty thousand, nine hundred cubic feet a second.'

About? I looked at the drifting chaos of the Mississippi and tried to make it fit that nigglingly precise figure: it wouldn't go.

The flood was breeding its own obsessive numerology. The more nature got out of control, the more people measured it. Across the enormous drainage area of the Mississippi and Missouri Rivers, people were stationed with rain gauges, rulers, hygrometers, knotmeters, probes. In the cities of St Paul, Rock Island and St Louis, people fed the data into computers. Each day at noon, the Corps of Engineers faxed out a new sheet of numbers. The sheet would tell you – among many other things – that the Mississippi was due to crest at Hannibal, Missouri, on Thursday at one-thirty p.m., at a height of 31.4 feet.

Each day, these sheets were posted up in city halls and riverside bars. They were treated exactly as opinion polls are treated in a neck-and-neck political campaign. Spin-doctors interpreted them. Strategies were changed by them. 'Thirty-one point four!' people said, and the number alone would excite fear or relief.

At noon next day, the number would be revised by a foot or more – and it wouldn't be Thursday, it would be Saturday or Tuesday. Yet still people clung to it. 'Twenty-nine point six!' they said, as if the prediction was itself a victory worth celebrating.

I asked the lockmaster how much warning he'd been given. Had he known about the flood for ages before it arrived?

'They didn't forecast it until it happened,' he said.

In March the river was high with normal spring run-off after the melting of the northern snows. One by one, the dams were raised – as usual – to give the Mississippi a free run to the Gulf of Mexico. Then the rain began.

'It just kept on coming and coming. It was unreal. In April, they were saying it would be all over by May. In May, things were getting real tight, but they said we'd be dry by June. And all through June, it rained and rained. And rained.'

As we spoke, five inches of rain had just been forecast for Nebraska; four or more in South Dakota; it was due to rain tomorrow in Minnesota, Wisconsin, Iowa, Illinois and Missouri. A *disaster* is a disorder in the heavens: *dis* + *astrum*, an unfavourable aspect of the stars or planets. Few 'disasters' are really *disasters*, but this one was – in 1993, the heavens were all to hell.

The road south crossed a dozen swollen creeks, and with the addition of each creek to the main stream, the infant flood grew stronger. It was on the boil now, moving in big greasy rolls and swirls. As the flood rose, the towns got emptier. 'It's not this bad in *January*' said the waitress in Lansing, Iowa. There were no cars, no tourists, no fishermen, no houseboaters. Shops were closed; roads were closed; and in the café where I remembered a merry breakfast crowd on my last visit, four Iowa ancients in plastic baseball caps sat silently in line, staring out at the Mississippi. The river unscrolled like a movie: in the middle distance, an uprooted tree sailed slowly past from left to right. It was followed by an oil-drum, a tractor-trailer wheel, another tree. The ancients watched closely, awaiting the next twist in the plot – a vagrant skiff, an outhouse, an interesting box. For half an hour, I watched them watch the river. Something over 235,620,000 cubic feet of Mississippi water slid past the window, bearing nothing worth the bother of salvaging it.

I spent the night at a motel in Prairie Du Chien, on the Wisconsin side, and had just fallen asleep when I was woken by thunder – a series of grumbling explosions directly overhead that made the second-floor room shake and waver in its flimsy timber frame. I found the switch on the bedside lamp, but the lamp was dead. The sound of thunder gave way to that of rain on the parking lot outside, like gravel pouring from a long chute. I groped my way to the window, from where I watched bursts of sheet lightning flicker over the roofs of the darkened town. My watch said that it was eight-fifty.

Soaked to the skin by a ten-yard dash to the car, I drove round to the candlelit motel office. The woman at the desk took my key and checked her ledger by flashlight to make sure that I'd paid. 'Come back and see us sometime,' she said, indifferently. 'Have a nice day.' No mention of the storm, the lightning, the power outage, the candles at mid-morning. This was evidently how summer days usually began in the year of the Deluge.

The roads were awash. A truck cruised slowly down US 18 like a clipper ship with a bone in its teeth. On the car radio, a tiresomely upbeat, top-of-the-morning announcer was enjoying himself, reading out flash-flood warnings for Crawford, Grant, Clayton and Allamakee Counties. 'Seek higher ground,' he said, as I crossed the river back into

Iowa and struck out south on a low-lying minor road that kept close company with the Mississippi. Having told everyone to run for the mountains, he then told them to head for the Free Sweet Corn Boil at Johnson market. 'Go on!' he urged, 'brave the rain! Take the kids! It's going to be a whole lot of fun!' If we were thinking of spending the day in Illinois, he said, we must be sure to dial a 1-800 number: 'They'll tell you if your favourite tourist destination is underwater.'

By ten a.m. the rain was thinning, and the sky took on the appearance of a wintry dawn. The Mississippi was like an enormous sheet of dirty gauze, spread flat across the landscape. It was now impossible to guess where its banks might have been, and hard to tell where the river left off and the unflooded land began. Fields of short corn ('knee-high by the fourth of July') brimmed like ponds, and as the Mississippi rose to meet them, there was a kind of fluid commingling between this river full of earth and this earth full of water.

I stopped for breakfast at a grocery store on a low hill, a mile or two inland, and was shocked by the heat of the day as I stepped out of the car. It looked like November, but the temperature was over ninety degrees, and the rain on my scalp was warm as sweat. The same four ancients, first seen in Lansing, or their four cousins, were seated at the breakfast counter.

From them I learned – slowly and with some difficulty – that:

> The floods were caused by paving. *Paving?* Parking lots. Malls. Condo blocks. Community colleges. People from the cities were covering the land with concrete and there was nowhere for the rain to go.

> The water-table was rising. It was now so close to the surface that crops were rotting from the roots up.

> Things were going to get worse. Much worse.

'You think it's bad now, you better come back next year. Then you'll see floods. I'm telling you. What we got now – that's nothing to what's coming. You wait till the year two thousand. Where they've got cities now, there'll be just swamps then. Levees won't hold the river in, not with the water-table where it's at – no way.' He looked as if he was going to make damned certain that he stayed alive until the year 2000, if only for the sour pleasure of seeing his prophecy come true.

When I went back to the car, the rain had turned to steam. Visibility was down to less than half a mile. The river smoked, the bluffs were shrouded in hot fog. The road ran along the edge of the flood, which had recently dropped a little, exposing a margin, ten or twelve feet wide, of shiny black goo – a compound of rotting grass and corn-stalks, drain-water, fertilizers, oil and dead fish. The smell was of the sort that glows in the dark.

The mayflies were doing well in it. A huge hatch was in progress, and the big clumsy flies pasted themselves against my windscreen, hundreds at a time. The wipers made a crunching sound and were caked solid with bits of wing and thorax. The stink, the insects, the bubbly, sewagey look of the uncovered ground, were the result of a drop of just a few inches in the level of the river. When the Mississippi really went down, it would leave a margin of fetid slime, miles wide on either side.

In 1979, an Iowa farmer, Harvey Schwartz, showed me the precious soil of his bottomlands farm between Davenport and Muscatine. He powdered it between his forefinger and thumb, and made me do the same. It was soft, brown, moist and pungent – almost as rich in nutrients as dung itself.

'Taste it,' said Harvey Schwartz.

I parked a few grains on the tip of my tongue.

'That's some of the richest soil in the whole world,' he said, as if the grains were caviare.

Now the river was only doing what rivers are supposed to do with their flood plains: enrich the soil with the long, slow work of regular flood, siltation and decomposition, coating the fields with smelly glop. At present, all the talk was of how the Mississippi had 'devastated' the land around it. Actually it was nourishing it, though with scant respect for the barns sunk to their eaves, or the farmers' homes where the river was now in possession of the bedrooms on the second floor. When Governor Branstad of Iowa spoke on the radio of the tragedy that had befallen his state, with eight million acres of land under water, he might have added that most of this land was being improved by the experience. When the flood finally went down, there would be a foot or more of fresh topsoil on the 'bottoms' – a fine-sifted mulch in which the wheat would stand as thickly as the bristles on a brush.

At Le Claire, I spotted a fisherman sitting in the picnic gazebo in the centre of a children's playground. I waded across to talk to him on his island. He'd brought sandwiches, Gatorade and a transistor radio to while the day away. He watched his rod tip. His bait, a plump nite-crawler, had been cast far out; it lay between the slide and the swings.

'Ain't nothing doing,' he said. 'I don't know why. I think it's because the fish don't like the river going down. Beginning of the week, when it was coming up, the fishing was real good – right over the road there ...' He pointed to where I'd parked the car.

'Catfish?'

'*Big* catfish. And perch. And croppies. It was good fishing.' He reeled in. His worm hung in a limp *U* from the hook. It looked stressed-out by the heat and the humidity. He took a fresh one from the can, threaded it past the barb, and flicked it out towards the jungle-gym.

His radio, on the picnic table, was full of advice and instructions. Volunteer sandbaggers were being issued with assembly points. They were told to bring plenty of mosquito-repellent and to swab down thoroughly afterwards. 'Remember,' the announcer said, 'this is tough, hot, smelly work.' For about seven seconds, I toyed with the idea of becoming a volunteer sandbagger in Des Moines – a two-and-a-half-hour drive to the west – but the only thing that I could seriously imagine doing out in the open air was steaming asparagus in it.

As the Mississippi spilled untidily southwards, it added more and more new rivers to the flow. There were the Wisconsin River, the Rock River, the Iowa River, the Des Moines River and – before the Mississippi reached St Louis – it was also joined by the Illinois River and the Missouri River. There were Indian rivers: the Maquoketa, the Wapsipinicon, the Kickapoo. There were animal rivers: the Turkey, the Fox, the Bear, the Skunk, the Buffalo. There were the Apple and Plum, the Cedar and Root, and smaller rivers, by the dozen and the score, piling into the Mississippi – and all the rivers were in flood.

According to the Corps of Engineers and their current meters, the Mississippi was moving at a speed and volume of 130,900 cubic feet per second at La Crosse; 400,000 cubic feet per second at Rock Island; 1,000,000 cubic feet per second at St Louis. Over the same stretch of river, the current was quickening from about three knots to about ten knots.

These figures make it sound as if the Mississippi was travelling downstream with the concentrated energy of a locomotive on a track, when its actual motion was more like that of the suds in a washing-machine. It spun and tumbled, gyre on whirling gyre, water rubbing against water. The friction generated strings of whirlpools, some big enough to trouble, if not quite swallow, a boat.

Wherever one looked, the water was moving in coils and wreaths, like smoke. The dead mayflies on its surface were drifting every which way on the turbulence. They raced, dawdled, described long lazy Ss, revolved in dizzy pirouettes. I focused on a single fly, one veined wing standing proud of the water like a windsurfer's sail. It would ... but it didn't. It feinted, sashayed, zig-zagged, confounding my predictions over every inch of the course.

From Davenport on down, the cities began to take to the waters in earnest. Muscatine and Port Madison were in the river up to their middles. Their downtown shopping streets had become canals. Parking meters had turned into convenient mooring-posts for the aluminium skiffs that served as gondolas in these new Venetian times. The boats moved silently. There was a ban on the use of outboards, whose wake might have toppled the sandbag walls, so people rowed and punted, as if they were doing it for the scenery and the exercise on this broiling Saturday afternoon. It's said that a change is as good as a rest, and most of the flood victims were in a larky holiday mood.

'Start your own business! Be your own boss! Fax machines! Answerphones . . .' sang out one jolly ferryman over the water, as he paddled a cargo of office equipment to higher ground.

The bottom end of each town petered out into a semiotic playground of signifiers, divorced from their referents, sticking out of the flood, TURN RIGHT FOR US 61. STOP, RAILROAD CROSSING. BUSINESS LOOP. NO PARKING. NO LEFT TURN. STRAIGHT AHEAD FOR THE MUSEUM, ONE WAY. YIELD, EXIT ONLY. Some of the signs had been knocked sideways by the Mississippi and leaned at forty-five-degree angles to the water. Some were completely submerged. The river ran placidly through the slough of antediluvian messages, the current making braids around every post.

All the shutterbugs in town were out with cameras, and the jumble of signs was everybody's favourite subject. Pictures of the signs would become one of the two or three key images of the Great Flood. They're happy pictures. They show the river making monkeys of City Hall, the Highway Department and the rest. They show authority wittily subverted by the water, which has robbed every imperious command of its meaning. They catch something important, about which little was said at the time: the glee that people felt as the river came up and played this gigantic practical joke on their world.

In Port Madison at dusk, with the mosquitoes beginning to sound like a string band, I was loitering at the edge of a flooded street, watching a line of sandbaggers build a wall around a threatened gas station. An elderly woman with a camera stood nearby, her Oxford shoes islanded. She was waving the bugs away with a handkerchief, and smiling, hugely. When she saw me see her smile, she felt called on to explain it. 'Well,' she said, 'everybody's got to look at the water, haven't they?'

On Sunday morning, I crossed the Iowa-Missouri state line. Now things looked like a war. Each tributary river ran higher and faster than the last. Big creosoted barns were pasted flat against trees, like stoved-in cardboard boxes. Lines of oddly foreshortened telephone poles led out to isolated farms that were sunk to their roof beams. From a distance, they looked like bivouacs, pitched on the water. Things were so bad in towns like La Grange that even the National Bank was in the river. US 61, the main highway to the west of the Mississippi, led down a hill and ran slap into the flood. At every turn, soldiers, in battle fatigues and camouflaged armoured cars, manned roadblocks and talked importantly into antique two-way radios. With the sodden fields, the National Guardsmen and the pensioned-off military equipment, it looked as if one had stumbled into the making of a movie set in Vietnam, *circa* 1968.

The National Guard was there to deter looters and turn sightseers away. But the sightseers were locals – farm families, still dressed for church; shrunken grandpa-figures in straw hats and oversize pick-ups – and the soldiers shrugged and let them through. Me, too. At one checkpoint, I pulled up and prepared to spin a story, but the sergeant in charge said only, 'We're going to have to start charging for tickets of admission soon.'

The families formed a slow promenade in the heat, leaving their cars to walk out to the end of a gravelled road that was now a pier. The sheet of water ahead, dotted here and there with roofs and treetops, stretched to the horizon, an inland sea. People said very little. There was some nervous joking among the adults, some rough-house capers from the kids, but the prevailing atmosphere was that of the church that most of them had just left. We squinted at the flood in silence.

Water not only finds its own level; it makes itself perfectly at home. The winding contour-line of the edge of the flood had the natural authority of any coast. It looked so *right*. It was not the water that was in the wrong place, but the strange, angular things that poked impertinently out of it. Wherever the water impinged on the man-made – on a road or a city parking lot – it resulted in a sweet curve across a surface that one would previously have thought of as flat. The flood redefined the land, and the dangerous thought came, unbidden, that the work of the flood was a beauty and a wonder.

Driving south through Missouri, as close to the water as I could manage, I had to brake several times for lumbering racoons. There were many dead, but all the bodies lay on the right hand side of the road. They looked like cuddly toys from an infant's crib – dead opossums, racoons, coyotes, chipmunks, fawns. They had all fled west to get out of the way of the rising river; racing to escape nature, they'd been felled by technology.

But on the whole, nature was doing well out of the flood. The fish were thriving, and the birds that ate the fish, like herons and ducks, were everywhere. People said they couldn't remember a time when so many birds were in residence on the river. The mosquitoes were in heaven, and the lower orders – viruses like *E. coli* and tetanus – were enjoying a rare taste of freedom from the constraints of civilization, breeding by the billions in the stagnant swampy water on the fringes of the flood. For the wandering tribes of freshwater plankton on whom the whole ecosystem of the Mississippi depended, life had never been better than in the summer of '93.

The flood was making many humans happy too. Door-to-door insurance salesmen were working round the clock, selling dubious policies to frightened home-owners in low-lying areas. On the Chicago stock market, commodity traders were making a killing on wheat and soybean futures. In St Louis, panhandlers were putting on their best clothes and representing themselves as charities collecting for flood-victims.

It was a wonderful time for prophets.

On the car radio, Randall Terry of Operation Rescue, the anti-abortion outfit, was being interviewed by Terry Gross of NPR's 'Fresh Air'. The floods in the Midwest were, he said, 'The first Call. The first Blast of the Trumpet.' There was a triumphant I-told-you-so squeak in his voice, and his tone was that of the mad lounge-bar logician who can prove that the moon-landings never took place and that Richard Nixon was a Communist spy. We had, according to Randall Terry, seen nothing yet. 'God has a *hundred* hurricanes, a *hundred* droughts, a *hundred* floods . . . ' And in His wrath over abortion, He would bowl them at America one by one.

Terry Gross pointed out that God's choice of the Midwest as the locus of His vengeance seemed a little unfair: had He not picked on the most god-fearing region in the whole United States? Why was He so punishing His own home team?

'When God judges a nation, innocent people suffer,' said Randall Terry, with frank relish. 'Innocent people suffer – for the sins of the child-killers, and for the sins of the homosexuals . . .'

A few days later, CNN financed a poll which found that one in five Americans – the same percentage as had voted for Ross Perot in the Presidential election – believed that the floods were God's judgement on the sins of the people of the US.

At Louisiana, Missouri, that Sunday evening, a Free Supper for Flood Victims was advertised on the noticeboard of the Masonic Temple. The feast was being scoffed by six perspiring National Guardsmen, each attended by a Mason's wife, looming with another dish.

I was barely inside the door before I was fending off an avalanche of ribs and wings. I explained that I hadn't come to eat, but that I would like to meet a flood victim, if any of the flood victims would care to talk to a stranger.

'There aren't too many flood victims here right now, but you *must* try these cookies.'

'Are you a vegetarian? We could make you up a special plate—'

I could see why the Masons themselves were all men of impressive substance, whose most noticeable clothing-items were their belts and suspenders. One man wore a particularly fine belt of strange devices proclaiming him to be a member of the Ancient Arabic Order of Nobles of the Mystic Shrine.

'You have to be in the photograph—' he said, and I was hustled into the group of waiting brethren. The picture was for a forthcoming issue of a Masonic magazine. In it, the Shriner and I have our arms around each other's shoulders; I am grinning weakly and billed, I fear, as a visiting Knight Templar from London, England. The reason for the picture is that we have all been helping flood victims.

When the photography was done, I asked the Shriner about the flood victims.

'Those people,' he said. 'Most of 'em, they just don't want to be helped.'

How many people had been washed out by the flood here?

'Oh, not too many. Down in the flats ... must be about thirty families, maybe?'

How were they coping?

'Oh, those people, they cope pretty good. They're used to it. They're the same people got flooded out in '73. They just move right back in: hang out the carpets to dry, hose down the furniture, and they're back in there, happy as clams.'

'Are these people – black?'

'Oh, no; some of 'em are – it's pretty much of an even mixture, down there in the flats. Between you, me and the gatepost, most blacks in this town have got more sense than to live there. The smart ones all live up on the bluff, as far away from the river as they can get. And good luck to 'em!'

The Masons' wives began, reluctantly, to shroud the bowls of food with Seranwrap, while the Masons folded up the tables, and the guardsmen returned to their roadblock on the flats.

I went for a stroll in the dusk. The cabins of the flats – people were deep in the river. The current spiralled through bedroom windows that had been smashed by floating railroad ties. At the corner of Alabama and 6th, a catfish was rootling down the centre of the street, its progress marked by the bursts of small bubbles that it sent up at steady intervals. Further down, where someone's yard shelved steeply into the river, I spotted what appeared to be a large pale halibut. It turned out – disappointingly – to be a submerged satellite dish.

The flats were on a back-eddy of the Mississippi, a natural assembly-point for drifting junk, and wherever the river touched dry land, it returned a broad selection of objects to the civilization from which they had been thrown away. On the little beach at the end of one quite narrow street, I counted more than twenty car tyres, a propane cylinder, a torn-out car headlight, a fishing float, a fifty-gallon oil drum, a glove, several super-economy-sized detergent bottles, numerous soft-drink cans, some lightbulbs, a clutch of aerosols, a toddler's yellow plastic tricycle, badly mauled and encrusted in gobs of tar, some broken honeycombs of polystyrene packing, and enough baulks of lumber with which to build at least one new cabin on the flats.

In the Downtown Lounge, a spry black man in his seventies was half-telling, half-miming, a flood story to an audience of two younger white men.

'And Duval – you know Duval – has that purple house down there? Duval's up on the levee, takin' pictures . . .' The storyteller was being Duval; prancing on tiptoe, his right hand curled into the shape of a viewfinder, while his left hand cranked on the imaginary handle of an old-fashioned movie camera. His head jerked to one side; he'd been interrupted in his filming. '"Oh, I ain't baggin'," says Duval, "I'm too busy takin' pictures of the water—." They're piling up the sandbags, fast as they can go, but Duval's *busy*. He's walking round his house, round and round, taking *pictures*. "I ain't baggin'," – the storyteller was wheezing with laughter. '"I ain't baggin'."' He stopped to sip his beer. 'And the river, he's *rising*, right around Duval's purple house. The river's through the door. Duval, he didn't get *nothing* out of there; he's taking pictures on the levee. And when it's too late, and the water's come right up, you shoulda heard him! "My TV! My couch! My rug! My clothes!" That Duval!'

He returned to his stool and hoisted himself up on it, shoulders shaking.

'I ain't baggin'!'

I asked the storyteller if his own house was safe. Did he live down by the river?

'Where's my house? Oh, my house is fine. I live way up the hill.'

At St Charles – in normal times – the Missouri River briefly runs parallel to the Mississippi, tucking behind a wide and leisurely bend of it. For more than twenty-five miles, the two rivers swing in consort, first north, then east, then south, before they tangle violently with one another, twelve miles before St Louis. But now they did not run parallel; their separate floods had met and washed across a flatland of industrial estates, trailer parks, farms and townships – a hazy shimmer of water, the same colour and texture as the sky.

I had wanted to reach Portage des Sioux, once on the Mississippi, now ten miles out across the lake, but still, just, connected to the mainland by a road that was only a few inches under water. I was turned back at the first roadblock: only residents and emergency workers were allowed to tackle this amphibious route, where jumbo pick-ups crawled like a line of ants traversing a mirror.

People here looked mugged.

In the small towns where I'd been stopping, people knew each other, knew the Mississippi, and had found in the flood a cause of anarchic Blitz humour. It was different in the Greater St Louis suburbs, where the river is normally little more than a glint of brown water with a towboat on it, seen out of the corner of one's eye from a car on the expressway. Tourists, doing the Gateway Arch thing, saw more of the Mississippi than most native St Louisans, for whom the river lay on the far edge of the known world, a convenient barrier between St Louis proper and the desperate no-go area of East St Louis over in Illinois. You could live in St Louis without giving the river a second thought from one year's end to the next; you might not even be aware that you had a river on your doorstep at all.

So when the Missouri, the Mississippi and the little Des Peres ganged up and moved into the suburbs, their arrival was a horrible surprise to people who had no memory or mythology to help them cope with the flood. The little one was the nastiest of the three. The Des Peres had backed up from its junction with the Mississippi, burst through its earthen levees and made itself at home in the middle of residential South St Louis. Headline writers renamed it the Despair.

I passed over the Des Peres on a freeway bridge. The river was being escorted through evacuated streets on a leaky aqueduct of sandbags and plastic sheeting; the area was surrounded by troops. Meanwhile, policemen were unrolling a floppy orange screen along the side of the freeway bridge to deter motorists from slowing for the view. The sight of a nice, quiet neighbourhood spectacularly ruined by the flood was bringing rush-hour traffic to a standstill.

The region around St Louis was suffering from another inundation, of journalists. The world's television crews had set up command positions in all the best hotels, and were fanning out across the countryside in search of stories. At Kimmswick, on the Mississippi, I reached the roadblock in time to catch the tail end of an altercation between *Time* magazine, the Houston *Post* and a captain of the National Guard. No one, said the captain, was to be allowed through: orders of the mayor.

'What about *Good Morning America*?' said *Time*. 'You let *Good Morning America* through.'

The captain allowed that an exception had been made for *Good Morning America*.

'It's typical,' said the Houston *Post*, 'this is what we're finding everywhere – discrimination against the print media. The breakfast shows are reporting from the levee, while national newspapers have to put up with "briefings" in the City Hall – and here we can't even get to City Hall.'

'It's not me,' said the captain. 'I'm here to carry out the instructions of the mayor. And that's what she says. No journalists beyond this point.'

'I want to speak to the mayor,' said *Time*.

The captain spoke into his radio. The message from downtown was that the mayor was out of her office and would not be back until the evening.

'But we have to file our stories by six,' said the *Post*, 'in the print media.'

'And they know that,' *Time* said, 'that's why she's out of her office. Can we reach her at home?'

The best that the captain could do, he said, was to report that the newspapermen had filed an urgent request for access. He spoke into his radio again. 'I've got *Time* magazine and the Houston *Post* and—' he turned to me: 'who are you with?'

'Oh, I'm not exactly ... *Granta*,' I said.

For a moment, the captain looked at me with a flicker of significant interest.

'That's *Time*, Houston *Post* and Greta,' he said.

Sainte Genevieve, Missouri, was lapped in a cloud of hot grey dust. This dust was everywhere: it turned the grass grey and greyed the faces of the people on the streets. In the town centre, the high school yard had become a sandbag factory, where dozens of small squads of volunteers were shovelling dust among the mounds. Dotted about the yard were more small squads, of cameramen and reporters, filming the sandbag brigade.

The dust was from the local lime-producing plants, whose trucks rolled through town on their way to the levees. The noise of their passage blended nicely with the sound of an enormous orchestra of two-stroke pumps. From end to end, Sainte Genevieve rumbled, coughed and snuffled in the dusty air, while the river drifted past, just overhead.

The Mississippi had already taken a large slice of the town, but a winding line of inner levees had so far stopped it from swamping the antique heart of the place – a pretty grid, five streets by five, of freshly painted antebellum houses, gift shops, restaurants and hotels. The river was on the rise. The water was now within a very few inches of the top of the sandbag-parapet, and it was coming up from below, puddling the streets and making ominous dark stains on the dry ground.

That day, Sainte Genevieve was where the story was. CNN were in town, with ITN and Swedish television hard on their heels, followed by a brilliant rabble of scribes and photographers, conspicuous in their Florida beach-vacation wear. Along the balcony of one old hotel had been strung a banner – STE. GENEVIEVE – DOING IT AGAIN BEATING OLE MAN RIVER – and the TV reporters were taking turns being filmed in front of it as they delivered their to-camera pieces about historic-town's-heroic-cliff-hanger-battle-with-mighty-Mississippi. Up on the levee, cameras slowly panned from the rooftop islands in the river to the sweating sandbaggers. *They fight a foot at a time. They fight a day at a time. They fight with grit and determination* ... And you could almost see the levee bulge and quake as the river threatened to sweep away this precious, candy-coloured piece of early Americana in a tide of foaming slurry.

It was a good image, and a valuable one. Sainte Genevieve had always wanted a 'federal levee' – a top-of-the-range model, built by the Corps of Engineers, with a solid clay core encased in layers of earth and rock. When the river eventually went down, there would be a tremendous contest between the flooded towns for federal money. In Sainte Genevieve, whose experience in the tourist industry had equipped it with more worldly cynicism than most towns of its size, it was thought that the money would flow naturally to those places that had been most prominently pictured on the evening news and on the breakfast shows.

Trying to catch the attention of senators and congressmen, Sainte Genevieve went fishing for journalists. Its little city hall was like the headquarters of a political campaign; in fact it was the headquarters of a political campaign. Under the slogan WE CAN DO IT the walls were decorated with factoids, written out in a big, round hand: '40,000 Sandbags Are Needed Every Day'; 'Number Of Sandbags Used So Far – 800,000'; 'Ste. G. Annual Budget, $1.4m – Estimated Flood Expenses, $15.3m And Rising.' Every journalist was supplied with a map and a fact sheet, which proved, beyond any journalist's reasonable doubt, that floods in Ste Genevieve, Mo., were usually caused and always exacerbated by the construction, in the 1940s, of federal levees on the Illinois side of the river.

The city had appointed a Media Coordinator – Jean Rissover, a local woman who had once been editor of the Ste Genevieve *Herald* and now ran her own PR firm – and it was hard to figure out quite how Ste

Genevieve had managed to contain Ms Rissover before the flood. She had the metropolitan knack of being able to maintain efficiently three conversations at once; she knew how to hobnob with purpose; she smoked; and she nourished the story of Ste Genevieve, as it was told on the networks and in the national press, adding just enough to it each day to keep it alive for many days on end. If there was a weak spot on a farm levee, or a dip in production at the sandbag factory, the fact – and the name Ste Genevieve – would appear on the ten o'clock news and in next morning's *New York Times*. Given the geographical extent of the floods and the intense competition for time on television and space in papers, it was extraordinary how Ste Genevieve managed to keep itself in the public eye. That was Ms Rissover's work.

Under her direction, the National Guard took the journalists off on helicopter rides, and the Coast Guard ferried them around in boats. She kept a team of local historians at the ready, to brief the journalists on the unique nature of the national treasure that was threatened by the flood. For Swedish television, she found a Swedish-speaking local historian.

Ms Rissover thumb-tacked newspaper stories datelined *Ste. Genevieve, Mo.* to the wall around her desk. They hung there in fat bunches of wilting newsprint, and the wall was fast growing too small for them. Some day soon, the City Administrator would cash them, for a correspondingly thick pile of tax-dollars and a new federal levee.

For *Granta*, Ms Rissover (who took the democratic line that a medium was a medium was a medium) laid on a boat trip. In the company of a photographer from FEMA, the Federal Emergency Management Agency, and another from the A.P. wire service, I got afloat on the flood, in an aluminium dory piloted by two Coast Guard reservists.

The current was running fast, even though we were two miles from where the map said the Mississippi was. Though there was no wind, the treetops shook as if in the grip of a gale, and a street lamp oscillated wildly on its stalk.

'Dancing light-pole,' said Petty Officer Mobley.

The boat gained slowly on the current, the fifty horse-power motor on tickover. If Mobley made a wake, he risked knocking sandbags off the levee. He was also navigating without a chart and without local knowledge, for the Coast Guard detachment assigned to Sainte Genevieve came from Louisville, Kentucky, and neither Mobley nor his crew, Able Seaman Felicia Berba, who sat up front with a five-foot boat-hook, had ever visited Sainte Genevieve before the flood. So we moved gingerly, in doubtful water, over foul ground, with the A.B. sounding for chimney-pots, parking-meters, heating vents, rock gardens, sheds, power-lines, trailers. Though there were plenty of roofs and utility poles in view, it was surprisingly hard to make out the safe, deep channel of a street.

The current, spooling through the shallows of an orchard, made the boat slew.

'Lot of eddies here,' FEMA said.

'By the time you get the current figured out – forget it,' said Mobley, weaving the dory between a gable-end and a submarine garage. 'Snake . . .' he called out. 'Snake in the water.' It moved like a spring, in quick spasms. A.B. Berba, sitting next to me, screwed up her face in pantomime disgust.

'What sort of snake is that?' I said. 'It's not a water-moccasin—'

'They got more snakes in this river than I ever heard of,' said Berba, 'and any kind of snake's a bad snake to me.'

'Snake . . .' said Mobley. 'Snake in the tree.' It was dangling from a branch, apparently trying to make up its mind as to whether to take the plunge. It plopped neatly into the water as we went past, ten feet clear.

After a few minutes of this, Mobley stopped alerting us to snakes; it was like shouting 'Fly!' on a warm evening in a barnyard. There were a lot of snakes. The mammals, ousted from their homes on the islands and wooded river banks, had fled inland, but the snakes were happy with any dry lodging they could find – a window-sill or chimney did nicely; an upstairs deck was snake heaven. So the flooded half of town had filled with copperheads, cottonmouths, rattlers. There were snakes sunning themselves on roofs, snakes on couches, in drawers and closets, in beds. The snakes – so sinuous and riverine in shape – were natural emblems of the Mississippi itself, and nothing so well represented people's sense of being violated by the river as the image of the cottonmouth in the child's crib. When people talked about going back to their houses after the flood, it was the snakes they mentioned first, and with good reason. The snakes were real, deadly and in residence.

Pacing the current, Mobley opened the throttle and immediately the boat ran into something soft and substantial. It reared, slid sideways over the obstruction, and nearly tipped Associated Press into the snake-infested river.

'I never hit that before,' Mobley said.

Berba, leaning over the bow, prodded about with the boat-hook, but it went cleanly down into deep water.

'It wasn't hard enough for a shed,' Berba said.

'It felt something like a dead cow,' I said.

'The things people have in their yards.'

The levee, seen from the perspective of the river, was only a shallow rim, no more than six inches high in places, of grey sandbags and torn plastic sheeting. We coasted to its edge and looked over at the flimsy streets below – at the pumps, the limestone piles, the dark wet patches on the ground. It was as if someone had tried to patch Holland together overnight

We ducked to clear the telephone lines and nosed out into open water, skinning a couple of shingles from a roof. As we headed for the main channel, Mobley ran the motor on full thrust, and the dory began to kick up a steep and curling wake. It slammed and bounced on the water as it climbed on to the plane, but the fringe of trees alongside barely moved. The engine roared, the wake streamed in a white V behind us, the boat pounded, but the land remained obstinately still.

We skidded from boil to boil as the Mississippi poured southwards under our feet. The surface of the river was a lacework of rips and swirls: oily mushroom-heads, a hundred feet or so across, bloomed and spun; little whirlpools raced away on private zig-zag tracks; everywhere the water was dividing, folding in on itself, spilling, breaking, spitting and sucking.

It was only when the down-draft from its rotor blades began to disrupt the patterns of the current that I saw the National Guard helicopter overhead. Associated Press was photographing it. I could see the picture he was taking, and it was a good one: the coastguard afloat, alone, on the raging flood; and, over his left shoulder, a military chopper on a rescue mission.

'Oh—' said A.P., and put his camera down. 'It's full of journalists.'

At the same time, the 'copter, having spotted the same problem, wheeled away into the sky.

'People taking pictures of people taking pictures,' said P.O. Mobley.

I was on the levee, making a sketch of how the river moved as it tried to flow through the middle of someone's house, when a small, raw-boned man in sunglasses approached me. 'Got all your notes?' he said, and put out his hand. His handshake was of the kind that people go to evening classes to learn. There was a lot of technique in it – the modulated pressure of the thumb; the palm-to-palm interface; the finger-lock; the terminal wrist-flip. It was a prolonged and multi-layered assertion of confidence, frankness, solicitude and firmness of intent.

'John Kasky,' the man said, with an intimate cough.

I took him for a travelling evangelist, and noticed that his limp moustache was interestingly out of character with the powerful handshake.

'R. & H. Service & Supply.'

He was a pump salesman. He was shortly going to demonstrate a pump to the City Administrator; in the meantime, he rehearsed his patter on me. The pump stood at the bottom of the levee, and looked like a shiny red tractor.

These were flush times. Mr Kasky could not recall exactly how many pumps he'd sold in the last three weeks, but it was over thirty. These were not tin-pot two-stroke jobs, but big industrial pumps, costing from 20,000 to 50,000 dollars apiece, and Mr Kasky was selling them, on commission, to cities up and down the river. The excitement of all these done deals had worked on him like speed. He was elated and twitchy.

This particular pump was a Godwin Dri-Prime 6-inch 65-horse-power model, with a throughput of 2.1 MGD.

'Million gallons a day,' said Mr Kasky.

'That's a lot of water.'

'Oh, we go way up. Take a twelve-inch pump, for instance. That'll give you a throughput of nine MGD – and that *is* a lot of water.'

I was curious to find out how much water had to be pumped out of Sainte Genevieve every day.

'You'd be talking hundreds of millions. Close on a billion. But don't quote me.'

He snapped open his briefcase and got out the literature on the Godwin. 'We just took on this line a little while back. Pretty fair timing ...' He gazed appreciatively over the levee and its lines of pumps, each with a hose poking over the top of the sandbags, spewing dirty water back into the flood. Beside the spanking new Godwin, they looked a sorry collection of rustbuckets.

Mr Kasky explained to me the poetry of the dry-prime system. A wet-prime pump – he flagged his hand dismissively at the hardware nearby – is a source of never-ending tribulation. It must be constantly tended. If you allow your wet-prime pump to suck dry, it will probably break its seals. With broken seals, it won't pump. And in any case, you'll have to reprime it. ⟵

On the other hand, suppose you go the extra mile and invest in something like the Godwin Dri-Prime? When there's water to suck, it sucks. When there's no water to suck, it quietly hums along, waiting for the next leak to spring. It requires no adjustment and no priming. Its seals don't break. If you wish, you may go away on vacation to Hawaii, leaving your trusty pump to do its work unattended in your absence. Everybody should have one.

'And it's made in England.' He read the name of the place, with some difficulty, from the promotional sheet: 'Cirencester, United Kingdom.'

'How much?'

'Twenty-three, just shy of twenty-four thousand dollars.'

I was still puzzled as to why, in this drowning and pump-hungry city, Mr Kasky had chosen to spend time selling his shiny red tractor to me.

'You're the media. It's like everything else – you need to get media coverage in this business if you're going to succeed. You never know: you could be doing yourself a favour if you work in a reference in your article to the Godwin Dri-Prime Pump.'

I have done my best.

I hung around for the demo. The pump worked. I saw water coming out of the other end. The city bought it.

At his house on South Gabouri Street, Mr Ish Scher had fifteen pumps, and they all ran out of gas at different times, so Mr Scher spent the day going from pump to pump with a two-gallon gasoline can. It was hard enough to keep the pumps supplied with fuel, but they were old and temperamental, and every day at least one pump would cough and die, and the water would begin to climb. Even when all the pumps were smoothly churring, the basement of the Scher house was ankle-deep in flood water, and a bit of muck in an impeller would bring the level to knee-height in a few minutes. If one stood in the sopping basement, the river was just above one's head; held off by a home-built wall of sandbags. Water dripped and bubbled through the cracks between the bags, and the bigger leaks were miniature cascades.

'It's a beautiful house,' said Mr Scher. 'It used to be.'

Over the din of the pumps there was the sound of purling mountain streams. The wallpaper had slid from the walls, and so had much of the plaster, exposing bricks that were black with wetness.

'The city told us to evacuate. But I couldn't do that – not when we're so near the end.'

Did he mean the end of life or the end of the flood? Perhaps both. Mr Scher was in his late seventies; his wife, a woman with vague, shocked eyes, was a few years younger, but looked older. 'Elaine's taken this very hard. She gets no sleep. She's in a bad state. But I'm fine – just fine.' His voice was southernly soft, and he smiled, out of polite habit, when he spoke. Trudging from pump to pump with his gasoline can, while the Mississippi leaned against his house and forced its way in, Mr Scher seemed at home with the flood: he might have been pottering in his garden on any sleepy summer afternoon.

His left arm ended in a bare stump below the elbow; his fortyish son was blind.

'We've been so lucky with our friends – I can't tell you. If it hadn't been for our friends, we'd have lost this house long ago.

They've been so good to us—'

The Schers were defending a line about thirty yards long. Their sandbag wall, over which the river was now so nearly spilling that the removal of one bag could easily have caused the whole wall to give way, stretched round the side and back of the house and across the yard, where it was shored up by the side of a trailer home.

Sandbagging is a skilled craft, like dry-stone-walling, and the nine-foot wall had been built by several sandbaggers in several styles. The good bits were dry; the bad bits sagged and dribbled.

In the trench at the foot of the wall, the water was the colour of beef bouillon; its surface was wrinkled and shivering in the contest between the leaks and the pumps. Measured against the coarse weave of a fallen sandbag, it was up a thread, down a thread, up two threads ... *winning – losing – winning – losing – losing*.

In City Hall I found Mr Kasky. The deal was done. He had the contract in his hand.

'I've found you a great media opportunity,' I said, and told him about the Schers. 'You could get on network television ...' I stressed how the story of one deserving family, saved in the nick of time by a pump salesman with a heart, would carry more weight than the loss or salvation of a whole suburb. I came as close as I dared to suggesting that Mr Kasky's face might make the cover of *Time*.

'I'm with you, I'm with you ... It is a good idea,' said Mr Kasky. 'But what a shame you didn't come up with it this morning. If you'd come to me then, I could have helped them out, no problem. Now, though,' he shook his head and chewed on his moustache. 'I haven't got a pump. I've sold it to the city.'

'You could get one by tomorrow.'

'That would be tricky.'

'Please—'

Mr Kasky consulted his watch and made a great show of being astounded by what he saw there. 'Sorry!' he said: 'I got to go!' And he was gone, the rat.

Jean Rissover was smoking on the loggia. When I told her about the Schers, she went off to talk with the city administrator, but came back with the news that there were no spare pumps of the right size for the job.

'Isn't there any way in which the Schers could make the city change its mind on that?'

'Oh, they *could*. But they'd need to get media coverage. If Mr Scher could go on a radio show and tell his story there . . .'

Next morning, the river was still only shin-deep in the Scher basement. The previous evening, 1,400 new sandbags had been added to the wall around the house. Half a dozen neighbours had turned out to form a chain, and we'd spent three hours slinging the bags up to an expert sandbagger on the top of the wall; some of the worst leaks were now staunched, though new ones had started overnight, and another pump – a hefty one, with a four-horsepower motor – was on the blink.

'It's looking good,' Mr Scher said. 'And the flood seems to be going down.'

It was, too. Up the street from the house, the river had found a new shoreline. There was a seven- or eight-inch margin of wet gravel, like an outgoing tide. A wooden stake in the water now showed a distinct dark band. As I watched, a whiskery splinter on the stake popped clear.

Suddenly there were a dozen people in the street, raptly, fondly watching the water as it exposed – first one crumb of gravel, then another, and another. We were witnessing a miracle.

'They were forecasting a rise—'

'What do they know?' said a woman with an exhausted face and a wild laugh. 'They've been wrong about everything.'

In ten minutes, the level of the water dropped by a full inch.

A uniformed coastguard, with a quacking VHF set holstered to his hip, arrived by bicycle. Half an hour ago, the levee at Kaskaskia Island, twelve miles downstream, had burst. Sainte Genevieve's few inches of remission were someone else's misfortune: thousands of acres had gone under; even now, the Mississippi was fanning out through the corn in a great wave.

'They're saying it's real bad down there,' the coastguard said.

'Excuse me!' said the woman with the laugh. 'My house is half underwater, and you're telling me to feel sorry for a *field*?'

Every time a levee went, it relieved the pressure of the river, for a few hours at least, on the towns nearby. This was tempting knowledge. In Quincy, Illinois, the breaching of the levee was said to be sabotage, and there was some unofficial talk of other levees that had burst with help and encouragement from the neighbours. Townspeople were prone to blame the farmers for unfairly constricting the river, as Missourians were inclined to blame the people of Illinois for flooding Missouri with their great federal levee.

It didn't take much to cause a breach. It was night-work, but easy to do, given a half-hour or so of privacy. You'd need to shift a dozen sandbags to create a good strong waterspout, and the river would do the rest. In no time at all, the hole in the levee would be big enough to float a barge through it. Then the whole soggy wall of softened earth would give way, and the river would swallow the long flat miles of flood plain, as it was always meant to do.

The river dropped four inches, then began to rise again. It crept back across the gravel until it was an inch or two further into town than it had been before it took Kaskaskia Island. The excitement and the ensuing lurch of disappointment of the morning had tired people, made them cranky and strange. I spoke to a woman whose basement had the usual assortment of pipes and hoses leading out from it to the river.

'How are things holding up in your house?'

'We've got everything in there but the alligators,' she said. 'Everything but the alligators!' she repeated. 'Everything but the alligators!'

A boy of eight or nine came out of the house next door. 'Did you hear the noise, mister?'

'What noise?'

'A weird noise. I was out here earlier. I heard it. It was weird.'

'What kind of weird?'

'Kind of like a frog-noise. But much louder. And weirder.'

We listened together. There was just the drone of the pumps in the heat and dust. The boy drifted away, his head full of monsters.

Out on the levee, I met a telephone engineer, working for Southwest Bell, whose job it was to visit a long string of river towns, inspecting their phone equipment for flood damage.

'It's interesting,' he said. 'Every town reacts differently. Some towns, it's just like what people say it is on TV: everybody pulling together, neighbour helping neighbour, all that. You can see that in Dutchtown – it's real cohesive. But there's the flipside: towns where people sit on the hill, watching television and saying, "Why do I have to lift a finger to help those dumb-asses down by the river?" A lot of towns are like that. I don't know what it is. Maybe it's in their history. But it seems that whatever was in that town before, the flood finds it and brings it out. It's bringing out a heap of meanness, a heap of resentment, a heap of pettiness. Have you been down to St Mary?'

'No.'

'You ought to. There's no National Guard there, and no media. It's just a town that was flooded, and nobody paid any attention. When folks from St Mary see Sainte Genevieve on the evening news, they'll tell you: they're *bitte*—'

He was interrupted by a mud-spattered farm pick-up, which jounced up the levee. From the driver, there were salutations for the telephone engineer and an irritable growl for me.

'*Ropawdah?*'

'Sort of.'

The farmer and the engineer grunted laconically at each other for a while, then fell to gazing at the water. Silence. The river flowed over shunting yards and through a factory. It was a placid floodscape; the ravelling whorls of current, the signs and telephone poles moored to their reflections. People might well come here with paint-boxes and easels.

'Repawdahs.' The farmer stared into the shining middle distance. Water chuckled under the eaves of a sunken house. The pumps grumbled and spat. 'They're making it out to be a whole lot worse than it is.' He put the truck into reverse and backed off the levee before I could say that I knew what he meant.

THE LIFE AND DEATH OF A HOMOSEXUAL

Pierre Clastres

Pierre Clastres was a young French anthropologist whose book,
Chronique des indiens Guayaki, *described the time he spent among*
some of the stone-age tribes who then still lived in the jungles of Paraguay
and Venezuela. It was published in 1972 and among the people intrigued
by it was Paul Auster, who was living in Paris. After Auster returned to
the United States, he began to translate Clastres' Chronicle *and to*
exchange letters with the author. Eventually an American publisher was
found. Then Clastres died in a car accident. The American publisher went
bankrupt; and the manuscript, of which Auster had no copy, was lost. There
the matter stood for the next fifteen years – a project consigned to oblivion –
until in 1996 Auster went to San Francisco to deliver a lecture. After the
lecture was over, a young man approached him and asked him to autograph
a set of bound galley proofs. The young man had bought them for five
dollars in a second-hand bookstore. Auster had never seen them before.
They were proofs of the long-lost Chronicle of the Guayaki Indians, *from*
which the following extract is taken.

There was no sweetness in the air that day: the corpse gave off a
terrible stench. The man had been dead for only a little while, but the

vultures had opened his belly, which accelerated the process of putrefaction, attracting numerous swarms of flies, and the flies had become drunk with everything oozing and flowing from the gashes. There were blood-splattered holes in the place of the eyes, which had been pecked out by the birds. The mouth was enlarged; the birds had forced their way through the teeth to get at the tongue. But even so we could recognize him: the length of his body left no doubt. It was a Stranger whose height had surprised me: he was four or five inches taller than the tallest hunter. And now he had become food for the vultures. The Atchei did not like to see this happen. He had left several days before, saying that he was going to meet up with two families who were hunting. He had been rather ill and had probably changed his mind on the way; but he had not been able to return to the camp at Arroyo Moroti. He had died all alone, and no doubt had seen the *briku* gather in the sky above and then swoop down on him one by one. The birds were motionless; bloody slivers of meat hung from their beaks. Hundreds of little yellow butterflies drily beat their wings around the corpse of Krembegi.

Unusual in many respects, he was immediately striking because of his exceptional height, which made him almost a giant compared to the little Atchei. But he was not proportionately more vigorous. He gave an overall impression of flabbiness. He had a broad, fat belly, whereas the bellies of the other men were hard and compact, even when relaxed. He was a strange hunter, to say the least.

But was this all? Krembegi came from one of the two small tribes of Atchei that belonged to the Guayaki 'nation'. Until recently, they had had no contact with one another, did not know one another, and even considered one another to be enemies. One tribe, the Atchei Gatu, knew the other tribe as the *Iroiangi*, meaning 'strangers'. Krembegi belonged to the Atchei Iroiangi or Strangers, and they did not like to talk about him, and when they did talk it was only with reticence. As for the Atchei Gatu, who were hardly more loquacious on the subject, their knowing looks and crafty smiles showed that even though they would not say anything, they had certainly devoted some thought to the matter. It seemed clear that Krembegi was not just anyone.

Because he wore his hair long like a woman (the men wore theirs short), I wanted to take his picture one day and asked him to hold his bow, which was standing nearby. He got up politely but refused to hold the weapon.

'Why?'

'It's not my bow.'

'Take it anyway.'

'I don't have a bow, I don't want to touch this bow.'

He spoke firmly and seemed disgusted, as if I had asked him to do something obscene. And then, to show that he did not feel any ill will, he pointed to something that I thought could not have been his.

'I'll hold my basket.'

This was the Atchei world turned upside down: a man with a basket and no bow! Who was Krembegi? As soon as I learned the secret of this man's strangeness, people were quite willing to talk to me about him. His story was told to me little by little, first by the Atchei Gatu, who were delighted to have another chance to show that they had good reasons for scorning the Strangers and that they would never allow someone like Krembegi to live among them. Later, the Iroiangi agreed with the portrait drawn by the Atchei Gatu and added details to it. But from the man himself I could get nothing. Timid and reserved, he would avoid talking to me. He died without having said anything.

The insistence of the Atchei tribes on instilling in their young men the idea of *bretete*, the great hunter, is the basic both of the groups' moral law and of individual honour; but it also arises from economic necessity. Since they are nomads in a forest that is rather limited in edible vegetation, the members of the two Guayaki tribes cannot subsist on gathering. Roots, berries, fruits, palm-hearts, honey and larvae unquestionably account for a considerable portion of their food: it is the women's responsibility to gather this hidden food, and all around their stopping places in the forest they are constantly foraging for it. But not all areas are rich in trees with edible fruit, and the forest is generous only during certain seasons. That is why the *kuja* sometimes return to the camp without their baskets pulling on their necks. There is very little to be found in the *naku*: a few larvae reserved for the children, especially the 'soft heads', because they are very nutritious, a rat, one or two frogs, and sometimes a snake, which is caught by the tail, quickly dashed against a tree before it can bite, and then roasted. Eating like this is all right once in a while, but if you make a steady diet of it you lose weight, and that is depressing.

The major portion of the food is produced by the men. In Guayaki society it is they who have the task of supplying the people with meat and fat, which are indispensable. *Bareka*, to hunt: this is their function; they identify themselves with it and define themselves by this activity. A man can think of himself only as a hunter, one cannot be a man and not a hunter at the same time. The entire symbolic space of masculinity unfolds in the act of *jyvo*, shooting an arrow, and from their earliest years the boys are prepared to enter their normal place, to fulfil their natural role. The long years of apprenticeship running along with their fathers through the woods, the initiation that confirms them as hunters, the women's preference for the best *bretete*, the night songs of the men loudly celebrating their exploits as archers – all these things combine to make the young men take on the collective will of the group as their own personal desire. They must become true hunters, for the survival of the tribe will depend on them. They know it, and in this knowledge lies their truth, their destiny as men: either one is a hunter or one does not exist. There is no choice.

Hunting is never considered a burden. Even though it is almost the exclusive occupation of the men, the most important thing they do every day, it is still practised as a 'sport'. There is work involved, of course, in endlessly tracking animals, in sitting still for hours watching the movements of a roebuck or a band of monkeys, in holding the bow poised for several minutes so that they will be ready for the brief instant when a bird or coati can be seen through the thickness of the foliage. They know that it is crouching in the branches above, but they can't see it: they have to wait until it shows itself, keeping their arrows at the ready. They must also dig holes for the tapir to fall into, and expand the armadillo's hole: the man digs, and the animal tries to escape by burrowing further into the tunnels. It is a race that the hunter usually wins, but only after considerable effort – sometimes he makes an excavation so big that he can disappear into it.

And then the hunters must keep replenishing the supply of arrows. The tips are made of very hard wood tempered by fire, but as they are used they wear out and break. They are often lost, either when a wounded animal gets away after being hit or when an arrow misses its mark and flies off into the vegetation and disappears. Whether the men are in the woods or resting in the camp, then, they are always involved with the work of hunting.

Hunting is always an adventure, sometimes a risky one, but constantly inspiring. Of course it is pleasant to take sweet-smelling honey from a hive or split a palm tree and find swarms of delicious *guchu* left behind by the scarabs. But everything is known in advance, there is no mystery, nothing unforeseen: it is absolutely routine.

Whereas tracking animals in the forest, proving that you are more clever than they are, approaching within arrow's range without revealing your presence, hearing the hum of the arrow in the air and then the dull thud as it strikes the animal – all these things are joys that have been experienced countless numbers of times, and yet they remain as fresh and exciting as they were on the first hunt. The Atchei do not grow weary of hunting. Nothing else is asked of them, and they love it more than anything else. Because of this they are at peace with themselves. They feel no internal division, no bitterness troubles their souls. They are what they do, their Self fearlessly achieves its fullness in doing what the group has always done since the beginning of time. One might say they are prisoners of fate. But from what point of view? The Atchei hunters themselves feel that they live in complete freedom.

To be a *bretete* requires strength, poise and agility: you have to reach a state in which the body and mind feel at ease, are sure of themselves. This is *pana*. *Pana: pané-at*, the opposite of *pané*. And *pané* is what frightens a man most. For once you have fallen victim to it, *bareka* is finished. Your arm has no strength, the arrow flies far from the target, useless and absurd. You can no longer kill anything. The return to camp is grim when your right shoulder is not straining under the weight of some animal. Instead of celebrating his catch with a sonorous chant, the empty-handed hunter sits in silence beside his fire. If *japa* – shooting wide of the mark – happens several times in a row, then measures must be taken, for *pané* has befallen the hunter. This is of course a painful humiliation, since it is an admission that he is incapable of being what he is: a hunter.

But it could be even more serious. A man never eats his own game: this is the law that provides for the distribution of food among the Atchei. A hunter kills an animal and his wife cuts it up, since he is forbidden to do it himself. She keeps a few pieces for herself and the children and the rest is given out, to relatives first, brothers and brothers-in-law, and then to the others. No one is forgotten, and if there is not much meat, then the shares are small, but each person gets something. In exchange the hunter receives a portion of the game brought back by the others. He feeds them with what he has killed, and they do the same for him. A hunter, then, spends his life hunting for others and eating what others have caught. His dependence is total, and the same is true of his companions. In this way things are equal, no one is ever wronged, because the men 'produce' equivalent quantities of meat. This is what is called *pepy*, exchange.

But if a man is *pané*, what can he give in return, how can he pay another man back for the game he has given him? You cannot receive without giving. It is impossible to be *pané* and to respect the law of reciprocity at the same time. In the end, your companions would grow weary of always giving without receiving anything in return. An old man who is too weak to hold a bow is given food. He deserves it, and a son never lets his father go hungry. If this parasitical existence goes on for too long, however, one day he will be left at the foot of a tree beside a fire. There he will wait patiently for death. But a strong male is not an old man. If he is *pané*, it is because he deserves it: he has certainly done something wrong. Every act against the order of things must be paid for, and this is how the imprudent man is punished. Why help a man who has been found guilty and condemned? It would not do any good.

Fortunately, long-term cases of *pané* are rare. Every man has his periods of bad luck, his hesitant arrow leaves too soon or too late, his hand does not draw back the bow with enough force. But this can be remedied. The young men's lips are pierced and their backs are scarred to confirm them in their condition of *pana*. If *pané* should occur, the operation is repeated. New scars are made, but much more superficial ones than the cruel stripes that were dug out of the skin before. They go around the biceps and crisscross with the old cuts: some men cut their forearms, others their thighs. Very little blood flows, and once the wounds have been smeared with wood ashes and have closed up, the shallow scars have the effect of attractive embroidery on the skin. This treatment is almost always successful: the *pané* leaves you and once again you become *bretete*. And if you become *pané* again, you begin all over. The causes of this type of bad luck are mysterious. It can happen to anyone, and there is not a single Atchei hunter who does not have therapeutic tattoos in addition to the *jaycha* on his back.

If the cause of *pané* is unknown in some cases, in others it is very clear. One cause – and this would be so fatal that no one even dreams of attempting it – would be to eat your own game, to refuse to participate in the exchange. To insist on keeping the animals you have killed leads to a total and permanent separation from the world of animals, since the *pané* will prevent you from ever killing one again. When you do not want to mediate your relationship with food through your relationship with other people, you risk being completely cut off from the natural world and placed outside of it, just as you are pushed out of the social universe by refusing to share your goods. This is the foundation of all Atchei knowledge. It is based on the awareness that an underlying brotherhood binds the world and men together and that what happens among men is echoed in the world. A single order rules them, and it must not be disrupted.

The Atchei therefore avoid doing things that will attract *pané*. Young hunters, for example, never eat animal brain. Although it is a great delicacy, it also causes bad luck. For this reason it is reserved for the *chyvaete*, who hunt little or not at all and therefore run no risk. Some kinds of honey are also forbidden to the young men because they bring on *pané*, such as the honey from the *tei* bee. The honey of the *tare*, on the other hand, only prevents the *kybuchu* from growing pubic hair. But there is something else. For what does it mean to be a great hunter but to identify one's very existence with the bow? And doesn't *pané* separate a man from his bow so that it becomes exterior to him, as if it had rebelled against its master? The bow is the hunter himself: an initiate's first task is to make his first adult bow by himself. This weapon is much more than a tool. When its owner dies, it becomes *ove enda*, the dwelling place of the departed soul, as do the arrows. The bow and arrows have now become dangerous, and are discarded. The bow is the sign and symbol of the man, the proof that he exists and the means of his existing. When he dies, then, his bow disappears as well, for it is that part of the man which could not survive him. Conversely, if the bow abandons him when he is *pané*, then he is no longer a hunter, he is no longer anything.

The very strength of the bow makes it vulnerable. It is not difficult for *pané* to affect a hunter: it has only to affect his bow: he will immediately suffer from it and be *pané*. A bow is the essence of virility, the irrevocable metaphor of masculinity. Because of this, it is one of the things that must be protected from their opposites. How far does the hunter's space extend, what is the boundary of the masculine world?

The boundary is the feminine world. An order presides over the lines of force in this geography and keeps the different regions separate. If some disorder causes them to interpenetrate, masculine space is contaminated, weakened and degraded by this contact with feminine space. In other words, if a woman touches a bow, *pané* befalls its owner. For this reason there is a severe taboo against women having any contact with a bow. They themselves run no risk, but for the men it can be fatal. Inversely, the equivalent of the bow for the *kuju* is the *naku*, the basket, which is the quintessence of a woman's femininity. After the ritual of seclusion and the scarring of her stomach, a young woman celebrates her entrance into the world of adults by weaving palms into her first basket. She knows how to do it because her mother has taught her; she made little ones when she was a girl. Now it is up to her to make it by herself, and until her death she will carry a basket. Just as the bow is the man, the basket is the woman. So that if a hunter touches a basket, or even thinks of carrying one – which would be even more absurd than comical – the result would be the same: *pané* would be his punishment for having contact with the basket.

It is always the men who suffer the consequences. The unwarranted overlapping of masculinity and femininity affects only the man. Of course the *kuja* will also suffer from the *pané* in the sense that the hunters will no longer have anything to give them to eat. But the women's power is so strong that it can be harmful to men. To be a hunter, that is to say a man, you must always be on your guard against women, even when they are not menstruating. You cannot be a man except by opposing yourself to women. When the distance separating men from women vanishes, when a man crosses the dividing line, a contagion is produced that makes him lose his worth, that wears away his masculinity: he finds himself within the sphere of women. Bowman, basket-woman, this is how people are divided up. What happens to a man without a bow? He becomes a basket person.

This is what had happened to Krembegi. He was not joking when he said 'my basket', because it really was his, made by his own hands with the help of one of the women. Why did he have a basket? Because he did not have a bow. And why didn't he have a bow? Because he was *pané*. But this had been the case for a long time; in fact, it had always been the case. He had never been able to kill an animal with a bow and arrow, and the matter became clear rather quickly: he was *pané* in the same way that the others were *bretete*. This was not an accident. It was his nature. But still, why, when circumstances had taken away his bow, did he provide himself with a basket? He could have had nothing at all, have remained, so to speak, between bow and basket. But is it possible to be neither a bow person nor a basket person?

Only in early childhood is there any space in which the difference between the sexes remains negligible. And Krembegi was a grown-up – he was no longer a *kromi*. He could no longer exist in this neuter universe. When one is an adult one is either a man or a woman, a bow or a basket: there is nothing in between, no third possibility. What, then, is a man without a bow? He is a non-man, and for this reason he becomes a basket-carrier.

There were two basket-carrying men at the camp at Arroyo Moroti where the tribes now lived, and both were Iroiangi. The second one was named Chachubutawachugi, the Great Wild Pig with the Long Beard. A very hairy beard covered his face. And since it often took him a long time to find a woman willing to shave him, his beard would grow quite prodigiously. I gave him a present of a mirror and some razor blades: he would put the blades in the middle of a split piece of bamboo and then fasten them tightly. In this way he could shave more often. In gratitude he gave me the name of *apaio*, father. Chachubuta-wachugi had a basket because he was *pané*. But unlike Krembegi he was very strong, and though he had not used a bow for several years because of the *pané*, he continued to hunt coatis by hand and to stalk armadillos in their burrows. He would distribute his catch and would receive presents from the other hunters in return. His shoulders, striped with thin black lines, attested to his efforts to overcome his bad luck with tattoos. But after repeated failures he had given up and resigned himself to his fate. One of his brothers' wives had made a basket for him. He lived with them, more tolerated than welcomed. When his sister-in-law was in a bad mood she wouldn't give him anything to eat. At those times he would cook for himself. No woman would have agreed to become the wife of a *pané* man; he therefore had to take on the feminine work himself. He had once been married, but his wife had died, leaving him alone. To judge by the evidence, Chachubutawachugi did not have the best of luck.

Krembegi, on the other hand, seemed comfortable with his situation. He did not say much, of course, but he looked serene. He lived with a family who accepted him completely. Cooking was not a question for him since he helped the wife in her daily household tasks. It was almost as if he was the co-wife of the man who lodged him. In the morning he would go off with the *kuja* to look for larvae, fruits and palm-hearts. His basket would be just as full as those of his companions when he came back. He would put it down, crouch on his heels, and diligently and efficiently begin to prepare the evening meal: husking berries, peeling roots, preparing *bruce*, a thick soup made of palm marrow mixed with larvae. He would fetch water and firewood.

When he had nothing to do he would rest or make necklaces with the teeth of the animals killed by his host. They were very pretty, far more attractive than those made by the women. The women were content to pierce the teeth of all the different animals killed by their husbands and to string them through with a thin cord. It amounted to little more than a collection of teeth of different sizes placed in the order in which the animals had been killed. These necklaces were sometimes very long, six feet or more, containing hundreds of teeth from monkeys, agoutis, and especially pacas – those from pigs and roebucks were not saved because they rattled against each other. When a woman is feeling happy she puts on her necklaces in several layers, glad to be able to wear the proof of her husband's prowess as a hunter. Then she puts them back in the bottom of her basket. Krembegi's necklaces showed more care. He would use only monkey canine teeth and only those that were more or less the same size. It is no small job to pierce all these tiny canines with nothing more than a paca tooth. But Krembegi had great patience.

No one in the camp paid any particular attention to him, he was like everyone else. He did only women's work, but this was known and taken for granted. Krembegi was no more or less anonymous than anyone else in the tribe, and he tranquilly filled the role destiny had given him. He lived with the women and did what they did; he did not cut his hair and carried a basket. He was at home in this role and could be himself. Why should he have been unhappy?

Chachubutawachugi was a different matter altogether. It was not at all assumed that he had found his niche, or that he was content with his lot. And the proof was that no one took him seriously. Whatever he said or did was greeted by the Atchei with condescension. They did not openly make fun of him, because that was not done, but they found him rather ridiculous and smiled behind his back. The men were somewhat wary of him and the women laughed into their hands when they saw him coming with his basket. The children, who were usually so respectful of their elders, forgot the rules of politeness and good conduct when they were with him. They ran wild, were insolent, and refused to obey him. Sometimes he would get angry and try to catch them, but they were always too fast; he would give up and sullenly take a walk in the woods or lie down somewhere off by himself. Everyone pretended to believe that he was stingy with what he brought back from the forest, while he was actually as generous as anyone else. For example, he had gone off in the morning one day saying that he was going to look for larvae. On his return he ran into a group of men. 'Well?' 'Nothing. No *guchu*.' And he walked on. When he was out of earshot one of the men said: 'Nothing? *U pa modo!* He ate everything up!' And they all burst out laughing. This was an unjust accusation.

Why were the Atchei so mean to poor Chachubutawachugi? It was true that they found him something of a clown, with his passion for adorning his neck and head with the most unexpected objects. If he saw a piece of metal, a cartridge case or a bottle, he couldn't resist; he would pick it up, attach it to a string and put it around his neck. He would walk around with his chest covered by a necklace made of a few dozen penicillin bottles, some sardine can keys, and formless pieces of scrap iron. He would wear it for a while, then abandon it and go to find other things. The *kybuchu* were once given a rubber ball. After a short time they had ruined it. For him it was a godsend. He cut it in two and made one of the pieces into a superb skullcap that covered his whole head down to the eyes. He was very happy with his idea. The Atchei, however, looked at the elegant fellow with an air of pity. 'Not at all surprising! That's his style, all right!' In other words, the victim of *pané* had found another way to call attention to himself through this rather awkward dandyism.

But there had to be another reason for the Atchei's ill will, for in the final analysis Chachubutawachugi's innocent faults were more than compensated for by his activity as a hunter of coatis and armadillos. This activity was of course limited; but it was by no means negligible. On the other hand, Krembegi, who never trapped animals, was not mistreated in the slightest way by the Atchei. This was why he was able to accept his fate with such placidity. What was the difference then, between these two *pané* men? What was the difference that made people adopt different attitudes towards two negatively similar individuals – similar in that they were both excluded from the circle of hunters? As a rule, the Atchei would have had the same attitude towards both of them. But it was not at all the same. Therefore, the fact that both these men were *pané* did not make them identical. As it turned out, they were not.

Man = hunter = bow; woman = gatherer = basket: these two equations strictly determine the course of Atchei life. There is no third equation, no additional space to protect those who belong neither to the bow nor the basket. By ceasing to become a hunter, one loses one's very masculinity; metaphorically one becomes a woman. This is what Krembegi understood and accepted: his radical renunciation of what he was incapable of becoming – a hunter – automatically put him on the side of the women; he was one of them, he accepted himself as a woman. He carried his basket in the same way they did, with a carrying strap around his forehead.

And Chachubutawachugi? It was simple: he hadn't understood a thing. For he, the innocent one, thought that he could remain in the masculine universe even after he had lost the right to do so, so blind was he in his desire to remain a man – he who was no longer a hunter, who was no longer considered a hunter. *Esse est percipi.* What did the others see when they saw him? Perhaps this is not the right question. Because from a certain point of view Chachubutawachugi was invisible. Why? Because he did not live anywhere: neither among the men, because of the *pané*, nor among the women, for in spite of his basket, he refused to incorporate himself into their group, to inhabit their space. But the place he was obstinately trying to occupy, midway between the two, did not exist. And so he did not exist any more either; he was a pathetic inhabitant of an impossible place. This was what made him 'invisible'; he was elsewhere, he was nowhere, he was everywhere. Chachubutawachugi's existence was unthinkable.

And this was what annoyed the Atchei. What they reproached the *pané* man for without their even knowing it was his incomprehensible refusal to let himself be taken along by the logical movement of events, which should have put him in his new and real place, among the women. When you have a basket, it is because you are a *kuja*. But he did not want to be one, and this created disorder in the group and upset the ideas of the people – not to speak of the man himself. This was why he often seemed so nervous, so ill at ease. He had not chosen the most comfortable position for himself, and he had thrown things out of order.

You had only to see how Chachubutawachugi carried his basket. He did not do it as the women and Krembegi did, with the carrying strap around his forehead. In this position the women walked with their heads lowered, somewhat bent, looking at the ground. But he carried his *naku* differently, with the strap in front and slung over his shoulders. Whenever he slipped he would painfully squeeze his neck. But in this way he walked like a man.

As for Krembegi, his relations with the bow were the same as those of the women: he never touched a bow because this would attract bad luck to the owner of the weapon. Nothing set him apart from the *kuja*. That was why he refused when I asked him to hold a bow for the photograph, and had picked up his basket instead. But this was not all. Krembegi, who was separated from the bow and masculinity, had gone the full symbolic distance into the feminine world. This accounted for the Strangers' reticence and the hints made by the Atchei Gatu. What did the Atchei know about him? Why did the one group refuse to speak about him and the other group make only sarcastic remarks about him? It was because Krembegi was a *kyrypy-meno*, an anus-lovemaker, a homosexual.

The people of his tribe accepted it naturally, even though they were somewhat annoyed by it. But that was because of the Atchei Gatu, who were very disapproving. 'There are no *kyrypy-meno* among us! You have to be Iroiangi for that!' But everyone agreed that if Krembegi was what he was, it was because he was *pané*. The Atchei Gatu felt no contempt for him personally. For them it was rather comic that a man would accept the compliments of another man by offering him his *kyrypy*. They laughed about it and saw in this yet another proof of their superiority over the Strangers. They could not recall any similar cases among their group. They only told the story of Bujamiarangi. It had happened a long time ago, when Paivagi was still a young man. An Atchei went out hunting and had the good fortune to fall upon a *kware*, which was caught unawares and did not have time to escape into the thickets. The man did not even have to use an arrow; he beat the animal with his bow and broke its spine. The vegetation in this spot was very dense, the underbrush a tangle of creepers and climbing plants. The hunter left behind his still-dying prey and tried to open a hole in the vegetation by using his bow to knock down the plants and shrubs. He had progressed a few dozen yards when he came upon a more open space and then went back to get the ant-eater and put it on his back. He saw someone next to the animal. It was Bujamiarangi, a very young man, who had been following him. And what was he doing there? The hunter could not believe his eyes: Bujamiarangi was making *meno* with the dead ant-eater! He was so absorbed in taking his pleasure that he did not hear the man approach. The hunter did not hesitate for a second. Mad with rage over what the other man was doing with his game, he shot an arrow, and Bujamiarangi collapsed on to the cadaver of the *kware*. No one, concluded the Atchei, ever saw him again.

But as for *kyrypy-meno*, no, they didn't know anything about it. To be insensitive to the charms of women was something that surpassed the understanding of the Atchei Gatu. But then, to give in to the assaults of other men, that was too much! And all that because of *pané*. What did they say about Krembegi? First of all, of course, that he never 'went' to women. But why? Because his penis was very small, like the penis of a coati. It was freely compared to the little barbs put on the tips of arrows: it was really not much of anything, he could not use it. It could well have been that this was simply malicious gossip. But who were Krembegi's partners? Were the Strangers also different from the Atchei Gatu in that their hunters all enjoyed *kyrypy-meno*? For obviously Krembegi could not be a homosexual all by himself.

He did have partners. But not many, and not those one would have thought. It would be logical to assume that, to the extent that a man like Krembegi represents a certain disorder in the ethico-sexual world of the Atchei, a subversion of all accepted and respected values, the field of his sexual activity would not be governed by any rules, that he could pursue his own pleasure at will: in other words, that any man of the tribe, if he so desired, could make love with Krembegi. But this was not at all the case; homosexual relations are not anarchic, they are governed by a very rigorous logic. Krembegi was the Atchei world upside down, but he was not its negation; he was part of another order, another group of rules which were the image – even though reversed – of the 'normal' order and rules.

The ultimate bases of Atchei social life are the alliances between family groups, relations which take form and are fulfilled in marriage exchanges, in the continual exchange of women. A woman exists in order to circulate, to become the wife of a man who is not her father, her brother or her son. It is in this manner that one makes *picha*, allies.

But can a man, even one who exists as a woman, 'circulate'? How could the gift of Krembegi, for example, be paid back? This was not even imaginable, since he was not a woman, but a homosexual. The chief law of all societies is the prohibition against incest. Because he was *kyrypy-meno*, Krembegi was outside this social order. In his case the logic of the social system – or, what amounts to the same thing, the logic of its reversal – was worked out to its very end: *Krembegi's partners were his own brothers. 'Picha kybai* (meaning *kyrypy-meno*) *menoia*: a *kyrypy-meno* man does not make love with his allies.' This injunction is the exact opposite of the rules governing the relations between men and women. Homosexuality can only be 'incestuous'; the brother sodomizes his brother and in this metaphor of incest the certainty that there can never be any real incest (between a man and a woman) without destroying the social body is confirmed and reinforced.

That is why Krembegi's partners were so few in number. Of course now and then a man without family ties would solicit his favours – the dissolute Bykygi for example. But these things rarely leave the family, so to speak. Such was Krembegi's fate: *pané*, homosexual, a complete inversion of the sexual and social order. But still, he was not too unhappy with his lot.

But now it was all over. He had run into his last bit of bad luck, and the vultures were in the process of devouring him. It would not have been a good idea to let them go on. Krembegi was going to be buried. One of the men went back to the camp to give the news. He would bring back several women so that they could do the death *chenga-ruvara*. In the meantime the others would prepare the grave. With a few quick blows of the machete they cleared a small space in the woods at the centre of which a hole was dug. It was a sort of well that was more or less cylindrical, just wide enough for a human body, and more than three feet deep. The thick humus that covered the ground of the forest was not hard to dig, and the machetes went into it easily.

The vultures were still waiting, not at all scared off by our activities. They did not try to get closer to the corpse. A man went off a little way under the trees to look for *chipo*, a fine creeper used as string.

The messenger came back, accompanied by three women. One was the wife of the chief, Karewachugi; she presided over all the tribe's rituals, she was always the first to intone the chants. The other two were Krembegi's sisters-in-law. Crouching on their heels, they burst forth in the *chenga-ruvara*. Their sobbing seemed even more lugubrious than it had the other times, because now it did not mingle with the quiet but constant noise of camp life. Silence, light, vultures. The men (among whom was a brother of the dead man) seemed indifferent. Krembegi's passing did not seem to affect them. Were the words they were speaking – so quickly that I could not understand them – an elegy to the dead man? I couldn't be sure, but I doubted it. When the farewell to Krembegi was finished, the men took over.

Working rapidly because of the stench, with almost brutal gestures they folded the legs high over the chest, having to force them a bit because rigor mortis had already set in. He was in the foetal position: as it is before birth, so it is after death. To keep the body in this position it was tied tightly with the creepers that had been gathered a little while before. The same process was repeated with the arms: they were folded in to the torso against the ribs, the forearms bent up to the shoulders, the elbows against the body. The head was last. The men pushed on the neck to lower it against the chest. The hands were then pushed against the temples with the fingers slightly separated and closed, like the claws of a bird of prey. The head was put between the hands and a solid knot of creepers fixed it in this position. Krembegi's large body now resembled a kind of ball caught in a net. It was ready for burial.

The Atchei always leave the area in which an adult is buried after destroying or burning his possessions: a woman's basket and mats, a hunter's bow and arrows. The bow is broken and thrown into the fire.

The arrows are not burned, but shot off at random in all directions. Aren't they *ove enda*, the dwelling place of the soul? After a person's death nothing must remain that belonged to him during his life. Those things are too dangerous. As soon as Krembegi's death was known, therefore, his basket was thrown into the fire.

THE SERAMPUR SCOTCH

Ian Jack

In Serampur I had an awful dream. I dreamed of my mother and brother. They stood on the slopes of a public park. Behind them lay a Victorian bandstand – octagonal with a curved roof like an onion – and behind that a line of trees. The landscape was in shades of green. The rich green of grass that has thrived on a summer's rain, the pale green of copper mould on the bandstand roof, the dark green foliage of oaks and elms. And all of this green under a sky of grey clouds which held the last of the evening's light. It looked like the end of an August day in Scotland, around nine o'clock, just before the street lamps string the towns with rosaries of bright orange and old people begin to mourn the passing of another summer, telling one another: 'Aye, the nights are fairly drawin' in.'

But this, the visual element, was only a dream within a dream. The larger dream had no pictures. It was simply a kind of soundtrack which said: 'These people and this scene are dead.' And so it was a cunning dream, a dream that told you that you were only dreaming, that the scene was not a real scene, and that the reality was that you would wake and never again see and hear the people in it.

I woke up in tears. I had lost my childhood, the people I loved, the kind of country I came from – there would be nobody else who knew me as these people had done, memories could no longer be exchanged, the sense of isolation from the past would be permanent and absolute. Only slowly did my surroundings penetrate and diminish this self-pity. First, the fan racing and creaking from its pivot on the ceiling, and then the chants of the Krishna worshippers who had set up camp a few hundred yards away on the banks of the Hooghly. Life began to fall into place. I looked at the luminous hands of my watch. It was two in the morning, a warm April night in Bengal, the year 1989. My mother and brother were alive, though my mother was old. By subtracting the time difference it seemed possible that they were settled in front of their gas fires and televisions in Fife and Edinburgh and watching the evening news. I crawled out from under the mosquito net and felt the coal smuts and tiny cinders on the floor scratch under my feet on the way to the bathroom, where I bathed in scoops of cold water from the bucket and, remembering my tears, thought ruefully: this was a dream of the middle-aged and homesick.

For the rest of the night there were no more memorable dreams. When I woke again at seven the Krishnaites were still chanting – they worked in relays – but now their shouts mingled with the sounds of Christianity from the chapel opposite my bathroom window. There a sparse congregation drawn from the Christian students and teachers of Serampur College was singing a hymn, a low murmur of piety easily pierced by the cymbals of Krishna and, for a moment or two, just as easily drowned by the steam hooter of the Serampur jute mill over the wall, which sounded to call the morning shift to work. Twenty minutes later the singing stopped and there was a knock on my door: my next-door neighbours the missionaries, having sung in the chapel, were summoning me to share their breakfast.

Mr and Mrs Knorr had said that this would be the best arrangement, otherwise I would have to share rice and dhal in the students' canteen. 'You should eat with us. It's no trouble. We've hired a cook.' The Knorrs were Baptists, energetic and practical Canadians with personalities so apparently unshaded by ambiguity or introspection or melancholy that they stood out in Serampur like a daub of primary colour on a sepia print. There was nothing false in them; to me, they were kind and direct. But Mr Das, their Bengali cook, seemed by contrast to represent a different race, separated not just by continent and colour but by an infinite wistfulness and obliqueness, as though he had stood in the wrong queue when the rations marked 'Energy' and 'Happiness' had been given out. Now he served the porridge with the silence and gravity, though not the precision, of an undertaker. Mrs Knorr arched her eyebrows. 'Poor Das,' she would say, 'he has simply no idea.' And then she bent her head as her husband said grace.

The Knorrs were not new to India – they had worked for decades in what they still spoke of as 'the mission fields' of the south – but they were new to Bengal and to this town thirteen miles upriver from Calcutta. They did not intend to stay long. Knorr said it was 'a kind of vacation'; he was here to consult the college archives for a book he was writing on early Baptist missions. They compared the district unfavourably with their old home in the uplands of southern India, a place of vigour and competence where the women wore flowers in their hair and the smell of fresh coffee drifted across station platforms to meet the morning train. The little they had seen of Bengal perplexed them. They saw lassitude and decay, a state government that was at least nominally Marxist and therefore perhaps nominally atheist, a lazy river in a flat landscape, small and squalid towns, tall mill chimneys made of brick, and a cook who made heavy weather of the porridge. On the journey from Calcutta they had passed station buildings and factory walls painted with hammers and sickles, portraits of Marx and Engels, and slogans urging the continuation of the class struggle. But Mrs Knorr discounted these as symptoms of energy. She said: 'I don't know why, but the people here have no go.'

We ate. Knorr said the college library was closed again that day, so we would have another day off: there would be no opportunities for research, either mine or his. Therefore the day guaranteed nothing but frequent meals. The Knorrs were hearty eaters. At breakfast, Das came out of his kitchen with bananas, tea and toast as well as porridge. At lunch there might be rice, vegetables, dhal, curried chicken, followed by fruit and a rich Bengali sweet of boiled sugar and milk. For afternoon tea, always promptly observed at half past four, the table was laid again with biscuits (Britannia brand), fruit, dishes of salty Indian mixtures made from lentil flour and dotted with bright green peas, and – perhaps the cook's greatest success – loops of sweet and sticky jelabis plucked crisp from the frying pan. Finally, for dinner, Das had been persuaded to switch to the old British mode which had reached him, perhaps more as a rumour than a recipe, via some previous employer. Soup would be followed by plates of chips, tomatoes and omelettes, rounded off with more fruit. Before each meal we bowed our heads as Knorr thanked Christ for what we were about to receive – almost, I began to think, more as a warning to the bowels than a blessing.

In the interval between eating that morning, I sluiced from the cold-water bucket again and walked along the river bank. I was grateful to the Knorrs. For the past three weeks I had been travelling alone up-country in Bihar on a diet of hard-boiled eggs and oranges, and now the profound weight of so much food and religious certainty had a dulling, convalescent effect, burying the embers of my dream like spadefuls of sand on a fire.

Early morning is always the best time in an Indian summer. The sun is still friendly. On the road beside the river I passed old men in their dhotis and sandals taking their daily exercise, while in the river itself families bathed from the muddy shore; the men struck out boldly into the river and held their noses and bobbed under, while the women stayed close to the bank and soaped themselves discreetly under wet saris. Each splash sparkled in the sun. Crows cawed and the horns of cycle-rickshaws honked like flocks of geese down the bumpy road from the bazaar. The jute mill chimney put out more smoke and a low hum emerged from the weaving sheds. From this distance it was almost a noble sound – industry as Victorian idealists liked to think of it, something akin to the busyness of bees – but inside the sheds, I knew, the hum became a hellish clatter of shuttles and looms, so loud that communication was confined to a crude sign language between loom-hands and their foremen.

By midday it was too hot to walk and by afternoon the fierce light had bleached the landscape. Trees that in the morning looked green now looked grey, the brown and blue of the river had turned to a sheet of silver. The crows and rickshaws fell silent, the lizards stuck motionless on my bedroom walls. Even the Krishnaites sounded defeated, their chants ragged and tired. I lay under the fan and read, and slept and sluiced again. 'Hot enough anyway,' said Mrs Knorr over the teatime jelabis, though by that time the sun had slid down the sky and Serampur was coming back to life. When I went out again there were groups of students smoking cigarettes in the shadows of the road that ran along the river and the rickshaw pullers were beginning to light the oil lamps that were suspended from the axles of their tricycles.

I walked to the end of one of the little jetties that carried narrow-gauge railway lines from the jute warehouses, where barges were loaded with finished jute and towed downstream to Calcutta docks. Once it had been a considerable traffic, dotting the river with barges and steam tugs trailing banners of smoke upstream and downstream for dozens of miles. Now the river traffic was much less considerable – most jute swayed down the Grand Trunk Road in large, elaborately decorated lorries – but the shine on the rails and the grease on the crane indicated that sometimes a fleet of barges would still arrive and coolies would still push wagons to the end of the jetty and attach bales to an iron hook and watch the bales swing into the hold.

The river had changed from silver to dark glass. Downstream on either side chimneys pricked the evening sky from mills which bore Scottish names: Dalhousie, Waverley, Angus, Kelvin, Caledonia. Nearer, a hundred yards or so upstream from the jetty on the same bank, stood a grand block of flats – impossibly grand for a place like Serampur; 'mansion flats' they would be called in London or Calcutta – with bay windows and balconies and crude classical pediments on the roof and the gateposts. That morning I had met an elderly Bengali out on his stroll and asked about this building: who had lived there? 'Scotch,' he said. The jute mill manager, perhaps? No, he said, the manager had a separate villa. Assistant managers, foremen, engineers, that kind of person had lived there. 'Scotchmen and their families, all of them. But they went away a long time back.' The flats were still occupied – I could see pale electric light shining through the shuttering on the third floor – but they did not look well kept. Damp from the monsoon had streaked the yellow lime-wash on the walls, the plaster of the facade was crumbling, the gardens had run riot.

The evening hooters began to sound, first from the Serampur mill and then from the other mills up, down and across the river. There was nothing alarming or rousing in the noise, nothing that suggested fires or air raids, or even that a day's work had been completed and a night's work was about to begin. It was a slow, reedy expulsion of steam and it resembled nothing more than a collective sigh, as though old men were turning in their sleep.

It completed a scene of the purest melancholy. I remembered my dream then, as I stood on the jetty and watched the flickering fire from the Krishna camp and the black silhouettes of the figures who walked and danced around it; the evening had renewed their vigour. That night I wrote in my diary of the dancers and the missionaries, Hindu and Christian: 'I suppose both are meant to supply a balm, if not an answer, to the universal human terror which seemed (was) so real to me last night. But in my family's case it failed and in my case it'll fail too. This morning I felt I'd grieve over this childhood memory of love and kinship until it died with me. And I suppose I shall – intermittently, of course, otherwise life would be both unbearable and insupportable. But I've too strong a sense of transience and what was, and almost none of what is to be.'

Did I really feel this commonplace so forcefully? I suppose I must have done; I wrote it down. The diaries of solitary travellers are often littered with banalities and depressions which seem unreal and overheated after the writer has come home to the distractions of the social present. And then there is the old Scottish problem, of minds held in thrall to their childhoods and the sentimentalization of the past (think of Scott, Stevenson, Buchan, Barrie, all of them gifted with imaginations which in some sense were immunized from adult life; children's writers). Perhaps my dream owed something to each of these, the loneliness plus what might be called the cultural disposition. But Serampur, and more than Serampur – Calcutta, Bengal, Bihar, Bangladesh; all these places were reflected in it too. Sometimes as I travelled that winter and spring it seemed that these might be the last places on earth which preserved the old industrial civilization of Britain, people as well as scenes, manners as well as objects, frozen in the Victorian economy of the lower Ganges. Sometimes it even seemed, particularly in a place such as Serampur at dusk, that I had come home; or if not home, then to some tropical version of the time and country that my Scottish parents and grandparents knew, as if I might turn a corner of a Serampur lane and meet them dressed in dhotis and saris. That was absurd. But among the mill chimneys and the steamboats and the hissing locomotives this waking dream persisted, like a tribal memory.

India is different now and my mother is dead. As I say, the year was 1989.

SIBERIA

Colin Thubron

The faintly clownish name of Omsk raises light-hearted expectations. The city lies where the railway crosses the Irtysh River on a massive cantilever bridge, and you see the curve of the water under a line of stooping cranes as it heads out among sandy islets and meadows, touching the city with an illusion of peace. But beyond, the suburbs bristle with petrochemical plants, textile combines and oil refineries, and the pollution is so thick that driving at night has sometimes been forbidden. They sprawl for miles above the river. Marx Prospect, Lenin Square, Partisan Street: the veteran names follow one another in relentless procession.

Yet the city has a modest distinction. Whereas the Second World War razed many western Russian towns to the ground, here in Siberia, untouched, they often attain a formal grandeur or rustic exuberance, and seem older than they are. I wandered the streets in surprise. The municipal flower beds were all in bloom, and fountains played between provincial ministries. Close above the river, nineteenth-century streets dipped and swung in icing-sugar facades of fawn and white. The air in the parks clattered with pop music. Clusters of mini-skirted girls paraded their irregular beauty, and children strolled with their parents in sleepy obedience; but their jeans and T-shirts were stamped with stars-and-stripes or Donald Duck. Every other pair of shoes or trousers sported a pirated Western logo. Fast-food restaurants had appeared, offering instant *pelmeni* – the Siberian ravioli – or anonymous steaks with stale mash, and a rash of small shops and kiosks had broken out, selling the same things.

Yet a feeling of boredom, or of waiting, pervaded everything. All style and music, the new paths to paradise, seemed synthetic, borrowed. Real life remained on hold. The pop songs had the scuttling vitality of shallow streams. The bus shelters and underpasses, stinking of urine, were rife with graffiti: POMPONIUS NAUTILUS – I LOVE YOU! AGATHA CHRISTIE! SEPULCHRE! THE PRODIGY! It took me some time to realize that these were pop groups; other graffiti accompanied them, sometimes scrawled in English, the lingua franca of youth, JIM MORRISON LIVES! NO! . . . I FUCKED THE BITCH! . . . COMMUNISTS ARE ALL BUGGERS . . . Then, in Russian, enigmatically: WHY TRAVEL WITH A CORPSE? . . . THE POINT OF LIFE IS TO PONDER THE CROSS ON YOUR GRAVE . . .

A pervasive frustration pronounced that freedom, once again, had proved illusory. Scarce jobs and high prices were the new slave-masters. The pavements were dotted with the new poor. Yet in this August sunlight I was touched by the traveller's confusion: the gulf between the inhabitant and the stranger. A little architectural charm, or a trick of the light, could turn other people's poverty to a bearable snapshot. The air was seductively still. Naked children were splashing in the polluted river.

I walked over the headland where the old fort had spread, but trees and terraces had blurred away the lines traced by its stockade, and only a stout, whitewashed gate remained. For four years Dostoevsky had languished here in a wooden prison, condemned to hard labour for activities in a naively revolutionary circle in St Petersburg. Sometimes he would gaze yearningly across the Irtysh at the nomad herdsmen, and would walk round the stockade every evening, counting off its stakes one by one as his sentence expired. He transmuted his life here into *The House of the Dead*, and it was here, among convicts who at first filled him with loathing but later with awe, that he experienced a half-mystical reconciliation with his own Russian people.

On the site of the vanished prison, fifty years later, rose a fantastical baroque theatre, painted white and green. Now it was showing *The Merry Wives of Windsor*, Alan Ayckbourn's *Season's Greetings* and Shelagh Delaney's *A Taste of Honey*. The only prison building to survive was the house of the governor, a purple-faced drunkard and sadist in Dostoevsky's day, who would have his prisoners flogged for any misdemeanour, or none. His home has been turned into a museum to the writer he hated.

A century after Dostoevsky's incarceration, Solzhenitsyn was escorted through Omsk on his way to a labour camp in Kazakhstan. He and his fellow prisoners were incarcerated in a vaulted stone dungeon whose single window opened from a deep shaft above them. He never forgot how they huddled together under a fifteen-watt bulb, while an elderly churchwarden sang to them, close to dying: how the old man's Adam's apple quivered as he stood beneath the mouth of the hopeless shaft, and his voice, trembling with death and feeling, floated out an old revolutionary song:

> *Though all's silent within,*
> *It's a jail, not a graveyard –*
> *Sentry, ah, sentry, beware!*

My hotel costs five dollars a night. The plaster falls in chunks from the walls of its corridors, and from the Stalinist mouldings of the ceiling. The night is close and humid. It is over 85°F. I lie on the bed and watch the full moon shining through a pattern of dainty flowers in the lace curtains. I cannot sleep. The sweat leaks from my chest and forehead. And this is Siberia.

Next morning, outside the big, unlovely cathedral, which in Stalin's day had been a cinema, I found a coachload of pilgrims setting off for a rural monastery. They welcomed me on board. The monastic foundations were only just being laid, they said, and they were going to attend the blessing of its waters. In 1987 an excavator at the site – near the state farm of Rechnoi – had unearthed a mass grave, and the place was revealed as a complex of labour camps, abandoned at Stalin's death. The inmates, mostly intelligentsia, had died of pneumonia and dysentery from working in the fields, and their graves still scattered its earth.

As our bus bowled through ramshackle villages, the pilgrims relayed the story with murmurs of motherly pity. They were elderly women for the most part, indestructible babushkas in flower-printed dresses and canvas shoes, whose gnarled hands were closed over prayer books and bead-strings, and whose headscarves enshrined faces of genial toughness. When a fresh-faced cantor began chanting a hymn in the front of the bus, their voices rose in answer one after another, like old memories, reedy and melodious from their heavy bodies, until the whole bus was filled with their singing.

We reached a birch grove on the Rechnoi farm. It was one of those ordinary rural spots whose particular darkness you would not guess. As the babushkas disembarked, still singing, the strains of other chanting echoed from a chapel beyond the trees. It was the first of four shrines which would one day mark the corners of an immense compound. Inside, a white-veiled choir was lilting the sad divisions of the Liturgy. As the pilgrims visited their favourite icons, a forest fire of votive candle-flame sprang up beneath the iconostasis, and two or three babushkas trembled to their knees.

In the south transept, still meohed in scaffolding, an unfinished fresco of the Deposition from the Cross loomed above us. It was almost complete; but the flesh tints were still missing, as if the artist were afraid to touch too closely on Divinity, and pots of pigment still lined the scaffold. So only the coloured garments of the disciples semaphored their grief, while their hands and features were empty silhouettes in the plaster: here a face uplifted in dismay, there a blank caress on the unpainted body of Christ, which remained a ghostly void, like something the onlookers had imagined.

Sometimes, whimsically, I felt as if this scene were echoed in the nave where I stood, where around the great silence left by God the worshippers lifted their heads and hands, crossed themselves, and wept a little.

From outside came the squeal of bulldozers in a distant field. They were smoothing the earth of the labour camps into monastery foundations. I strained to catch the sounds, but our singing drowned them in the sad decrescendos of the Russian rite. And out of the mouths of these ancient women – whose sins, I imagined, could barely exceed a little malicious gossip – rose the endless primal guilt, 'O Lord forgive us!', over and over, as if from some deep recess in the national psyche, a need for helplessness.

The sanctuary curtains parted on an incense-clouded region inhabited by a very small priest. His hair shimmered down his head like a Restoration wig and melted into a droop of violet-clad shoulders. Occasionally, feebly, one of his arms swung a censer; in the stillness between responses its coals made a noise like suppressed laughter. As he intoned the prayers he constantly forgot or lost his place, until his chanting dithered into confused conversation, and three deacons in raspberry robes prompted his responses with slips of paper. He would stare at these through enormous spectacles stranded in his hair like the eyes of a bush-baby, and try again. But the cause of his panic was plain to see. Enthroned beside him, giant and motionless, sat Feodosy, Archbishop of Omsk.

Towards noon a procession unwound from the church and started across the pasturelands towards the unblessed waters. It moved with a shuffling, dislocated pomp. Behind its uplifted cross, whose gilded plaques wobbled unhinged, the Archbishop advanced in a blaze of turquoise and crimson, his globular crown webbed in jewels. He marked off each stride with the stab of a dragon-headed stave, and his chest shone with purple- and gold-embossed frontlets, and a clash of enamelled crosses. He looked huge. Beside him went the quaint, dishevelled celebrant, and behind tripped a huddle of young priests in mauve, and the trio of raspberry-silk deacons.

I fell in line with the pilgrims following. It was oddly comforting. An agnostic among believers, I felt close to them. I, too, wanted their waters blessed. I wanted that tormented earth quietened, the past acknowledged and shriven. I helped the old woman beside me carry her bottles. My feeling of hypocrisy, of masquerading in others' faith, evaporated. As I took her arm over the puddles and our procession stretched out over the wet grass, Russia's atheist past seemed no more than an overcast day in the long Orthodox summer, and the whole country appeared to be reverting automatically, painlessly, to its old nature. This wandering ceremonial, I felt, sprang not from an evangelical revolution but from a simple cultural relapse into the ancient personality of the motherland – the hierarchical, half-magic trust of its forefathers, the natural way to be.

I had already seen it everywhere. Every other market, airport or bus station was staked out by a babushka selling prints of icons and religious pamphlets, and nursing an offertory for the restoration of the local church or cathedral. Holy pictures dangled from the dashboards of taxis, decorated people's rooms. God had re-entered the vocabulary, the home, the gestures of beggars crossing themselves in the streets. Far away in Moscow the Church was growing fat on concessions to import tax-free alcohol and cigarettes; while here in Siberia, traditionally independent but conservative, this corrupting embrace of Church and State was paying (I imagined) for our monastery. But the cross wavered and glistened confidently

among the birches. Authority, as always here, was salvation. It sold
peace in place of thought, as if these people were not worthy of
thought.

Yet after the Communist hiatus, what had God become? Was He
not now very old? And hadn't He lost too many children? On a road
beyond the trees a troop of young men and girls were watching us
from their parked cars, without expression, as tourists look at
something strange.

How had these devotees survived? For sixty years scarcely a
church was open in Siberia; the priests had been dispossessed, exiled
or shot. Even the oldest pilgrims trudging through these meadows
could scarcely have remembered the Liturgy from childhood. How
had they kept faith?

'We had icons in my home, hidden in the roof.' The young priest
was pasty and shy, with absent eyes. He had joined the procession
late. 'My father worked in the stone quarries of Kazakhstan, so we
lived miles from anywhere. But parents pass these icons down to their
children, you see, and my grandmother's family had kept theirs.
That's how I came to God, through the icons, through my
grandmother. Not suddenly, but out of the heart' – he touched his
chest – 'bit by bit. It's very simple. God calls you out.'

We reached a place where a silver pipe, propped on an old lorry
tyre, was spilling warm water into a pool. A blond deacon like a
Nordic Christ planted the processional cross on the far side, and the
archbishop, the priests, the acolytes and pilgrims, the babushkas with
their bags and bottles, a few war veterans and one mesmerized
foreigner made a wavering crescent round the water's rim.

The unkempt celebrant, clutching a jewelled cross, was ordered
to wade in. From time to time he glanced up pathetically at
Archbishop Feodosy, who gave no signal for him to stop. Deeper and
deeper he went, while his vestments fanned out over the surface, their
mauve silk waterlogged to indigo, until he was spread below us like

an outlandish bird over the pool. At last Feodosy lifted his finger. The priest floundered, stared up at us – or at the sky – in momentary despair, recovered his balance and went motionless. Then, with a ghostly frown, he traced a trembling cross beneath the water.

A deep, collective sigh seemed to escape the pilgrims. Again the cavalcade unfurled around the pool, while the archbishop, grasping a silver chalice, sprinkled the surface with its own water, and the wobbly cross led the way back towards the noise of the bulldozers.

But the babushkas stayed put. As the procession glimmered and died through the darkness of the trees, and the archbishop went safely out of sight, a new excitement brewed up. They began to peel off their thick stockings and fling away their shoes. They were ready. They tugged empty bottles (labelled Fanta or Coca-Cola) from their bags. Then they clambered and slid down the muddy banks and waded into the newly blessed water. At first they only scooped it from the shallows. It was mineral water, muddied and warm. They drank in deep gulps from their laced hands, and winched themselves back to stow the bottles on shore.

Then it all went to their heads. Six or seven old women flung off first their cardigans, then their kerchiefs and skirts until, at last, stripped down to flowery underpants and bras, they made headlong for the waters. All inhibition was lost. Their massive legs, welted in varicose veins, carried them juddering down the banks. Their thighs tapered to small, rather delicate feet. Little gold crosses were lost between their breasts. They plunged mountainously in. I stood above them in astonishment, wondering if I was meant to be here. But they were shouting and jubilant. They cradled the water in cupped hands and dashed it over their faces. Holiness had turned liquid, palpable. You could drink it, drown in it, bring it home like a bouquet for the sick.

Two of the boldest women – cheery, barrel-chested ancients – made for the gushing silver pipe and thrust their heads under it. They sloshed its torrent exultantly over one another, then submerged in it and drank it wholesale. They shouted at their friends still on land, until one or two of the younger women lifted their skirts and edged in. Bottle after bottle was filled and lugged to shore. But it was the young, not the old, who hesitated. The old were in high spirits. One of them shouted at me to join them, but I was caught between laughter and tears. These were women who had survived all the Stalin years, the deprivation, the institutional suffering, into a long widowhood and breadline pensions. Their exuberance struck me dumb. Perhaps, in this sacred and chaotic waterhole, the world seemed finally to make sense to them, and all this aching, weary flesh at last found absolution.

The procession, meanwhile, had reached the open fields where the bulldozers worked. All the way to the future cathedral, which would stand in the compound's heart, the tarred pipes lay ready alongside their trenches, and the channel was blessed. I caught up with the remaining pilgrims clustered in the big meadows, beside the ghost-cathedral. Here Feodosy, above the lonely swing of a censer, blessed the terrible site 'where nameless thousands had laboured and died', and we stared across fields lacquered in blue and white flowers while the incense vanished over them. Sometimes I wondered if the past were being laid too easily to sleep, forgotten. But the monastery would countermand this, said the shy priest. In future years people would ask: Why is it here? and recognize its building both as a cleansing and a memorial. This was being done for the dead.

The procession moved on. I fell behind with a puckish war veteran hobbling on a stick, and found myself wondering aloud again: why, why had this faith been resurrected out of nothing, as if a guillotined head had been stuck back on its body? Some vital artery had preserved it. And as I watched the pilgrims filtering back towards us from the pool, I thought: it was the women. 'Yes,' the soldierly old man answered. 'For me it was my mother. We lived in a remote region near Voronezh – not in a town at all, you understand, just a country village. No church for hundreds of miles. My mother was illiterate, but she remembered all the prayers from the old days, and taught me them.'

I tried to imagine his old face young, and found an impish boy there. A dust of hair was still brown over his scalp. He said: 'And in the war, when I was on the front, she prayed for me and I for her, secretly. She gave me one of these' – he pulled a miniature icon from his wallet. 'Marshal Zhukov kept one in his pocket all through the war – and so did other generals. And nobody knew it.'

He paused from the pain in his foot. Neither his icon nor his mother's prayers had saved him from a German sniper. The bullet had opened up a ten-inch wound, and now he had this trouble walking. 'We didn't have bullets like that in Russia, it was a type of shrapnel. When it hit me, it exploded and shattered the leg bones. Now I try to walk like this ... or this ... but nothing works.' He said: 'God must have been looking away.'

When we arrived back at the chapel we found a long table laden with salads and jams in the shade. The babushkas had returned. Their serried hands were ready beside their soup plates in two ranks of sun-cracked knuckles and broken nails. The archbishop, presiding at the head, commanded me to sit beside him – 'We have a guest from England!' he boomed. 'We must make him welcome!' – and I stared down an avenue of scarfed and nodding heads, which turned to gaze at me as one, and murmured 'England ... England ...' Their cheeks bunched into smiles, and faltering lines of teeth parted in welcome.

Feodosy pounded the table with a bottle. 'This is for you!' he said. 'It's our monastery water! It cures everything!' He read off the label. 'Chronic colitis and enterocolitis! Liver ailments! All gastric problems! Cystitis! Non-cancerous stomach ulcers! Duodenal ulcers ...'

The babushkas crossed themselves and commended me to God. They looked deeply respectable. Nobody would have guessed that half an hour before they had been ducking one another half-naked in a waterhole. Yet under the benches their bags bulged with bottles of holy water and they were sitting becalmed, almost smug, in the warmth of their success.

Around me at the table's head the priests had turned pallid in the desanctifying light. Stripped to simple soutanes, they fingered their cutlery nervously around the archbishop. On his far side the celebrant appeared to be defensively asleep. His beard, I noticed, was fringed with white but auburn at the roots, as if it had turned white after some shock and he was getting over it now. Only Feodosy still looked formidable. His black eyes and aquiline nose broke imperiously through the gush of grey hair and beard which swamped his pectoral crosses and lapped at his nape. He hammered out commands at the nuns who had appeared from nowhere to serve us, or shouted down the table. 'Brothers and sisters! Pass the mineral water round! ... Sisters, bring on the *kasha*.' The vegetable soup was gone in a trice, and soon he was ramming the rice into his mouth with giant wedges of bread. 'And no water! Sisters ...' I wondered if he had been promoted for his looks. A burst of jet-black eyebrows lent him the glamour of a converted Mephistopheles. Nobody dared ask him questions. He addressed me in explosions of German which I could rarely understand. 'The man who found the first mass grave here – this was the hand of God – it was the local Party Secretary! And now he's become a priest, yes! He's chaplain to a Cossack regiment in Omsk. Sisters! Where is the bread? ...'

He ladled a dollop of strawberry jam on to my bowl of rice. It was like being back at school. 'And in the spring we'll start the building of the cathedral, yes, God is in this place of tragedy!'

I gestured out to the fields. 'Built on graves?'

'Yes, there are dead out there.' He turned sombre. 'And everywhere. The monastery will gather information on them, and the monks will pray for their souls.'

'And what will you do with so much space?'

'Do?' he bellowed. 'We'll plant it with roses! Nothing but roses!' The enamel crosses trembled on his paunch. 'An ocean of roses!'

All down the table the faces broke into smiles again, and stray wisps of hair shivered free of their headscarves. As the meal broke up, one of the women tapped my arm and held out a thin blue sash stamped with prayers. 'This is for you,' she said, 'to wear on your train.' Then she committed me to God, and went back among her friends.

I spread the sash in my hands and read: 'He shall give his angels charge over thee, to keep thee in all thy ways. They shall bear thee up in their hands . . .'

Yes, I thought, I would wear it as a belt. I must have grown thinner, because my trousers were loose. I knotted it round my waist.

A light intoxication, something welcome and unexpected (for we had drunk only water) descended on me out of the half-healed land. A priest was tolling a carillon of bells on a makeshift scaffold near the chapel, but softly (perhaps he was practising) as if to lay to rest the spirits, and the pilgrims, by twos and threes, were returning to the coach. I climbed in among them. For a moment I wanted to believe that everything was as they believed. I was thankful for their stubborn needs and passions. I sat stifled between two babushkas (there was a shortage of seats) and they began to sing. 'Sing! Sing!' they cried. I hitched up my sash: 'He shall cover thee with his feathers,' it went on, 'and under his wings shalt thou trust . . .' Yes, I thought, everything will get better. We will abrogate reason and love one another. Perhaps monastic water will turn us near-immortal. The past will forgive us, and the earth will bear roses . . .

A land of interlaced earth and water, mutable, near-colourless – the sway of fescue grass above the swamps, the wrung-out platinum of winter wheat – spread from the train window to a thin sky. Halfway to Novosibirsk, the Baraba steppe was once a place of exiles and Tartar nomads, crossed by a string of Cossack forts. Now wild geese and coots flew from the marshes over a glint of lakes fringed by salinated soil. Here and there the old collectives were spread in long white barns, but they looked uninhabited. The villages, too, empty. Distance resolved them into the hamlets of Russian fairy tale, where the witch Baba Yaga might appear, or a formation of swan-princesses fly in. ⟵

In 400 miles we stopped only three times. I stared out to a faint, light horizon where the forest made charcoal lines. Occasionally a horseman watched his cattle, or a field of rapeseed broke into buttery flower. More often, for mile after mile, the late summer haze turned this into looking-glass country, refracting and confused. Its water-smeared earth wobbled against the sky. All matter looked temporary and dissoluble, all liquid so silted that it was halfway to being earth. Yet a farmer beside me said that the summer rains had been too few, and I noticed how low the rivers dawdled in their banks, and how the shrubs were already taking on the burnish of autumn.

We were following the line eastward of the Trakt post road, the precursor of the Trans-Siberian, laid in the 1760s from the Urals to the Pacific. In those days the bone-crunching journey – by horse-cart or sleigh – might take a year. When Chekhov embarked on his long tarantass ride towards Sakhalin, coughing up blood and sinking deep into depression, it was raining day and night, the rivers flooded, the ferries groping back and forth in howling wind, and ice floes on the move. Now, as we rumbled towards Novosibirsk, the largest city in Siberia, trains passed us every three minutes on the busiest freight line in the world, bringing coal from the Kuzbass basin to the smelting furnaces of the Urals.

You disembark at Siberia's biggest station, then taxi into the third most spacious city in Russia. Space is the sterile luxury of

Novosibirsk. In summer it hangs in vacant stillness over the flattened boulevards. In winter it starts to move, and howls between the islanded buildings and across the squares. The city is a claustrophobe's dream. Its roads sweep emptily between miles of apartment blocks and Stalinist hulks moaning with prefabricated pilasters and cornices. As for the people, there are a million and a half of them, but they seem lost in space; they trickle along the pavements to work. You become one of them, reduced. The traffic seems sparse and far away, wandering over a delta of stone and tarmac.

Longing for intimacy, you avoid the 888-room Hotel Novosibirsk. But instead you find yourself in the void of Lenin Square, where the man himself stands in windswept defiance, his bronze coat flying out as if in a winter gale. Behind him the largest opera house in Russia, bulkier even than the Bolshoi, crouches like a square-headed tortoise under a dome of silver scales. To reach it you have to sprint two hundred yards across the traffic-sprinkled square. Then you are turned away. It is closed in August.

So you stand, a little ashamed of your indifference – for this, after all, is Siberia's industrial giant, its centre of heavy metallurgy and machine-tool manufacture, of international trade conferences and joint ventures – you stand on a traffic island christened by a gold-domed chapel: because here, it has been calculated, lies the geographical centre of Russia. You wait, as visitors wait in Times Square or Piccadilly Circus, expecting something to happen. But nothing does, of course. And you are alone. The streets reel away on either side. From the granite steps of the chapel you gaze miles down the main street at the shadow of a bridge over the Ob River, to where on the far bank glimmers a suburb of smokestacks and apartment blocks built in Khrushchev's time, now misted in smog. Here the Ob, the fourth-longest river in the world, moves imperceptibly towards the Arctic – dropping only two inches a mile; soon it is filled with industrial waste and toxic oil, becoming so polluted that in winter it sometimes fails to freeze.

Space, in the end, may be all you remember of Novosibirsk. It is Siberia's gift. The vacancy of the land seems to infiltrate every town, or license it to sprawl. The apartment blocks carry on for mile after monotonous mile. Railway stations, whose tracks and sidings multiply ten or fourteen abreast, lie far from their town centres. And the rivers wind in enigmatically from nowhere like sky-coloured lakes, and curl out again to nowhere. The eye is met by eternal sameness. It begins to glaze.

Like the city outside, the restaurant is near-empty. A man and a woman sit alone four tables away. He is narrow-shouldered and rat-like, his eyes so small that they are almost snuffed out. She is a dyed blonde, running to fat. She is starting to weep. When she rubs her eyes, the mascara rings them quaintly, panda-like. I hear only snatches of their talk. Their right hands, each with a cigarette, are raised between them. 'Who with? . . . Have you understood? . . . Only too well . . . A lot, a terrible lot, too much . . .' Her thighs stir in their polka-dot dress. A two-man band – synthesizer and guitar – is playing from a gaudily lit rostrum. The woman lumbers to her feet and asks the guitarist to play something. Perhaps it is 'their' song. He starts up in the whining, nasal tones of Western pop singing.

Dancing in the streets of New Orleans
Dancing cheek to cheek in New Orleans

Her feet in their acrylic shoes start to tap unseen under the table. His do not. He turns away from the music and from her, smoking. Then her head slumps and her body gives a shudder. For the first time she stares at her bowl of undrunk soup instead of at him.

Dancing cheek to cheek in New Orleans
Dancing with the Queen of New Orleans

The salad and cold meat lie untouched in front of them. They smoke from the same box of cigarettes. To me they seem less present than the spaces around them, the distances that are too great.

In the mid-1950s, when the Soviet Union reached middle age, the rise of Khrushchev resurrected the old vision of a purpose-built city dedicated to science. This Utopian artifice would solve the problems of pure knowledge; but it would also deploy its genius in the service of technology and economics, devoting itself in particular to the vast resources of Siberia, by which Russia would at last outstrip the West.

The embodiment of this awesome concept was planned twenty miles south of Novosibirsk in the Golden Valley by the Ob River. Building began in 1958, and within seven years 40,000 scientists, executives and their families had poured in to fifteen newly opened research academies. A garden city grew up in six micro-regions, with its own schools and supermarkets, an elite university, an artificial beach on the Ob reservoir, even ski runs illuminated at night.

Here in the taiga, far from the watchful Party apparatus in Moscow, a brief, intoxicating freedom sprang up. Akademgorodok became the brain of Russia. It attracted a host of young, sometimes maverick scientists, many from Siberia. It opened up fields of study previously forbidden. The Institutes of Nuclear Physics and Economics, of Hydrodynamics and Catalysis, shared the forest with academies devoted to geology, automation, thermophysics (for the tapping of volcanic energy beneath permafrost) and a Physiological Institute working on the adaptation of animals and plants to the Siberian climate. And at the centre of this cerebral spider's-web the Institute of Abstract Mathematics sat like a cool agony aunt, advising on the problems of all the rest. Informal communication between institutes was the touchstone of the place's founder, the mathematician Lavrentiev. There were breakthroughs in physics, biology and computer studies. For a few heady years it seemed as if the science-fiction city could fulfil its promise.

Then, with the fall of Khrushchev, ideological controls began to tighten. Science became yoked to industry and was commandeered to show direct economic returns. The heart went out of things. But in a sense the clampdown came too late. There were people working in Akademgorodok – the economist Aganbegyan, the sociologist Zaslavskaya – whose thought became seminal to perestroika. Yet ironically it was the chaotic results of Gorbachev's revolution that laid waste the powerhouse whose institutes I tramped for two days.

They rose in mixed styles, prefabricated, sometimes handsome, recessed among their trees along irregular avenues. There were now twenty-three of them, but the only map I found catered for visitors shopping in the town's handful of emporia. I scanned it in bewilderment. In Soviet times, I knew, maps were often falsified or full of blanks. This one featured greengrocers and shoe shops, even the smallest bakery and café. But the institutes had become ghosts. Not one was named. Were they too important to divulge, I wondered? Or were they just forgotten?

I wandered them in ignorance, staring at their name boards. INSTITUTE OF SOLID-STATE CHEMISTRY ... CYTOLOGY AND GENETICS ... INSTITUTE OF CHEMICAL KINETICS ... We barely shared a language. In between, woodland paths wound among silver birch and pine trees, their trunks intermingled like confused regiments. The earth sent up a damp fragrance. It was obscurely comforting. A few professors strolled between institutes, carrying shapeless bags and satchels, and fell pleasantly into conversation.

One of these chance meetings landed me unprepared in the Akademgorodok Praesidium. The professor who introduced me soon disappeared, and I was left in a passage outside the General Secretary's office, like a schoolboy waiting to be beaten. I thought I knew these interviews. From the far side of his desk a sterile apparatchik would tell me that all was well. The only signs of truth would be chance ones: damp wallpaper or indiscreet secretaries or the way the man's hands wrenched together. But I waited with suppressed hope. I wanted to know the outcome of several key Siberian projects, and sieved my brain for the Russian equivalent of 'nuclear reaction' or 'electric light stimulant', then fell into despondency. I wasn't even dressed right. I was still wearing my Orthodox prayer-belt, and one of my climbing boots had developed a foolish squeak.

When the General Secretary's door opened, my heart sank. He loomed big and surly behind his desk, in shirtsleeves. His features were obscure oases in the blank of his face: pin-prick eyes, a tiny, pouting mouth. I squeaked across the room to shake his hand. It was soft and wary. It motioned me to sit down.

Where could I tactfully begin? He wasn't going to help. He was gazing at me in passive suspicion. So I asked after the institute's recent successes.

He went on staring. All his answers came slowly, pronounced in the gravelly bass of authority. Progress had been made in the climatic adaptation of livestock, especially sheep, he said, and in a biochemical substance to stimulate the growth of wheat and rice ... But he did not enlarge on this. I thought he looked faintly angry.

Then I hunted for projects safely past, and alighted on the perilous Soviet scheme for steering Siberian rivers away from the Arctic to irrigate Central Asia and replenish the Aral Sea. He said: 'It was a useless scheme, horrible. It would have been an ecological disaster for both Siberia and Kazakhstan. Our scientists here were categorically against it, and the project was scrapped.'

I shifted nervously (my boot squeaked back) in the face of his morose stillness. There had been a project, I continued, in which artificial daylight was used to increase fertility in minks, foxes, pigs ... It had something to do with the relationship between the retina and the pituitary gland, I remembered, and sounded faintly repellent; but the General Secretary might approve.

He said: 'I only know they breed different coloured Arctic fox-furs now.' He tossed a batch of imagined stoles dismissively over his shoulder. 'Blue, navy blue, green. Any colour.'

But the remembered words of Soviet apologists, of Lavrentiev himself, were crowding back into my head. Some thirty years ago they promised that nuclear power would by now be centrally heating enormous tracts of Siberia and flooding Arctic towns with artificial sunlight. *Dramatic changes in Siberia will astound the world, changes that will make Siberia ideally suitable for human habitation.'*

I said: 'There was an idea for melting permafrost by controlled nuclear power . . .'

The Secretary was unmoved.

'That was just an idea,' he said.

I felt grateful for this honesty. But the voices of the old enthusiasts went on clamouring in me. 'It was proposed to fire coal underground,' I continued, 'to feed hydroelectric stations from underground funnels.'

A cigarette waggled unlit between the Secretary's fingers. 'It didn't work. It was impossible.'

'Then what about the scheme for fuelling power stations with steam, using the Kamchatka volcanoes?'

He shrugged. 'I haven't even heard of it. And it doesn't fall within the province of this institution . . .' He was slumped deeper behind his desk, huge in the slope of his beer gut. His eyes were ice-pale. I imagined they had no pupils. I felt at sea. My jacket had fallen open on my prayer-belt, which guaranteed me immunity from pestilence and the cockatrice's den. I hid it with my arm. I was unsure what a cockatrice was, but the General Secretary might know. He continued to glare at me.

By now my questions, his answers, and the voices from the still-recent past seemed to be interlocked in a formal dance. I lit despairingly on an old success story. 'The hydrodynamic cannon ...'

'*It slices off whole layers of hard earth*,' Lavrentiev had said, '*and opens coal deposits in a matter of hours*.'

'They were discontinued years ago,' answered the General Secretary. 'They couldn't really do the job. The principle is now used only to press matter, not cut it open. The cannon could only drill a small hole ...'

We had reached a strange impasse. It was I who was believing in a future, it seemed, and he who was denying it. But I floated out a last fantasy, something I had childishly hoped to see. Twenty years ago plans were afoot for a whole Arctic town enjoying its own microclimate. Named Udachny, 'Fortunate', it would either rise in a transparent pyramid or shelter beneath a glass dome or spread along a sealed web of avenues and gardens. It had been promised within ten years. (Lavrentiev: '*Siberia will become the science centre not only of the Soviet Union, but of the world*.')

I asked: 'Where is this town? Wasn't there a scheme?'

'There was a scheme,' said the General Secretary remorselessly. 'But there is no town.'

I went quiet, foolishly dispirited. The voices of the failed future mewed faintly, faded away. Suddenly the Secretary leaned forward. 'Look,' he growled. 'Look ...' I had no idea what to expect. His face was heavy with anger. 'We have one overriding problem here. *Money*. We receive no money for new equipment, hardly enough for our salaries. There are people who haven't been paid for six months.' Then his anger overflowed. He was barking like a drill-sergeant. 'This year we requested funds for six or seven different programmes! And not one has been accepted by the government! Not one!'

I stared at him, astonished. I realized that all this time his bitterness had been directed not at me, but at Moscow. Far from being a passive mouthpiece for his masters, he was furious with them. 'I don't know what policy drives our government, or even if it has one! Science is now as cut off from the State as the Church used to be. As far as I can see everything's run by Mafia!'

He delved into a box and found me a book about the past achievements of Akademgorodok. It was richly illustrated with bursting corn-heads and fattened sheep. 'We used to accomplish things,' he said, as I got up to go. Then, as if a boil had been lanced, his anger evaporated. All his face's features, which had seemed numb or absent before, creased and wrinkled into sad life. How curious, I thought, bewildered. He was almost charming.

'The future?' he said. 'When we have a government that realizes no country can do without science, Akademgorodok will flourish again.'

He accompanied me to the Praesidium steps, perhaps reluctant to stay in his gaunt office. I started, too late, to like him. As I shook his hand I no longer sensed the brooding menace of the apparatchik; in his place was an ageing caretaker, dreaming of other times.

I walk along the Ob Sea with a young scientist from the Institute of Physics. This is not truly a sea but a giant reservoir, which sparkles tidelessly. And he is not quite a scientist (although he calls himself one) but a research student from the once-prestigious university. He is wondering what to do with his life. The sand under our feet is not naturally there either, but was imported – two and a half million cubic yards of it – to complete the town's amenities.

And now everything is in ruins, he says. 'The younger scientists are leaving in droves, mostly for business. In business you can earn five times the salary you're offered here. Others have emigrated to the States and Germany. All the bright ones have gone.'

Gone to the countries their parents feared, I thought. 'And you?'

A stammer surfaces in his speech, like some distress signal. 'I'll go too.'

'To work in science?'

'No. Most of us can't use our scientific expertise. We just want a decently paid job, and a future.'

Our feet drag in the sand. The enormous beach is dotted with sunbathers, and some women are walking their dogs along the shallows. He says: 'A few years ago, you know, when people left university, there was terrible competition to get into the institutes. But now they'll take anyone. They'll give you a flat, of course, but what's the point of that if you can hardly afford to eat?' The question is not quite rhetorical. He wants to be a scientist still. But he doesn't see how. 'Only the dim ones stay. They do laboratory work for a pittance. The equipment's getting old. And nobody's working properly.'

We stop by the water's edge. For miles it is fringed by a flotsam of logs, broken loose from their booms somewhere upriver. For a heady moment their resinous smell returns me to my childhood by a Canadian river, where the stray logs became the playthings of a small, naked boy, years before Akademgorodok was even conceived.

The student is saying without conviction, without love: 'I'll go into business.'

He was an only child. Reclusive, almost biblically innocent. During the war his mother had escaped with him from the siege of Leningrad; his father had been killed. I had been given his telephone number by chance, and when he clattered up in his institute's car – a professional perk – I had no idea what to expect.

Where did Sasha belong? Not with Russia's troubled present, I think, but with the dreamers who scatter its nineteenth-century novels. His work consumed him. Many evenings he toiled through the night in a big, bleak building called the Institute of Clinical and Experimental Medicine. Even now, during the August break, the receptionist acknowledged him with pert familiarity. He studied in the basement, in a chain of dim grottoes – their electricity had failed – poring over data on magnetic fields. Beside his desk stood a rusty stove and an exercise bike, and two or three machines loomed against the walls in a fretwork of tubes and wires. But there must have been electricity somewhere because a fridge wheezed in one corner, and after a while Sasha disappeared to make tea. I waited. I might have been in the den of some harmless wizard. The walls were hung with prints by the mystic painter Nikolai Roerich – grainy mountains inhabited by hermits or traversed by pilgrims.

We drank tepid tea in the dark. Sasha was fifty-six, but boyish, bursting with enthusiasm and trust. A pelmet of chestnut hair fell over his forehead and his eyes were brown and puppyish. He was sad that he could not measure my magnetic sensitivity on the Heath-Robinson machine beside us ('No electricity!'), but he hoped I would enter the hypomagnetic chamber next door. 'You've seen these photographs?' He pointed to a cabinet. 'Those detect energy flowing from a patient's fingertips after just three sessions in the chamber!'

I stared at them: they seemed to show a jellyfish haloed in hair. I said doubtfully: 'What diseases can it cure?'

'It treats epilepsy, but the subject needs to be very sensitive. It's also helped with nervous paralysis and cancer.'

'*Cancer?*'

'Well, it's helped in diagnosis.'

'But what does the chamber actually do?'

Even to myself I sounded peremptory, but Sasha was breathless with evangelism. 'The chamber almost eliminates the body's natural magnetic waves! They decrease by six hundred times! And this allows *other things* to happen – purer waves. Things we can't be sure about.' He was beaming his boy's smile. 'But before treatment we need to know your prenatal development in each of the weeks between conception and birth. The interplanetary magnetic field, phases of the moon and so on . . .' He stared at me as if I must have this data on me, perhaps in my passport.

'I'm afraid . . .'

But he rushed on: 'The field-structure of our organism is very dynamic. Sometimes it is closed, sometimes not. Recently, for instance, we had a conference in Martinique, and the people there were very open, very. Their magnetic sensitivity, when we tested them, was first-rate. People need to unlock, you see. To open up!'

I began to feel jittery. I stared down at myself, wondering if I would open up, but saw only a scruffy shirt and a prayer-belt. The magnetic waves to which I would be exposed owed much, it seemed, to the astrophysicist N. A. Kozyrev, who had set up telescopic mirrors to record starlight simultaneously from the past, present and future. Kozyrev was Sasha's god. The astronomer seems to have believed that the universe was awash with a unified time-energy, in which intellect, matter and cosmic forces were bundled up in some Hegelian process which fascinated Sasha but eluded me.

'It all depends on your responsiveness,' Sasha said, leading me to the next room. 'The machine opens up psychophysical recesses not normally explored.' We stood before two identical chambers: grey, open-mouthed tunnels for the patient to lie in. They resembled MRI scanners or huge, open-ended washing machines, but were utterly plain.

I said stupidly: 'There are two.'

'Yes, but one is a dummy,' he said. 'If you lie quietly in each, you will sense which is which.' He straightened the mattresses inside them. 'Of course there are some people who stay closed up. Yes. There are, I should say, cosmophiles and cosmophobes. But seventy per cent are sensitive to it. Some get a feeling of flying, others of being lifted out of themselves. It depends on your sensitivity.'

His trust invited mine. I was determined to be sensitive. I climbed into one of the tunnels, feeling like dirty washing, and lay down. 'Lie quietly,' he said. 'Meditate.' I tried to empty my mind, but instead found myself scanning the arc of ceiling above me for some tell-tale sign. Was this the dummy or the real one, I wondered? I thought I discerned a trickle of wiring under its plaster, but decided this was only a structural joint. I lay still. A mill-race of thoughts started up, subsided. I closed my eyes and concentrated only on the darkness under their lids, where an odd grey plasma was floating. The room was silent. My mind attempted a thought or two, then gave up. But I felt nothing. Nothing. After a while I stared down at the circle of light beyond my feet, hoping for some sensation, anything, but saw only Sasha's face peering in. 'Relax. Meditate for five minutes. I have to check my fax machine.'

I meditated. But no, this was the dummy machine, I realized. I simply wanted to go to sleep. So I climbed out and confronted its twin. They both looked makeshift and somehow unreal, like stage props. But as I crawled into the second chamber, I felt a tremor of unease. Now I would be passing (Sasha had said) from Einstein's space into Kozyrev's space. Living matter would enter an immaterial dimension. Hesitantly I lay down and gazed up. I imagined a white blank. A long time seemed to go by. I tried to float. Again, nothing.

Now I heard a steady, rhythmic whirring. For a moment I could not locate it, then realized it came not from my head, nor from the tunnel ceiling above me, but from the next-door room. I thought: Sasha is pumping something, a generator perhaps. He is trying to activate my tunnel. So at least I know I'm in the right one. I lay down and tried again. The whirring continued, but instead of flying I seemed to be sinking into a bored catalepsy. My next thought was: the Russian Academy of Sciences is actually paying for this stuff, has been paying for years . . .

After a few minutes, tiredly, I climbed out. Despite myself, an irritated sense of failure arose. I fought it off. I'm not cosmophobic, I thought grumpily, I'm just English. I scrutinized the chambers for any difference: a give-away trail of cables or an extra metal coat. But there was none. The rhythmic whirring still sounded next door. I peered in and discovered its source: Sasha was riding his exercise bike.

'How was it? How was it?' He jumped off, sweating and jubilant.

I hazarded a guess at which was the real machine, but got it wrong. 'Maybe I'm tired,' I said. 'I didn't feel anything.' I hated to disappoint him. Momentarily I wanted the world to be as he wished it, riddled with cosmic benevolence. 'At least I don't think I did . . .'

I had fallen plumb into the insensitive thirty per cent. But Sasha brushed this aside. 'Let me show you something else . . .' My statistic, I could tell, would be lost in his own certainty. He had a way of discounting failure, I sensed. His wife and son, he had mentioned, lived far away in Estonia – she had returned to the town of her childhood. Yet he shied away from the word 'separated'. They just were not together. He had sealed the subject with a hazy smile. Sadness made him afraid, perhaps.

'You know there are certain trajectories of extraordinary magnetic power . . .' He was burrowing among his files. 'Just look at these, from Stonehenge. I find these most interesting.'

On to my lap he spilled sheaves of paper covered with random sketches. They were the result of an arcane experiment. Here in Akademgorodok one of his colleagues had sat encased in a curved aluminium chamber called 'Kozyrev's Mirrors', constructed to heighten the transmission of his 'time-energy waves'. While he concentrated his mind on a selection of ancient Sumerian images, other participants – sitting among the monoliths of Stonehenge over 3,000 miles away – had attempted to receive and sketch his thought-pictures.

'Look, look,' said Sasha. 'This is remarkable.' He pointed to a Sumerian original, which resembled a pair of gnats, then he riffled through the sketches. I saw spirals, boats, dogs, phalli, suns, stickmen, flowers, stars. At last: 'There!' Someone in Stonehenge had come up with a hovering bird. 'You see? You see?' He was glittering with faith. Never mind that all the other sketches – page upon page – bore no relation to anything envisioned, or that the gnats and the bird only dimly corresponded. Sasha was smiling at them like a cherub. He scarcely needed proof. He already knew. For him they were joining mankind to the cosmos, earth to heaven.

An old man sits in his dacha in the Golden Valley. These country homes are given only to the elite – he is an Academician – and all along the avenue their stucco facades rear from tangled gardens, until the road gives out against wooded hills. The Academician's sitting room is filled with kitsch: glass animals, sentimental pictures, statuettes of the Medici Venus, the Capitoline Venus, the Venus de Milo. But there are icons too, and tense, miniature landscapes painted by a Gulag prisoner. I wonder vaguely what these contradictions mean. Sasha, who has brought me here like a trophy, has gone silent. He listens to the Academician, his mentor, with hushed respect. So do the Academician's wife and middle-aged son. The whole house smells of a damp dog, which is hurtling through the undergrowth outside.

For a while we sit nibbling *zakuski* snacks and drinking vodka. The Academician hands me his latest book, *Cosmic Consciousness of Humanity*. Then they toast my future Siberian travels ('It's dangerous now, you know') and I begin to squirm in my traveller's disguise, because they want to convert me to their beliefs. Unnoticed I open the Academician's book and read: 'The total world human Intellect in its cosmoplanetary motion is neither derivative from, nor some pro-creation of, the social movement (social-cultural historic development). It is a peculiar cosmoplanetary phenomenon in the organization and motion of the Universe Living Matter in its earth-adapted manifestation . . .'

Fearing an attack of cosmophobia, I close it up, and now, impatient with the trivia of eating, of small talk, the Academician announces: 'We must go upstairs and discuss.'

Years of deference, I suppose, have wrecked him. An old pedagogy and a new evangelism smooth his thinking to unchallenged monologue. In the study where we sit – his son, Sasha, myself – his books are stacked in avenues from floor to ceiling, all nestled in dust. While his wife stays downstairs, washing up, he explains how man's spiritual and mental life is shot through by galactic waves, and I cannot decide if this idea is a vanity or humility (and the Academician does not take questions). He often lifts his finger as he advances point by point, and his message grows in urgency.

'We are at a crisis in the world's development. The West is powerless, blinded by money. It can't *see* anything. *It can't think new.* It is only Russia which can show the way. Point Three: she can do this precisely, and only, because everything has been taken from her, and she is open! Yes, open! This is the moment! We have just a brief chance – now! In a few years it will be too late. Now is the moment for classical thinking and cosmic thinking to converge. We must save the world – not only Russia! – and unleash new ways of thought!'

He speaks as if in an echo chamber, and the message which he finds so new is resonantly old. It rings through the works of the nineteenth-century Slavophils, who half-mystically enjoined the ancient values of the Russian soul. It is the vision of Dostoevsky, Herzen, Tolstoy. Yes, Russia will save the earth! Truth will rise through suffering! Europe – rational, individualist Europe – is benighted by affluence. Only impoverished Russia can touch the heart of things, and rescue mankind.

I start to lose the Academician's thread. He seems to be talking about experiments with cosmic waves in a Thracian sanctuary in Bulgaria, and in the Arctic Circle north of Dudinka where I will be going. He drops sweeping abstracts and magisterial generalizations. His audience is solemn, grateful. Stray concepts surface in English, sink again. 'Spatio-temporal waves ... Point Six ... distant-image interaction ...' Then he says to me: 'When you sail down the Yenisei, if you go with an open mind, you'll discover a new Siberia! We conducted experiments in Dikson in the Arctic Circle, and you'll find the magnetic channels between there and here are very powerful.' He asks: 'You've heard of Yuri Mochanov?'

To my surprise, I have. He is a Russian archaeologist whose excavations in the lower Lena have uncovered evidence of an ancient Siberian people. Controversially he has set the date of their stone tools at more than 2,000,000 BC, matching Leakey's Africans in the van of civilization. He still worked in the town of Yakutsk in East Siberia, where I meant to find him.

The Academician is fired up. 'A civilization at least as old as Africa's! So what does that do to Darwinism? Now the classic view is that man evolved out of Africa, then spread east and north into Asia. But the excavations of Mochanov and others prove something different. They prove that Intelligence emerged in several regions simultaneously – in Siberia, in Africa, in Central Asia. In fact Siberia was the first!'

It all fits beautifully, of course. Here in Siberia – the symbol and repository of Russia's otherness – civilization itself began. And here the cosmic flow, the great communion, will be reaffirmed. Not that the Academician repudiates science (although he lives in its ruins). In fact, his finger is raised again. 'I hold that cosmic influences accompanied by changes in the earth's magnetic field were responsible for a sudden maturation in men's brains at that time. These early civilizations were in tune with the cosmos, but due to various factors they could not, in the end, survive . . .' His hands return comfortably to his lap. 'Darwin, you understand, is nonsense.'

I sit opposite him, writhing with rebellion at first, then oddly sad. Sasha is glowing. But I see an old man in tracksuit trousers and threadbare socks, who has gone off the rails. Sometimes I feel that he is talking not to us, but to himself, and that he is very lonely. I imagine him the victim of that self-hypnosis which sustained the great illusion of Communism itself – where ideas and dreams hover delusively over the wasteland of fact.

HOW IT ENDS

Andrew O'Hagan

The Clyde used to be one of the noisiest rivers. Thirty or forty years ago you could hear the strike of metal against metal, the riveter's bedlam, down most of the narrow channel from Glasgow, and at several other shipbuilding towns on the estuary. There was a sound of horns on the water, and of engines turning. Chains unfurled and cargoes were lifted; there was chatter on the piers. But it is very quiet now. Seagulls murmur overhead, and nip at the banks. You can hear almost nothing. The water might lap a little, or ripple when pushed by the wind. But mostly it sits still.

This quietness is broken, five days a week, by the passage of the two ships which carry one of the Clyde's last cargoes: human effluent, sewage, sludge.

Glaswegians call these ships the sludge boats. Every morning, they sail west down the river to turn, eventually, south into the estuary's mouth, the Firth, where they will drop their load into the sea. By this stage of the voyage, their elderly passengers may be dancing on the deck, or, if the weather is wet or windy, playing bingo in the lounge. Underneath them, a few thousand tons of human sewage (perhaps some of their own, transported from their homes) will be slopping in the holds.

There was a time when passengers and cargo set sail from the Clyde to New York, Montreal, Buenos Aires, Calcutta and Bombay in liners equipped to carry awkward things like railway locomotives and difficult people like tea planters. And now, almost alone upon the river, this: tons of shit accompanied by an average complement of seventy old-age pensioners enjoying a grand day out, and travelling free.

This morning it was the ladies – and several gentlemen – of the Holy Redeemer's Senior Citizens' Club of Clydebank who were taking a trip down the river. I'd watched them ambling on to the boat from the wharf at Shieldhall sewage works, each of them with a plastic bag filled with sandwiches and sweets. Now I could hear the party arranging itself on the deck above me, as I stood down below to watch the sludge being loaded into the ship's eight tanks. It came from the wharf through an enormous red pipe, then into a funnel, and then from the funnel into a hopper, which channelled the sludge evenly through the ship's basement. It took about an hour and thirty minutes to load up. As the ship filled – with wakeful passengers and tired sludge – a little fountain of perfume sprinkled silently over the hopper's top.

We were on board the *Garroch Head*, a handsome ship named after the point near the dumping ground forty miles downstream, and built on the Clyde, as was her sister ship, the *Dalmarnock* (named after a sewage works). The *Garroch Head* can carry three and a half thousand tons of sludge; the *Dalmarnock* three thousand tons. They are not particularly old ships – both were launched in the 1970s – but neither seems likely to survive the century. After 1998, the process of dumping at sea will be outlawed by a directive from the European Union on grounds of ecology and public health. And yet this quiet disposal, this burial of a city's intimate wastes in ninety fathoms halfway between the islands of Bute and Arran, once seemed such a neat and clean solution.

Until the 1890s, Glasgow's untreated sewage went straight into the river's upper reaches, where it bubbled under the surface and crept ashore as black mud. Civic concern arose with the stench; the population was still growing in a city made by the first industrial revolution and popularly described as 'the workshop of the world'. In 1889, the city's engineer, Alexander Frew, read a paper on the sewage question to the Glasgow Philosophical Society, and then addressed increasingly heated questions about what was to be done. He opposed dumping at sea, and suggested instead that the sewage be spread along the banks of the Clyde, where it would come to form fine agricultural land. The city rejected this scheme, though a feeling persisted that something *useful* (and profitable) might be done with Glasgow's swelling effluent; in London at that time, the Native Guano Company of Kingston-upon-Thames appeared to be setting a trend with this sort of thing. Glasgow's own brand, Globe Fertilizer, was popular for a short while. But here, science was ahead of the game – or behind it – with new artificial fertilizers that were more powerful and cheaper than the processed human stuff.

How did other cities arrange their disposal? A delegation went from Glasgow to Paris to find out, and there discovered a great tunnel on either side of the river Seine. Sewage poured out of pipes into these tunnels, which then poured into the Seine some miles from the city. The Seine, however, was clean when compared with the Clyde, because (as the delegation noted) the current carried the effluent away from the city to less fortunate towns further downstream, and then to the sea. The Clyde, on the other hand, was tidal; sewage went with the ebb and came back up with the flood – a mess that, like an unwanted stray dog, could not be shooed away. There was also another reason for the Seine's relative purity, which perversely had to do with Glasgow's greater progress in sanitation. Paris had six hundred thousand closets, or lavatories, but only a third of them were water-closets; the rest were dry, their waste carried away by night-soil carts to fields and dumps. Glasgow, thanks to its climate and municipal reservoirs and pipes, had most of its lavatories flushed by water. It had wet sewage rather than dry, and much more of it to get rid of.

In 1898, nine years after the Paris trip, another delegation travelled south, this time to London, where they were shown the system of sewers, sewage works and, lastly, sewage ships which carried the capital's waste to its destination far out in the Thames estuary. They were impressed, and by 1910 Glasgow had a similar system in place – the second largest (after London) in the world, with three great sewage works sending their produce down the Clyde in ships.

The passengers came later, just after the First World War, when a benevolent but cost-conscious Glasgow city council (then called the Glasgow Corporation) decided that convalescing servicemen would benefit from a day out on the Clyde. Cruising on pleasure steamers up and down the estuary and across to its islands was then Glasgow's great summer pastime; the sludge boats offered the city council the prospect of killing two birds with one stone. Their voyages were already paid for out of the rates. The servicemen could travel free. It was seen as an expression of socialist goodwill – allied with the enlightened Victorian municipalism that had given Glasgow its lavish water supply and so many public parks. The vessels were rebuilt to carry passengers, fitted out with more lifeboats and saloons, equipped with deck quoits. By and by, their traffic in convalescing servicemen died away, to be replaced, thanks to the charitable offices of Glasgow Corporation, by old people who couldn't afford cruises on the regular steamships, but who may have been encouraged by the doctor to take the air.

And so it was, in the summer of 1995, that I came to be travelling with the Clydebank Holy Redeemers on top of three and a half thousand tons of sludge.

Everything – or everything visible to the passenger – on the *Garroch Head* was scrupulously clean. The wooden table and chairs in the lounge shone with polish; the urinals gleamed; the deck was as free of dirt as any deck could be. The haphazard filth and toxic stews of Glasgow were kept well out of sight. There was a sense among the crew that it was this opposition of cleanliness to filth that carried them and their ship forward on each voyage.

We sailed past the grass and rubble where the shipyards used to be – Connell's and Blythswood to starboard, Simons and Lobnitz to port – and I talked to a woman who was leaning on the ship's rail and enjoying the breeze. She was called Mary Kay McRory, she was eighty, and she had a big green cardigan pulled across her chest. Her eyes ran, but she laughed a lot as she spoke. She said the first time she had sailed on the Clyde was in 1921, when she had travelled as a six-year-old with her family on the steamer that took cattle and people from Derry in Ireland to Glasgow, and very seldom took the same ones back again. Mary Kay's father was escaping some bother in Donegal; he heard of work in Glasgow, came over and was employed right away as a lamplighter. Then he summoned his wife and the six children. 'We came away from Donegal with biscuits,' Mary Kay said. 'Everybody would throw biscuits over the wall to you. They were good biscuits. The food over there was good.'

She had worked as a waitress, when the city was still full of tearooms, and then on the Glasgow trams for twenty-five years. I asked her if Glasgow had changed much, and she got me by the arm. 'Ye can say what ye like,' she said, 'but there's no poverty now, none.' She talked a lot about sanitation, about toilets and baths, in the way many old Glaswegians do. Those who remember lavatories shared with neighbours and trips to the public bathhouse tend to talk more about these matters than people like me who grew up thinking it was nothing special to have porcelain bits at the top of the stairs stamped ARMITAGE SHANKS.

Plastic bags were being rustled in the lounge. Out of them came the day's supplies: sandwiches of white bread cut into quarters and filled variously with slates of corned beef, chicken breast, shiny squares of gammon, salmon paste and cheese spreads. And then the treats to follow: Paris buns, Blue Riband biscuits, Tunnock's Teacakes, Bourbon creams. Some of the women dropped sweeteners into their tea and stirred melodically for a long time after. Others placed ginger snaps at the edge of their saucers, or unwrapped tight wads of shortbread, ready for distribution. Neat stacks of white bread and sweet acres of treats stretched on the table, in front of every passenger. All the mouths were going – shredding meat and sloshing tea – like washing machines on a full load.

This was not lunch for the Holy Redeemers; merely elevenses.

Sludge, in the particular sense of our sludge boat's cargo, comes about like this. The sewage pumped into Glasgow's three sewage works is twice screened. The first screening takes out large objects – lumps of wood, rags, metal – that somehow find their way into the sewers. The second screening extracts smaller, abrasive materials such as glass and sand. Then comes the first separation process, designed to make the organic component of the sewage sink to the bottom of the tank (just as sediment will settle in a bottle of wine). They call this the stage of primary settlement. The heavy stuff at the bottom is called raw sludge; the clearer liquid above is settled sewage.

The raw sludge is not ready to dispose of; it needs further modification and is subject to biochemical breakdown. Some of it goes through a process called digestion. Bacteria are allowed into the holding chambers, where they feed energetically on the proteins and carbohydrates, diminishing the organic matter until the sludge is fit to be spread on farmland or made ready for dumping at sea. Then, at the works near the wharf at Shieldhall, the sludge is 'settled' one last time, to increase the content of sinkable solids in the watery mix. The stuff in the hold has passed through many systems – biological and mechanical – and it will have no final rest from the biological, even at the bottom of the sea. It degrades there to feed marine life (the fishing near the dumping ground is said to be fairly good) and continue its journey through the ecosystem.

There has, however, been an awful lot of it dumped, and all in the same place. In the first year of the sludge boats, 213,867 tons were carried down the Clyde. In 1995, the figure was 1.8 million tons. The total for this century is 82.6 million tons. The seabed at the dump's centre is said to be damaged, its organisms contaminated. The EU has delivered its verdict. Glasgow needs a new venue for the sludge, and old ideas are being re-examined. Fertilizer, for example. Sludge is rich in nitrates (four per cent), phosphate (three per cent) and potassium (one per cent), and full of nutrients – it could do a good job on the land, and farmers seem willing to try it for free. It is also well suited to grass-growing and is already being spread on derelict industrial sites to prepare them for reclamation. A new product range – sludge cakes, sludge pellets – will be tried on the waste ground that was once the Ravenscraig steelworks, the largest and last of Scotland's steel plants, where the soil has been poisoned by decades of metal wastes. Sludge used there could make a meadow grow.

We passed Greenock, which used to make ships and sugar, and then veered left into the Firth proper. The *Garroch Head* was going at a fair pelt now, and most of the passengers had their eyes down, playing a restive round or two of bingo. Some were nibbling still at the corners of buns and sandwiches. From the saloon porthole the water looked silver, as if some giant shoal of mackerel swam just beneath the surface. The islands of Great and Little Cumbrae stood out, like two large boulders only recently dropped into the sea.

We passed them. Up on the bridge, they were slowing the vessel down, ready to discharge their load. We had reached the dumping ground, and as soon as the position was right a crewman on the bridge flicked a switch, and I heard a little rumble. The valves were opening. I thought I could feel the cargo starting to be pulled by gravity from its tanks.

I went down from the bridge to the deck nearest the water, and saw the first of the billowing columns. Fierce puffs, great Turner clouds of wayward brown matter, rose up and spread in an instant over the surface. The waters of the Firth were all at once rusty and thick, and the boat was an island in a sea of sludge. This was all in the first few minutes.

We moved off, leaning to port, aiming to complete a full circle as the sludge descended. A group of pensioners stood in a row looking out, covering their mouths and noses with white hankies. All the worst odour of a modern city, until now stored and battened down, was released in this time-stopping, comical stench. I looked up at the coast and wondered for a second where it had all begun, because this was an ending, and the sense of an ending was as palpable and strong as the brew in the sea before us.

The ship turned about and headed home. Its emptying had taken ten minutes. Back in the saloon, the pensioners were dancing to a song called 'Campbeltown Loch, I Wish Ye Were Whisky'. My tea sat just where I'd left it, and I was happy to notice it was still quite warm.

the first of the following

Farbe der Augen
Colour of eyes
Couleur des yeux

BRAUN

Größe / Height / Taille

184   cm

Unterschrift des Paßinhabers / Signature of bearer / Signature du titulaire

Länder, für die dieser Paß gilt / Countries for which this passport is valid
Pays pour lesquels ce passeport est valable

Für alle Länder / For all countries / Pour tous pays

Paßausstellende Behörde / Issuing authority / Autorité ayant délivré le passeport

Ausgestellt (Ort) / Issued at / Délivré à

GENERALKONSULAT
DER BUNDESREPUBLIK DEUTSCHLAND
MAILAND

Datum / Date / Date

04. AUGUST 1987

Unterschrift / Signature / Signature

Nr. H 3560586

3

GOING ABROAD

W. G. Sebald

Translated from the German by Michael Hulse

In October 1980 I travelled from England, where I had then been living for nearly twenty-five years in a county which was almost always under grey skies, to Vienna, hoping that a change of place would help me get over a particularly difficult period in my life. In Vienna, however, I found that the days proved inordinately long, now they were not taken up by my customary routine of writing and gardening tasks, and I literally did not know where to turn. Early every morning I would set out and walk without aim or purpose through the streets of the inner city, through the Leopoldstadt and the Josefstadt. Later, when I looked at the map, I saw to my astonishment that none of my journeys had taken me beyond a precisely defined sickle- or crescent-shaped area, the outermost points of which were the Venediger Au by the Praterstern and the great hospital precincts of the Alsergrund. If the paths I had followed had been inked in, it would have seemed as though a man had kept trying out new tracks and connections over and over, only to be thwarted each time by the limitations of his reason, imagination or will power, and obliged to turn back again. My quartering of the city, often continuing for hours, thus had very clear bounds, and yet at no point did my incomprehensible behaviour become apparent to me: that is to say, my continual walking and my reluctance to cross certain lines which were both invisible and, I presume, wholly arbitrary. All I know is that I found it impossible even to use public transport and, say, simply take the 41 tram out to Pötzleinsdorf or the 58 to Schönbrunn and take a stroll in the Pötzleinsdorf Park, the Dorotheerwald or the Fasangarten, as I had frequently done in the past. Turning in to a coffee house or bar, on the other hand, presented no particular problem. Indeed, whenever I was somewhat fortified and refreshed I regained a sense of normality for a while and, buoyed up by a touch of confidence, there were moments when I supposed that I could put an end to the muted condition I had been in for days, and make a telephone call. As it happened, however, the three or four people I might have cared to talk to were never there, and could not be induced to pick up the receiver no matter how long I let the phone ring. There is something peculiarly dispiriting about the emptiness that wells up when, in a strange city, one dials the same telephone numbers in vain. If no one answers, it is a disappointment of huge significance, quite as if these few random ciphers were a matter of life or death. So what else could I do, when I had put the coins that jingled out of the box back into my pocket, but wander aimlessly around until well into the night. Often, probably because I was so very tired, I believed I saw someone I knew walking ahead of me. Those who appeared in these hallucinations, for that is what they were, were always people I had not thought of for years, or who had long since departed, such as Mathild Seelos or the one-armed village clerk Fürgut. On one occasion, in Gonzagagasse, I even thought I recognized the poet Dante, banished from his home town on pain of burning at the stake. For some considerable time he walked a short distance ahead of me, with the familiar cowl on his

head, distinctly taller than the people in the street, yet he passed by
them unnoticed. When I walked faster in order to catch him up he
went down Heinrichgasse, but when I reached the corner he was
nowhere to be seen.

After one or two turns of this kind I began to feel a vague
apprehension, which manifested itself as a feeling of vertigo. The
outlines on which I tried to focus dissolved, and my thoughts
disintegrated before I could fully grasp them. Although at times,
when obliged to lean against a wall or seek refuge in the doorway of
a building, fearing that mental paralysis was beginning to take a
hold of me, I could think of no way of resisting it but to walk until
late into the night, till I was utterly worn out. In the ten days or so
that I spent in Vienna I visited none of the sights and spoke not a
word to a soul except for waiters and waitresses. The only creatures
I talked to, if I remember correctly, were the jackdaws in the gardens
by the city hall, and a white-headed blackbird that shared the
jackdaws' interest in my grapes. Sitting for long periods on park
benches and aimlessly wandering about the city, tending increasingly to avoid coffee houses and restaurants and take a snack
at a stand wherever I happened to be, or simply eat something out
of paper – all of this had already begun to change me without my
being aware of it. The fact that I still lived in a hotel was at ever
greater variance with the woeful state I was now in. I began to carry
all kinds of useless things around with me in a plastic bag I had
brought with me from England, things I found it more impossible to
part with as every day went by. Returning from my excursions at a
late hour, I felt the eyes of the night porter at my back subjecting me
to a long and questioning scrutiny as I stood in the hotel lobby
waiting for the lift, hugging the bag to my chest. I no longer dared
switch on the television in my room, and I cannot say whether I
would ever have come out of this decline if one night as I slowly
undressed, sitting on the edge of the bed, I had not been shocked by

the sight of my shoes, which were literally falling apart. I felt
queasy, and my eyes dimmed as they had once before on that day,
when I reached the Ruprechtplatz after a long trail round the
Leopoldstadt that had finally brought me through Ferdinandstrasse
and over the Schwedenbrücke into the first district. The windows of
the Jewish community centre, on the first floor of the building
which also houses the synagogue and a kosher restaurant, were
wide open, it being an unusually fine, indeed summery autumn day,
and there were children within singing, unaccountably, 'Jingle Bells'
and 'Silent Night' in English. The voices of singing children, and
now in front of me my tattered and, as it seemed, ownerless shoes.
Heaps of shoes and snow piled high – with these words in my head
I lay down. When I awoke the next morning from a deep and
dreamless sleep, which not even the surging roar of traffic on the
Ring had been able to disturb, I felt as if I had crossed a wide stretch
of water during the hours of my nocturnal absence. Before I opened
my eyes I could see myself descending the gangway of a large ferry,
and hardly had I stepped ashore but I resolved to take the evening
train to Venice, and before that to spend the day with Ernst Herbeck
in Klosterneuburg.

Ernst Herbeck has been afflicted with mental disorders ever since
his twentieth year. He was first committed to an institution in 1940.
At that time he was employed as an unskilled worker in a munitions
factory. Suddenly he could hardly eat or sleep any more. He lay
awake at night, counting aloud. His body was racked with cramps.
Life in the family, and especially his father's incisive thinking, were
corroding his nerves, as he put it. In the end he lost control of
himself, knocked his plate away at meal times or tipped his soup
under the bed. Occasionally his condition would improve for a
while. In October 1944 he was even called up, only to be discharged
in March 1945. One year after the war was over he was committed
for the fourth and final time. He had been wandering the streets of

Vienna at night, attracting attention by his behaviour, and had made
incoherent and confused statements to the police. In the autumn of
1980, after thirty-four years in an institution, tormented for most
of that time by the smallness of his own thoughts and perceiving
everything as though through a veil drawn over his eyes, Ernst
Herbeck was, so to speak, discharged from his illness and allowed
to move into a pensioners' home in the town, among the inmates
of which he was scarcely conspicuous. When I arrived at the home
shortly before half past nine he was already standing waiting at
the top of the steps that ran up to the entrance. I waved to him from
the other side of the street, whereupon he raised his arm in welcome
and, keeping it outstretched, came down the steps. He was wearing
a glencheck suit with a hiking badge on the lapel. On his head he
wore a narrow-brimmed hat, a kind of trilby, which he later took
off when it grew too warm for him and carried beside him, just as
my grandfather often used to do on summer walks.

At my suggestion we took the train to Altenberg, a few kilometres
up the Danube. We were the only passengers in the carriage. Outside
in the flood plain there were willows, poplars, alders and ash trees,
allotment gardens and occasionally a little house raised on pillars
against the water. Now and then we caught a glimpse of the river.

Ernst let it all go by without venturing a word. The breeze that came
in at the open window played about his forehead. His lids were half
closed over his large eyes. When we arrived in Altenberg we walked
back along the road a little in the direction we had come and then,
turning off to the right, climbed the shady path to Burg Greifenstein,
a medieval fortress that plays a significant part not only in my own

imagination but also, to this day, in that of the people of Greifenstein
who live at the foot of the cliff. I had first visited the castle in the late
1960s, and from the terrace of the restaurant had looked down across
the gleaming river and the waterlands, on which the shadows of
evening were falling.

Now, on that bright October day when Ernst and I, sitting beside each other, savoured that wonderful view, a blue haze lay upon the sea of foliage that reaches right up to the walls of the castle. Currents of air were stirring the tops of the trees, and stray leaves were riding the breeze so high that little by little they vanished from sight. At times, Ernst was very far away. For minutes on end he left his fork sticking upright in his pastry. In the old days, he observed at one point, he had collected postage stamps, from Austria, Switzerland and the Argentine. Then he smoked another cigarette in silence, and when he stubbed it out he repeated, as if in amazement at his entire past life, that single word 'Argentine', which possibly struck him as far too outlandish. That morning, I think, we were both within an inch of learning to fly, or at least I might have managed as much as is required for a decent crash. But we never catch the propitious moment. – I only know that the view from Burg Greifenstein is no longer the same. A dam has been built below the castle. The course of the river was

straightened, and the sad sight of it now will soon extinguish the memory of what it once was.

We made our way back on foot. For both of us the walk proved too long. Downcast we strode on in the autumn sunshine, side by side. The houses of Kritzendorf seemed to go on for ever. Of the people who lived there not a sign was to be seen. They were all having lunch, clattering the cutlery and plates. A dog leaped at a green-painted iron gate, quite beside itself, as if it had taken leave of its senses. It was a large black Newfoundland, its natural gentleness broken by

ill-treatment, long confinement or even the crystal clarity of the
autumn day. In the villa behind the iron fence nothing stirred. Nobody
came to the window, not even a curtain moved. Again and again the
animal ran up and hurled itself at the gate, only occasionally pausing
to eye us where we stood as if transfixed. As we walked on I could feel
the chill of terror in my limbs. Ernst turned to look back once more at
the black dog, which had now stopped barking and was standing
motionless in the midday sun. Perhaps we should have let it out. It
would probably have ambled along beside us, like a good beast, while
its evil spirit might have stalked among the people of Kritzendorf in
search of another host, and indeed might have entered them all
simultaneously, so not one of them would have been able to lift a
spoon or fork again.

We finally reached Klosterneuburg by way of Albrechtstrasse at
the upper end of which there is a gruesome building banged together
out of breeze-blocks and prefab panels.
The ground-floor windows are boarded
up. Where the roof should be, only a
rusty array of iron bars protrude into the
sky. Looking at it was like witnessing a
hideous crime. Ernst put his best foot
forward, averting his eyes from this
fearful monument. A little further on, the
children inside the primary school were
singing, the most appealing sounds
coming from those who could not quite
manage to hit the right notes. Ernst stood

still, turned to me as though we were both actors on a stage, and in
a theatrical manner uttered a statement which appeared to me as if he
had committed it to memory a long time ago: That is a very fine
sound, borne upon the air, and uplifts one's heart. – Some two years
previously I had stood once before outside that school. I had gone to

Klosterneuburg with Clara to visit her grandmother, who had been taken into the old people's home in Martinsstrasse. On the way back we went down Albrechtstrasse and Clara gave in to the temptation to visit the school she had attended as a child. In one of the classrooms, the very one where she had been taught in the early 1950s, the selfsame schoolmistress was still teaching, almost thirty years later, her voice quite unchanged – still warning the children to keep at their work, as she had done then, and also not to chatter. Alone in the entrance hall, surrounded by closed doors that had seemed at one time like mighty portals, Clara was overcome by tears, as she later told me. At all events, when she came out she was in such a state of distress as I had never seen her in before. We returned to her grandmother's flat in Ottakring, and neither on the way there nor that entire evening did she regain her composure following this unexpected encounter with her past.

The St Martin's home is a large, rectangular building with massive stone walls dating from the seventeenth or eighteenth century. Clara's grandmother, Anna Goldsteiner, who was afflicted with that extreme kind of forgetfulness which soon renders even the simplest of everyday tasks impossible to perform, shared a dormitory on the fourth floor. Through the barred, deeply recessed windows there was a view down onto the tops of the trees on the steeply sloping ground to the rear of the house. It was like looking upon a heaving sea. The mainland, it seemed to me, had already sunk below the horizon. A foghorn droned. Further and further out the ship plied its passage upon the waters. From the engine room came the steady throb of the turbines. Out in the corridor, stray passengers went past, some of them on the arm of a nurse. It took an eternity, on these slow-motion walks, for them to cross from one side of the doorway to the other. How strange it is, to be standing leaning against the current of time. The parquet floor shifted beneath my feet. A low murmuring, rustling, dragging, praying and moaning filled the room. Clara was sitting

beside her grandmother, stroking her hand. The semolina was doled
out. The foghorn sounded again. A little way further out in the green
and hilly water landscape, another steamer passed. On the bridge, his
legs astride and the ribbons on his cap flying, stood a mariner,
signalling in semaphore with two colourful flags. Clara held her
grandmother close as they parted, and promised to come again soon.
But barely three weeks later Anna Goldsteiner, who in the end, to her
own amazement, could no longer even remember the names of the
three husbands she had survived, died of a slight cold. At times it does
not take much. For weeks after we learned of her death I could not put
out of my mind the blue, half-empty pack of Bad Ischl salt under the
sink in her council flat in Lorenz Mandl Gasse which she would never
now be able to use up.

Footsore from our walk, Ernst and I emerged from Albrechtstrasse
on to the town square, which sloped slightly to one side. For a while
we stood irresolute on the kerb in the dazzling midday sun before
trying, like two strangers, to cross the road amid the infernal traffic,
almost being run down by a gravel truck. Once we were on the shady
side of the street we dived into a bar. At first the dark that enveloped
us as we entered was so impenetrable for eyes accustomed to the
midday glare that we were obliged to sit down at the first table we
came to. Only gradually and partially did our sight return and other
people become apparent in the gloom, some of them bent low over
their plates, others sitting curiously upright or leaning back, but all of
them without exception on their own, a silent gathering, the shadow
of the waitress threading among them, as if she were the bearer of
secret messages between the several guests and the corpulent
landlord. Ernst declined to eat anything, and instead took one of the
cigarettes I offered him. A time or two he appreciatively turned the
packet with its English wording in his hands. He inhaled the smoke
deeply, with the air of a connoisseur. The cigarette, he had written in
one of his poems,

is a monopoly and must
be smoked. So that it
goes up in flames.

And, putting down his beer glass after taking a first draught, he observed that he had dreamed about English Boy Scouts last night. What I then told him about England, about the county in East Anglia where I live, the great wheatfields which in the autumn are transformed into a barren brown expanse stretching further than the eye can see, the rivers up which the incoming tide drives the sea water, and the times when the land is flooded and one can cross the fields in boats, as the Egyptians once did – all of this Ernst listened to with the patient lack of interest of a man who has long been familiar with every detail he is being told. I then asked if he would write something in my notebook, and this he did without the slightest hesitation with the ballpoint which he took from his jacket pocket, resting his left hand on the open page. His head to one side, his brow furrowed in concentration, his eyelids half-closed, he wrote:

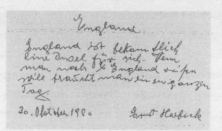

England. England, as is well known, is an island unto itself. Travelling to England takes an entire day. 30 October 1980 Ernst Herbeck. – We left. It was not far now to the St Agnes home. When we parted, Ernst, standing on tiptoe and bowing slightly, took his hat from his head and with it, as he turned away, executed a sweeping motion which ended with him putting the hat back on; a performance which seemed to be, at the same time, both childishly easy and an astonishing feat of artistry. This gesture, like the manner in which he had greeted me that morning, put me in mind of someone who had travelled with a circus for many years.

The train journey from Vienna to Venice has left scarcely any trace in my memory. For what may have been an hour I watched the lights of the southwestern metropolitan sprawl pass by, till at length, lulled by the speed of the train, which was like an analgesic after the never-ending tramping through Vienna, I fell asleep. And it was in that sleep, with everything outside long since plunged into darkness, that I beheld a landscape that I have never forgotten. The lower portion of the scene was well-nigh immersed in the approaching night. A woman was pushing a pram along a field track towards a group of buildings, on one of which, a dilapidated pub, the name Josef Jelinek was painted in large letters over the gabled entrance. Mountains dark with forests rose above the rooftops, the jagged black summits silhouetted against the evening light. Higher than them all, though, was the tip of the Schneeberg, glowing, translucent, throwing out fire and sparks, towering into the dying brightness of a sky across which the strangest of greyish-pink cloud formations were moving, while visible between them were the winter planets and a crescent moon. In my dream I was in no doubt that the volcano was the Schneeberg, any more than I doubted that the countryside, above which I presently rose through a glittering shower of rain, was Argentina, an infinitely vast and deep green pastureland with clumps of trees and countless herds of horses. I awoke only as the train, which for so long had been threading the valleys at a steady pace, was racing out of the mountains and down to the plains below. I pulled down the window. Swathes of mist were ripping past me. We were hurtling onwards at breakneck speed. Pointed wedges of blue-black rock thrust up against the train. I leaned out and looked upward, trying in vain to make out the tops of the

fearful formations. Dark, narrow, ragged valleys opened up, mountain streams and waterfalls threw up white spray in a night on the
edge of dawn, so close that their cold breath against my face made me
shiver. It occurred to me that this was the Friaul, and with that
thought came naturally the memory of the destruction which that
region had suffered some few months before. Gradually the daybreak
revealed landslides, great boulders, collapsed buildings, mounds of
rubble and piles of stones, and here and there encampments of people
living in tents. Scarcely a light was burning anywhere in the entire
area. The low-lying cloud drifting in from the Alpine valleys and
across that desolated country was conjoined in my mind's eye with a
Tiepolo painting which I have often looked at for hours. It shows the
plague-ravaged town of Este on the plain, seemingly unscathed. In the
background are mountains, and a smoking summit. The light diffused
through the picture seems to have been painted as if through a veil of
ash. One could almost suppose it was this light that drove the people
out of the town into the open fields, where, after reeling about for
some time, they were finally laid low by the scourge they carried
within them. In the centre foreground of the painting lies a mother
dead of the plague, her child still alive in her arms. Kneeling to the left
is St Thecla, interceding for the inhabitants of the town, her face
upturned to where the heavenly hosts are traversing the aether. Holy
Thecla, pray for us, that we may be safely delivered from all contagion
and sudden death and most mercifully saved from perdition. Amen.

When the train had arrived in Venice, I first went to the station
barber's for a shave, and then stepped out into the forecourt of
Ferrovia Santa Lucia. The dampness of the autumn morning still hung
thick among the houses and over the Grand Canal. Heavily laden, the
boats went by, sitting low in the water. With a surging rush they came
from out of the mist, pushing ahead of them the aspic-green waves,
and disappearing again in the white swathes of the air. The helmsmen
stood erect and motionless at the stern. Their hands on the tiller, they

gazed fixedly ahead. I walked from the Fondamenta across the broad square, up Rio Terrà Lista di Spagna and across the Canale di Cannaregio. As you enter into the heart of that city, you cannot tell what you will see next or indeed who will see you the very next moment. Scarcely has someone made an appearance but he has quit the stage again by another exit. These brief exhibitions are of an almost theatrical obscenity and at the same time have an air of conspiracy about them, into which one is drawn against one's will. If you walk behind someone in a deserted alleyway, you have only to quicken your step slightly to instil a little fear into the person you are following. And equally, you can feel like a quarry yourself. Confusion and ice-cold terror alternate. It was with a certain feeling of liberation, therefore, that I came upon the Grand Canal once again, near San Marcuola, after wandering about for the best part of an hour below the tall houses of the ghetto. Hurriedly, like the native Venetians on their way to work, I boarded a vaporetto. The mist had now dispersed. Not far from me, on one of the rear benches, there sat, and in fact very nearly lay, a man in a worn green loden coat whom I immediately recognized as King Ludwig II of Bavaria. He had grown somewhat older and rather gaunt, and curiously he was talking to a dwarfish lady in the strongly nasal English of the upper classes, but otherwise everything about him was right: the sickly pallor of the face, the wide-open childlike eyes, the wavy hair, the carious teeth. *Il re Lodovico* to the life. In all likelihood, I thought to myself, he had come by water to the *città inquinata Venezia merda*. After we had alighted I watched him walk away down the Riva degli Schiavoni in his billowing Tyrolean cloak, becoming smaller and smaller not only on account of the increasing distance but also because, as he went on talking incessantly, he bent down deeper and deeper to his diminutive companion. I did not follow them, but instead took my morning coffee in one of the bars on the Riva, reading the *Gazzettino*, making notes for a treatise on King Ludwig in Venice, and leafing through Grillparzer's

Italian Diary, written in 1819. I had bought it in Vienna, because when I am travelling I often feel as Grillparzer did on his journeys. Nothing pleases me, any more than it did him; the sights I find infinitely disappointing, one and all; and I sometimes think that I would have done far better to stay at home with my maps and timetables. Grillparzer paid even the Doge's Palace no more than a distinctly grudging respect. Despite its delicately crafted arcades and turrets, he wrote, the Doge's Palace was inelegant and reminded him of a crocodile. What put this comparison into his head he did not know. The resolutions passed here by the Council of State must surely be mysterious, immutable and harsh, he observed, calling the palace an enigma in stone. The nature of that enigma was apparently dread, and for as long as he was in Venice Grillparzer could not shake off a sense of the uncanny. Trained in the law himself, he dwelt on that palace where the legal authorities resided and in the inmost cavern of which, as he put it, the Invisible Principle brooded. And those who had faded away, the persecutors and the persecuted, the murderers and the victims, rose up before him with their heads enshrouded. Shivers of fever beset the poor hypersensitive man.

One of the victims of Venetian justice was Giacomo Casanova. His *Histoire de ma fuite des prisons de la République de Venise qu'on appelle Les Plombs écrite à Dux en Bohème l'année 1787*, first published in Prague in 1788, affords an excellent insight into the inventiveness of penal justice at the time. For example, Casanova describes a type of garrotte. The victim is positioned with his back to a wall on which a horseshoe-shaped brace is mounted, and his head is jammed into this brace in such a way that it half encloses the neck. A silken band is passed around the neck and secured to a spool which a henchman turns slowly till at length the last throes of the condemned man are over. This strangulating apparatus is in the prison chambers below the lead roofs of the Doge's Palace. Casanova was in his thirtieth year when he was taken there. On the morning of 26 July 1755, the

Messergrande entered his room. Casanova was ordered to surrender
any writings by himself or others that he possessed, to get dressed
and to follow the Master of the Keys. The word 'tribunal', he writes,
completely paralysed me and left me only such physical strength as
was essential if I were to obey. Mechanically he performed his
ablutions and donned his best shirt and a new coat that had only just
left the tailor's hands, as if he were off to a wedding. Shortly after he
found himself in the loft space of the palace, in a cell measuring
twelve feet by twelve. The ceiling was so low that he could not stand,
and there was not a stick of furniture. A plank no more than a foot
wide was fixed to the wall, to serve as both table and bed, and on it
he laid his elegant silk mantle, the coat, inaugurated on so
inauspicious an occasion, and his hat adorned with Spanish lace and
an egret's plume. The heat was appalling. Through the bars,
Casanova could see rats as big as hares scuttling about. He crossed to
the window sill, from which he could see but a patch of sky. There he
remained motionless for a full eight hours. Never in his life, he
recorded, had the taste in his mouth been as bitter. Melancholy had
him in its grip and would not let go. The dog days came. The sweat
ran down him. For two weeks he did not move his bowels. When at
last the stone-hard excrement was passed, he thought the pain would
kill him. Casanova considered the limits of human reason. He
established that, while it might be rare for a man to be driven insane,
little was required to tip the balance. All that was needed was a slight
shift, and nothing would be as it formerly was. In these
deliberations, Casanova likened a lucid mind to a glass, which does
not break of its own accord. Yet how easily it is shattered. One wrong
move is all that it takes. This being so, he resolved to regain his
composure and find a way of comprehending his situation. It was
soon apparent that the condemned in that gaol were honourable
persons to a man, but for reasons which were known only to their
Excellencies, and were not disclosed to the detainees, they had had to

be removed from society. When the tribunal seized a criminal, it was already convinced of his guilt. After all, the rules by which the tribunal proceeded were underwritten by senators elected from among the most capable and virtuous of men. Casanova realized that he would have to come to terms with the fact that the standards which now applied were those of the legal system of the Republic rather than of his own sense of justice. Fantasies of revenge of the kind he had entertained in the early days of his detention – such as rousing the people and, with himself at their head, slaughtering the government and the aristocracy – were out of the question. Soon he was prepared to forgive the injustice done to him, always providing he would some day be released. He found that, within certain limits, he was able to reach an accommodation with the powers who had confined him in that place. Everyday necessities, food and a few books were brought to his cell, at his own expense. In early November the great earthquake hit Lisbon, raising tidal waves as far away as Holland. One of the sturdiest roof joists visible through the window of Casanova's gaol began to turn, only to move back to its former position. After this, with no means of knowing whether his sentence might not be life, he abandoned all hope of release. All his thinking was now directed to preparing his escape from prison, and this occupied him for a full year. He was now permitted to take a daily walk around the attics, where a good deal of lumber lay about, and contrived to obtain a number of things that could serve his purpose. He came across piles of old ledgers with records of trials held in the previous century. They contained charges brought against confessors who had extorted penances for improper ends of their own, described in detail the habits of schoolmasters convicted of pederasty, and were full of the most extraordinary accounts of transgressions, evidently detailed for the delectation solely of the legal profession. Casanova observed that one kind of case that occurred with particular frequency in those old pages concerned the deflowering of virgins in the city's orphanages, among them the very one whose young ladies were heard every day in Santa Maria della Visitazione, on the Riva degli Schiavoni, uplifting their voices to the ceiling fresco of the three cardinal virtues, to which Tiepolo had put the finishing touches shortly after Casanova was arrested. No doubt the dispensation of justice in those days, as also in later times, was largely concerned with regulating the libidinous instinct, and presumably not a few of the prisoners slowly perishing beneath the leaden roof of the palace will have been of that irrepressible species whose desires drive them on, time after time, to the very same point.

In the autumn of his second year of imprisonment, Casanova's preparations had reached a point at which he could contemplate an escape. The moment was propitious, since the inquisitors were to cross to the *terra firma* at that time, and Lorenzo, the warder, always got drunk when his superiors were away. In order to decide on the precise day and hour, Casanova consulted Ariosto's *Orlando Furioso*, using a system comparable to the *sortes Virgilianae*. First he wrote down his question, then he derived numbers from the words and arranged these in an inverse pyramid, and finally, in a threefold procedure that involved subtracting nine from every pair of figures, he arrived at the first line of the seventh stanza of the ninth canto of *Orlando Furioso*, which runs: *Tra il fin d'ottobre e il capo di novembre*. This instruction, pinpointing the very hour, was the all-decisive sign Casanova had wanted, for he believed that a law was at work in so extraordinary a coincidence, inaccessible to even the most incisive thought, to which he must therefore defer. For my part, Casanova's attempt to plumb the unknown by means of a seemingly random operation of words and numbers later caused me to leaf back through my own diary for that year, whereupon I discovered to my amazement, and indeed to my considerable alarm, that the day in 1980 on which I was reading Grillparzer's journal in a bar on the Riva degli Schiavoni between the Danieli and Santa Maria della Visitazione, in other words near the

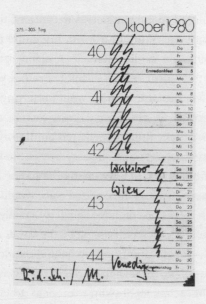

Doge's Palace, was the very last day of October, and thus the anniversary of the day (or rather, night) on which Casanova, with the words *E quindi uscimmo a rimirar le stelle* on his lips, broke out of the lead-plated crocodile. Later that evening I returned to the bar on the Riva and fell into conversation with a Venetian by the name of Malachio, who had studied astrophysics at Cambridge and, as shortly transpired, saw everything from a great distance, not only the stars. Towards midnight we took his boat, which was moored outside, up the dragon's tail of the Grand Canal, past the Ferrovia and the Tronchetto, and out on to the open water, from where one has a view of the lights of the Mestre refineries stretching for miles along the coast. Malachio turned off the engine. The boat rose and fell with the waves, and it seemed to me that a long time passed. Before us lay the fading lustre of our world, at which we never tire of looking, as though it were a celestial city. The miracle of life born of carbon, I heard Malachio say, going up in flames. The engine started up once more, the bow of the boat lifted in the water, and we entered the Canale della Giudecca in a wide arc. Without a word, my guide pointed out the Inceneritore Comunale on the nameless island westward of the Giudecca. A deathly silent concrete shell beneath a white swathe of smoke. I asked whether the burning went on throughout the night, and Malachio replied: *Sí, di continuo. Brucia continuamente*. The fires never go out. The Stucky flour mill entered our line of vision, built in the nineteenth century from millions of bricks, its blind windows staring across from the Giudecca to the Stazione Marittima. The structure is so enormous that the Doge's Palace would fit into it many times over, which leaves one wondering if it was really only grain that was milled in there. As we were passing by the facade, looming above us in the dark, the moon came out from behind the clouds and struck a gleam from the golden mosaic under the left gable, which shows the female figure of a reaper holding a sheaf of wheat, a most disconcerting image in this landscape of water and stone. Malachio told me that he had been giving a great deal of thought to the resurrection, and was pondering what the Book of Ezekiel could mean by saying that our bones and flesh would be carried into the domain of the prophet. He had no answers, but believed the questions were quite sufficient for him. The flour mill dissolved into the darkness, and ahead of us appeared the tower of San Giorgio and the dome of Santa Maria della Salute. Malachio steered the boat back to my hotel. There was nothing more to be said. The boat berthed. We shook hands. I stepped ashore. The waves slapped against the stones, which were overgrown with shaggy moss. The boat set about in the water. Malachio waved one more time and called out: *Ci vediamo a Gerusalemme*. And, a little further out, he repeated somewhat louder: Next year in Jerusalem! I crossed the forecourt of the hotel. There was not a soul about. Even the night porter had abandoned his post and was lying on a narrow bed in a kind of doorless den behind the reception, looking as if his body had been laid out. The test card was

flickering softly on the television. Machines alone have realized that
sleep is no longer permitted, I thought as I ascended to my room,
where tiredness soon overcame me too.

Waking up in Venice is unlike waking up in any other place. The day
begins quietly. Only a stray shout here and there may break the calm, or
the sound of a shutter being raised, or the wing-beat of the pigeons.
How often, I thought to myself, had I lain thus in a hotel room, in Vienna
or Frankfurt or Brussels, with my hands clasped under my head,
listening not to the stillness, as in Venice, but to the roar of the traffic,
with a mounting sense of panic. That, then, I thought on such occasions,
is the new ocean. Ceaselessly, in great surges, the waves roll in over the
length and breadth of our cities, rising higher and higher, breaking in a
kind of frenzy when the roar reaches its peak and then discharging
across the stones and the asphalt even as the next onrush is being
released from where it was held by the traffic lights. For some time now
I have been convinced that it is out of this din that the life is being born
which will come after us and will spell our gradual destruction, just as
we have been gradually destroying what was there long before us. Thus
it was that the silence which hung over the city of Venice that All Saints'
morning seemed wholly unreal, as if it were about to be shattered, while
I lay submerged in the white air that drifted in at my half-open window.
The village of W., where I spent the first nine years of my life, I now
remember, was always shrouded in the densest fog on All Saints' Day
and on All Souls'. And the villagers, without exception, wore their black
clothes and went out to the graves which they had put in order the day
before, removing the summer planting, pulling up the weeds, raking the
gravel paths, and mixing soot in with the soil. Nothing in my childhood
seemed to possess more meaning than those two days of remembrance
devoted to the suffering of the sainted martyrs and poor unredeemed
souls, days on which the dark shapes of the villagers moved about in the
mist, strangely bent over, as if they had been banished from their houses.

What particularly affected me every year was eating the *Seelenwecken*, the special rolls that Mayrbeck baked on those commemorative days only, precisely one apiece, for every man, woman and child in the village. These *Seelenwecken* were made of white bread dough and were so tiny that they could easily be hidden in the fist. There were four to a row on the baking tray. They were dusted with flour, and I remember one occasion when the flour dust that remained on my fingers after I had eaten one of these *Seelenwecken* seemed like a revelation. That evening, I spent a long time digging in the flour barrel in my grandparents' bedroom with a wooden spoon, hoping to fathom the mystery which I supposed to be hidden there.

On that first day of November in 1980, preoccupied as I was with my notes and the ever widening and contracting circles of my thoughts, I became enveloped by a sense of utter emptiness and never once left my room. It seemed to me then that one could well end one's life simply through thinking and retreating into one's mind, for, although I had closed the windows and the room was warm, my limbs were growing progressively colder and stiffer with my lack of movement, so that when at length the waiter arrived with the red wine and sandwiches I had ordered, I felt as if I had already been interred or laid out for burial, silently grateful for the proffered libation, but no longer capable of consuming it. I imagined how it would be if I crossed the grey lagoon to the island of the departed, to Murano or further still to San Erasmo or to the Isola San Francesco del Deserto, among the marshes of St Catherine. With these thoughts, I drifted into a light sleep. The fog lifted and I beheld the green lagoon outspread in the May sunshine and the green islets like clumps of herbage surfacing from out of the placid expanse of water. I saw the hospital island of La Grazia with its circular panoptic building, from the windows of which thousands of madmen were waving, as though they were aboard a great ship sailing away. St Francis lay face down in the water of a trembling reed-bed, and across the swamps St Catherine came walking, in her hand a model of the wheel on which she had been broken. It was mounted on a stick and went round in the wind with a humming sound. The crimson dusk gathered above the lagoon, and when I awoke I lay in deep darkness. I thought about what Malachio had meant by *Ci vediamo a Gerusalemme*, tried in vain to recall his face or his eyes, and wondered whether I should go back to the bar on the Riva, but the more I deliberated, the less was I able to make any move at all. The second night in Venice went by, then All Souls' Day, and a third night, and not until the Monday morning did I come round, in a curious condition of weightlessness. A hot bath, yesterday's sandwiches and red wine, and a newspaper I had asked for, restored me sufficiently to be able to pack my bag and be on my way again.

The buffet at St Lucia station was surrounded by an infernal upheaval. A steadfast island, it held out against a crowd of people swaying like a field of corn in the wind, passing in and out of the doors, pushing against the food counter, and surging on to the cashiers who sat some way off at their elevated posts. If one did not have a ticket, one had to shout up to these enthroned women, who, clad only in the thinnest of overalls, with curled-up hair and half-lowered gaze, appeared to float, quite unaffected by the general commotion, above the heads of the supplicants and would pick out at random one of the pleas emerging from this crossfire of voices, repeat it over the uproar with a loud assurance that denied all possibility of doubt, and then, bending down a little, indulgent and at the same time disdainful, hand over the ticket together with the change. Once in possession of this scrap of paper, which had by now come to seem a matter of life and death, one had to fight one's way out of the crowd and across to the middle of the cafeteria, where the male employees of this awesome gastronomic establishment, positioned behind a circular food counter, faced the jostling masses with withering contempt, performing their duties in an unperturbed manner which, given the prevailing panic, gave an impression of a film in slow motion. In their freshly starched white linen jackets, this impassive corps of attendants, like their sisters, mothers and daughters at the cash registers, resembled some strange company of higher beings sitting in judgement, under the rules of an obscure system, on the endemic greed of a corrupted species, an impression that was reinforced by the fact that the buffet reached only to the waists of these earnest, white-aproned men, who were evidently standing on a raised platform inside the circle, whereas the clients on the outside could barely see over the counter. The staff, remarkably restrained as they appeared, had a way of setting down the glasses, saucers and ashtrays on the marble surface with such vehemence, it seemed they were determined to all but shatter them. My cappuccino was served, and for a moment I felt that having achieved this distinction constituted the supreme victory of my life. I surveyed the scene and immediately saw my mistake, for the people around me now looked like a circle of severed heads. I should not have been surprised, and indeed it would have seemed justified, even as I expired, if one of the white-breasted waiters had swept those severed heads, my own not excepted, off the smooth marble top into a knacker's pit, since every single one of them was intent on gorging itself to the last. A prey to unpleasant observations and far-fetched notions of this sort, I suddenly had a feeling that, amid this circle of spectres consuming their *colazione*, I had attracted somebody's attention. And indeed it transpired that the eyes of two young men were on me. They were leaning on the bar across from me, the one with his chin propped in his right hand, the other in his left. Just as the shadow of a cloud passes across a field, so the fear passed across my mind that these two men who were looking at me now had already crossed my path more than once since my arrival in Venice. They had also been in the bar on the Riva where I had met Malachio. The hands of the clock moved towards half past ten. I finished my cappuccino, went out to the platform, glancing back over my shoulder now and then, and boarded the train for Milan as I had intended.

I travelled as far as Verona, and there, having taken a room at the Golden Dove, went immediately to the Giardino Giusti, a long-standing habit of mine. There I spent the early hours of the afternoon lying on a stone bench below a cedar tree. I heard the soughing of the breeze among the branches and the delicate sound of the gardener raking the gravel paths between the low box hedges, the subtle scent of which still filled the air even in autumn. I had not experienced such

GIARDINO GIUSTI
VERONA
———

BIGLIETTO D'INGRESSO

№ 52314

a sense of well-being for a long time. Nonetheless, I got up after a while. As I left the gardens I paused to watch a pair of white Turkish doves soaring again and again into the sky above the tree tops with only a few brisk beatings of their wings, remaining at those blue heights for a small eternity, and then, dropping with a barely audible gurgling call, gliding down on the air in sweeping arcs around the lovely cypresses, some of which had been growing there for as long as 200 years. The everlasting green of the trees put me in mind of the

yews in the churchyards of the county where I live. Yews grow more slowly even than cypresses. One inch of yew wood will often have upwards of a hundred annual growth rings, and there are said to be trees that have outlasted a full millennium and seem to have quite forgotten about dying. I went out into the forecourt, washed my face and hands at the fountain set in the ivy-covered garden wall, as I had done before going in, cast a last glance back at the garden and, at the exit, waved a greeting to the keeper of the gate, who nodded to me from her gloomy cabin. Across the Ponte Nuovo and by way of the Via Nizza and the Via Stelle I walked down to the Piazza Bra. Entering the arena, I suddenly had a sense of being entangled in some dark web of intrigue. The arena was deserted but for a group of late-season excursionists to whom an aged cicerone was describing the unique qualities of this monumental theatre in a voice grown thin and cracked. I climbed to the topmost tiers and looked down at the group, which now appeared very small. The old man, who could not have been more than four feet, was wearing a jacket far too big for him, and, since he was hunchbacked and walked with a stoop, the front hem hung down to the ground. With a remarkable clarity, I heard him say, more clearly perhaps than those who stood around him, that in the arena one could discern, *grazie a un'acustica perfetta, l'assolo più impalpabile di un violino, la mezza voce più eterea di un soprano, il gemito più intimo di una Mimi morente sulla scena*. The excursionists were not greatly impressed by the enthusiasm for architecture and opera evinced by their misshapen guide, who continued to add this or that point to his account as he moved towards the exit, pausing every now and then as he turned to the group, which had also stopped, and raising his right forefinger like a tiny schoolmaster confronting a pack of children taller by a head than himself. By now the evening light came in very low over the arena, and for a while after the old man and his flock had left the stage I sat on alone, surrounded by the reddish shimmer of the marble. At least I thought I was alone, but as time went on I became aware of two figures in the deep shadow on the other side of the arena. They were without a doubt the same two young men who had kept their eyes on me that morning at the station in Venice. Like two watchmen they remained motionless at their posts until the sunlight had all but faded. Then they stood up, and I had the impression that they bowed to each other before descending from the tiers and vanishing in the darkness of the exit. At first I could not move from the spot, so ominous did these probably quite coincidental encounters appear to me. I could already see myself sitting in the arena all night, paralysed by fear and the cold. I had to muster all my rational powers before at length I was able to get up and make my way to the exit. When I was almost there I had a compulsive vision of an arrow whistling through the grey air, about to pierce my left shoulder blade and, with a distinctive, sickening sound, penetrate my heart.

On the third day of my stay in Verona, I took my evening meal in a pizzeria in the Via Roma. I do not know how I go about choosing the restaurants where I should eat in unfamiliar cities. On the one hand I am too fastidious and wander the streets broad and narrow for hours on end before I make up my mind; on the other hand I generally finish up turning in simply anywhere, and then, in dreary surroundings and with a sense of discontent, select some dish that does not in the least appeal. That was how it was on that evening of 5 November. If I had heeded my first inclination, I would never have crossed the threshold of that establishment, which even from the outside made a disreputable impression. But now there I sat, on a kitchen chair with a cover of red marbled plastic, at a rickety table, in a grotto festooned with fishing nets. The decor of the floor and walls was a hideous marine blue which put an end to all hope I might have entertained of ever seeing dry land again. The sense of being wholly surrounded by water was rendered complete by a sea piece that hung right below the ceiling opposite me, in a frame painted a golden bronze. As is

commonly the case with such sea pieces, it showed a ship, on the crest
of a turquoise wave crowned with snow-white foam, about to plunge
into the yawning depths that gaped beneath her bows. Plainly this
was the moment immediately before a disaster. A mounting sense of
unease took possession of me. I was obliged to push aside the plate,
barely half of the pizza eaten, and grip the table edge, as a seasick man
might grip a ship's rail. I sensed my brow running cold with fear, but
was quite unable to call the waiter over and ask for the bill. Instead,
in order to focus on reality once more, I pulled the newspaper I had
bought that afternoon, the Venice *Gazzettino*, out of my jacket pocket
and unfolded it on the table as best I could. The first article that caught
my attention was an editorial report to the effect that yesterday, 4
November, a letter in strange runic writing had been received by the
newspaper, in which a hitherto unknown group by the name of

ORGANIZZAZIONE LUDWIG

claimed responsibility for a number of murders that had been committed in Verona and other northern Italian cities since 1977. The
article brought these as yet unsolved cases back to the memories of its
readers. In late August 1977, a Romany named Guerrino Spinelli had
died in a Verona hospital of severe burns sustained when the old Alfa
in which he customarily spent the night on the outskirts of the city
was set on fire by persons unknown. A good year later, a waiter,
Luciano Stefanato, was found dead in Padua with two 25-centimetre
stab wounds in the neck, and another year after that a twenty-two-
year-old heroin addict, Claudio Costa, was found dead with thirty-
nine knife wounds. It was now the late autumn of 1980. The waiter
brought me the bill. It was folded and I opened it out. The letters and
numbers blurred before my eyes. 5 November 1980. Via Roma.
Pizzeria Verona. Di Cadavero Carlo e Patierno Vittorio. Patierno and

Cadavero. – The telephone rang. The waiter wiped a glass dry and held it up to the light. Not until I felt I could stand the ringing no

longer did he pick up the receiver. Then, jamming it between his shoulder and his chin, he paced to and fro behind the bar as far as the cable would let him. Only when he was speaking himself did he stop, and at these times he would lift his eyes to the ceiling. No, he said, Vittorio wasn't there. He was hunting. Yes, that was right, it was him, Carlo. Who else would it be? Who else would be in the restaurant? No, nobody. Not a soul all day. And now there was only one diner. *Un inglese*, he said, and looked across at me with what I took to be a touch of contempt. No wonder, he said, the days were getting shorter. The lean times were on the way. *L'inverno è alle porte. Sí, sí, l'inverno*, he shouted once more, looking over at me again. My heart missed a beat. I left 10,000 lire on the plate, folded up the paper, hurried out into the street and across the piazza, went into a brightly lit bar and had them call a taxi, returned to my hotel, packed my things in a rush, and fled by the night train to Innsbruck. Prepared for the very worst, I sat in my compartment unable to read and unable to close my eyes, listening to the rhythm of the wheels. At Rovereto an old Tyrolean woman carrying a shopping bag made of leather patches sewn together joined me, accompanied by her son, who might have been forty. I was immeasurably grateful to them when they came in and sat down. The son leaned his head back against the seat. Eyelids lowered, he smiled blissfully most of the time. At intervals, though, he would be seized by a spasm, and his mother would then make signs in the palm of his left hand, which lay in her lap, open, like an unwritten page. The train hauled onwards, uphill. Gradually I began to feel better. I went out into the corridor. We were in Bolzano. The Tyrolean woman and her son got out. Hand in hand the two of them headed towards the subway. Even before they had vanished from sight, the train started off again. It was now beginning to feel distinctly colder. The train moved more slowly, there were fewer lights, and the darkness was thicker. Franzensfeste station passed. I saw scenes of a bygone war: the assault on the pass – Vall'Inferno – 26 May 1915. Bursts of gunfire in the mountains and a forest shot to shreds. Rain hatched the windowpanes. The train changed track at points. The pallid glow of arc lamps suffused the compartment. We stopped at the Brenner. No one got out and no one got in. The frontier guards in their grey greatcoats paced to and fro on the platform. We remained there for at least a quarter of an hour. Across on the other side were the silver ribbons of the rails. The rain turned to snow. And a heavy silence lay upon 'the place, broken only by the bellowing of some nameless animals waiting in a siding to be transported onward.

THE LAZY RIVER

Ryszard Kapuściński

Translated from the Polish by Klara Glowczewska

I am met in Yaoundé by a young Dominican missionary named Stanislaw Gurgul. He will take me into the forests of Cameroon. 'But first,' he says, 'we will go to Bertoua.' Bertoua? I have no idea where this is. Until now I had no idea it even existed! Our world consists of thousands – no, millions – of places with their own distinct names (names, moreover, that are written or pronounced differently in different languages, creating the impression of even greater multiplicity), and their numbers are so overwhelming that travelling around the globe we cannot commit to memory even a small percentage of them. Or – which also often happens – our minds are awash with the names of towns, regions, and countries that we are no longer able to connect meaningfully with any image, view or landscape, with any event or human face. Everything becomes confused, twisted, blurred. We place the Sodori oases in Libya instead of in Sudan, the town of Tefé in Laos instead of in Brazil, the small fishing port of Galle in Portugal instead of where it actually lies – in Sri Lanka. The oneness of the world, so unachievable in the realm of empirical reality, lives in our minds, in the superimposed layers of tangled and confused memories.

It is 350 kilometres from Yaoundé to Bertoua, along a road that runs east, towards the Central African Republic and Chad, over gentle, green hills, through plantations of coffee, cacao, bananas and pineapples. Along the way, as is usual in Africa, we encounter police guard posts. Stanislaw stops the car, leans his head out of the window, and says: *'Evêché Bertoua!'* (the bishopric of Bertoua!). This has an instantaneous and magical effect. Anything to do with religion – with the supernatural, with the world of ceremony and spirits, with that which one cannot see or touch but which exists, and exists more profoundly than anything in the material world – is treated with great seriousness here, and immediately elicits reverence, respect and a little bit of fear. Everyone knows how toying with something higher and mysterious, powerful and incomprehensible, ends: it ends badly, always. But there is more to it. It is about the way in which the origins and nature of existence are perceived. Africans, at least those I've encountered over the years, are deeply religious. *'Croyez-vous en Dieu, monsieur?'* I would always wait for this question, because I knew that it would be posed, having been asked it so many times already. And I knew that the one questioning me would at the same time be observing me carefully, registering every twitch of my face. I realized the seriousness of this moment, the meaning with which it was imbued. And I sensed that the way in which I answered would determine our relationship. And so when I said, *'Oui, j'en crois'* (yes, I believe), I would see in his face the relief this brought him, see the tension and fear attending this scene dissipate, see how close it brought us, how it allowed us to overcome the barriers of skin colour, status, age. Africans valued and liked to make contact on this higher, spiritual plane, to which often they could not give verbal definition, but whose existence and importance each one sensed instinctively and spontaneously.

Generally, it isn't a matter of belief in any one particular god, the kind one can name, and whose appearance or characteristics one can describe. It is more an abiding faith in the existence of a Highest Being, one that creates and rules and also imbues man with a spiritual essence that elevates him above the world of irrational beasts and inanimate objects. This humble and ardent belief in the Highest Being trickles down to its messengers and earthly representatives, who as a consequence are held in special esteem and granted reverential acceptance. This privilege extends to Africa's entire multitudinous layer of clergymen from the most varied sects, faiths, churches and groups, of which the Catholic missionaries constitute only a small percentage. For there are countless Islamic mullahs and marabouts here, ministers of hundreds of Christian sects and splinter groups, not to mention the priests of African gods and cults. Despite a certain degree of competition, the level of tolerance between them is astonishingly high, and respect for them among the general population universal.

That is why, when Father Stanislaw stops the car and tells the policemen, '*Evêché Bertoua!*' they don't check our documents, do not inspect the car, do not demand a bribe. They only smile and make a consenting gesture with their hand: we can drive on.

After a night in the chancery building in Bertoua, we drove to a village called Ngura, 120 kilometres away. Measuring distances in kilometres, however, is misleading and essentially meaningless here. If you happen upon a stretch of good asphalt, you can traverse that distance in an hour, but if you are in the middle of a roadless, unfrequented expanse, you will need a day's driving, and in the rainy season even two or three. That is why in Africa you usually do not say, 'How many kilometres is it?' but rather 'How much time will it take?' At the same time, you instinctively look at the sky: if the sun is shining, you will need only three, four hours, but if clouds are advancing and a downpour looks imminent, you really cannot predict when you will reach your destination.

Ngura is the parish of the missionary Stanislaw Stanislawek, whose car we are now following. Without him, we would never be able to find our way here. In Africa, if you leave the few main roads, you are lost. There are no guideposts, signs, markings. There are no detailed maps. Furthermore, the same roads run differently depending on the time of year, the weather, the level of water, the reach of the constant fires.

Your only hope is someone local, someone who knows the area intimately and can decipher the landscape, which for you is merely a baffling collection of signs and symbols, as unintelligible and bewildering as Chinese characters to a non-Chinese. 'What does this tree tell you?' 'Nothing!' 'Nothing? Why, it says that you must now turn left, or otherwise you will be lost. And this rock?' 'This rock? Also nothing!' 'Nothing? Don't you see that it is telling you to make a sharp right, at once, because straight ahead lies wilderness, a wasteland, death?'

In this way the native, that unprepossessing, barefoot expert on the writing of the landscape, the fluent reader of its inscrutable hieroglyphics, becomes your guide and your saviour. Each one carries in his head a small geography, a private picture of the world that surrounds him, a most priceless knowledge and art, because in the worst tempest, in the deepest darkness, it enables him to find his way home and thus be saved, survive.

Father Stanislawek has lived here for years, and so guides us without effort through this remote region's intricate labyrinth. We arrive at his rectory. It is a poor, shabby barracks, once a country school but now closed for lack of a teacher. One classroom is now the priest's apartment: a bed and a table, a little stove, an oil lamp. The other classroom is the chapel. Next door stand the ruins of a little church, which collapsed. The missionary's task, his main occupation, is the construction of a new church. An unimaginable struggle, years of labour. There is no money, no workers, no materials, no effective means of transport. Everything depends on the priest's old car. What if it breaks down, falls apart, stops? Then everything will come to a standstill: the construction of the church, the teaching of the gospel, the saving of souls.

Later, we drove along the hilltops (below us stretched a plain covered in a thick green carpet of forest, enormous, endless, like the sea) to a settlement of gold diggers, who were searching for treasure in the bed of the winding and lazy Ngabadi River. It was afternoon already, and because there is no dusk here, and darkness can descend with sudden abruptness, we went first to where the diggers were working.

The river flows along the bottom of a deep gorge. Its bed is shallow, sandy, and gravelly. Its every centimetre has been ploughed, and you can see everywhere deep craters, pits, holes, ravines. Over this battlefield swarm crowds of half-naked, black-skinned people, streaming with sweat and water, all of them feverish, in a trance. For there is a peculiar climate here, one of excitement, desire, greed, risk, an atmosphere not unlike that of a darkly lit casino. It's as though an invisible roulette wheel were spinning somewhere near, capriciously whirling. But the dominant noises here are the hollow tapping of hoes digging through the gravel, the rustle of sand shaken through handheld sieves, and the monotonous utterances, neither calls nor songs, made by the men working at the bottom of the gorge. It doesn't look as if these diggers are finding anything much, putting much aside. They shake the troughs, pour water into them, strain them, inspect the sand in the palm of their hand, hold it up to the light, throw everything back into the river.

And yet sometimes they do find something. If you gaze up to the top of the gorge, to the slopes of the hills that it intersects, you will see, in the shade of mango trees, under the thin umbrellas of acacias and tattered palms, the tents of Arabs. They are gold merchants from the

Sahara, from neighbouring Niger, from Nidjamena and from Nubia. Dressed in white djellabas and snowy, gorgeously wound turbans, they sit idly in tent entrances drinking tea and smoking ornate water pipes. From time to time, one of the exhausted, sinewy black diggers climbs up to them from the bottom of the crowded gorge. He squats in front of an Arab, takes out and unrolls a piece of paper. In its crease lie several grains of gold sand. The Arab looks at them indifferently, deliberates, calculates, then names a figure. The grime-covered black Cameroonian, master of this land and of this river – it is, after all, his country and his gold – cannot contest the price, or argue for a higher one. Another Arab would give him the same measly sum. And the next one, too. There is only one price. This is a monopoly.

Darkness descends, the gorge empties and grows quiet, and one can no longer see its interior, now a black, undifferentiated chasm. We walk to the settlement, called Colomine. It is a hastily thrown together little town, so makeshift and scruffy that its inhabitants will have no qualms abandoning it once the gold in the river runs out. Shack leaning against shack, hovel against hovel, the streets of slums all emptying into the main one, which has bars and shops and where evening and nightlife take place. There is no electricity. Oil lamps, torches, fires and candles are burning everywhere. What their glow picks out from the darkness is flickering and wobbly. Here, some silhouettes slip by; over there, someone's face suddenly appears, an eye glitters, a hand emerges. That piece of tin, that's a roof. That flash you just saw, that's a knife. And that piece of plank – who knows what it's from and what purpose it serves. Nothing connects, arranges itself, can be composed into a whole. We know only that this darkness all around us is in motion, that it has shapes and emits sounds; that with the assistance of light we can bring bits of it up to the surface and momentarily observe them, but that as soon as the light goes out, everything will escape us and vanish. I saw hundreds of faces in Colomine, heard dozens of conversations, passed countless people walking, bustling about, sitting. But because of the way the images shimmered in the flickering flames of the lamps, because of their augmentation and the speed with which they followed one another, I am unable to connect a single face with a distinct individual or a single voice with some particular person that I met there.

In the morning we drove south, to the great forest. First, however, was the Kadeï River, which runs through the jungle (it is a tributary of the Sangha River, which flows into the Congo River at Yumbi and Bolobo). In keeping with the operative local principle that a thing broken will never be repaired, our ferry looked like something fit only for the scrap heap. But the three little boys scampering around it knew exactly how to compel the monster into motion. The ferry: a huge, rectangular, flat metal box. Above it, a metal wire stretching across the river. Turning a squeaky crank, alternately tightening and releasing the wire, the boys move the ferry (with us and the car on board) – slowly, ever so slowly – from one bank to the other. Of course, this operation can succeed only when the current is sluggish and somnolent. Were it to twitch, to come alive, suddenly we would end up, carried off by the Kadeï, the Sangha and the Congo, somewhere in the Atlantic.

After that – driving, plunging into the forest – sinking, slipping, into the labyrinths, tunnels and underworlds of some alien, green, dusky, impenetrable realm. One cannot compare the tropical forest with any European forest or with any equatorial jungle. Europe's forests are beautiful and rich, but they are of average scale and their trees are of moderate height: we can imagine ourselves climbing to the top of even the highest ash or oak. And the jungle is a vortex, a giant knot of tangled branches, roots, shrubs and vines, a heated and compressed nature endlessly proliferating, a green cosmos.

This forest is different. It is monumental, its trees – thirty, fifty, and more metres high – are gigantic, perfectly straight, loosely positioned, maintaining clearly delineated distances between one another and growing out of the ground with virtually no undercover. Driving into the forest, in between these sky-high sequoias, mahogany trees, and others I do not recognize, I have the sensation of stepping across the threshold of a great cathedral, squeezing into the interior of an Egyptian pyramid, or standing suddenly amid the skyscrapers of Fifth Avenue.

The journey here is often a torment. There are stretches of road so pitted and rough that for all intents and purposes one cannot drive, and the car is flung about like a boat on a stormy sea. The only vehicles that can deal with these surfaces are the gigantic machines with engines like the underbellies of steam locomotives, which the French, Italians, Greeks and Dutch use to export timber from here to Europe. For the forest is being cut down day and night, its surface shrinking, its trees disappearing. You constantly come across large, empty clearings, with huge fresh stumps sticking out of the earth. The screech of saws, their whistling, penetrating echo, carries for kilometres.

Somewhere in this forest, in which we all appear so small, live others smaller still – its permanent inhabitants. It is rare to see them. We pass their straw huts along the way. But there is no one around. The owners are somewhere deep in the forest. They are hunting birds, gathering berries, chasing lizards, searching for honey. In front of each house, hanging on a stick or stretched out on a line, are owls' feathers, the claws of an anteater, the corpse of a scorpion, or the tooth of a snake. The message is in the manner in which these trifles are arranged: they probably tell of the owners' whereabouts.

At nightfall we spotted a simple country church and beside it a humble house, the rectory. We had arrived at our destination. Somewhere, in one of the rooms, an oil lamp was burning, and a small, wavering glow fell through the open door on to the porch. We entered. It was dark and quiet inside. After a moment, a tall, thin man in a light habit came out to greet us: Father Jan, from southern Poland. He had an emaciated, sweaty face with large, blazing eyes. He had malaria, was clearly running a fever, his body probably wracked by chills and cramps. Suffering, weak and listless, he spoke in a quiet voice. He wanted to play the host somehow, to offer us something, but from his embarrassed gestures and aimless puttering about it was plain he didn't have the means, and didn't know how. An old woman arrived from the village and began to warm up some rice for us. We drank water, then a boy brought a bottle of banana beer. 'Why do you stay here, father?' I asked. 'Why don't you leave?' He gave the impression of a man in whom some small part had already died. There was already something missing. 'I cannot,' he answered. 'Someone has to guard the church.' And he gestured with his hand towards the black shape visible through the window.

I went to lie down in the adjoining room. I couldn't sleep. Suddenly, the words of an old altar boy's response started to play in my head: *Pater noster, qui es in caeli ... Fiat voluntas tua ... sed libera nos a malo ...*

In the morning, the boy whom I had seen the previous evening beat with a hammer on a dented metal wheel rim hanging on a wire. This served as the bell. Stanislaw and Jan were celebrating morning mass in the church, a mass in which the boy and I were the sole participants.

LOVELY GIRLS, VERY CHEAP

Decca Aitkenhead

The Oriental Hotel in Bangkok is proud of its aristocratic past. It describes itself as colonial, though Thailand has never been a colony, and is staffed by bellboys in magnificent pantaloons who wring their hands when they bow. We arrived there on our first night in Thailand and were immediately presented with personalized gold-embossed stationery, so that we could write letters to prove to our friends that we had stayed at the Bangkok Oriental.

The bar was a hushed, burgundy room, and that evening a jazz band was playing. A young Thai woman sheathed in sequins sang Western love songs, and from every table middle-aged white couples watched in silence. The women sipped cocktails through straws, holding their glasses with both hands, never taking their eyes off the band. The men leaned backwards, arms locked straight out in front, palms flat, and from time to time their heads would swivel, as though every one of them was stranded on a blind date that was not working out. We took a table and ordered a Mai Tai. Its arrival was noted by one of the men, and his face lit up in delight.

'Eh, that looks good. What's that one then? A what?' He studied his cocktail menu, then held it up for us, pointing. 'We had this one last.

This one's next on my list.' My husband took a sip of his Mai Tai, and the man practically leaped out of the sofa.

'Eh, when I saw that I thought, oh, he's spoiling the wife. But it's for him! And she's got a lemonade, and you've got that!' He laughed and laughed, shaking his head. When he'd subsided he leaned across to Paul. 'Beer man, normally, are you?'

Satisfied, he went on, 'When did you get in? We got in this morning. Saw the King's palace. It's definitely not to be missed. Full of lots of different cultures. Different influences. Thai influences ...' There was a long pause. 'Um, Cambodian. Very spectacular. Then we went to Papong.' His wife was perched stiffly at right angles to the conversation. She was small, with a frosted blonde hood of hair, and didn't shift or turn her head. 'Patpong,' she corrected softly.

'Yeah, Patpong. Anyway, market were 'eaving, absolutely 'eaving. But it weren't as bad as what I'd thought it would be.' Patpong is Bangkok's famous red-light district. If he'd thought the vice would be bad, I wondered why he'd wanted to go there. 'But the shopping were amazing. We saw this bag,' – his wife wordlessly produced a fake Prada handbag – 'and we got the price right down to four hundred baht. Didn't we, love?' He talked us through the haggle like a fisherman reliving how he landed a shark, while his wife murmured, 'You've got to be hard.' She repeated it to herself. 'You've just got to be hard.'

Four hundred baht, at sixty-five to the pound, is roughly equivalent to six pounds, or nine dollars.

'And it's flame-resistant!' cried the man, and she held it up like a magician's assistant, and lit a match to it for us to see.

'Normally we go to the Caribbean,' he went on. 'This is our first time East. The wife likes cocktails, you see, so we thought, well, let's go to Fooket. Eh, where are you going?' Paul told him we were aiming for Ko Samui and Ko Pha-Ngan, and he looked momentarily thrown.

'So you're on a three-centre holiday, then? Bangkok, Ko Samui, and – and the other one. Phew.'

We flew south the next day. I had heard about Thailand for most of my adult life, but not of a fallen tiger economy feasted on by herds of package tourists. Friends had described Ko Samui as a hedonist's wonderland, and its neighbour, Ko Pha-Ngan, as a place of dreamy charm. Ko Pha-Ngan had become famous for its Full Moon rave, said by some to be a quasi-spiritual experience. In the course of the Nineties it had assumed the status of Mecca for the Ecstasy generation.

Thus it was that Paul and I found ourselves landing in a small clearing of palm trees later that afternoon. We had undertaken a sort of Ecstasy pilgrimage across the globe in order that I should write a travel book about clubbing, and the trail had naturally led us to Ko Samui. Paul had spent a week there ten years ago, before the gap year or *The Beach* had been invented, and stayed in a town called Chaweng. He remembered it as rustic and charming.

The airport taxi let us out in a resort that looked like Magaluf, Majorca. It had a main strip – two miles of potholed road running parallel to the beach – lined with concrete restaurants and shops, and pubs with names such as Fawlty Towers. Neon signs advertised PUB GRUB, cold beer in a PINT GLASS, and WESTERN TOILETS FOR THE LADIES. On one side of the strip, short muddy tracks led off to collections of bungalows that sprawled down to the beach. Some were built of wood rather than breeze blocks, and we chose the first one with a vacancy. An Italian with a shiny pink head was in charge; he called himself Papa, and showed us to our bungalow, a single creaky room only inches larger than the bed, with sheets of wallpaper for carpet. We unpacked as night fell and then set off back up the track through the dark.

'Hello, welcome! Welcome, hello! Hello, welcome!' As we turned the corner and stepped into the neon glare of the strip, about a dozen young Thai women came running at us. They bumped into each other as they pulled up a yard short, and some clasped each other's shoulders and pretended to double up in giggles, like teenage girls on a dare, astonished at their own audacity. They pointed at a small bar behind them. 'Come! Come!' Twenty yards further down the street this happened again, and then again, and then again. Some of the girls wore tight jeans and halter-neck tops, and others wore little Lycra dresses, but all of them had long glossy hair, which they tossed from side to side, and laughing kitten eyes with which they pleaded. They were stationed at the entrance to every bar, and when we walked past they spilled off their stools and took a run at us. 'Hello, welcome! Hello! Where you from?'

It is a tribute to them that they could make themselves heard at all. Trance and techno blasted out from the bars, and car horns seemed never to stop blaring, but still the cries of 'Welcome!' triumphed, and every few yards a new troop of girls came charging out. The assault was so relentless that we were a good way down the strip before we noticed anything else. Westerners streamed past us, but they were not the backpackers we'd expected to see, yet they didn't look quite like tourists, either, and then it dawned on us that this was because they were all men.

If we really had been in Majorca, they would have been about eighteen. Instead, these men were twenty years older, with grey faces, cropped hair and purple smudges under their eyes. At eighteen they would have been light on their feet with a suggestion of violence, but these men carried themselves heavily. They wore regulation sportswear and looked like discreet criminals. They filled the pubs and restaurants, drinking slowly and deliberately, and on their laps sat Thai bar girls.

We walked on, startled into silence, past bars called Black Jack and O'Malleys showing Premiership football, and then a tattoo parlour (TEN YEARS EXPERIENCE, NEW NEEDLE). There were videos showing in every restaurant and the amplified soundtracks poured on to the street and curdled in the racket, so that it sounded as if we were walking through a gigantic amusement arcade. Several pharmacies were open, doing a brisk trade despite the late hour. They looked like little old-fashioned sweet shops, except that they had posters in the windows offering CLEAN WOUND, PREG TEST.

We stopped for a drink and noticed two men sitting in the next-door bar, both in their early thirties and unmistakably English. One looked amiable enough – dirty blond, with a boxer's nose – but the other had bulging eyes and pumping cheeks and his whole face was working, sending ripples of fat and sweat down his belly. You couldn't say he was smiling – his mouth was too busy to form any definite expression – but his face was a billboard of enjoyment. Both of them were emptying what looked like brown glass medicine bottles into their mouths. I asked what was in them and the fat man hurled himself at the conversation.

'Picks you right up when you've 'ad a few, an' you're spinning, like. Down one of these and you're fackin' bang right, innit? Sorts you right out. Look,' and he pointed to the list of ingredients printed in Thai on the label. 'All herbal, innit? Really good for you stuff, healthy like. Herbs and stuff. Look, it's only 0.5 amphetamine.'

'So it's not speed, then?' Paul asked doubtfully.

'Nah,' he said. 'I had about ten last night. Proper good.' His friend nodded happily. A few minutes later he mentioned that they hadn't been to sleep for four days.

The fat man was called Sean. He was from Reigate and he had been in Chaweng for a few weeks. He had friends waiting for him on another island, but bad weather had prevented the ferry from running, so here he was, stuck on Ko Samui, a state of affairs that didn't seem to trouble him. Eight bar girls were gathered around his stool.

'You come in 'ere,' he exclaimed, gesturing to the bar, 'and they look after you like a prince. They get a wet towel, they wipe yer face ... '*Ere!*' He summoned the barmaid to give Paul a wet towel. 'I tell you, these girls do everyfing for you.' How much does everything cost, I asked. 'Five hundred baht and they do everyfing. They'll do' – he took a deep breath – 'your nails, they'll barf you, do your toenails, clean your hotel room. Everyfing! They're diamonds. Mind you, this one here,' and he nodded, 'she keeps saying, "I love you."' He pulled a disgusted face, shoved her away, then gathered up another into a noisy, wet kiss. All the girls beamed.

'This is Sue,' he went on. 'Sue's a nanny from Bangkok, down here on holiday. Well, I wasn't to know that, was I? I say, "How much?" She says, "Nuffing – I ain't a bar girl, it's for *free*."' His eyes popped even wider. '*Fa*-ckin' ree-*sult*!' Sean couldn't keep still for the wonder of it all, and swayed clean off his stool twice in the telling.

We bought a round of drinks. A few of the girls sneaked cocktails on to the order and Sean exploded in the fashion of a man never happier than when a friend has been slighted. He pretended to shoot the bar girls. He seemed to have developed a proprietorial role towards them, but presently he explained that in fact the Thai man at the door looked after them. 'And 'e won't touch them cos he's *bent*. It's ideal, innit?' Sean gazed about him. His eye fell on his friend, who was now shadow-boxing alone in the corner. 'Diamond geezer, diamond geezer. Wouldn't hurt a fly.'

'Ever been to Goa?' he asked suddenly. 'Now that's cheap, that's fackin' cheap. Beer, 30p! And the Es! Fack me. If you've got the money, get yourself on a plane to Goa, I'm tellin' you. Cheap or fackin' what?' The memory of Goa's prices temporarily silenced him, and in the pause Paul said that we'd wondered about the Ecstasy situation here. Sean was off again.

'Five hundred, mate! Five fackin' hundred.' Overflowing with happiness, he explained that he had smuggled 500 Es in with him. He'd packed them into hollow plastic balls found inside Kinder eggs, a hundred to a ball, and secreted them in his rectum. He mimed the act, indicating chronic pain all the way up to his chest and hopping from foot to foot. I asked if he was selling them in clubs here. 'You fink I'm mad? One hit and I'm done, mate. I'll sell the lot to a dealer, and see how long the money lasts. They're wicked, mind. You can have a couple if you like.' He glanced down and noticed the size of the camera on Paul's arm.

'You're not from the papers are you?' he asked. 'You're not from the *Sun*?' and he roared with laughter, then turned and gathered up another girl for an almighty kiss. From where I was standing, it looked as if he'd simply bent down and eaten her up.

A bar girl in Ko Samui is employed to attract customers. Almost every bar has at least one girl, and some of the larger bars have up to twenty. You don't see them during the day. This is when they sleep. But by sundown they are back in place on their high stools, ready for another long night. 'Come, come!' they beckon, on just the right side of insistence, thereby ensuring that the effect is girlishly charming rather than sluttish. And come men do, with faces full of wolfish delight at the joy of this amazing arrangement which lets them make-believe they are sexually appealing.

The overall impression is more naughty schoolgirl than call girl, and this is no accident, because 'of course', as everyone will tell you, 'they are not prostitutes'. The girls' official job description is notionally innocent. They are paid a percentage of the price of every drink that is bought by a customer whom they entice in and entertain. The longer they can keep the customer happy, the more drinks he will buy, and the more the girls will earn. To this end, they fawn and swoon over the men, who can grope and fondle them, sit them on their laps, and bore them to tears with conversation; wisely, the girls have come up with an inventive deterrent to the latter by playing endless games of Kerplunk or backgammon with their partners instead.

This is the basic system. However, if a man wants to take a girl off and have sex with her, all he has to do is pay the bar a fine of about four pounds, and agree a price with the girl. This money she is allowed to keep. More popular than the one-off transaction, which costs ten to twenty pounds all-in, is to start what the men refer to as a 'relationship'. Under this arrangement, the bar girl becomes a 'girlfriend' for the duration of the man's stay – a tirelessly devoted, obliging girlfriend, and a distinct improvement, you might say, on the real thing. In return, the man buys her meals and clothes and so on, as well as presents for her family – in theory her parents, but in practice usually her children, since most bar girls end up in the profession because they are single mothers. So Ko Samui is full of fat and unattractive European men driving around on mopeds with beautiful young Thai women on the back.

There are obvious difficulties in trying to calculate how much a bar girl earns. A recent Thai university survey put the national monthly average for a 'sex worker' at $125, but a Patpong bar girl can earn $150–$200 a month directly from the bar where she works, plus twenty dollars or more per session for sex with private clients. If she strikes lucky with a generous 'boyfriend', there is no limit to what he might give her. Compared to the official per capita income in Bangkok of $580, these sums are still relatively modest, but most bar girls are young, uneducated, and come from rural villages where the legal minimum wage can be as low as three dollars a day. Even in Bangkok, it is only four dollars a day. A hot meal of egg and noodles from a pavement food trolley will cost less than the equivalent of fifty cents, even in a touristy part of town, which means the bar girls are relatively wealthy – though nowhere near as wealthy as the average foreign tourist, who spends a hundred dollars in Thailand every day.

Tourists in Chaweng hadn't a bad word to say about the bar girls. How could they, the girls made everybody feel so good about themselves. The men felt irresistible and went around with faces stuffed with self-congratulation. Their mood was so good, they found themselves behaving nicely to one another, and this novelty put them in a better mood still. They were positively gallant towards white women, who in turn were delighted to be spared the usual advances.

There weren't many white women in Chaweng. Occasionally we would see young European backpackers, stopping off en route to other islands, but most of the women were older and came in groups with their husbands and boyfriends – big beery gangs, on holiday for a month or two. The women made a great fuss of getting along with the bar girls. At night, they would dance on the tables with them, curl their bodies together, laughing. In the day they could be heard remarking loudly on how pretty this or that one looked. Being seen to be sisterly was very important, although it was never clear if this was meant to be read as compassion, or as proof that they felt no sexual threat. Either way, they were thrilled that the girls smiled back, and took it to mean that they liked them.

The only club in Chaweng still open beyond two in the morning would usually run on until dawn, jammed and chaotic. Empty, it would have been a more sophisticated venue than most, with elegant open-air terraces and wicker tables softly lit by lanterns. It was never empty, though, but full of bar girls who came along after their own establishments closed, hoping to pick up some late freelance business. In the crush as we were sitting down, one accidentally put her cigarette out on the tail of a Dalmatian dog that had wandered in from the street. Then another with legs like pipe cleaners pushed past us and vomited into a pot plant. The man sharing our table didn't notice either mishap, for his eyes were locked on two others dancing on stage in lime-green bikinis.

'Lovely girls,' he murmured dreamily.

'What, the prostitutes?' Paul asked. The man turned, shocked.

'Prostitutes? They're not prostitutes. They're bar girls.' And he looked angry, as if Paul had just insulted him.

This would happen whenever anyone said the word 'prostitute'. The men on holiday in Chaweng thought the girls were so lovely, the least one could do was lie about what they did for a living. This lie was to protect the girls' honour, and there was never any doubt that it was the girls who would be shamed by the truth. Their unflagging loveliness made it easy for everyone to uphold the consensus of deceit; nevertheless, at some level the men knew it wasn't true, and so liked to feel that their lie was chivalrous.

The chivalry had its limits. Later that night a scuffle broke out between one of the lime-green-bikini girls and a stocky German. He slapped her, she bristled, everyone stared – and then she gave a short, tired shrug and walked away. Nobody intervened on her behalf – and in the many similar scenes we witnessed afterwards, nobody ever did.

We quickly stopped noticing the girls, but I became obsessed with the men, and took to quizzing them in the street. Paul thought I was mad and left me to it, but at first I didn't get far because I kept meeting Belgians and Germans, who were polite but offered only pidgin clichés. Then one evening I was sitting in a café when a man leaned across and asked: 'Would you like to join us? You are by yourself.' He had his arms around a bar girl, and was smiling broadly. I smiled back.

Rory was a handsome Australian in his mid-thirties. He pulled out a chair and shook my hand.

'And is this your girlfriend?' I said.

'Yes, this is Yah,' he agreed, closing his fingers over her forearm. Yah was about his age, not especially glamorous and gave me a warm smile but said nothing. I asked the usual holiday questions and Rory explained that he had come to Ko Samui with ten men friends from Australia, but on the night they were leaving he had met Yah. That was nearly ten weeks ago. 'I would never have stayed if it wasn't for Yah,' he said, squeezing her arm again. He seemed proud of her, and also proud of this statement of his love.

'Aren't relationships like this compromised from the very beginning?' I asked him.

'Well, yes,' he agreed quickly, nodding. 'You do have to

compromise, obviously. I mean, I have to come to terms with ... you know, overlook her past. And now I'm going to speak very quickly, so she won't understand what I'm saying to you. There is the intellectual side, that's of course a disappointment, maybe a problem, and I have to overlook that, so that's another compromise.'

'I'm sorry, that's not quite what I meant. Isn't a relationship like this fundamentally corrupted?'

'Well,' he considered, 'I expect it raises your hackles as a Western woman. I feel uncomfortable with Western women now, I do sense their disapproval.'

'And how does that make you feel?'

'It makes me think ...' He paused, and pulled a series of weary, injured, irritated faces. 'It makes me think: Why? You see, I care about this lady a lot. I care about her. A lot.' He took her hand and stroked it. Yah was wearing a pleasant, blank smile, but facing away from the table. Rory talked as though she wasn't there. He seemed to be enjoying the conversation, measuring his opinions and pausing to admire the sound of each one as it came out. I asked if he would ever have expected to find himself in this situation.

'God no! Never! I would never have condoned it. I mean, I don't condone it. But when you travel, you know, you have to adapt, you have to examine your ideas, you know? And I think, well, if it makes a man happy for a few weeks, well then ...'

'Well then, what?'

'Well then, that's a good thing, isn't it? And you know what? A lot of the ugliest men here, it turns out they're the nicest men. The really fat, ugly men, they treat their girl so well, they just want to be good to her.' I asked if he thought Yah would be with him if she was Australian.

'Oh, if she was Australian I would have left her weeks ago!'

'No, you misunderstand me. I mean, would she still choose to be with you if she was an Australian?'

'Ah. Oh, well ... That's a tough one, I don't know.' He thought. 'You know, she could walk away whenever she wanted. She's as free as I am.'

'You believe all that?'

'Oh yeah. Y'see, I'd take a good argument over a pretty face any day. I want a wife, not a maid.' Rory said he was going back to Australia in two weeks' time. I asked if he was taking Yah with him. He said there were no plans for that as yet.

When we left, he said he hoped that we'd see each other again, and I think he meant it, for he was pleased with his performance and would have liked another chance to make his case. I found his presence disproportionately upsetting and avoided him, which was surprisingly easy to do in Chaweng. In spite – or perhaps because – of the town's boundless sexual licence, visitors seemed to need rituals, and one of these was a tendency to single out a particular bar and make it their local. I had met Rory in his local, and we never went back.

Paul and I had a local, too. Each night we would drop in at a tiny bamboo bar hidden down a mud track. It had just one bar girl, seldom any customers, and a young Swedish barman called Stefan, who was both boyishly sweet and fluent in all Chaweng's delusions. If the bar girl wanted to have sex for money, he said, it was nothing to do with him. 'I just want her to eat and be happy. I don't want to feel like a pimp.' When the girl did disappear with a man one night, though, he blustered and pretended not to know where they'd gone. He said the girls in Chaweng were treated wonderfully, but he was embarrassed when we asked if they were paid anything if no customers came in. 'That's not my side of the business.' The only time it seemed to count as prostitution for Stefan was the night a pair of particularly gross men, all paws and wet lips, took turns mauling the girl at the bar. 'That makes me so angry,' he shuddered. 'Urgh, they're so *big*.'

The girl in Stefan's bar had a buck-toothed smile that was too boisterous to be sexy and podgy legs dimpled like a baby's. Her walk was a playful waddle, more like a puppy's than a prostitute's. She beamed at us and chattered away to us every night, and because she looked so ungainly, so artless, we couldn't help ourselves. We began to believe she genuinely liked us.

'The girls, you know,' Stefan said quietly, in a rare lapse into honesty. 'They are not so nice. They really think about money, you know?' He meant it to be derogatory, but it was the only genuine compliment we ever heard the girls paid.

The night we arrived in Chaweng, it began to rain, and by dawn everywhere was knee-deep in water. Quite amused by the mess, we went out and bought raincoats – bright pink sheets of plastic with a hole in the middle for your head – and I was delighted by my new outfit, but would have been less so had I known it would be weeks before I could take it off. In the evenings the rain eased to a drizzle, but the deluge returned each morning and the town was rapidly reduced to a bog of rubbish and mud. For much of the time the electricity was down, so there were no showers or fans, and beneath our pink plastic we began to smell. This was unpleasant, but unimportant, because the whole strip stank. Miles of empty sand stretched out not twenty yards away, but we all stuck to the same septic gutter of concrete.

Tourists would start the day in the restaurants, where breakfast blurred into lunch, and movies were shown back to back. Diners tended to pick at their food, but stared intently at the television screen; violence was the staple theme. Afterwards, they drifted into shops and bought fake Nike trainers and fake Gucci belts, or they would start drinking again. The only reason why anyone was here – more than sunshine, more than bar girls, even – was that life on Ko Samui was cheap.

A man we met in a bar had calculated that his rent was 2.25 pence a night. His body was soldered on to a bar stool, but he swivelled round as soon as he heard Paul's Glasgow accent and introduced himself as Lenny from Falkirk. He was with five friends. 'This is my gang.' Lenny ran a pub in Spain called the Rovers' Return, and his friends were all landlords. Every winter they spent two or three months in Ko Samui while their Spanish pubs were closed. Most of them were staying in the bungalows near ours, though one was staying in the more expensive bungalows further up the beach. Lenny looked embarrassed. 'Wife's five months pregnant, you see.' We ran into Lenny and his gang every day, and the encounter always opened with a brief report of how much each of them had drunk the previous night. It was like calling a class register. They never seemed to get over how cheap the beer was, although they were knocked sideways one afternoon by a rumour that it was cheaper in Manila.

Besides cheap beer there was also Thailand's pharmaceutical free-for-all. Ko Samui's chemist's shops are as famous as Amsterdam's coffee shops in certain circles, and inspire the same sort of guzzling excitement. Sean took us to his favourite shop. The queue stretched to the door and a woman in a white coat was spooning pills out of large jars into plastic bags beneath a blackboard advertising VALIUM, VIAGRA, PROZAC, THE PILL, like a pub menu. A man in front of us asked about amphetamine pills and she frowned, said they were banned, then took a scoop of capsules out of a jar under the counter and slipped them into a bag with a wink. He pointed to some purple sleeping pills. 'Very good,' she nodded. 'When you wake up, there is nothing left in your brain.'

Sean's 'one-hit' sale had been forgotten in the fun of handing out free Es to bar girls and his stock of pills was dwindling fast. There was something touching about his willingness to believe everything the girls told him. 'They'd never had an E before they met me!' he boomed with pride. We passed his local one afternoon and saw him leaning over, kissing a tiny girl who lay slumped on a chair. Her matchstick arm stuck out at an unnatural angle, like the limb of a dead child protruding from the scene of an accident.

*

The Full Moon rave was still almost a fortnight away, but we had lost
the heart to wait any longer on Ko Samui, and so we sailed to Ko Pha-
Ngan. Bar owners there had come up with an enterprising invention,
the Half Moon party, thereby licensing themselves to hold three raves
a month instead of one. Party-goers had proved relaxed about the
finer points of lunar ritual, and around 10,000 flooded into the island
every time. The next was due in a few days.

The ferry left from a dock near Chaweng. During the night the rain
had finally ended and we found the upper deck jammed tight with
backpackers fresh in from Bangkok and heading straight to Ko Pha-
Ngan. A couple standing along the rail from us cracked Essex-girl-
style jokes about Ko Samui, tossing fag ends into the water and
lamenting the ruin of the island we were leaving behind. Most people
said nothing at all, but put on sunglasses and did crosswords, or lay
down to sleep. Even when the mountains and white sands of Ko Pha-
Ngan came into view, mockingly beautiful, like an old Bounty Bar
advert, nobody seemed to notice. Sunglasses and Walkmans stayed on
as we docked in a shimmering sandy cove, and rucksacks were set
down in silence on the jetty. Then along bounced a dozen or so pick-
up trucks; the drivers jumped out, called 'Taxi!' and everyone came to
life.

'A hundred baht?' This was £1.50. 'Each? For ten of us?' Young men
who five minutes earlier had been fast asleep swarmed around the
drivers, waving their bronzed arms about in a pantomime of disgust.
Rucksacks were thrown on to a truck, then snatched back when the
driver refused to lower his price. 'Ten times a hundred – that makes
a thousand baht!' a young Israeli screamed. He was tall and sinewy,
wrapped in a kaftan, and the muscles in his neck stood taut with rage.
He bent right down into the driver's face. 'A thousand baht! That's a
lot of money for you.'

We decided to walk. The track to the main town of Had Rin was lined with single-storey shacks; some were bars, but most were either flip-flop shops or Internet cafés or both. MOSQUITO NET, read a sign outside one store, then: FAST SCREEN, SEVENTEEN-INCH, NON-RADIATION. There was no traffic or tarmac or bar girls, just a peaceful simplicity, but when we reached Had Rin we were still unprepared for the great sweep of beach facing us. It was long and creamy, framed by pearly boulders and turquoise surf, a cliché of tropical perfection. Pretty wooden huts on stilts were built into the cliff above us, and as we stood and stared, a man called down from the steps of one.

'You've got to be here, right. It'll go off here for sure. Best beach party in the world. Gotta be here. Unless you go to Goa, mind – you could be there, it'll go off in Goa too. But it goes off here all right, goes off every night.' He tipped a bottle of beer in welcome, and his friends waved hello. 'M'name's Neesy, we're from New Zealand. Between us we've got fourteen years' travelling experience, and forty-three years' drinking experience. I think that's enough.' His friends nodded. 'Yep, hard core. But we're still working on it, for sure.'

Neesy was hard core all right. His nose was so badly burned that it looked like a crusty purple scab hanging on to his face. We would see him sauntering up and down the beach every day, commanding awe among more junior travellers, although also a little secret alarm. They would gaze in admiration as he passed, then hiss, 'Christ, did you see his nose?' when he was gone.

Backpackers on Ko Pha-Ngan looked nothing like the tourists on Ko Samui. At first glance, though, they did all look like each other. Everyone looked good, in the way young people do when they have lost a stone and grown used to wearing hardly any clothes. They were scuffed with bites and bruises, but these imperfections were all part of the look and so didn't really stand out. The Italians had good skin and wild hair, the Dutch had tattoos, and Americans came in rather serious, thirty-something couples, or as galumphing college boys, but this was as much as we noticed at first. To the naked eye, the Ko Pha-Ngan dress code appeared to be entirely relaxed.

It took a day or so to grasp the full hierarchy of style rules. A sensible Netherlands sandal was unsexy, but an obviously sexy shoe was out of the question, so anything involving straps or heels was unwise. A flip-flop worked best, implying frugality as well as beach bum/mountain goat agility. It was also important to have a tan deep enough to suggest you took being a backpacker seriously. The correct positioning of the knot in one's sarong was evidently a fraught issue; we watched one girl discreetly tie and retie hers using the reflection of a window for fifteen minutes. Bikinis were strictly of the stringy sort, thongs being too *Baywatch*, and underwired cups too C&A, and ethnic jewellery was essential, although too much betrayed amateurish enthusiasm. Combat shorts were all right for boys, if worn topless with a good tan, and the classier girl traveller rolled the waistband of her skirt down into a hipster. Here and there you would spy pale-skinned boys who had been thoughtless enough to come to Thailand wearing long trousers and Ben Sherman shirts. They stood about awkwardly, studying everyone else's outfits with dismay.

Friendliness was taken for inexperience, and considered shamefully gauche. It was safer to send emails than risk making conversation with each other, and this is what people spent a great deal of their time doing. The Internet cafés were so crowded that it was easy to spy on people's mail, and this revealed as much as anything we accomplished face to face. A high percentage of all emails began with 'Subject: Hangover', and a surprising number of those written by men gave rather arch and worldly accounts of the Bangkok sex industry. Middle-class boys composed wry emails to their fathers ('went to see women perform interesting acts with ping-pong balls'), and sauce to their mothers ('was offered sex for two hundred baht!!!'), followed by equally breezy but more graphic accounts to their friends of what happened when they accepted.

Few male backpackers had made it through Bangkok without paying to watch women eject ping-pong balls from their vaginas. Most were young men who would not visit a stripper or a prostitute at home, let alone tell their parents if they did, and yet Patpong was just part of the global itinerary, a morally neutral must-see. But there were no emails about the Thai tradition of eating dog, nor any other adventure in cultural relativism. Just a lot of emails about bargain sex.

Backpackers didn't talk about this. Nor did they explore any other anomaly in their lifestyle. As far as we could gather, the social code imposed a strict embargo on any discussion that could be considered controversial; what hippies would once have called 'heavy' was now discredited as inappropriate and girls in particular made quite a performance out of rolling their eyes at the first sign of trouble. Boys liked to boast about how little they knew of what was going on in the world, for to be caught knowing what was in the news was worse than tying your sarong the wrong way. Instead the favourite, if not the only conversation would always begin in the same way. 'Such and such a place,' someone would volunteer, 'is supposed to be *really* cheap.' And then everybody would sit up and listen.

Mountain Sea Bungalows were supposed to be really cheap. It was our first day on Ko Pha-Ngan and we were in a bar discussing where to stay when a French girl offered this advice. At once, two tall English blondes were at her table firing questions – how cheap? where? what were they like? – and shortly we were making our way to Mountain Sea together. We found the owner on the veranda, being shouted at by a beautiful Italian about her bill. 'Look around us! Look at where we are!' The Italian girl's arm swept across the bay and the beach, and she stamped her foot. 'Look at all this – and we are talking about money!' The problem seemed to be that Mountain Sea had put up its rate by a few baht because of the Half Moon party. As backpackers out-numbered beds on the island, this was standard practice among the guest houses each time there was a party. Paul and I took a room. The two girls from London refused, 'on principle', and shared a supportive cigarette with the Italian. We agreed to look after their bags while they went to look elsewhere.

Each time they returned, they had bad news about another hotel hiking its prices by thirty pence a night. 'It's disgusting,' they said. 'They shouldn't be allowed to get away with it.'

Kate and Suzie were law graduates from the Home Counties, halfway round the world, and indignation seemed to be the theme of their tour. Time and again, Kate said, they'd arrived in a new place only to discover that the prices were way higher than anything they had been told to expect. Suzie wished they had gone straight to India now. Thais were just too greedy. Thailand was finished, she said. Ruined.

They ended up sleeping on our floor. During the day they dozed on the beach, practised their new hobby of juggling, or did sums in the flyleaves of their paperbacks to calculate how much they had spent. Their world tour was going to take them twelve months, but most of this time, it seemed, was going to be spent trying to save money, a pursuit they endowed with moral significance. 'Don't buy that there!' Suzie would chide strangers in shops. 'They're selling it for ten baht less over there.' She and Kate liked to show off their concave midriffs, not out of conventional vanity but as a boast of how little they'd managed to spend on food. They would sit up until the early hours trading tips with other backpackers on where in the world one could best avoid spending money.

Kate and Suzie expected to become lawyers. In the meantime, however, having volunteered to survive on eight pounds a day, they chose to think of themselves as poor people. 'Look, I've only got eight pounds a day, all right?' Suzie would remind anyone whom she felt was failing to make every possible concession to her self-imposed poverty. Thais should give her a break, she thought, and she was forever losing her temper with another shopkeeper who didn't seem to understand that she was on a budget. 'Fucking rip-off merchants,' she would hiss to Kate, handing over her coins with a scowl.

It was true that eight pounds, or 500 baht, was not a lot to get by on in Thailand. A beer cost sixty baht, a meal maybe 200, and our bungalow in Chaweng had been 450 baht a night. But if Kate and Suzie were facing a measure of austerity, it was nothing to what the Thais had suffered after the crash of 1997. Since that summer, when the baht lost almost half its value and the economy practically collapsed, unemployment had more than doubled and inflation was running at seven per cent. For a time this had represented a jackpot for backpackers, the devalued baht making Thailand a tropical bargain to rival even Goa. Word had spread that one could live like a king on 200 baht a day. Happily for Thailand, this was no longer true, but backpackers seemed to treat this development like a broken promise. Most of them regarded the tentative recovery with outright indignation, and attributed the price rises to downright greed.

I suggested to Suzie that if she had come away for less time, she could have had a bigger budget and would not have had to spend her journey thinking about money. 'But you have to have a year,' she corrected me, looking confused. 'I mean, that's what you get, isn't it?' To Suzie, the year out was the constitutional right of all young professionals, and it was the duty of the Third World to keep her within her budget.

After a couple of days we left our room to the two of them and travelled up the coast, to a guest house tucked away in the jungle where, it had been suggested, we might find the true spirit of Thailand.

The Sanctuary styled itself as a retreat for travellers who had come to experience a culture rather than a discount economy. It was a picturesque cluster of wooden platforms on stilts built into the cliffs of a deserted cove; low tables and cushions and hammocks were dotted about, ethnic trance music played softly in the background, and the waves lapped below. A board behind the curved stone bar was reserved for a THOUGHT FOR THE DAY. When we arrived, the thought was: ONCE YOU REALIZE GOD KNOWS EVERYTHING, YOU ARE TRULY FREE. Another sign suggested: TRY TO REALIZE YOU ARE A DIVINE TRAVELLER. YOU ARE ONLY HERE FOR A LITTLE WHILE, THEN DEPART FOR A DISSIMILAR AND FASCINATING WORLD.

The woman in charge spoke in a low, dreamy voice, and appeared to float rather than walk, as though the gravity had been turned down wherever she went. Most of the guests were trying to copy her, and greeted our arrival with slow-motion nods of the head and whispered half-smiles. One of them led us to the library, a corner of bookshelves lodged into the rocks, and encouraged us to try a book about the mystical significance of birthdays, but by this point we were ravenous, having not liked to be caught eating anything in Had Rin, so we declined the book and ordered a mountain of food. When we had finished eating, we had to say 'Paul and Decca' to the waitress. No money changed hands until it was time to check out, and our tab was filed under our names instead of our room number. 'When you stay at the Sanctuary,' they would remind any guest who needed it spelled out, 'you are not a number, you are an indiv . . .' and so on.

It was a relief to go whole days without hearing anybody mention money. It was prudent of the owners to operate such a system, though, as their prices were at least double the going rate everywhere else. The Sanctuary belonged to an Irishman, and the staff in charge were all Westerners. They sold the Sanctuary as an experience of pure Thailand, yet were alone among Thai businesses in having contrived not only to overcharge backpackers, but to get them to pay without complaining.

Most of the guests were British. They worked in the arts or media, liked yoga and boiled rice, and tied their sarongs in inventively new twists. Most were subtly possessive about the Sanctuary. They sighed about 'other' backpackers, the *Lonely Planet* hordes in Had Rin who showed no respect for Thailand, and in an interesting inversion of tradition, they took pride in paying Sanctuary prices. It was as though by spending more rather than less, they hoped to prove their authenticity as travellers.

In the next bay along lived a Thai housewife in a Robinson Crusoe-style shack. She spoke no English, but would rustle up an omelette for thirty baht – a fraction of the price charged at the Sanctuary – but its guests seldom climbed the headland to eat her food. Like all the travellers we met, they spoke not a word of Thai, so they preferred to swing in hammocks at the Sanctuary, enthusing among themselves and the staff about the beauty of 'real' Thailand. One man was worried when he saw Paul taking photographs. 'Don't say the name of the beach,' he murmured confidentially. 'Just say, "a beach".'

The Half Moon party took place the following night. We caught a small boat down the coast to Had Rin with two Australian nurses who were taking the night off from their meditation studies at the Sanctuary. They urged us to try it, calling it 'cosmic'. Arriving at Had Rin, the boatman asked for a hundred baht each. 'A hundred baht?' shouted one of them. 'It's a fifty-baht ride! Right, take us back, you wanker, and we'll get a fifty-baht ride.' The other nurse stood over him and wagged a finger, repeating: '*Bad* business. *Bad* business,' in a voice you might use to talk to a dog. 'Nice meeting ya. Have a great party!' she called to us as we climbed ashore, then turned back to the man. '*Bad* business.'

And so here at last was the famous Ko Pha-Ngan party. The beach had been refashioned into a late-Eighties warehouse party, with fairy lights glowing in the cliffs, and strobes raking the beach, catching luminous crescent moons of silk staked along the sand. The effect was spooky, and unexpectedly pretty – although perhaps not as un-expected as the lengths everyone had gone to to dress up for the occasion. As if by secret pre-arrangement, they had come as ravers circa 1988. Girls wore spray-tight trousers in amusingly lurid patterns, boys came as ironic tramps in woolly hats, and both wore gigantic trainers and strode up and down in tight little groups, faces hardened by expectation. Those wearing the wrong outfit hovered on the edges, gratifying the others with their abject inferiority.

People drank beer, and took speed and magic mushrooms, and apart from the unlucky few whose hallucinogens made them stand by themselves and scowl at the sand, they danced. I recognized the dance from raves a decade ago; it looked like a small child's impersonation of a mentally handicapped person, and it skidded around in a circle, incoherent and demented. Round and round everyone spun, all the way down the beach, most narrowly managing to miss the beat, and some apparently dancing to a different record altogether. As the night wore on the dancing thinned, and thousands of people lay back in the sand on their elbows, smoking cigarettes and gazing about them in wonder. 'Wicked,' they nodded, grinning at each other. 'Wicked.'

Drifting from one cluster to the next, I realized the conversations were also familiar from old raves, when everyone used to laugh about discos and girls who wore make-up. Here, it was Ko Samui they were mocking – tatty, tarty Ko Samui, lavishly scorned with the same lazy pleasure all the way along the beach. One group was unable to let the matter go, and as the night wore on its members became worked up about the need to protect Ko Pha-Ngan from the vulgar tribe over the water. As custodians of paradise, everyone agreed, they had a duty to keep out the beer bellies and credit cards.

In the dark I lay and listened. I was reminded of Sean and his friends on Ko Samui, and after a while I found I couldn't see any difference between them and the backpackers, except that Sean's lot paid up for their pleasures without complaining. As the temperature dropped before dawn, and they kept on talking, I realized I couldn't see any difference between the backpackers and us, either. I had taken it for granted that the Thais were happier to have Paul and me there, rather than the other tourists, because we weren't rude. But the backpackers assumed that prostitutes preferred sleeping with them rather than with men like Sean because they weren't ugly, and I had thought them contemptible for flattering themselves about it.

All any of us had done in Thailand was buy things. Travelling like this is a euphemism for shopping, an endless spree, and whether we were buying breakfast or sex, we were doing it primarily because it was cheap. Paul and I had thought it funny and slightly tragic that the couple in the hotel bar in Bangkok had come all this way for a fake handbag, believing themselves to be on an exotic adventure. It hadn't occurred to us that we might be the same.

And if we were, then the great debate about who was to blame for spoiling Thailand was meaningless. Everyone who came to Thailand to spend foreign earnings on fun was defined by the gap between their wealth and Thailand's poverty. Despite the backpackers' belief in their own poverty, what they actually take from Thailand is the experience of being immensely rich. They behave in the same careless, bored and discontented way as rich people anywhere, with no purpose but their own amusement. Guarding their money like millionaires, they greet every Thai with suspicion, and mix only with their own. It is a cruel irony for those who set off imagining they will find themselves by travelling, and find instead their identities are reduced to the sum of their traveller's cheques.

Long-haul travel on this scale is scarcely a generation old. It began in the Seventies, in overland lorries to Kathmandu, and it was only in the Eighties that around-the-world tickets became commonplace. The expression 'gap year' wasn't heard outside public schools until the Nineties. Yet already it is accepted without question that a long stint away from home, in somewhere like Thailand, is an essential and improving experience. And so here we all were on a beach, observing the convention, impersonating the time of our lives.

*

The sun rose slowly over a rubbish tip of empty bottles and debris and raddled dancers. Their basic move had evolved into a hunched stomp by now, like the posture of an elderly woman who has just heard a mugger coming up behind her, and their eyes were pink and bloodshot. Men were standing knee-deep in the ocean, peeing. A scattering of girls lay sobbing on the sand, wretched with exhaustion now the drugs had worn off, and at the far end of the beach taxi drivers were herding the unsteady into pick-up trucks. We threaded our way through the casualties and boarded one, but just as we were pulling away, a skinny young man stumbled up and threw himself in over the tailgate, face first.

'I just wanna wind them up, like,' he slurred at our feet, in a thick Welsh accent. 'Say I won't pay more than thirty baht.'

The driver said quietly that the fare was sixty baht. The Welshman took a swig from a bottle of whisky, levered himself on to his elbows, and told him to fuck off. A laugh and cheer went up in the truck – and there was a noisy commotion, then we were all out of the truck, and then we were all in again, minus the Welshman, and agreeing to pay the fare. But by now the driver wanted it in advance, and as we were paying the Welshman came flying in again, head first, crash-landing between our legs with the whisky bottle held safely aloft in an outstretched hand. Calmly, the driver leaned in again, and asked for the fare.

'Fuck off,' spat the Welshman.

'Just pay him,' I pleaded.

'No, I like to wind them up.'

'Please, pay him the fare.'

'Shut up, it's a laugh.'

'For Christ's sake, *pay him*!' I screamed. He blinked, startled, and Paul's hand closed on my arm as I made to fly at him. The other passengers stared at me in amazement, and the two women on board slid supportive hands on to the Welshman's shoulder. Still the driver waited for his fare. At the front, two Swedish skinheads lost their tempers.

'Drive the car! Drive the car!' they roared in unison at the driver. Their hairless pink faces were twisted with fury, and they were stamping their feet on the floor. '*Fuck-ing drive the fuck-ing car! Drive! The! Car!*' Then everyone was shouting at the driver, and in the uproar someone paid for the Welshman, and suddenly we were off, bumping along a dusty track through the jungle in the raw morning sunshine. For a few minutes the surprise of being under way silenced us all, and I realized that I was shaking.

The bundle at our feet stirred. The Welshman pulled himself upright, gazed around, rubbed his eyes, took another swig, and offered the bottle around. 'It's only a laugh, stupid,' he grinned, catching sight of my expression. 'It's only a laugh. They're thieving bastards anyway.'

'How much do you earn?'

'Fifteen hundred pounds a month. So what?'

'There's not one person in this vehicle who earns as little as the man driving it. Why do you think you can treat him like that?'

'I don't want to be lectured. I'm travelling.'

'That doesn't give you a licence to act like a cunt.'

A shock jolted around the truck, and I felt hostile eyes settle on me. The two girls stroked the Welshman's neck, and a man at the back shook his head slowly and let out a low whistle. The skinhead boys squared their shoulders and then one of them said, 'I think you'd better mind your manners, young lady, don't you? There's no need to be rude.'

DERVISHES

Rory Stewart

'Dervish are an abomination,' said Navaid.

'What do you mean by a Dervish?' I asked.

'Dervish? Don't you know? It's a very old concept. Fakir? Pir-Baba?
Sufi? Silsilah Malang – that beggar doing magic tricks ...?' Navaid
was staring at a man who was sitting cross-legged in the street with
a ten-foot black python wrapped round his neck. 'That beggar –
medieval mystics like Shahbaz Qalander – the people who live and
dance at his tomb. They are all Dervish.'

When I first met Navaid at the tomb of Datta Ganj Baksh a week
earlier, he had been examining the same snake man. Now Navaid was
standing very still, stroking his white beard. The python was asleep
and so was its owner and no one except Navaid seemed to notice
them. For the last ten years he had spent his days at the mosques of
the old city of Lahore. He had neither a family nor a job. His voice was
quick, anxious, slightly high-pitched, as though he were worried I
would leave before he had finished his sentence.

'You foreigners love the idea of Dervish – whirling Dervish,
wandering Dervish, howling Dervish – exotic – like belly dancers and
dancing camels,' he insisted, ' – surely you understand what I mean?'

'But what's that beggar there got in common with a medieval Sufi poet?'

'One thing anyway — they are both irrelevant,' replied Navaid. 'They have nothing to do with Islam or Pakistan. They barely exist any more and, if they do, they don't matter. Forget about Dervish.'

Two weeks later I was walking alone along a canal in the Southern Punjab. It had been five months since I started walking across Asia but I had only been in the Punjab for a few days. The arid mountains of Iran had been replaced by a flat, fertile land and I was struggling to turn my limited Persian into Urdu. I was also getting used to new clothes. I was trying to dress in a way that did not attract attention. I was, like everyone else, wearing a loose, thin Pakistani salwar kameez suit and, because of the 120-degree heat, a turban. I had swapped my backpack for a small cheap shoulder bag and I carried a traditional iron-shod staff. In Iran I was frequently accused of being a smuggler, a resistance fighter or a grave robber. In the Punjab, because of my clothes, black hair and fair skin I was often mistaken for one of the millions of Afghani refugees now living in Pakistan. Afghanis have a reputation as dangerous men and this may partly have explained why I had not (so far) felt threatened, walking alone along the Punjab canals.

A snake was swimming down the canal, its head held high over its own reflection, shedding bars of water thick with sunlight in its wake. In a hollow between the towpath and the wheat field was a stunted peepul tree draped with green cloth and beneath it the earth grave of a 'Dervish'. A thin bare-chested man dragged a bucket through the canal, staggered to the edge of the path and threw water on the dry track. I watched him weaving up and down the grass bank towards me. The history of his labour was laid across the path in thick bars of colour. In front of him, where I was walking, was pale sand; at his feet was a band of black mud. Behind him stripe after stripe, each slightly paler than its successor, faded through orange clay until, where he had worked an hour before, nothing remained but pale sand. This was his job in the Canal Department.

'*Salaam alaikum.*'

'*Wa alaikum as-salaam,*' he replied. 'Where are you going?'

'To the canal rest-house.'

'Respected one,' he smiled and his voice was nervous, 'most kind one. Give me a sacred charm.'

'I'm sorry, I don't have one.'

'Look at me. This work. This sun.' He was still smiling.

'I'm very sorry. *Hoda Hafez,* God be with you.'

I turned away and he grabbed me by the arm. I hit him with my stick. He backed off and we looked at each other. I hadn't hurt him but I was embarrassed.

Navaid had warned me I would be attacked walking across Pakistan. 'Violent? Pakistan is a very violent country – the Baluch caught a young Frenchman who was trying to walk here last year and killed him. Or look at today's newspaper – you can be killed by your father for sleeping around, you can be killed by other Muslims for being a Shi'a, you can be killed for being a policeman, you can be killed for being a tourist.'

But I could see that the man I'd hit wasn't dangerous.

He was now smiling apologetically, 'Please, sir, at least let me have some of your water.'

I poured some water from my bottle into his hands. He bowed to me, passed it in front of his lips and then brushed it through his hair.

'And now a charm: a short one will be enough . . .'

'No, I'm sorry. I can't.'

I couldn't. I wouldn't play the role of a holy man. '*Hoda Hafez.*' A hundred yards further on I looked back through the midday glare and saw him still staring at me. He had, it seemed, perhaps because I was walking in Pakistani clothes, mistaken me for what Navaid would call a wandering Dervish.

An hour later, I turned off the towpath down a tree-lined avenue. There was a peepul, with its pointed leaves, trembling forty feet above. This one had outgrown its pink bark but its trunk was thin, its canopy small. It looked as though it had been planted when the canal was completed in 1913, and it would probably outlast the canal, since part of the peepul under which the Buddha achieved enlightenment, 2,500 years ago, is still alive in Sri Lanka. Further on, among the banyans, the ruby flowers of the dak trees, and the yellow of the laburnum, was the electric-blue spray of a Brazilian jacaranda imported I assumed by some extravagant engineer. Two men and two boys were sitting on the lawn.

'Salaam alaikum.'

'Wa alaikum as-salaam. We had been told to expect someone. Please sit down.' I sat on the charpoy string bed and we looked at each other. They knew nothing about me and I knew nothing about them. They were looking at a twenty-eight-year-old Briton, seated on a colonial lawn, in a turban and a sweat-soaked salwar kameez shirt. I was looking at a man, also in salwar kameez, but with a ball-point pen in his breast pocket – an important symbol in an area where less than half the men can write their own name. The other man, standing on the balls of his bare feet, staring at me with his hands forward like a wrestler, looked about sixty. He had shoulder-length grey, curly hair and a short beard. He was wearing an emerald-green kemis shirt and a dark green sarong, a silver ankle ring, four long bead necklaces and an earring in his left ear. I asked if I could boil some water.

'Acha, acha, boil water,' said the old man with the earring and immediately loped off in a half-run, with his hands still held in front of him, to the peepul tree. I watched him build a fire and shout to a boy to bring a bucket of water from the canal. He and the column of smoke seem small beneath the Buddha's tree. The man in green returned with the handleless pot of boiling water in his hands. When

I took it from him, I burned my fingers and nearly dropped the pot. He asked if I'd like some honey and I said I would very much.

Ten minutes later, he returned breathless and sweating with part of a cone of dark wild honey in his hands.

'Where did you get it from?'

'From there,' he pointed to the peepul, 'I just climbed up there to get it.' I thought I could see where the cone must be – it was on a branch, some way out, about forty feet above the ground. It was a difficult climb for a sixty-year-old, even without the bees.

'What do you do?'

'Me?' He laughed and looked at the others, who laughed also. 'Why, I'm a Malang – a Dervish, a follower of Shahbaz Qalander of Sewhan Sharif.'

'And what does it mean to be a Dervish follower of Shahbaz Qalander of Sewhan Sharif?'

'Why, to dance and sing.' And he began to hop from foot to foot, clicking his fingers in the air, and singing in a high-pitched voice:

Sbudam Badnam Dar Ishq,
Biya Paarsa Ikanoon,
The Tarsam Za Ruswaee,
Bi Har Bazaar Me Raqsam.

(Come, behold how I am slandered for my love of God
But slander means nothing to me,
That's why I'll dance in the crowd, my friend
And prance throughout the bazaar.)

'Who wrote that?'

'My sheikh, my master, Shahbaz Qalander, when he lived in the street of the whores.'

'And where are you from?'

'Me? Well my family is originally from Iran not Pakistan – we came like Shahbaz Qalander.'

Laal Shahbaz Qalander was a twelfth-century mystic, what Navaid would call a Dervish. He belonged to a monastic order, wandered from Iran to Pakistan preaching Islam, performed miracles, wrote poems like the one above, and was buried in a magnificent medieval tomb in Sewhan Sharif, a city founded by Alexander the Great. His name, Laal Shahbaz, they say records his brilliant red clothes and his spirit, free as the Shahbaz falcon. He is one of the most famous of a group of mystics who arrived in Pakistan between the eleventh and fourteenth centuries. Their poetry and teachings often celebrate an intoxication with and almost erotic love of God that appears at times to transcend all details of religious doctrine. Their mystical ideas seem to have passed, like the use of rosary beads and the repetition of a single phrase for meditation, from the sub-continent through the Islamic world, and from the crusaders into Christianity. It is they, not the Arab conquerors of the earlier centuries, who are credited with peacefully converting the Hindus of Pakistan to Islam. Indeed, if the shirt of the man in front of me was like Shahbaz's red, not green, he would look, with his long hair and jewellery, exactly like a Hindu sadhu. And he is one of half a million Pakistanis who gather at Shahbaz's tomb once a year to celebrate with dancing and singing.

'Do you not have land?' I asked. 'Work as a farmer?'

'I used to but I gave it all away – I have nothing now.'

'Nothing?'

'I need nothing else. As the prophet says, "Poverty is my pride,"' he replied, smiling so broadly that I wasn't sure whether I believed him.

When it was time to go, the Dervish accompanied me to the gate hobbling slightly on his bare feet.

'Have you always been a Dervish?' I asked.

'No, I was a civil servant in the Customs Department. I worked in the baggage inspection hall of Lahore airport for fifteen years.'

At the canal bank, I took out some money to thank him for the cooking and the honey. But he was horrified.

'Please,' I said, employing a Persian euphemism, 'take it for the children.'

'There are no children here,' the Dervish said firmly. 'Good luck and goodbye.' He shook my hand and, bringing his palm up to his chest, added in a friendlier voice, 'God be with you – walking is a kind of dancing, too.'

When I walked back into Lahore, I met a very different kind of Muslim civil servant. 'Umar is a most influential person,' said Navaid. 'He knows everyone in Lahore, parties all night – meets Imran Khan all the time. And you must see his library. He will explain to you about Islam.'

I was invited to Umar's house at ten at night because he had had three parties to attend earlier in the evening. As I arrived, I saw a heavily built, bearded man in his mid-thirties stepping down from a battered transit van. He was talking on his mobile and holding up his arms so his driver could wrap a baggy, brown pinstriped jacket round him but he managed to hold out a hand to greet me. Still clutching my hand, he led me into a government bungalow of a very similar age and style to the canal rest-house. We removed our shoes and entered a small room, with shelves of English-language books covering all the walls and no chairs. Umar put down the phone, sat on the floor and invited me to sit beside him.

'*Salaam alaikum*, good evening. Please make yourself comfortable. I will tell the servant to get a blanket for you. This is my son, Salman,' he added. The eight-year-old was playing a video game. He waved vaguely but his focus was on trying to persuade a miniature David Beckham to kick with his left foot.

Umar's eyes were bloodshot and he looked tired and anxious. He never smiled, but instead produced rhetorical questions and suggestions at a speed that was difficult to follow.

'*Multan*, but of course,' he said, 'you must meet the Gilanis, the Qureshis, the Gardezis – perhaps as you move up the Punjab – Shah

Jeevna. I know them all. I can do it for you.' All these people were descendants of the famous medieval saints who had converted Pakistan – Navaid's Dervish or Pirs. It was said that they had inherited a great deal of their ancestors' spiritual charisma – villagers still touched them to be cured of illnesses or drank water they blessed to ensure the birth of a male son. They had certainly inherited a great deal of land and wealth from donations to their ancestors' shrines. But Umar, it seemed, was not interested in their Dervish connections. He was concerned with the fact that they were currently leading politicians. Thus the female descendant of a medieval mystic, who once stood in a Punjabi river for twelve years reciting the Qur'an, had just served as Pakistan's ambassador to Washington. Another Dervish, who it is said entered Multan riding on a lion and whipping it with live snakes, and 600 years later is still supposed to stick his hand out of the tomb to greet pious pilgrims, has descendants who have served as ministers in both the federal and provincial governments. Umar knew them all and perhaps because he was rising fast in the interior ministry he was able to help them occasionally.

Umar's mobile rang again. He applauded one of his son's virtual goals, dragged off his shiny silver tie, dark brown shirt and brown pinstriped trousers for a servant to take away, pulled a copy of V. S. Naipaul's *Beyond Belief* off the shelves and pointed me to a chapter, which I slowly realized was about himself – all this while still talking on the phone.

I had seen Umar earlier in the evening at the large marble-floored house of a wealthy landowner and Dervish descendant. A group of clean-shaven young Pakistani men in casual Gucci shirts had been standing beside Umar drinking illegal whisky, smoking joints and talking about Manhattan. And there he had been, in his brown suit and brown shirt, bearded and with a glass of fruit juice in his hand, not only because he was not educated abroad but also, it seemed, because he had very different views about religion.

'My son,' said Umar proudly, putting down the phone, 'is studying at an Islamic school – his basic syllabus is that he must memorize the whole book of the Qur'an – more than 150,000 words by heart – I chose this school for him.' The boy concerned was trying to decide which members of the Swedish squad to include in his dream team. 'You know our relationship with our families is one of the strengths of Islamic culture. I am sorry it will not be possible for you to meet my wife – but she and my parents and children form such a close unit. When you think of the collapse of families in the West, the fact that there is (I am sorry to say it but I know because I have been to the West) no respect for parents – almost everyone is getting divorced, there is rape on the streets – suicide – you put your people in "Old People Homes" while we look after them in the family – in America and perhaps Britain as well I think, there is rape and free sex, divorce and drugs. Have you had a girlfriend? Are you a virgin?'

'No, I'm not.'

'My friend,' he said, leaning forward, 'I was in a car with a friend the other day, we stopped at the traffic lights and there was a beautiful girl in the car next to us. We wanted to gaze at her but I said, and my friend agreed – do not glance at her – for if you do not stare now you will be able to have that woman in heaven.' He paused for effect. 'That is what religion gives to me. It is very late, my friend, I suggest you sleep here tonight and I will drive you back in the morning.'

'Thank you very much.'

'No problem.' He shouted something. The servant entered, laid two mattresses and some sheets on the floor and led Umar's son out. Umar lay on his mattress, propping himself on one arm, looked at me with half-closed eyes and asked, yawning, 'What do you think of American policy in Iraq?'

His phone rang again and he switched on the TV.

I reopened Naipaul's *Beyond Belief*. Naipaul portrays Umar as a junior civil servant from a rural background with naive and narrow

views about religion, living in a squalid house. He does not mention
Umar's social ambitions, his library, his political connections, his 'close
friends' in the Lahore elite. He implies that Umar's father had tracked
down and murdered a female in his family for eloping without
consent.

When Umar had finished on the phone I asked whether he was
happy with this portrait.

'Yes, of course I am – I have great respect for Naipaul – he is a true
gentleman – did so much research into my family. You know most
people's perspectives are so limited on Pakistan. But I try to help
many journalists. All of them say the same things about Pakistan.
They only write about terrorism, about extremism, the Taliban, about
feudalism, illiteracy, about Bin Laden, corruption and bearbaiting and
about our military dictatorship. They have nothing positive to say
about our future or our culture. Why, I want to know?'

He pointed to the television news which showed a Palestinian body
being carried by an angry crowd. 'Three killed today by Israel – why
is America supporting that? Why did they intervene so late in Bosnia
and not in Chechnya? Can you defend the British giving Kashmir to
the Hindus when the majority of the population is Muslim? Is it a
coincidence that all these problems concern Muslims?'

I tried to say that the West had supported Muslims in Kosovo but
he interrupted again.

'Let me tell you what it means to be a Muslim,' he said, lying on his
back and looking at the ceiling. 'Look at me, I am a normal man, I
have all your tastes, I like to go to parties. Two months ago, a friend
of mine said to me, "Umar, you are a man who likes designer clothes,
Ralph Lauren suits, Pierre Cardin ties, Italian shoes, Burberry socks –
why don't you do something for Allah – he has done everything for
you – why don't you do something for him – just one symbol – grow
a beard."' He fingered his beard. 'This is why it is here – just a little
something for Allah.' He was now lying on his mattress in a white

vest and Y-fronts. I didn't really remember his designer clothes.
Perhaps he had been wearing Burberry socks. The new facial hair was,
however, clearly an issue for him. I wondered whether as an
ambitious civil servant he thought a beard might be useful in a more
Islamic Pakistan. But I asked him instead about Dervish tombs. He
immediately recommended five which I had not seen.

'What do you think of the Dervish tradition in Pakistan?' I asked.

'What do you mean?'

I repeated Navaid's definition.

'Oh I see – this kind of thing does not exist so much any more
except in illiterate areas. But I could introduce you to a historian who
could tell you more about it.'

'But what about their kind of Islam?'

'What do you mean? Islam is one faith with one God. There are no
different types. You must have seen the common themes that bind
Muslims together when you walked from Iran to Pakistan. For
example the generosity of Muslims – our attitude to guests.'

'But my experience hasn't been the same everywhere. Iranians, for
example, are happy to let me sleep in their mosques but I am never
allowed to sleep in a mosque in Pakistan.'

'They let you sleep in mosques in Iran? That is very strange. The
mosque is a very clean place and if you sleep in a mosque you might
have impure thoughts during the night . . .'

'Anyway, basically,' I continued, 'villagers have been very relaxed
and hospitable in Pakistan. Every night they take me in without
question, give me food and a bed and never ask for payment. It's
much easier walking here than in Iran. Iranians could be very
suspicious and hostile, partly because they are all afraid of the
government there. In some Iranian villages they even refused to sell
me bread and water.'

'Really, I don't believe this – this is propaganda. I think the Iranian
people are very happy with their government and are very generous

people. I cannot believe they would refuse you bread and water.'

'Listen to me – they did.'

'Well, this may be because of the Iran–Iraq war which you and the Americans started and financed. Do you know how many were killed in that war? That is why Iranians are a little wary of foreigners. But look how the Iranians behaved . . .'

The phone rang again and he talked for perhaps ten minutes this time. I examined the bookcase while I waited. Many of the books were parts of boxed sets with new leather bindings and had names like *Masterpieces of the West, volumes 1–11*.

When he turned back to me again, Umar seemed much more animated. He sat cross-legged on the mattress and leaned towards me. 'My friend,' he said. 'There is one thing you will never understand. We Muslims, all of us – including me – are prepared to die for our faith – we know we will go immediately to heaven. That is why we are not afraid of you. We want to be martyrs. In Iran, twelve-year-old boys cleared minefields by stepping on the mines in front of the troops – tens of thousands died in this way. Such faith and courage does not exist in Britain. That is why you must pray there will never be a "Clash of Civilizations" because you cannot defeat a Muslim: one of us can defeat ten of your soldiers.'

'This is nonsense,' I interrupted uselessly. What was this over-weight man in his Y-fronts, who boasted of his social life and foreign friends, doing presenting Islam in this way and posing as a holy warrior. It sounded as though he was reciting from some boxed set of leather books called *Diatribes against Your Foreign Guest*. And I think he sensed this too because his tone changed.

'We are educated, loving people,' he concluded. 'I am very active with a charity here, we educate the poor, help them, teach them about religion. If only we can both work together to destroy prejudice – that is why people like you and me are so important. All I ask is that the West recognize that it too has its faults – that it lectures us on religious freedom and then the French prohibit Muslim girls from wearing headscarves in school.'

'Do you think Pakistan will become an Islamic state on the Iranian model?' I asked.

'My friend, things must change. There is so much corruption here. The state has almost collapsed. This is partly the fault of what you British did here. But it is also because of our politicians. That is why people like me want more Islam in our state. Islam is our only chance to root out corruption so we can finally have a chance to develop.'

I fell asleep wondering whether this is what he really believed and whether he said such things to his wealthy political friends.

When he dropped me off the next morning, Umar's phone rang again and as I walked away I heard him saying in English:

'Two months ago, a friend of mine said to me, "Umar, you are a man who likes designer clothes, Ralph Lauren suits, Pierre Cardin ties, Italian shoes, Burberry socks – why don't you do something for Allah . . ."'

'A beard?' said Navaid, stroking his own, when I went to meet him again that afternoon at the tomb of Datta Ganj Baksh. 'When people like Umar start growing beards, something is changing. But he must have enjoyed meeting you. His closest friends are foreigners.'

I told Navaid what Umar had said about a clash of civilizations and Navaid shook his head. 'Forget it – don't pay any attention. He was only trying to impress you. He doesn't mean it. People should spend less time worrying about non-Muslims and more time making Muslims into real Muslims. Look at this tomb for example. It is a scandal. They should dynamite this tomb. That would be more useful than fighting Americans.'

Behind us were the tomb gates which Navaid swore were solid gold and which had been erected in the saint's honour by the secular leftist prime minister Zulfiqar Ali Bhutto, Benazir's father. He gave gold gates to the tomb of Shahbaz Qalander in Sewhan Sharif as well. 'That beautiful glass-and-marble mosque in front of us,' continued Navaid, 'was built by General Zia after he executed Bhutto and took power. Then the CIA killed Zia by making his airplane crash. So the marble courtyard we are standing on was built by our last elected prime minister Nawaz Sharif. It hasn't been finished because of the military coup.

'But,' he reflected, 'this Dervish of Shahbaz Qalander is all nonsense. This tomb of Datta Ganj Baksh is nonsense. It has nothing to do with Islam, nothing at all. There is nothing in Islam about it. Islam is a very simple religion, the simplest in the world.'

Beside us a man was forcing his goat to perform a full prostration to the tomb of the saint, before dragging it off to be sacrificed.

'But what do people want from these saints' tombs?' I asked.

'Babies, money – but the Prophet, peace be upon him, teaches that we should not build tombs. They tempt us to worship men not God.'

'And the Dervish?'

'They are cheaters, beggars and tricksters, who sit at the tombs becoming rich by selling stupid medicines.' He led me to the balustrade. 'Look at him, for example.' There was a half-naked man in the dust below the courtyard, where the snake-charmer usually sat. His upper body was tattooed with the ninety-nine names of Allah. 'He's probably got a snake in that box, and,' Navaid dropped his voice prudishly, 'has intercourse with his clients.'

'And the history of these saints, their local traditions?'

'I think looking too much at history is like worshipping a man's tomb. Allah exists outside time. And we should not look at local things too much because Allah does not have a nationality.'

'People say there are seventy-four forms of Islam in Pakistan, what do they mean?'

'Nonsense.' Navaid was being very patient with me. 'Islam is one – one God – one book – one faith.'

'But what do they mean? Are they referring to Qadianis?'

'Of course not ... Qadianis are heretics, they are not Muslims. General Zia has confirmed this in law.'

'Or are they talking about differences between Naqshbandiyah, Wahhibis, Shi'as ...?'

'Pakistani Shi'as are not true Muslims – they are terrorists and extremists – worshipping tombs – they are responsible for these Dervish. But in fact there is only one Islam. We are all the same.' He turned away from the beggar. 'There are no real differences because our God is one.'

The politicians had spent millions on this tomb to win the support of the saint or his followers. But it was only superficially a tribute to the older Pakistan of wandering holy men. Ten years ago, the courtyard of this tomb was the meeting-place for all the diverse groups which Navaid calls Dervish. There was Datta Ganj Baksh, the medieval Sufi himself in his grave, and around him were pilgrims, beggars, mystics, sellers of pious artefacts, drummers, tattooists, dancers, snake-charmers, fortune-tellers, men in trances. But most of these figures were now hidden in the narrow streets below the marble balustrade. The politician's gift both asserted the significance of the saint's tomb and obliterated the cultural environment which surrounded it. Their new architecture seemed to be echoing Navaid's vision of a single simple global Islam – a plain white empty courtyard and a marble-and-glass mosque, bland, clean, expensive – the 'Islamic' architecture of a Middle Eastern airport.

But I still could not understand why Navaid wanted to link these modern Dervishes, one of whom was now shouting drunkenly at us from the street, to the medieval saints. 'Navaid, what do you mean by a Dervish? Are you complaining only about mystics, who belong to a monastic order?'

'Of course not.' Navaid gestured at the man who was now cursing our descendants. 'You think he is a mystic in a monastic order?'

'Then what's he got in common with a Sufi poet or a medieval saint?' I was confused by the way he put medieval intellectuals, mystics and poets in the same group as magicians on the fringes of modern society.

'They're all Dervish – you know where that word comes from, from the Old Persian word *derew*, "to beg"? What they have in common is that they are all rich idle beggars.'

I presumed that explained why he didn't call them 'Fakir', which means 'poor', or 'Sufi', which refers to their clothes.

'But why have you got such a problem with them?' I asked.

'What do you think? Those people down there,' he said pointing at the varied activities in the street, 'wear jewellery, take drugs, believe in miracles, con pilgrims, worship tombs – they are illiterate blasphemers.'

'Alright. But why do you reduce the Sufi saints to the same level?'

'Partly because people like you like them so much. Western hippies love Sufis. You think they are beautiful little bits of a medieval culture. You're much happier with them than with modern Islam. And you like the kind of things they say. What is it the Delhi Dervish Amir Khosrow says?' Navaid recites:

I am a pagan worshipper of love,
Islam I do not need,
My every vein is taut as a wire
And I reject the pagan's girdle.

'That's why I don't like them. Medieval Islamic mystics have no relevance to Islam in Pakistan.'

'Then why do you keep attacking them? Or comparing them to these men in the street?'

Navaid just smiled and wandered off down the courtyard.

Medieval mystics were, I was convinced, not irrelevant. It was they (not Arab invaders) who had converted the bulk of the Hindus to Islam in the first place, while their clothes, practices, poetry and prayers showed strong Indian influences. They were thus both the cause of Pakistani Islam and a reminder of its Hindu past. Furthermore, by drawing the link to the present, Navaid was conceding that the medieval 'Dervish' remained a live tradition in rural Pakistan.

Umar, by contrast, had not felt the need to recognize this. His modern Islam flourished among migrants into Pakistan's cities. He could thus ignore the half a million people who still danced at the tomb of Shahbaz Qalander, and the fact that his friends the politicians were credited with inheriting miraculous spiritual powers from men six centuries dead. His Islam, he felt, was the future. He could safely leave the Dervish behind in a marginalized, illiterate, impoverished world – leave them, in other words, in the rural communities where seventy per cent of Pakistanis still lived.

At last Navaid turned back towards me. 'When I said that Dervish were irrelevant, I meant that Islam is simple, anyone can understand it, it is public, it helps in politics, it does practical things for people. But for a Dervish, religion is all about some direct mystical experience of God – very personal, difficult to explain. Islam is not like that at all – it's there to be found easily in the Qur'an – we don't need some special path, some spiritual master, complicated fasting, dancing, whirling and meditating to see God.'

I could not imagine Navaid dancing. He was a reserved man, basically a puritan by temperament. When he admitted to being anything other than 'a Muslim pure and simple' he said he was a Wahhibi. His Islam, like Umar's, was in a modern Saudi tradition, the tradition of the plain white mosque. It rested on a close attention to the words of the Qur'an, it refused to be tied to any particular place or historical period, it was concerned with 'family life', the creation of Islamic states – an approach that was underwritten by extensive global funding networks. I could guess, therefore, why Navaid was troubled by an otherworldly medieval tradition with strong local roots, personal and apolitical, celebrating poverty, mystical joy, tolerance and a direct experience of God. I could also guess why he wanted to reduce this tradition to a roadside magic trick.

But I might have been wrong. Although Navaid was fifty he was, unusually for a Pakistani man, not married. He claimed never to have had a girlfriend. He was very poor but he did not get a job. Instead he spent his days discussing religion in the courtyards of the ancient mosques in the old city. He could recite a great deal of Persian poetry as well as most of the Qur'an. He was a wanderer and had lived for eleven years in Iran, from just after the revolution. He was a very calm and peaceful man, he had few criticisms of the West and he rejected most of the religious leaders in Pakistan. Although he attacked Dervishes, he knew the name of every obscure Dervish grave in Lahore. I left him by the outdoor mosque of Shah Jehan. He had seated himself under a large peepul tree, to recite a *dhikr*, a repetitive mantra for meditation favoured by the Sufis. As I walked off, I heard him repeating, 'There is no God but God . . .' with a half-smile on his face, entirely absorbed in the words and I was no longer certain who was the Dervish.

TRESPASS

Paul Theroux

This took place forty years ago in Africa, and still I ponder it – the opportunity, the self-deception, the sex, the power, the fear, the confrontation, the foolishness, all the wrongness. The incident has informed one of my early novels and several short stories. It was something like First Contact, the classic encounter between the wanderer and the hidden indigenous person, the meeting of people who are such utter strangers to each other that one side sees a ghost and the other side suspects an opportunity. It won't leave my mind.

I had gone from America to Africa and had been there for almost a year: Nyasaland. Independence came and with it a new name, Malawi. I was a teacher in a small school. I spoke the language, Chichewa. I had a house and even a cook, a Yao Muslim named Jika. My cook had a cook of his own, a young boy, Ismail. We were content in the bush, a corner of the southern highlands, red dust, bad roads, ragged people. Apart from the clammy cold season, June to August, none of this seemed strange. I had been expecting this Africa and I liked it. I used to say: I'll get culture shock when I go back home.

With Christmas approaching I went via a roundabout route to Zambia and on Christmas Eve was sitting in an almost empty and rather dirty bar outside Lusaka, talking to the only other drinkers, a man and woman.

'This is for you,' I said, giving the man a bottle of beer. 'And this is for your wife. Happy Christmas.'

'Happy Christmas to you,' the man said. 'But she is not my wife. She is my sister. And she likes you very much.'

At closing time they invited me to their house. This involved a long taxi ride into the bush. 'Happy Christmas. You give him money.' I paid. They led me to a hut. I was shown a small room, the woman followed me in. I stepped on a sleeping child – there was a squawk – and the woman woke him and shooed him from his blanket into the next room. Then she sat me down, and she undressed me, and we made love on the warm patch on the blanket where the child had been lying.

That was pleasant. I had had a year of women in Malawi, the casual okay, the smiles, the fooling, Jika's bantering, Ismail's leers. But, in the morning, when I said I had to leave, to go to my hotel in Lusaka, the woman – Nina – said, 'No. It is Christmas,' and made a fuss.

The brother – George – overhearing, came into the room and said that it was time to go to the bar. It was hardly eight in the morning; yet we went, and drank all day, and whenever beer was ordered, they said, 'Mzungu' – the white man is paying, and I paid. We were all drunk by mid-afternoon. The woman was taunted for being with a white man. She answered back, drunkenly. The brother stopped several angry men from hitting her. Loud, drunken fights began in the bar.

We went back to the village hut and I lay half-sick in the stinking room. Nina undressed me and sat on me and laughed, and jeered at me.

I was dressing in the morning when she asked me where I was going. Once again, I said I had to leave.

'No. It is Boxing Day.' And she summoned her brother.

'We go,' George said and tapped my shoulder and smiled. His smile meant: You do what I tell you to do. We spent Boxing Day as we had done Christmas: the bar, beer, fights, abuse, and finally that dizzy nauseating feeling of mid-afternoon drunkenness. Another night, Nina's laughter in her orgasm and in the morning the reminder that I was trapped. 'You stay!'

In her refusal to let me go was not just nastiness but a hint of threat. And her brother backed her up, sometimes accusing me of not respecting them. 'You don't like us!'

When I protested that of course I did, they smiled and we ate boiled eggs or cold peeled cassava roots or a whitish porridge, and then off we went to the bar, to get drunk again in the filthy place. And as she grew drunker she pawed me and promised me sex – now an almost frightening thought. Another day passed and I realized I did not know these people at all. The food was disgusting. The hut was horrible. The village was unfriendly, the bar was outright hostile. The beer drinking was making me ill. I was the only *mzungu* in the place – as far as I knew, the only one for miles around. The language that I knew – Chichewa – was not their language, though they spoke it. Their own language – Bemba, I think – was incomprehensible to me, and I knew they were plotting against me when they spoke it – quickly, muttering, so that I wouldn't know what they were saying. I belonged to them, like a valuable animal they had poached. Whenever they wanted money for beer, for snacks, for presents, for whatever reason, they demanded it from me. When I handed it over they were excessively friendly, the woman kissing me, licking my face, pretending to be submissive; her brother and the hangers-on praising me, praising America, saying Britain was bloody shit and asking me to let them wear my sunglasses.

That first night I had been wearing a light-coloured suit. The suit was now rumpled and stained; my shirt was a sweaty mess. They were the only clothes I had.

They said what a great friend I was, but I knew better: I was a captive. They were out of money. My weakness and arrogance had sent me straying into their world from my own world. And I represented something to them – money, certainly; prestige, perhaps; style, maybe. After the first night we never had a sober conversation. I was a colour, a white man, a *mzungu*. I had been captured and they wanted to keep me: I was useful. When they said, as they often did, 'You no go!' I was afraid, because they spoke with such irrational loudness and threat. The boldness in Nina that had attracted me I now feared as wildness. Drinking deafened her and made her a bully as cruel as her brother. George peered at me with odd brown-spotted eyes, as though at an enemy. Sometimes at night I was wakened by the human stinks in the hut.

I think it was the fourth day. My terror was so great and the days so similar I lost track of time. We went to the bar in the morning and at noon they were still drinking – I had lost my taste for it, as I had lost my libido; I just stood there and paid with my diminishing wad okwacha notes. I said, 'I'm going to the *chimbudzi*.'

'Go with him,' Nina said to one of the tough boys hovering near. I protested.

'He will not come back,' she said, and I realized how shrewd she was. She had read my mind, another suggestion of her malevolence. I took off my suit jacket and folded it on the bar.

'Here's my jacket, here's some money. Buy me a beer, get some for yourselves, and hand over the jacket when I get back.' The *chimbudzi* was outside the bar, a roofless shed behind the tin-roofed building, upright bamboos and poles. Maggots squirmed in the shallow bog hole. I stood there and was too disgusted even to unzip, and then I stepped outside, looked around, and seeing no one, I ran – at first cautiously, then really hard until I got to the road and flagged down a car. Of course the man stopped. He was African, I was white, it was Christmas, he needed money for petrol. He took me to my hotel: I had not slept even one night there. I asked him to wait, I paid my bill and got in again and when the driver said where, I said, 'Just keep going.' He drove me twenty miles outside town and dropped me at a roadhouse, where I spent a sleepless night.

What a fool I had been to trespass. The time I spent had not helped me to understand them. Apart from my initial sexual desire, my curiosity, my recklessness, there was no common ground, other than mutual exploitation. I was reminded of who I really was, a presumptuous American. In spite of my politics and my teaching in the bush school, I was little more than a tourist, taking advantage. To me they were desperate Africans, seizing their chance to possess me. It was Tarzan turned inside out, and redefining itself. I saw nothing more. I had simply feared them and I wanted to get out of there. Later the incident kept resonating, telling me who I was. Much more dangerous things happened to me in Africa – serious fights, deportations, gunplay – was there anything more upsetting than being held at gunpoint? But this was my first true experience of captivity and difference, memorable for being horribly satirical. It had shocked me and made me feel American.

WHEN I WAS LOST

↓

James Hamilton-Paterson

Lowly creatures that are watched for a time often seem purposeless in their movements. Time-lapse photography and pheromone detectors can, however, reveal that slugs dash about on explicable courses, criss-crossing their fellows' trails and apparently able to meet or avoid suitors and predators. An analogous overview can equally come to someone passing his fiftieth birthday. On looking back he can see similar patterns emerge from the ostensibly random comings-and-goings of his life so far. In my own case I am unable to ignore the significance of all those unmade roads down which I have chosen to live. The tarmac stops and gives way to a track leading into a forest where, after a mile or two, some paths intersect, one of which heads towards an abode from which no neighbours can be seen. This has been as true of a hillside in Italy as it has for a forgotten province in the Far East. I must recognize that in a trivial sense, at least, I have a need to become lost.

Judging from most accounts, whether in psychoanalytical texts or travellers' tales, to become lost involuntarily is a frightening or unpleasant experience. Being lost in the desert with a dwindling supply of water is a reasonable cause for fear, but mostly the circumstances of becoming lost are not life-threatening. Yet the distress caused seems out of proportion to the temporary inconvenience. Control has failed, vulnerability increases ... One wonders at people's feeble grip on their sense of self, that their entire ontology can be so easily eroded. Suddenly one has an impression of the great energy they must expend daily in order to hold themselves together, an energy which if challenged by unfamiliar surroundings swerves at once to produce rising panic. I note this with curiosity, being by nature rather the opposite: not only content to live in some degree of isolation but on occasion revelling in finding myself stranded in strange territory and out of touch with the rest of the world. This seems to be the one consistent pattern that has emerged from years of slug-like meanderings about the globe.

In fact it is not at all easy nowadays to become physically lost to the extent that one's position cannot be known or one's presence detected. Sadly, the days are pretty much over when travellers could vanish on expeditions with faulty maps and broken compasses, when confronting fate demanded self-reliance and stoicism. A little GPS (Global Positioning System) instrument that tucks into a rucksack pocket will place you anywhere on the planet's surface to within fifty metres; a radio beacon will bounce that position up to a satellite which relays it to emergency services, or else a mobile phone will enable you to swap banalities with your family from the middle of the Gibson Desert. It is the sudden recent spawning of mobile telephones and their babble that eloquently testifies to a deep general insecurity, to a yearning to remain constantly 'in touch'. From all this it is clear that being truly lost has to do with a more than merely physical state; but becoming physically mislaid is a good place to start. I shall not easily forget the exhilaration of a few years ago when for a couple of hours I effectively vanished from the known universe, having fallen through all technological safety nets and being quite beyond finding or rescue.

*

This happened in 1995 on a dive I was making in a Russian manned submersible, one of the twin MIRs deployed by the research vessel *Mstislav Keldysh*. These were the same MIRs used in filming the *Titanic*: two of only four submersibles in the world rated able to descend 6,000 metres (the other two being French and Japanese). I was part of an expedition searching for the Second World War Japanese submarine *I-52* that had been sunk off the coast of West Africa in 1944 while ferrying – among other things – raw opium and two tons of gold from Japan to Occupied France to aid the German war effort. Our expedition had lapsed into the routine of slow sonar searches as it looked for the wreck: days of ploughing up and down in mid-Atlantic on tightly controlled courses, gradually mapping a likely swathe of the ocean floor in a technique jocularly known as 'mowing the lawn'. Each evening the printouts of these scans were examined and possible targets identified. No one knew whether the submarine had reached the bottom intact or as scattered debris. The sea at this point averaged 5,000 metres in depth. Sonar resolution of any object smaller than ten metres long was unreliable. Every few days the *Keldysh* would heave to and prepare to send the submersibles down to see if these blips on the printout were seabed features or pieces of Japanese submarine.

Sending three people in a tiny MIR down into that lightless and crushing pressure five kilometres beneath the ship's keel required careful preparation. At such a depth and distance from help there is really no hierarchy of priorities. Anything from a dozen different kinds of mechanical failure to becoming entangled in wreckage could have fatal consequences. The MIRs had been beautifully designed for full mobility and independence. No wires or cables connected them to the *Keldysh*. Once they had been launched, they were entirely in the hands of their two Russian pilots. Externally they resembled the fuselages of little helicopters, the 'cockpit' being a titanium pressure sphere two metres in diameter into which the three occupants fitted like spacemen of the Sixties surrounded by dials, controls and life-support systems. The rest of the 'fuselage' consisted of mouldings of syntactic foam (a buoyant material which would supposedly always bring the MIR to the surface) and directional motors whose propellers gave the craft complete manoeuvrability. It was this self-contained independence that also gave the MIRs their inherent ability to become lost. The first of the preparations, therefore, was for the ship to drop a pattern of transponder buoys to enable the submersibles to navigate in their dark and unmapped world. These buoys were each tethered to float a hundred feet or so above the seabed. After the dive was over a signal would be sent to them to trigger a release mechanism that would jettison their pig-iron ballast and they would come back up to the surface for recovery. When deployed, each buoy sent out its own signal at a distinctive frequency. The MIR's onboard computers would then interpret this net of signals three-dimensionally so that provided they were within range the crews would always know where they were in relation to the buoys. That, at any rate, was the theory.

Three hours after the hatch had closed on a blue, tropical sky *MIR 1* reached the end of its silent descent, having fallen five kilometres to a precise point on the planet's surface that no human eye had ever seen. This is a strange and wonderful sensation, rare in these post-explorer days. Seen through a porthole in the small circle of light cast by our external lamps the Atlantic bed was a reddish-grey rolling desert. But it was certainly not a lifeless world. Everywhere the dunes and hillocks were scarred with holes and casts that testified to the worms and other biota living in the topmost few feet of the sediment. Shrimp, copepods and occasional rat-tail fish were attracted to the MIR, swimming in and out of its illumination; but whether they were drawn by its lights, its sounds or its faint mechanical smells was anybody's guess. The submersible must have been the noisiest thing to have alighted in those parts since the ocean's formation – or at least since a dying Japanese submarine had sunk there almost forty years ago, its last watertight spaces imploding under the pressure and leaking all manner of sonic energy as well as heat and oil, blood and opium. We were planning to search down here for twelve hours, after which it would take a further three to ascend. Having worked out our position from the transponder buoys, we set off towards the spot where, if the *Keldysh*'s GPS reckoning was correct, we would find the first of the targets we were scheduled to investigate.

As the hours went by and each of the targets was revealed as nothing more than an outcrop of pillow lava or a small dune, our gliding progress a few feet above the seabed became more dreamlike and felt less and less like anything as purposeful as a search. Occasionally our navigator became confused, and we would set down to recalculate our position. Sometimes our slug-like meanderings took us across our previous track and we either saw the marks of our own skids or else passed through a cloud of reddish silt we had disturbed. It was the colour of the Sahara, the sand having fallen there from the winds that blow out of Africa westward across the Atlantic and which often deposit the same desert dust on Florida. I stared and stared through the thick perspex plug that was my window on the primordial world outside, sunk into my own thoughts with an alertness that was attuned entirely to this unknown place into which I had fallen and not at all to finding a piece of military wreckage. Our cramped spherical chamber, around whose icy surface my body was bent on the observer's couch, unaccountably seemed to expand until it became roomy, far too large for the eyeball into which I myself had shrunk. The growing sense of majestic isolation was helped by problems of communication. In an immediate sense, I couldn't converse much with my two crewmates since I spoke no Russian and they scarcely any English. But our difficulties turned out to be more radical than that. During the descent the pilots had been in intermittent voice contact with the *Keldysh* as she basked in the sunshine somewhere miles overhead. Water is, of course, an excellent conductor of sound, though a poor one of radio waves. The MIR's communication system was therefore not based on radio. Instead, it converted ordinary speech to a higher frequency, amplified it and broadcast the sounds into the water column. Far away the *Keldysh* received them, converted them back to the frequency of normal speech, and could hear our crew's voices. Likewise, we could hear Control. Any nearby creatures such as fish or whales would have heard our speech as a shrill babbling squeal. As we were going down our shipmates' voices had become more and more faint and distorted as the gulf between us opened up. Now, nothing so intensified the feeling of having landed on an unknown planet beyond all human reach as the occasional ghostly voices of our friends speaking from brilliant tropic air. Gradually, their remarks became unintelligible, the vestiges of syllables echoing away into the limitless deep that encased us. I remember a story by Ray Bradbury that used to affect me very much as a teenager. There is an explosion aboard a spaceship not far from earth, and several of the crew are scattered into space in their suits, each helplessly propelled on his own trajectory away from the others. For as long as they remain within range of each other the doomed men talk over their radios, their voices growing ever more distant until one by one they fall silent. Before they do, they variously try to bring about hurried reconciliations or are amazed at the grandeur of their fate. One is swept up in a cloud of asteroids to be carried along for eternity in their orbit about the sun. Another is captured by earth's gravity and knows he will burn up on re-entry. The story ends when at dusk somewhere in Illinois a child looks up and sees a shooting star. Some residue of this tale inhabited me on the bottom of the Atlantic as the voices of our shipmates faded. The MIR had drifted into a complex of valleys formed by high dunes. Suddenly, no external sound was breaking the loudspeaker's soft hiss. At the same time, the transponders' navigation signals were likewise blocked.

From this moment we became lost to the world, lost to humanity and to the twentieth century. We had fallen off all known maps. We were as out of touch as a space capsule passing behind the moon, our presence no more than inferred from our last known position and supposed trajectory. The two Russians lay imperturbably as we hummed along, the pilot gazing through his port and his colleague fiddling on a borrowed laptop computer. They munched peanuts and from time to time exchanged a comment I couldn't understand. I had never felt more alone, more at the mercy of natural physics, more exhilarated. How many times in my choirboy days on that far-off planet earth had I sung the words '*Justorum animae in manu dei sunt*'? The souls of the righteous are in the hands of the Lord. I was not righteous; I did not think I had a soul; I did not believe there were any merciful hands out there where our halogen lamps shed a crawling speck of light on creation's primordial darkness. Indeed, it seemed probable that creation had yet to take place fully. Despite the occasional fish and the ubiquitous signs of other life being lived at a pressure of 500 atmospheres, the world beyond our titanium sphere was somehow pre-Genesis. The Garden of Eden was yet to come. I was an anachronism, a time traveller, non-existent. We were more than lost: we were expunged from the record. And yet I felt secure.

One need not have read Anna Freud's paper *About Losing and Being Lost* to sense that this state is not a simple proposition, either psychologically or philosophically. To take her example of a child becoming separated from its parents in a department store: the boy might have found a toy in which he is engrossed, while his parents who can't see him fall into a complete panic, at once imagining all kinds of horrors have befallen their child. From the boy's perspective he is not lost at all until the toy no longer distracts him and he begins to miss his parents. In other words one is never lost until one feels lost. My first remembered experience of this prosaic oddity was during the Festival of Britain in 1951. My parents had taken me, aged nine, to the

South Bank Exhibition where I was having an interesting time looking
at the Dome of Discovery and the Skylon when suddenly I became
aware of loudspeakers. As soon as I heard them I realized I had been
hearing them on and off for the previous ten minutes, repeating the
same message which I had ignored. The message they were repeating
was my own name; followed by instructions on how to find my
parents. The news to me was not only that I was officially lost, but that
I hadn't recognized my own name when it was spoken by a public
address system because public address systems spoke only other
people's names. I was me, myself, the world; but I needed no public
identity. It was only then I felt suddenly alone amid the swirl of
strangers, the lights and noise. When we were finally reunited my
father was, inevitably, furious in a way that seemed to me entirely
unjust. After all, he had lost me, not I him.

Such things came back to me more than forty years later aboard
MIR 1 as we and our mother ship became lost to one another. I began
to muse about the pleasure I was taking in our predicament; about
how I didn't feel lost, had never really felt lost in my entire life, only
disorientated in a strange place. At this moment I was merely out
of touch, which I experienced as a form of being freed. What made
others panic was for me a solace. The echiuroid worms beyond the
porthole were endlessly fascinating. Everywhere were hillocks of
sand with a hole from which little puffs of sediment were emitted from
time to time, like smoke signals telling of absorbed life processes going
on inside. It was as if the whole burden of my previous life – friends,
loves, pleasures, interests – had been shed like a lump of pig iron and
I was free to roam for ever in this pre-Genesis landscape in a kind
of weightless trance. Many hours later, when I had been restored
to the upper air and the late twentieth century, I was amazed that I
should ever have contemplated sacrificing my identity for permanent
communion with that dark and primitive dimension. And yet enough
of the experience's pungency lingered – lingers still – to remind me that

I had been neither hallucinating nor anoxic but had briefly crossed a threshold that led to a world whose profound interest to me depended on neither thought nor desire. I would never have believed such a thing possible. In some way it approached a state of complete satisfaction, which certainly threw an ironic cast over our mission in the MIR as well as over the entire expedition.

For down there in the eternal chill of blank and fathomless water we were looking for a lost object, a Japanese submarine; and anyone who has dipped into Freud (or Zen Buddhism) will know that the search for lost objects is always doomed because they can never be found. The Lost Object is the outcome of the structure of desire, and being party to this is the lot of all mortals. Unbelievably, it is a form of loss that can even precede possession, as witness ultrasound scans showing infants *in utero* sucking their thumbs as a substitute for the breast they have yet to encounter. As adults, of course, we can satisfy our wishes imaginatively if sadly, summoning back our dead or fantasizing ourselves rich or erotically triumphant; but such attempts do not depend on reality. Needs and urges can be fulfilled; desire, never. I had plenty of time in the weeks aboard the *Mstislav Keldysh* to speculate about this expensive search for the *I-52*. Whenever I wondered about what it was we were really looking for, our professed target seemed to give a smart sideways jump. It was like trying to focus one's eye on a piece of retinal debris. We were looking for the submarine, of course. Only no; we were actually looking for the two tons of gold she was allegedly carrying. But nobody really wants gold, the stuff itself, which is useful only for being locked in vaults as dark as the one it was currently lying in. What one wants are the things it stands for, the things it can buy. But the things one can buy with it are never quite what one thought one wanted, and themselves stand for something else ... And on and on it skids, pursuing itself relentlessly around the desire that can never be fully satisfied. The one thing people believe they

most long for, and then get, always carries within it a tiny seed of
disappointment. Even a Nobel turns out to be a second prize after all.
No one ever gets their hands on complete fulfilment. Thus desiring
and losing turn into a single topological figure that chases its own tail.
There is no lost object without desire; there is no desire without the
lost object. The circle cannot be broken. But for a strange long moment
it can perhaps be sidestepped, as when I stared out of *MIR 1*'s
porthole on to a world that was not lost, and which I was not finding,
but whose busy physics and skeins of phosphorescence underlay
things much as the galaxies and nebulae of the night sky overhang life
on dry land.

Our expedition never did find the Japanese submarine, as it
happened, but a subsequent expedition did. Ah, it might be said:
surely those others found the thing they were looking for, the object
that had been lost? But no. They found the submarine all right, but to
date they have not found the gold. Not a single ingot. Not even
enough to make a pen nib. Given the accelerating costs of deep-sea
recovery and the diminishing price of gold, it may no longer be worth
launching another expedition. Besides, dark rumours are circulating
of top-secret wartime hoodwinking that hint the gold was perhaps no
longer on board the submarine when she sank. The desire goes on, but
sometimes the pursuit has to be dropped from sheer weariness or
inanition and a new goal fixed.

For almost two of our seventeen hours' dive *MIR 1* remained lost to
the world, threading the maze of dunes in silence, searching with-out
success for our third target. At last our pilot took us up above the
sedimentary hilltops, and there we once again picked up the far-off
pinging of the transponder pattern. The world had returned to us. The
instant our onboard navigation equipment began buzzing and winking
and resetting its coordinates we re-entered the dimension of normality.
Where we next investigated, a mile or two away, the terrain was gently
undulating, like Home Counties pastureland done in ochre. There were

the same echiuroids, the same little crabs, starfish and holothurians; but now they could be assigned a position. Now, too, voices began ebbing faintly back through the loudspeaker. 'They are asking how you are,' the co-pilot told me in halting German. Once again I had failed to recognize my name over a PA system, although there was some excuse this time since the speaker was Russian and the mournful echoes were bouncing around the water column as though we were being addressed at the bottom of the world's deepest well.

So what of that world among the dunes where for a while we had been truly lost? Had the same vast tonnage of ocean that had cut us off from all signals and voices from the upper world also attenuated desire and rendered meaningless notions of loss and being lost? It had certainly felt like that: a dimension so different as to abrogate the norms of the human psyche. (It must be said, however, that the human body had remained cheerfully unaffected, inconveniently asserting its desire to pee, its pleasure in eating peanuts, and its susceptibility to the cold that penetrated the sphere.) It could only be called a lost world in the sense that it had never before been found. Its fascination for me was that it nevertheless felt like something familiar after which I had always hankered, and which I would now safely carry with me to the grave.

In the three chill hours as we slowly ascended like a bubble rising in a tower of oil, I wondered how it would be to have done the trip alone, to have found oneself alone and cut off on the ocean floor: a fantasy that was always punctured by sharp actuality. The whole experience had only been possible because of skilfully manipulated technology. If I had never felt fear it was surely because I had complete faith in the capsule and its pilots, despite all the pre-trip warnings and disclaimers of responsibility, and despite accepting that the chances of catastrophic failure or a trapped death from oxygen starvation were always there. However often the *Keldysh* deployed her submersibles it was never treated as a humdrum or routine matter. It was a solemn thing to visit the roots of the sea. No MIR ever went down without two highly qualified and sober pilots. The only imaginable way in which I might have found myself alone on the seabed would have been if both pilots had been struck down simultaneously by fatal food poisoning or something, in which case merely being lost would have been the least of my worries. In order to examine the true implications of getting lost one obviously needed to discount all those cases where one's life was in real danger, when fear was justified. Actually, the only interesting component of getting lost was irrational fear, and I was now sure this was something that happened to other people rather than to me.

The best thing about the end of our dive was that we came up well after midnight, so we were not greeted by blinding sunshine and rows of faces lining the decks. It was a more private affair. The necessary crew and a few colleagues were there beyond the puddle of light cast by the deck lamps on the black and rocking ocean. This grateful darkness helped the transition to the everyday world in which one was going to have to do the rest of one's living. The MIR was winched up, swung inboard, and deposited gently on its cradle. The hatch was popped and we emerged, a little stiff and breathing in the fresh Atlantic breeze with pleasure after so many hours of canned and recycled air. The mother ship seemed not inclined to be punitive about its precious child having strayed out of contact for so long. Instead, we were congratulated on our safe return and commiserated with over our failure to find the submarine. Submarine? Oh, that submarine ... I had completely forgotten about the pretext for our dive, our search for the lost naval object. Well, yes, I said; that was a bit of a disappointment. But it wasn't, of course. The entire experience had been so amazing I had scarcely given the *I-52* a thought.

I carried with me back to my cabin a bottle of pee and the knowledge that I had been well and truly lost, but had never felt it and now knew why. Or at least, I knew it was a consistent and lifelong quirk of mine never to be completely lost, despite having no sense of direction and a laughable ability to have no idea where I am. But that is not being lost, and it seldom produces in me more than minor irritation and quite often a serendipitous pleasure. A secure sense of one's identity does not depend on geographical whereabouts, after all. Anna Freud seemed to think the children she studied felt lost largely because they had not been securely enough loved, and promptly *got* lost to prove it. I note that a recent report by the University of Maastricht on primary-school children's fears cites the commonest of these as spiders, blood and getting lost, which suggests phobias rather than something more rational. Global positioning systems cannot help orient the psyche, and for the susceptible there is an awful lot of Elsewhere in the world. Luckily for slugs they don't get lost. Maybe the trick is to find your surroundings so engrossing, so diverting, as to be unaware that anyone is missing you. The chances are nobody is.

CAPTAIN SCOTT'S BISCUIT

Thomas Keneally

I first went to Antarctica in 1968, for somewhat under a fortnight. In those days one could visit Antarctica only as a member of an official group, and the American ambassador in Canberra, a noble soul who would later give his life to a disease caught while working for an Episcopalian aid agency in Ethiopia, invited me to go with him, as a member of his party. He was also taking his twelve-year-old son, whom he hoped would become the youngest person ever to stand at the South Pole itself. I am for ever grateful to this man, the sober and genial Bill Crook, through whom I was able to experience Antarctica in so profound a way that it recurred in my dreams for decades to come. In particular, the huge Transantarctic Mountains, complicated peaks and glaciers which start behind Cape Adare on the northern limit of the Ross Sea and run south across the continent, returned to me in sleep. Scott's own beloved and much researched Royal Society Range, visible from the bases across McMurdo Sound, are just one part of this transcendent chain.

Another companion on the 1968 trip was a young US Air Force colonel named Alex Butterfield. We and Mr Crook and his son shared the giant landscapes and improbable, barely polluted vistas of

Antarctica. Only at McMurdo Sound was there any garbage, including a litter of crashed aircraft piled up on the edge of the tide crack's jumbled ice. While Antarctica seems apolitical, and was and still is managed, apparently fraternally, according to principles framed by the 1959 Antarctic Treaty, political realities foreshortened our 1968 journey a little. Nixon was elected President, and Bill Crook, a Democrat, needed to resign his position in Canberra, while Alex Butterfield would go to Nixon's White House as deputy assistant to the President, and would have a not inestimable part in the Watergate scandal. When asked by the Senate Watergate Committee whether there were any recording devices in the White House, he said he had hoped he would not be asked that, but admitted there were tapes, and so, with a word, changed history and became a Republican Party pariah.

But none of this happened before the Crook group had experienced the bulk of Ross Island, that historic mass in McMurdo Sound which is cemented to the rest of Antarctica by the Ross Ice Shelf, an august shelf of ice the size of France. Nor before we had visited Scott's two huts – one of them on the edge of the McMurdo Sound station – and Shackleton's haunted Cape Royds hut, and lived beneath the midnight sun, and been to the South Pole on a plane which landed and took off on skids. And at that featureless, 10,000-feet-high South Pole, the younger Crook stood, suffering from mild altitude sickness; a sturdy lad though, who did not flinch in the glare of the polar plateau. We lined up around the striped barber's pole which had been put in place during the International Geophysical Year (IGY), ten years before. In that decade, it had moved a little off ninety degrees south. The great ice sheet covering the Pole was always moving infinitesimally outwards down to the sea.

This trip augmented a tendency of mine to see Antarctica as another state of being. Nobody was a native of the place. Only in the past sixty or seventy years had a scatter of human myths become associated with it. But even in its massiveness it had made no tribe unto itself. It had provoked no native tongue, no rites, no art, no jingoism. Its landscapes existed without the permission of humanity. And everything I looked at, even the nullity of the pole, produced jolts of insomniac chemicals into my system. It was not landscape, it was not light. It was super-landscape, super-light, and it would not let you sleep.

In 1968, among all the science and bulldozers and energy of the McMurdo Sound station, no one seemed to be doing much for the huts of the 'Heroic Era'. On the northern point of the bay next to the McMurdo Sound station stood, unattended, Scott's Hut Point hut, the *Discovery* hut. This hut had been used by Scott's 1901–04 party, and been pressed into use again by Shackleton in 1908, and then once more during Scott's journey to the Pole in 1910–12. During the First World War, Shackleton's tragic Ross Sea party had sheltered in it as well. Symbolizing all this Antarctic peril undertaken willingly, a cross on the small hill above the hut commemorated Seaman Vince, one of Scott's men, who perished of hypothermia in 1902.

Standing utterly unlocked in 1968, the hut was sunk in its old, ice-dried timbers in a bank of ice. There was accumulated ice inside sections of the hut as well, but also the remnants of Edwardian derring-do: boxes of Fry's cocoa, preserved fruit, condiments, tins of Huntley & Palmers biscuits, items of harness, old magazines and fragments of newspapers. There was no organization taking responsibility for Scott's huts at Hut Point and Cape Evans, or for Shackleton's at Cape Royds.

Those who took anything out of any of the huts could excuse themselves in the belief that they were merely saving a relic from gradual climatic destruction. Thus, glibly self-absolved, I approached an open tin of Huntley & Palmers hard-tack biscuit, the hard tack which soldiers from 1914 to 1918 ate in the trenches. I took two-thirds of a biscuit as a souvenir. Antarctic explorers, including Scott and his doomed four, subsisted on a diet of this biscuit, often mixed with and softened by water and pemmican, that is, chunks of compacted, dried meat. These staples, hard tack and pemmican, proved an inadequate diet, and helped weaken the young Shackleton to the point that Scott sent him home from the 1901 expedition. Ultimately, the limitations of pemmican and hard tack would stop Shackleton ninety-seven miles from the Pole in 1909, and then destroy Scott himself in 1912.

The two-thirds of a biscuit I took, hard to begin with when manufactured in the late nineteenth or early twentieth century, had been near ossified by Antarctica's perpetual freeze. So I brought it home with me as if it were more a fossil than a food, and displayed it, in a glass case.

It has only been as time went by that I, like other members of the general public, became educated by an increasing awareness of conservation. I began to feel Scott's biscuit should be returned. I saw the 1985 television series, *The Last Place on Earth*, and the scenes of Scott's big man, Petty Officer Taffy Evans, raving and howling in the wake of the sledge returning from the Pole, and dying in his tracks. For a second it was as if he was making a claim on my biscuit. But to whom to return the hard tack, and by what mechanism? I decided I would take it back to the hut myself, if ever I got to Antarctica again.

The resolve to return to Antarctica grew in me as I got older. Some friends went on a Russian ship from Ushaia in Argentina down to the Antarctic Peninsula. The Peninsula is the Antarctic continent's tadpole tail, and has beautiful glaciers and hence beautiful mountains, and much subantarctic wildlife. But it is not beyond the Antarctic Circle, and is on the wrong side of Antarctica for anything to do with Scott. I decided last year I would try to go anyway. Ships commonly used in these excursions are ice-breaking or hull-strengthened Russian vessels chartered by American, Australian and other adventure-travel companies. These companies came up readily on the Internet. I found that journeys from South America to the Peninsula and to South Georgia, the island on which Shackleton is buried, are largely booked up a year ahead, and it was only by accident that I discovered that journeys to the other side of Antarctica, to the area I felt I knew and from which I'd taken Scott's biscuit – the Ross Sea, McMurdo Sound, Ross Island, the great volcano Erebus, the Transantarctic Mountains and the Ross Ice Shelf which was the path to the Pole – were also planned.

I found there was a berth available on the last trip for the summer season, throughout February, on an ice-breaker named the *Kapitan Khlebnikov*.

I fell for the *Khlebnikov* the first time I saw a picture of it. It had an honest look, as if one would not need to dress for dinner – indeed the sort of ship on which there would be a good, rowdy bar operating during Antarctic midnights, as well as ample deck-space upon which to stand alone, rugged-up, in awe and exaltation. It weighed 12,000 tons and its bows were blunt and potent for crushing fields of ice. Its high castle, in which the cabins were placed, would guarantee that on the way to and beyond the Antarctic convergence, the zone of turbulence where Antarctic waters meet the waters of temperate oceans, we would experience a testing roll. Six Zodiacs were lashed down on the flight deck to take us to shore, and two helicopters. Its eighty crew members abounded with Arctic and Antarctic experience. This stubby, twenty-year-old ice-breaker promised to deal with the great radial skirts of ice which gird Antarctica.

So I was still in a childlike state of excitement as we drove through the tunnel in the mountain south of Christchurch, in New Zealand's South Island, and came down to Lyttelton, the exquisite, emerald, volcanic caldera which served Scott and Shackleton as their point of departure for the voyage south. Through a banal, corrugated-iron fence at the bunkering wharf of Lyttelton we lugged our luggage with half-smiles, like children entering a secret garden. Stepping over oil hoses, we climbed the stairs from the wharf to our ice-breaker. The air was filled with the shouts and talk of Russian seamen. A young ship's doctor, a Tasmanian, helped us get our gear to our two-bunk cabin. It was all wonderful. We exclaimed. The en suite bathroom seemed a miraculous luxury in such a romantic, journeyman lump of steel as the *Khlebnikov*.

The first night and day at sea were benign. We met our sixty or so fellow passengers – Americans, Australians, British, Germans, a Belgian or two, New Zealanders and a solitary Canadian. A blessed company, we thought, and so it proved to be. We exclaimed about the quality of the food – we had presumed that we would be eating tough-guy style to match the expedition; that it would be borscht and herring. The choice of three menus astonished us, and seemed in comforting tension with the colder and colder seas, the icier and icier air, the polar memoirs we were all immersed in, and the unarguable Antarctic conditions into which we were being taken.

The second night introduced us to the circumpolar current, a definite but irregular line in the ocean, visible from space as a huge pleat. The colder Antarctic waters here begin their dive beneath the warmer waters from the northern oceans, and the zone is full of the turbulence and violence of this meeting. Wind howled and the ship rolled to angles of more than thirty-five degrees. The passengers might have been temporarily sick but were generally delighted by the experience. Many of them had been here before. Their memory of things was validated by wind and rough seas. They were returning to the most intense of their memories. They drank merrily, but were slightly awed to meet the ship's officers, Captain Petr Golikov, the mates, the radio officer, the engineering officer, the two helicopter pilots. As the swell mounted, these were to be our guides to the underworld. In the morning, the expedition leader, Kate Adie, an American, greeted us by intercom with a resonating '*Dobroe Utro!* Good morning!' She and the captain, in consultation, would determine where the *Khlebnikov* would take us. To celebrate our southern-ocean initiation, the ship's notice board sported the words of Samuel Taylor Coleridge: 'The fair breeze blew, the white foam flew, the furrow followed free,/We were the first that ever burst into that silent sea.' Well, maybe not the first, but at least it felt like it when we stood on the flying bridge seeking ice, and Antarctica's first scalding air numbed our faces.

Among our company was a Scot who was researching a book on the lesser-known Antarctic explorers, and five Australian scientists who were being accompanied to the Australian subantarctic island, Macquarie Island, to pursue research into the irregularities of the earth's magnetic field, geology, marine biology, seals, penguins, albatrosses, etc. The presence of the scientists gave us tourists a sense of being part of a noble cause. We were also to pick up a group of four men, three New Zealanders and an Englishman, stuck by ice at Cape Adare, our first point of contact with the Antarctic coast. The drama of genuine Antarctic need augmented our long days.

The earliest icebergs we spotted were irregular in shape – eroded, conical, or else rather like ruined fortresses. But then large tabular bergs, higher than the ship, and some hundreds of metres long, appeared and displayed their water-level blue caverns. The first whales we met were orcas, and orcas and minke whales would accompany us the rest of our journey, with humpbacks and an occasional southern right whale thrown in. The populations seemed enthusiastic and numerous, but further north the whaling fleet of Japan, which had not signed the International Whaling Commission's Charter, awaited their arrival.

The ship traversed and broke ice bars and then met solid banks of ice, and began to break it, growling, transferring seventy tons of ballast water back to the stern to raise the ship by the bows, then pumping it forward at great speed to bring the bows crashing down. I stood in the bows transfixed by the fracture of ice, the way it moved, its sundry, plastic varieties. And distantly, a mere ice blink, Cape Adare, the Transantarctic Mountains and the coast running west-wards, began to show themselves. Cape Adare grew more and more massive throughout the day. We could see the tops of mountains fifty miles away, and all distance was foreshortened by the clarity of air, so that the chain of coast seemed not mere geology but the instantly legible manifesto of gods. Amid the mountains ran the broad all-altering hands of glaciers. Everything one had ever expected of the inhuman continent, all in a second's glance!

Adare, a black volcanic cape at the western entrance to the Ross Sea, was the site of the landing of the first European, Carsten Borchgrevink, in 1895. Borchgrevink, a Norwegian who had settled in Australia as a schoolteacher, in 1899 had built the first hut of the Heroic Era there on unsuitable Cape Adare, a venue for vicious gravity-fed winds. The four men we were to collect were working on the restoration of the hut, and the *Khlebnikov* was to take them off when we called there. We received instructions on how to visit the fragile hut – there are now protocols in place – and what our demeanour should be towards the some 4,000 Adélie penguins who lived on the strand beneath the high plug of granite – no sudden disturbing advances amongst the chicks of the rookery; photographs to be reflectively taken, not from a challenging human level, but from penguin level.

By mid-afternoon the captain had got the ship to work, slicing open areas in the ice, but we reached a point where there was nowhere for the ice we penetrated and cracked to go. We could see, beneath the huge black-and-white face of Adare, the fast ice with its necklace of brilliant but dominant icebergs. In the end, the helicopters went to get the men and their gear, and they were welcomed aboard, telling us how it had been camping in tents by Borchgrevink's hut in 200-kilometre-per-hour gales. I mentioned that from my lay-perspective across the sea ice, it looked as if they were captives of the Erl King. 'That's how we bloody felt,' they told me.

The fourth member of the group was, improbably, an urbane British heritage architect who genially confessed that at the height of their discomfort on the Cape, he had made a slighting remark about his life's task having been to restore some of Britain's finest buildings, and his having no interest in restoring garden sheds in Antarctica. To the New Zealanders, however, these Ross Sea huts of the Heroic Era were the garden sheds of the gods.

Captain Golikov assured us he would do his best to get us into Cape Adare on our way back north again. We took off in helicopters in teams of eight and inspected the region – huge Mount Minto in Australian Antarctica, Mount Melbourne, the Rennick Glacier, and such a glut of ice, and the bergs golden in the high late-afternoon sun. ↴

Satellite pictures had recently shown two enormous icebergs, slabs of the Ross Ice Shelf itself, which were preventing ice from escaping from the Ross Sea. Icebergs feature in the popular mind as the accused in the sinking of the *Titanic*, and thus a North Atlantic phenomenon. But ninety-three per cent of the world's icebergs are Antarctic, and genuinely titanic. The one named B15 guarded the approaches of the southern Ross Sea. (These bergs, by the way, are given code letters according to the section of the Ross Ice Shelf they break away from.) B15 was said to be the size of Jamaica. Then, at an inconvenient angle far out in the Ross Sea, C19 lay diagonally, like a 200-kilometre-long lock gate, completing the job of blocking in the ice of Antarctica's classic quarter. The captain took us looking for C19, yet it seemed that it found us, a perfect tabular wall of ice, fifty metres high and filling the horizon. This great vehicle had earlier, according to satellite pictures, collided with the penguin rookery at Cape Crozier, producing a seismic effect picked up in Hawaii, and a cataclysm for the penguins. Collisions with other hefty icebergs had also affected its drift. We could not see atop it, and its cliffs had not been indented by waves or by melt, so that it was possible to look at its flanks as representing the point at which it had broken from the Ross Ice Shelf, along one clean, enormous crack. The captain, to make up for our non-landing at

Adare, decided that his helicopters would transport us up there, to the top.

Heavily dressed, we flew up over the coast of this republic-unto-itself, and on inland, if *inland* is the term, to an uncrevassed area marked out by the ship's staff with red flags. An ice bar and an igloo had been built there, on C19. Landed, we could not see the edges of the berg, nor sea ice, nor the ship, so that C19 had become a new version of the earth, limitless white tending away into a sky clear to the south and to threatening snow clouds at the north. It was a strange, vertiginous and unearthly experience. In the immaculate snow, I carved my grandchildren's names, in the hope that subsequent snowfalls and giant gales would sweep loose squally snow from them, and treat the indentations lightly for a while. It will takes decades for it to break up and melt.

The sea ice was only a year old, but the ice of this berg was from water that fell on Antarctica when our ancestors lived as nomads in Central Asia, some 10,000 to 15,000 years ago, and the air bubbles trapped within were fossil air, a guide to the atmosphere, lower in carbon dioxide, the air that early Sumerians, the first Chinese farmers, and the few thousand migratory ancestors of Europeans were fortunate to breathe. By 2050, they say, carbon dioxide will have reached twice the level, 550 parts per million, that existed before the Industrial Revolution. There is argument about the effect of this on earth – powerful scientific opinion predicting a rise in temperature, a severe global warming beyond our previous experience. Hence CO^2 readings of the bubbles in such great ice masses as C19 are considered indicators of danger, even though some scientists argue that our CO^2-laced modern atmosphere has given increased benefit to plants. Laypeople, confused by conflicting scientific opinion – the scientists, like us, being too recent in their observations of the Antarctic continent – we celebrated this ice and air from before human cultural self-consciousness! We played, like stiffly dressed children, on an antiquity.

*

Whenever I could, I stood in the bows of the *Khlebnikov* feeling the impact in my spine as it growled its way in sunshine, shattering ice apart. We moved into a canyon in the huge Campbell Ice Tongue, just to have a look, and saw a world of heroic ice-fractures. This was not seamless and immaculate ice, like the ice of C19, but ice dramatically marked with the soil it had picked up years past, while grinding its way down from the Campbell Glacier. It was full of cracks and arches of pressure, and the soil streaks were vertical, not horizontal, such was the pressure under which this ice had travelled.

Terra Nova Bay, where the Italians have a base, lay nearby, between the Campbell and Drygalski Ice Tongues. Many of the ship's passengers, including my wife, would make their first footfall on the Antarctic continent at the base, which is said to be a model of its kind. It is occupied only in the summer, with all its geodesic and other equipment maintained throughout the winter by computer from Italy. All waste is shipped out, which is also the rule with the *Khlebnikov*. When one of the passengers threw up while crossing sea ice in McMurdo, that waste too was shovelled up, to be returned ultimately to the outer world.

The *Khlebnikov* had made its way to within a few kilometres of shore at Cape Royds, the protected cove where Shackleton's 1908 *Nimrod* hut stood, when we saw – another ship! This unfamiliar vessel, parked in the sea ice, was a psychological challenge to all we felt. It revealed us to be tourists, like those others over there. Their ship was merely ice-strengthened, and we pitied them for being on it when we saw them take off for Cape Evans across the ice in open people-movers – the Antarctic version of a tourist bus. The sight opened the question, how much tourism can Antarctica stand? That is, how much could it take of us?

The Americans intend to attempt to put down a track – to call it a road is perhaps melodramatic – across the Ross Ice Shelf, up the

Beardmore Glacier, and to the Pole. There are logistical reasons for it, all to do with the support of the base at the South Pole. Many argue that anything artificial would not survive for long on the fractured face of the Beardmore: the track wouldn't last. But even the idea of such a track sucks the myth out of the Pole, the myth on which every Westerner of my generation has been raised. And the existence of fast-ice airports, such as Williams Base at McMurdo, which could hold the weight of commercial planes, raises the possibility of fly-in tourism, by whose standards our approach by sea might one day look blessedly idyllic, primitive and adventurous. The idea of large-scale tourist operations in McMurdo Sound is absolutely possible and, to most even of the *Khlebnikov*'s passengers, horrifying in conservation terms. Will conservation win out over tourism? I seem to remember that it never has. Boeing has been the great democratizer of travel experience. And each of us would willingly exclude others, while excusing ourselves, the essential tourists, from any such edict. So the Ross Sea Novotel and McMurdo Sheraton could be built within this century. Children will gambol on the ice shelf where Scott exhaled his last, pained breath.

We walked to Shackleton's hut on a track laid across sea ice that seemed solid as earth. The hut itself lies in a depression in black rock, not far from an Adélie penguin rookery. It was the base for Shackleton's 1909 journey to within ninety-seven miles of the Pole. Its interior is, like all of them, full of intimate presences, but the vulnerability of the supplies and belongings that men left here is still obvious. Tinned peas stacked by the hut wall are rusting open and displaying their desiccated contents. A question for the preservationists: what should be done with this sort of artefact, and artefacts of all kinds scattered about the site? For example, by the pony stable still stands a wheel of the first automobile introduced in Antarctica, a Johnson. Where should it be placed, and how maintained? Scott's Cape Evans hut presents the Antarctic Heritage Trust with the same sort of problems. This is the one from which he left to go to his death, and is far more spacious than Shackleton's, and more openly 'atmospheric'. No other expedition produced so many known names – Dr Wilson, the two Evanses, Birdy Bowers, Ponting the photographer, Oates, Cherry-Garrard, author of the ultimate Antarctic text, *The Worst Journey in the World*, Petty Officer Crean, etc., etc. This hut, too, lies in a depression north of its cape, but not really enough of one to provide much protection. Scott somehow fitted in many 'gentlemen explorers' who had separate quarters from the 'men' – seamen, craftsmen, pony handlers. All was very skilfully and intimately secreted within the hut. In the pony stables next door, metal sheets were hammered against the timber to stop the continual kicking of the ponies from disturbing the sleep of the expeditioners.

Scott's bed in his personal alcove, and his study-table with its notebooks and newspapers, are affecting to this day, to the point that some of our fellow passengers found our night-time visit the central experience of their journey. From the hill above, where there is a monument to Shackleton's dead, it was the sight of the hunched hut amid the massive indifference of the Sound's ice, and the streaks of volcanic black and white which delineated offshore islands, that resonated most profoundly for me.

The Dry Valleys of Antarctica have some bearing on the question of whether the ice cap is likely to melt. The melting of the cap would accelerate global warming and obliterate the coastal civilizations of the world, raising the water level an average of seventy metres, ultimately drowning London, coastal Western Europe, Manhattan, sections of Sydney, Shanghai, Hong Kong. It will not do so overnight. When it last happened, at the end of the last Ice Age, the meltdown took 200 years, and ice loss at the moment is one hundred times slower than that, and, as some scientists say, it may merely be a random fluctuation, not a harbinger of disaster.

The Dry Valleys, discovered by Scott, lie on the Antarctic mainland across McMurdo Sound. Professor Barry McKelvey, the Australian geologist on the *Khlebnikov*, has specialized in these cold desert valleys since he was a young geologist. One of them is named after him. They are ground from which the glaciers have retreated leaving moraine, an intimidatingly broad vacancy, and tiny, isolated small patches of mosses and lichen never more than a few millimetres high, which McKelvey referred to ironically as 'the forests of Antarctica'. Large mountains separate the valleys, and they are still impinged upon by muscular glaciers, the Canada, the Commonwealth, whose faces do not melt away into trickles of water but which stand sixty or seventy metres high. One knows, and can feel the ache, that something more than this is meant to be here. For one thing, you don't need to walk far here to find the mummified corpses of crab-eater and other seals, some of them 3,000 or more years dead. They have come up here compelled by some ancestral memory, and they have died here, after a twenty- or thirty-mile journey from the Ross Sea, all achieved on flippers and out of their element, over the harshest land.

Though the Dry Valleys offer clues to the question of the ice cap's history, according to Professor McKelvey the answer is still unclear. McKelvey has come to the conclusion that the ice sheet has never been stable – two million years ago it went into serious decline, and in retracting, dumped its debris even on top of present-day mountains. It has grown considerably again since then. McKelvey's studies have convinced him that the ice cap is like a living thing, expanding sometimes, retracting at others, but strong enough to sustain itself through previous periods of global warming. It is a comforting hypothesis which I hope is true, and material I've read since seems to give strength to it. In the last thirty-five years the temperature of Antarctica has been dropping by 0.7 degrees Celsius (1.8 degrees Fahrenheit) per decade, further mystifying those who are trying to predict what will happen to us in a warming world.

Because of all the ice in McMurdo, we were helicoptered rather than boated to the great American base, which resembles an exceptionally tidy mining camp (unless one enters the enormous Crary Science and Engineering Centre, in which case one would believe oneself on a campus of the University of California).

Here and at the more intimate New Zealand base, Scott Base, which lies nearby, researchers share their findings on all Antarctic issues. At both bases they are aware of a diminution in the hole in the ozone layer. Winter over the Antarctic creates the chemical conditions in which the return of sunlight is the catalyst for destroying ozone at six to thirty miles above the earth. The hole split in two in 2002, and was now, in 2003, merely a fraction of its size in 2001, when it was the size of Canada, the United States and Mexico. It seems that the attack on the manufacture of CFCs and halons – chlorine and bromine chemicals – through the Montreal Protocol might have contributed directly to the improvement. Some scientists believe, however, that it's too early to judge, that the chlorine and bromine take years to disappear anyhow, and that the size of the hole each year is influenced by air temperatures. The New Zealand woman directing research at Scott Base, however, seemed reasonably sanguine that the hole, which has created wide DNA damage in the eggs and larvae of Antarctic fish and other Antarctic creatures and is a threat ultimately to all DNA on earth, might disappear altogether by 2050.

We were shown genially around the base, but I felt that our being barred from Hut Point, the home of my purloined biscuit, because a store ship had docked and the road was too busy, was symptomatic of the tension between Antarctic tourism and Antarctic bases. So too, perhaps, was an incident involving Captain Golikov. Some miles out in McMurdo lay a big tanker, which would supply the base with its winter oil. Because of the extraordinary extent of the ice, the US Coast Guard ice-breakers could not make a path for it, and Golikov offered to do so, very confident that the design of the *Kapitan Khlebnikov* fitted it better for these conditions. He was rebuffed. Perhaps jingoism had something to do with it, as well as the fact that the *KK* had fallen from the high office of Arctic ice-breaker to become an Antarctic tourist ship.

And now the admission cannot be delayed. What about the biscuit? Having set myself up to return the biscuit, and having told a number of people about my purpose, and having been assured that I would almost certainly meet someone on the trip associated with the preservation of the huts of the so-called Heroic Era, on the day we left for New Zealand to meet the boat, I went without it.

It was inexplicable, even to me. Maybe it was that, a loose-lipped confessor, I'd told so many people about my intention that I thought the thing had actually been packed already. Whereas thermal underwear and waterproof pants demanded to be packed physically one by one, my brain may have fooled me into believing the biscuit was part of my baggage, since it had an emotional and moral weight which I'd already hefted.

But, once aboard, I had consoled myself rather easily, I have to say. Not only because I was sure that somewhere in Antarctica I would meet an authoritative person who had something to do with the maintenance and preservation of the historic huts. It would be better if they handled it anyhow, rather than if I, during a visit to Hut Point, simply tried to slip it into a hard-tack tin.

One of the New Zealanders we had collected from ice-bound Cape Adare, Nigel Watson, was the head of the operations of the Heritage Trust. I took him aside the evening he was rescued from Cape Adare and made my hard-tack confession. He told me that American naval personnel had taken much greater plunder from Hut Point, and one man had returned canned goods and books to him. I made the point that there had been no equivalent to him around in 1968. Of course, he said, I understand. But in case he let me off too lightly, and reduced me to the status of minor polar pillager, I confessed to him the venality, vanity and greed which underpinned my crime. He bought me a drink to calm me down. It was agreed I would send him the biscuit for assessment. I had met the man. I felt that Antarctica could now be unambiguously enjoyed.

So consoled, I climbed Observation Hill with some friendly American Hercules pilots for guides. Members of Scott's expedition had placed on top of here a large wooden cross, facing out across the ice shelf on which they had found his body. Observation Hill is a relatively modest volcanic tor, a mere child of Mount Erebus, but the view is superb, and the last great one we had before the *Khlebnikov* turned north again.

From that point on, storms and ice prevented any further landings. The sea off Cape Adare had an extraordinary look – a conglomerated solid ice surface in which there were, nonetheless, deep swells, serving as a promise of how rough the weather would be northwards. No one sane would have tried landing. At Macquarie Island, our six young scientists were taken ashore at some peril to all parties, in seas which sometimes had the Russian sailors on the ship's stairs armpit-deep in water.

We had seen our last iceberg and, after a while, our last heroic wandering albatross. After Antarctica, nothing is the same, I decided; that was the real reason I went back, to refresh my wellspring of images: the size of the ice fields and mountains, their air of calm self-absorption (they are so free, still, of the usages of the human race) as they fill your sight like an independent and immaculate planet. As for the biscuit, it is now in the hands of the New Zealand Heritage Trust, Christchurch, New Zealand, who are assessing it for its return to the Antarctic.

THIS IS CENTERVILLE

James Buchan

In the imagination of strangers there is a small town in America which represents not just itself but the whole country. It will have a strip mall and a high-school band and a Pancake Day in the fall. It will be known on its Chamber of Commerce website as America's Hometown.

On a map of the United States, the town of Centerville, Iowa, 'America's Hometown' – looks promising. It stands midway between the Missouri River and the Mississippi, perhaps a hundred miles from Des Moines and 200 from Kansas City and about as far from the ocean as it is possible to be. In the Midwest's simple geography, with its tiers of counties stacked like supermarket boxes and highways straight as section lines, Centerville appears to be as ordinary as ordinary.

As Highway 5 runs south from Des Moines airport, the prairie flats begin to roll and break into wooded valleys. The prehistoric ice sheets that flattened northern and central Iowa and ground it up into six or seven feet of the deepest, blackest, richest agricultural soil on earth, here melted and gouged out bluffs and valleys. Monotonous fields of Monsanto corn and soybeans – fields flogged by agriculture as if they had done something unspeakably wicked – give way to black cattle sheltering under oaks, hog sheds, overgrown creeks, rough pasture, hunting ground for turkey, quail and white-tailed deer, see-through towns.

Centerville, the only place of any size in Appanoose County, arrives in a stately procession of chain stores: Wal-Mart, McDonald's, Sonic, Subway, a shuttered mall, one-room insurance brokers, a John Deere dealership, a Hy-Vee supermarket. From the highway, you can see down to a big old-fashioned courthouse square, where at fifty-yard intervals between the cast-iron lamp standards there is an American flag to tell you in which jurisdiction you find yourself.

Around the square, each side of it a double-block long, are lunch-rooms, a J. C. Penney, bank buildings, five-and-dimes you thought had vanished before the Second World War, clothing stores, chiropractors, doctors, a pair of pharmacists, optometrists, furniture stores. On the brick facades are the faded symbols of small-town fraternities – Masons, Shriners, the Independent Order of Oddfellows, Rotary – from the epoch before television. You wonder why nobody bothered to knock the place down. A couple of blocks north, east, south and west, the streets run out past one-storey houses cluttered with swingseats, wind chimes and bank mortgages worth $20,000 on a good day, some in a kind of everlasting yard sale – till they lose themselves in weedy oak and hickory woods or cornfields.

Centerville has twenty-two churches, some of Baptist subsects evidently invented just for articles such as this one, two motels with rooms for cleaning game, two banks, the neo-Romanesque courthouse with its stopped clock, and half a dozen saloons. Its factories make plastic yard furniture and sheds, sterile packaging for food, automotive spare parts, steel wire and mesh and muzzle-loading rifles. It has a high school and community college, a cattle auction, one jail with eighteen inmates, a museum, a movie palace, an old folks' home, a broadband service run by the water company, a National Guard (militia) transportation unit now in Iraq and about

800 family farms. It also has the largest per-capita use of homemade metamphetamine in the state of Iowa.

The 6,000 Americans of Centerville live on beef, pork and potatoes, eat dinner exactly at noon and supper exactly at six. For all the prejudice of Europeans, they are not noticeably overweight. In ten days I saw nobody read a book, eat an apple, use a cellphone (but once) or drink anything stronger than beer (except Jim Milani, a lawyer and rancher, and that was only by way of hospitality). Few men wear neckties even to church or lock their vehicles. The farmers and their wives drive early-model pick-ups round the courthouse square at fifteen miles an hour as if they were in horse-drawn buggies. More than twenty per cent of the population is over sixty-five, and at the factories middle-aged farmers put in a shift for benefits and health insurance and then go back to their row crops. There is at least one Puerto Rican and one African-American. Apart from a young Albanian woman just arrived in town, the nearest Muslim is a doctor in Unionville, ten miles away. People talked of this person as they would an indigo bunting in the woods.

Yet the bland, flat, American surface of Centerville, Iowa, is full of depths. In the parking lot of Hy-Vee there is a depression where (according to Gary Craver, who lost his job as a police dispatcher and now investigates the town's history) the ceiling of a longwall mine collapsed. Out to the west on Highway 2, just behind the Pale Moon supper club, there is a grassed-over slag pit where the Sunshine Coal Company ('For Economical Heat, Always Good') once undermined nearly 300 acres and employed 150 men and boys. The ground under Centerville becomes a dimension, like its history.

Certain institutions appear grossly oversized in a town of just 5,924 in the decennial census of 2000: a sixty-bed charity hospital with a CT scanner, the *Daily Iowegian* newspaper, a fifth-generation hometown bank with $100 million in deposits, and the city's very own freight railroad with two dozen miles of track, two diesel locomotives and a ballast car. Imagine such things in a British market town of the size, say, of Selkirk in Lanark or Wallingford, Berkshire. You sense that the town must have been quite rich once.

In reality, Centerville is poised in the balance between boom and failure and always has been. With not many more people than at the time of the War Between the States – 11,931 in 1860, 13,721 in 2000 – Appanoose County has risen and fallen and fallen and risen on convulsions of commerce or politics.

First there were natives, then pioneers and Mormons, coal, railroads and cattle, then Union Carbide and the Corps of Engineers, then Newell Rubbermaid. In a small town 1,000 miles from the Atlantic, hundreds of Croats, Slovaks, Italians, Germans, Austrians and Jews became good Americans. Just as the people of Centerville know where they are by the compass, and can direct a stranger twelve blocks north or eight to the east, and say which side of the square you can eat French toast and pancakes, they know where they stand in history. That is: that Dad raised a family on 120 acres and I can't make much of a living on 2,000, and I milked two cows before school each day and I delivered coal on Saturdays to the houses in Moravia.

Jeff Young is the fifth member of the Bradley-Young family to run the town bank, Iowa Trust and Savings, and can tell how his great-great-grandfather took the business through the crash of 1873, and his grandfather through the Depression 'though he was not an educated man' and his father and Dave Taylor through the farm crisis of the 1980s without initiating a single farm foreclosure. To hear the phrase 'great-great-grandfather' in modern America is a surprise. Rich or poor, the people of Centerville know they are actors in a colossal economic drama which started before them and will see them out and extends far beyond American borders to places they have never seen even in the Service: Canada, Mexico, Brazil, Europe, China, the Middle East.

Iowa was always prolific of soldiers. In the courthouse square, called in Centerville but nowhere else The Largest Square in the World, young men marched off behind the flags and pipes to fight and die at Vicksburg and Marks Mill, Arkansas; Cuba; France; Belgium and Germany; the Pacific. The day the Bloomington newspaper came into the Post Office with the news of the capture of the Confederate fortress at Vicksburg, the blacksmiths and farriers in the lanes behind the square that now carry the transmission lines rang and rang their anvils and the copperheads pulled down their blinds. When the Iowa National Guard 2133rd Transportation Company set off for Kuwait earlier this year, the highway north to Albia was lined for twenty-five miles by men, women and children waving flags. The National Guard armoury out by the industrial park is now deserted, but for a single woman sergeant, back home on family discharge to look after a teenage son with special needs. Iraq does not come naturally into conversation. Once introduced, it casts a shadow. In this small town in the centre of a powerful country, a disaster in the making reverberates like a telephone two rooms away that rings and rings and rings.

Once known as Chaldea, then as Senterville (which was taken to be a misspelling at the State offices in Iowa City), the town of Centerville was surveyed or 'platted' in 1847. The first log-cabin courthouse was built that summer, and within ten years there was the Bradley bank, grocers, blacksmiths, general stores, three hotels and an insurance agent. In 1857, the first bituminous coal mine was worked at the outcropping of the seam at Mystic in Walnut Township to the north-west.

With the coming of the rails from the 1870s, there was a ready market for the coal to fire locomotives. Two railroads came into Centerville, the Chicago, Rock Island and Pacific from Unionville and the Missouri, Iowa and Northern from Keokuk, and crossed at a place about a mile south of the courthouse square called The Levee, and still a place of bars and saloons: after Pancake Day on the last Saturday of

September, Sheriff Gary Anderson gets in his vehicle and drives real slow 'so they finish their fighting before I get there'.

By 1906, the mines were bringing up more than a million tons of coal a year. They attracted miners and their families from Central and Eastern Europe, whose names, somewhat Americanized, make a sort of layer above the old legal and merchant aristocracy of Bradleys, Youngs and Woodens. Jim Milani, whose forebears kept an ice cream parlour on the north side of the square, pronounced his family name Mullaney till he learned better on a visit to North Italy. By then, it would have been an affectation to change. There is not much affectation in Centerville, Iowa.

Because the coal seam was never more than twenty-eight inches deep, the miners dug it out by hand on their knees, sides or bellies. Shetland ponies drew the coal cars up to daylight. Some spent all winter down the mine and lost their sight. The slag hauled out and heaped was fired and then used to surface the gravel back roads. It is hard to imagine that the endless grey roads between the farms were once a brilliant red.

The last brick building on the square, now the Dannco sporting goods store on the east side, went up in 1912. In 1917, seventy-four mines produced a peak tonnage of 1,663,454 tons of coal. That year the railroads began to switch to diesel to fuel their locomotives, and the town entered a decline that lasted until the 1960s. The banks survived by lending not to local people but to Uncle Sam, taking in the public's deposits to buy risk-free Treasury bills. There was no money to build or knock anything down. Centerville was becalmed.

Coalmining lingered on, even if was sometimes just a man and his sons working what was called a dog mine. Dean Kaster, county supervisor, whose father operated the Kaster Coal Company in the Chariton River valley which closed in 1952, as a boy used to unload two mine-trucks after school and on Saturdays took coal to the houses in Moravia to the north. A large fan blew fresh air into the mine which on cold days condensed into a fog at the mine entry. 'When it steamed, that's when you knew it was safe from the blackdamp to go in,' he said. The last mine in Centerville, located just behind the commercial strip on Highway 5, closed in 1966. In the Appanoose County Historical Society Museum, which was set up in the old US Mail building east of the courthouse square, there is a film of the last shifts at the New Gladstone mine, to the west of town, which was the last to shut, in 1971. The men trudging down the slope with their carbide lamps and lunch pails look like grandfathers and probably were. 'In later years,' said Bill Heusinkveld, a local historian who showed me round, 'young men didn't want to go into the mines so we ended up with nothing but older men who had worked in that mine all their lives.' Rollic Reznicek, proprietor of the Owl Pharmacy on the east side of the square and a former mayor of Centerville, said, 'The end of the mines persuaded people in the town they had to work together.'

The Sixties brought a revival in the town's fortunes. In 1962, Union Carbide, a chemicals company with headquarters in the east, chose Centerville for a factory to make shrink packaging for meat from high-density polyethylene pellets delivered from the oil companies by railroad car. The plant employed 400 people. Two years later, the United States Army Corps of Engineers began building the two-mile-long Rathbun Dam to control flooding in the Chariton valley just to the north.

But in the early 1980s, Centerville was down again. In 1980, the bankrupt Rock Island line was shut down and the CBQ Burlington Northern, which had inherited the other track into town, announced that it would close its spur to Centerville in March 1982. To keep Carbide in town, Centerville had to find more than $2 million to buy the track and right of way to a Norfolk and Western junction at Moulton, ten miles to the east. Led by Dave Taylor, who had been brought in by the Youngs to manage Iowa Trust and Savings, and Bob

Beck, then publisher of the *Daily Iowegian*, the people of Centerville subscribed part of the money and raised the rest from state and federal grants. In 1993, when the railroad now known as Norfolk Southern abandoned part of its line, the Appanoose County Community Railroad bought twenty-six more miles of track to connect to the interstate network at Albia to the north. Carbide stayed, though the plant now operates under the name of Curwood. In 1985, Rubbermaid Corp., a consumer products company based in Freeport, Illinois, took over an abandoned factory next door to make outdoor storage bins and sheds, wheelbarrows and cattle drinkers from the same polyethylene that supplied Union Carbide. After three expansions, the factory now employs 500 people at rates of $10.60 an hour, which is not bad for the rural Midwest. A third company, Releo Locomotives, will next year open a works to recondition old locomotives and test them on the lightly used track. 'Without these industries,' said Jim Senior, manager of the Appanoose County Community Railroad, 'Centerville would be a ghost town.' Mr Senior employs seven grizzled old railwaymen and two fifty-year-old locomotives that haul about 500 cars a year and unload directly into silos at the back of the industrial park. Out on the track are two open-sided cars, used once a year for a town excursion that seems to belong to some golden age of jollification before the invention of liability insurance.

The same people who saved the railroad are now restoring the courthouse square, with the help of a local benefactor. Morgan Cline grew up in Centerville, studied pharmacology at Drake University in Des Moines, practised for a while in the town before moving to New York where he went into pharmaceutical advertising. His practice, Cline, Davis & Mann, has $500 million in customer billings, including the account of the largest pharmaceutical company in the world, Pfizer Inc. Mr Cline is credited with persuading the former Senate majority leader, Bob Dole, to advertise Viagra. Mr Cline began with the restoration of the best building on the square, the Continental

Hotel of 1893, which had become a flophouse. According to Bill Burch, who handles Mr Cline's business in Centerville, he has spent some $15 million in the district, and it shows. On every side of the square, the aluminium siding is coming down. 'He's the one,' said Linda Howard, who is active in civic affairs, 'who's shown us we can save these beautiful old buildings. We were more worried about having a strip mall, maybe because that's what the people saw when they went to Kansas City – a mall. Morgan helped us turn that corner.' The city now wants to convert an old movie house in the Spanish colonial style into a concert hall and do up the town's bandshell and a library built by General Francis M. Drake, who was wounded at Marks Mill in 1864 and went on to be Governor of Iowa. A group of white men in their seventies are restoring by hand the Baptist church that was used by the African-Americans in town. Thus a tonic for male impotence revives a fatigued old town in the Midwest.

To see what Centerville could have been and might still be, travel east along Highway 2 to Sunshine Corner then turn north to the old coal-mining town of Mystic. Mystic, named by a railway engineer for his hometown in Connecticut, is a place where the transformation from boom town to ghost town so evident across Appanoose County is not quite complete. On the railroad is an old water tower for the steam locomotives, and the sort of gas station Bonnie Parker and Clyde Barrow might have robbed and driven away laughing. Under the brilliant starlit nights, the long freights wail and the coyotes yip.

On what was once Nob Hill, where the mine owners and their lawyers lived, there are trailers among broken-down palaces. The mud roads and vanished subdivisions are overwhelmed with second-growth timber, where, walking in the rain, I came on a Mountain Dew bottle stopped with duct tape with a long, clear tube coming out the top.

Sheriff Anderson sent two officers to pick it up the next day. It was the remains of a homemade lab to make the speed known as metamphetamine or more generally 'crank'. Farm-country crack, it is, say the police and hospital people, just as savage, antisocial and habit-forming as its counterpart in the ghetto. Its active pharmaceutical is the decongestant ephedrine. Users buy Sudafed from the Fareway or Hy-Vee, then cook it up into rock or paste with a mixture of anhydrous ammonia from off the farm, acetone, hydrochloric acid, alkaline battery fluid and lye. Every now and then, according to Sheriff Anderson, a shed or garage out in the woods goes up to high heaven. Originally an overtime drug of factory workers and long-distance truckers, it has colonized the underclasses of the rural Midwest. 'I guess the meth epidemic is rather like the crack epidemic a few years back, except it is out in the rural parts of Iowa, Missouri, Indiana, out in the chicken coops, so it doesn't stand out,' said Dr Paul Novak, a senior doctor in the emergency room at Mercy Medical Center on Highway 5. Its most lurid symptom, it seems, is the delusion among users that insects have got under their skin. Dennis Sturms, ambulance manager, said, 'Unless you're with the police or medical services, you wouldn't know it was going on. But go into Wal-Mart, and look for people with scabs on their arms.' Mary Lou Sales, manager of the emergency-room clinic, said that children were at risk from fumes or spillages, or where chemicals had seeped into the walls of microwave ovens, from lye stored in pop bottles, and from the violent and unpredictable behaviour of users.

Mystic's Main Street is paved with brick, but only a few solid buildings survive like teeth among the weeds: the American Legion or the Coalminers Inn where a young man tried to pick a fight with me in the gloom, but did not know enough about Britain to find a cause. Up the street, beyond a chain-link fence, was a scuffed park and playground and a civilian notice: NO FIGHTING, NO PROFANITY. NO ALCOHOL.

On a vacant lot opposite, a small crowd had gathered in the rain for an auction of domestic furnishings out of the back of a truck.

'Dollar-bill-dollar-bill-half-dollar-half-dollar-dollar-bill-two-dollar-dollar-bill.'

The auctioneer, his long straight hair held by a baseball cap, called for a cigarette. A man in the truck, as sunburned and worn out as a Confederate infantryman at Appomatox Courthouse, manhandled an exercise treadmill from the truck. Jim Buban, the chief automobile dealer in Centerville, stalked round the crowd till greeted by me, when he jumped.

'Treadmill. Works,' he said. 'Dollar-bill-two-dollar-two-dollar. Nobody want it. Put it back.'

Each item brought down or taken up again – golf clubs, a grade-school desk, mechanical drill, a metal table, two snowboards (eight dollars) – carried traces of foreclosure or some other domestic failure. For this was the end of the road. Here, in Mystic and places like Mystic, the surplus objects of a society in surplus had come to rest, discharging their last vestige of value in commerce – the final half-dollar – into the wet American air.

'Dollar-bill-dollar-bill-half-dollar-half-dollar. Nobody want it. Put it back.'

In the modern suburbs of, say, Atlanta, Georgia, Americans do much of their business by hand signals from vehicles or formulaic conversations across store counters. Centerville, in contrast, is a partly pedestrian civilization. People walk, on their legs, along the sidewalks of the courthouse square or stop to view its little dramas: Sheriff Anderson bringing in two cuffed and orange-jumpsuited prisoners for arraignment and, a little later, Judge Dan Wilson stepping out in his suit and tie for his dinner. Everybody knows far too much about everybody else's business and that, for example, Tom Johnson, one of two optometrists in town, was late for his 9.30 Friday because he took that British writer to watch ospreys at the lake and came in still in his rubber boots. At night, teenagers lounge by their trucks as late as nine o'clock. Centerville is a town where people still make their own amusements, in church suppers, band suppers, drive-through dinners. It is not the fragmented and isolated American suburbs of Robert D. Putnam's *Bowling Alone*.

Beside the courthouse, the third on the site after No. 2 burned down in the Fourth of July fireworks of 1881, you might at any time see a man in a Hawaiian shirt and drooping moustache, carrying a digital camera. He looks like Dennis Hopper in *Apocalypse Now*, minus the shakes, and indeed the man once served in Vietnam and Germany as a military photographer. His hair is long and lank, for which he was once fined a dollar at Rotary. This is Dan Ehl, current managing editor of the *Daily Iowegian*. A liberal Democrat, a passionate opponent of the war in Iraq, pro-UN, pro-France even, Mr Ehl likes to write editorials in favour of such causes as legalizing marijuana. For a while, the cops used to flag down his truck and examine his tongue for something or other, but now Sheriff Anderson has come round to him. In reality, Mr Ehl is the life and soul of Centerville, a symbol of its tolerance and self-absorption, and of the ability of small-town America to convert rebellion into light comedy or corn pone. Mr Ehl recently hitchhiked from Des Moines just to show it could still be done as in the days when America was young.

Centerville was not always a political backwater. In the 1860s it found itself just thirty miles from the border of a slave state, and every cellar step and peeling outhouse, it now seems, was a station on the underground railroad to Canada for runaway slaves from Missouri. In the depressed conditions of the 1920s, the Ku Klux Klan set up on 12th Street and for a few years tried to make a political programme out of anti-Semitism and a ban on immigration. The Republican hold on the state of Iowa established at the Civil War broke down in the mid-twentieth century, and in the presidential election of 2000, Appanoose County voted by only 432 votes for George W. Bush and

Al Gore took the state's votes in the electoral college. As this January's Iowa Caucuses swung into view, and one by one the Democratic challengers to Mr Bush broke cover, Centerville found a party-political language in which to talk about America's place in the world and the Middle East.

It was as if the tremendous shock of September 11 still reverberated. 'I would say we in the Midwest are pretty patriotic people,' said Bill Belden, local manager of the Iowa Farm Bureau and an active Republican. 'I would say at this point we don't want to see terrorism in our shores again.' Democrats, in contrast, saw the Iraq invasion as only making matters worse, and impugned Mr Bush's motives. 'It just all felt so powerless,' Ms Howard said. 'He [Mr Bush] was going to do it [invade Iraq], it didn't matter what anybody said. And he just did it, playing cowboy. And now we have the burden of helping those people [Iraqis] recreate their country and we don't know how to do that.' Ms Howard, who has spent most of her life outside Centerville and has just returned, paused: 'But you know 9/11 upset us. It was so frightening and so unpredictable. It was like all the rules were gone. Any Joe Blow on a plane ...'

At Bruce Dickerson's US History class at Indian Hills Community College, a majority of students did not believe that Iraq had any hand in the assault on the USA on September 11, 2001. A small majority, and not just those from army and National Guard families, believed that the United States and the United Kingdom should stay in Iraq to install an American-style democracy. Nobody seemed very proud of what had occurred. 'I guess we were on a roll after Afghanistan and already wound up,' a young woman said. 'We're a pretty aggressive country, I think.' The students were shy, for Americans, and reluctant to express an opinion.

What unites both parties in town is lip service to the safety and welfare of the Iowans in Iraq. The unit had its first fatality when David M. Kirchhoff died on August 14 as a result of heatstroke in Kuwait.

The National Guard unit is now stationed a hundred miles west of Baghdad, backing up operations in the insurrectionary Sunni towns and villages of central Iraq, ferrying back front-line personnel for leave or to call home by satphone, transporting prisoners.

Attending the Moravia Fall Festival in her Humvee and fatigues, Sergeant Robin Page of the National Guard said, 'One thing that Dan [Mr Ehl] and I can agree on is that we must support our people over in Iraq.' This common loyalty keeps the peace in a small town and allows people to sit down together at the Farm Bureau steak supper. In truth, people are deeply shocked by the cost in lives and money of the expedition. They try not to think too much about it.

At the First Presbyterian Church on North Main Street, the minister, Dr Beverley Leonard prayed for rain for the crops but not for Iraq. She said it slipped her mind. Older people have their own anxieties. Pat Clark, a former athlete and navy rating, said in a saloon one night, 'One here, one there. Two here, two there. Pff.' He sighted down an imaginary sniper's rifle and squeezed the trigger. 'There's one word that explains it all. V-I-E-T-N-A-M.'

The word 'powerless', once uttered, seemed to describe many aspects of life in Centerville. In the dog days of coal mining in the 1940s and 1950s, labour unions gained a hold in Centerville but the modern factories are ununionized. At Rubbermaid, the work is hard, heavy and noisy. To cut the flash off the stamped plastic panels, the workers use hunting knives, as if they were cutting meat or field-dressing a deer, and there is a constant danger of injury. 'It's probably the most physical of our plants,' said Kevin Wiskus, plant manager.

What attracts employers such as Newell Rubbermaid and Curwood to Centerville is a tradition of hard physical labour from the farms. Phyllis More, a packer of 7ft x 7ft tool sheds at Rubbermaid, laughed at the exertion: 'This is no harder than dairy farming.' Yet Centerville must compete with similar hard-working small towns in

Oklahoma, Texas, Alabama, Mississippi. Centerville knows that its muscle is a mere American commodity, and, that should labour unions ever gain a hold in town, the industrial employers would leave and take with them 1,800 ten-dollar-an-hour jobs.

The farmers have no more control over their lives than the men and women stacking pallets of flat-pack storage bins at Rubbermaid. According to Bill Belden, Iowa farmers get to keep about eight cents of each dollar spent on food at the supermarket. Prices of beef were at all-time highs this autumn, but none of the cattle ranchers seemed to know why and many had sold forward at lower prices. Corn and beans looked good on the Fourth of July, but a scalding August without rain meant both crops would be short.

Pretty well all the large farmers in Appanoose County grow Roundup Ready crops: that is, corn and soybeans genetically modified by Monsanto of St Louis so they can be treated safely with the Monsanto glyphosate herbicide Roundup. It keeps the weeds down, they say, but not as much as it used to and they must buy seed anew each season and pay Monsanto a royalty on the seed, known as a tech fee. If they hold back seed from their own harvest to sow themselves, Monsanto will prosecute them. At harvest, they sell the corn to colossal merchant-processors such as Cargill Corp. of Minneapolis, Minnesota, and Archer Daniels Midland of Decatur, Illinois. The farmers complain they are squeezed on price at both ends. 'Cargill and Monsanto own the country,' says Tom Teno, who farms 2,000 acres of row crops and cattle just across the county line in Monroe County.

Mr Teno is a handsome man, who talks like John Wayne (born at Winterset, Iowa, some forty years before Mr Teno). The night before, he had broken a metacarpal in his right hand vaccinating his cows, and it pained him, though that didn't stop him talking or preparing the combine to harvest his corn.

Mr Teno is by all accounts one of the very best farmers in southern

Iowa but even he finds the going tough. 'Crop prices are the same now as when my dad raised five kids on one hundred and twenty acres,' he said. 'In 1952, Dad bought a tractor and all the train for eighteen hundred dollars. Now you have to spend hundreds of thousands on machinery and farm half the county to make any sort of living. It's one hell of a battle. Yet if I die tonight, people round here would be fighting for the land I cash-rent before I was cold. We should all refuse to sell crops at these prices, but it will never happen.' As well as cutting one another's throats, the farmers are conservative to the point of obstinacy. Mr Teno was once asked to grow just forty acres of artichokes. He refused unless the seedsman guaranteed to take the crop. Even now, he pronounces the word 'artichoke' as if it somehow did not belong in the English language. There is almost no conception in Centerville that there might be some other way to farm other than selling manipulated commodity foods into a fast-food culture, drawing subsidies that beggar other nations and seeking evanescent savings from genetic modification. Iowa farmers have had more than $10 billion in farm subsidies since 1996, more than those of any state in the Union. They latch on to any new use – ethanol, bio-diesel – that Cargill discovers for corn and beans. When a visitor says that in England families pay premiums for a species of uncooked ham from Parma, Italy, and red wine from Bordeaux, France, they say, Well, I'll be damned. And so it goes round: corn, beans, cattle, hogs, as God or Cargill has ordained until the greatest agricultural province on earth goes to hell or is displaced by Brazil.

Across in Highland Township of Wapello County, Larry Kinsinger takes a while to reveal just how down he is on his luck. A lean, bright man in his fifties, Mr Kinsinger quit farrowing 500 sows in February. In July his wife said she wanted to leave him. By December, he will have sold the last of his fat hogs, and be working at a job in the town of Ottumwa, probably at the meat-packer, Excel Corp., which is owned by Cargill. For the moment, Mr Kinsinger still has 1,200 hogs to fatten on contract. The hogs (Yorks, Large Whites, and lots in between) are packed tight on concrete slats in a long barn, about eight square feet or less per animal, fed wholly on concentrated feed from silos ranged along the barn. The hogs have their tails cut to discourage cannibalism and that is largely successful. Such 'hog confinements' are unpopular in Iowa, less for the hyper-intensive husbandry than for the stink. The smell of pigshit clings to clothes and rental cars for days on end. It is not a soft heart that brought Mr Kinsinger to grief.

After a spell as an army pharmacist, Mr Kinsinger took over from his father in 1975. In 1994, against his father's advice, he borrowed a couple of hundred thousand dollars to build the hog barn and to buy two neighbouring farms. In 1998, the hog market all but collapsed, with prices falling for a time under ten dollars a hundredweight. Mr Kinsinger sold the two farms and will have soon sold everything else except the barn. He hopes a neighbour might work it for him, such as Dwight Lowenberg, whose 4,000-head sheds gleam brutally white on the horizon.

It is hard to fail when your neighbours succeed. It is hard to work at a meat-packer that treats farmers like employees, specifies breed, genetics and feed and won't buy from independent farmers. It is hard to have your money in pork, when your wife has her money in the stock market. It'll be harder still this winter in town to watch the cattlemen driving round in their new-model trucks. It is hardest of all not to take your sons with you. 'Our house was three-quarters of a mile from the farm,' Mr Kinsinger said, 'and my sons would see me go off in the truck, but they'd stay and maybe help my wife around the house. They might have been living in a city. I remember back when Tom broke his arm at football, he was waiting around in the doctor's office and the nurses said what are you going to do when you're grown. He said, "Somebody'll have to work the farm." I said,

"Nobody *has* to work the farm, Tom.'" Tom Kinsinger is now a freshman at Iowa State.

The truck passed a couple of cornbins, lopsided in the weeds, where a farm had been, and failed, like this one. Mr Kinsinger turned to his visitor. 'I didn't fail, the farm failed. I've been reading about George Washington and Abraham Lincoln. You can lose and lose, but it's the last battle that matters; only the last.'

Centerville is a town the American founding fathers might have dreamed of building on the prairie: civic, self-reliant and law-abiding. Yet those very virtues have their shadow existences as arrogance, overconfidence and naivety. A sojourn in a British small town would turn up a different composition of virtue and vice. And both towns would have contributed to the catastrophe in Iraq.

There was one more visit to pay. This was to the Vanderlinden place, south of Centerville towards the Missouri state line. The long gravel road that is 600th Street was deserted, except for mourning doves on the wires and turkey vultures quartering the corn. A cloud of dust ahead resolved itself into an Amish sulky returning from school, a boy driving in his straw hat, his two sisters in their blue bonnets behind. The Amish are moving into Appanoose County, paying top dollar for land, and paying in cash. Their aloofness makes them unpopular. Out on the gravel roads, they look no more exotic than the drifts of monarch butterflies.

Kirk Vanderlinden is a large, tow-haired man with big spectacles that slide down his nose, fattening 300 cattle (mostly Angus) in a long trough on a muddy feed-lot behind his father's farmstead. He buys the cattle at the Ballanger auction in Centerville. He has 200 acres under corn, 200 under beans, and the rest under sown grasses. His grandfather bought the farm off an insurance company in 1948, and not a whole lot has changed since then, but a new steel silo ($7,500) and cutter for the cattle feed ($7,000). His wife, Debbie, teaches elementary school, which brings in $30,000 a year plus health benefits. They have a son, Evan, who is nine. Last spring, to the astonishment of every single person in Centerville, Kirk and Debbie Vanderlinden travelled to St Petersburg, Russia, and adopted four children out of a state orphanage. 'Actually,' Marilyn Vanderlinden, his mother, said at church, 'we thought Kirk had gone mad.' The youngest of the Russian children, a little girl named Roselana, raced ahead into the machinery barn, crying 'Kombin! Kombin!' at the harvester.

Kirk Vanderlinden worked in fibre optics in North Carolina before taking over three-quarters of the farm in 1990. With the price of cattle up at nearly one hundred cents per pound, he had done very well. (He would have done better, he said with a smile, if he hadn't sold some forward at seventy-four cents and vowed in future not to spend so long at his computer.) 'I wouldn't recommend this life to anybody. I have five hundred thousand dollars' worth of capital, another seven hundred and fifty thousand in land, maybe a hundred thousand in machinery, that's one point five million dollars in assets that if you're lucky makes a return of thirty thousand dollars. It's just the lifestyle. My kids enjoy some of the lifestyle I had as a kid. That's all you can ask.'

Roselana cried out. Beyond the yard and the house, beneath an immense elm tree, a yellow school bus was drawing gently to a stop. Roselana bolted and Mr Vanderlinden and his visitor ran after her. Their muddy boots slowed them down. As the bus started up and pulled away, four children were standing on the grass, a pretty girl of about seventeen and three sturdy boys. They stood with their lunch boxes and satchels, looking at Mr Vanderlinden with the most intense yearning. Mr Vanderlinden looked back. 'How was school?'

'Good,' said Liza.

'Good,' said Ivan.

'Fine,' said Ilya.

'Good,' said Evan.

Roselana chattered away.

Something about the children was altering beyond all restitution. In the yellow Midwestern light, under the colossal elm tree, I could see that they were ceasing to be what they had been and that they were becoming something else. They were becoming Americans.

OSAMA'S WAR

Wendell Steavenson

Osama was his real name, although all other names have been changed. Osama was slightly built, almost concave, and he wore checked shirts and pressed trousers, always clean and neat; he looked anonymously ordinary. His eyes were large and roamed the public places in which we met – hotel cafés, mainly – like sweeping radar, picking up on the blond man with a Walkman who didn't look like a journalist, the table of South African security mercenaries with guns and walkie-talkies strapped to their thighs, the lone wandering Arabs who glanced at us once and then again, and, on one occasion, two American GIs, helmets and M16s clattering, buying some chicken to take away. Osama would note these threats and I would ask him if he was okay, or if he wanted to move or to leave, and he would tut at my worry and assure me that he was not afraid of such things; fear and jihad were incompatible.

We talked many times between the end of April and the beginning of June – the months the insurgency took hold. Osama had begun fighting the Americans in a mujahideen cell in Baghdad a few months after the invasion in 2003. We met through a mutual friend whom we both trusted. Because of this, because I eventually met nearly all his

family, including cousins, because I cross-questioned him and because
I found what I could check of what he told me to be true, I believed
him. His manner was always polite and modest, usually serious.
Occasionally he would smile at something. If anything he was boring,
a sort of Everyman template for a set of beliefs and opinions and
actions that have enveloped his generation of Arabs. In the end I liked
him. I told him I'd be upset if he was killed. He smiled at me and said
that was because I had no belief. He, of course, had nothing to be
frightened of; if he died as a mujahid he was going to a paradise
heaven.⟵

Shut in, circumscribed, lied to, bitter, proud and angry: Osama was
an Iraqi. He'd had twelve years – half his life – of scraping sanctions
and UN handouts of bad-quality flour, which baked tough bread that
ground grit into the cavities of your molars. He was the married elder
son of a kebab restaurant owner on a street full of mechanics, the child
of a poorish, mixed Shi'a and Sunni neighbourhood. He was a Sunni,
he followed the path, he was sure, and he kept his belief wrapped
tight around him. It was a blanket-wall I could not penetrate. No
matter how much he tried to explain the logic of morality that the
Qur'an provided for him, I could not sympathize with his beliefs – I
did not believe in them. The best I could do was to put them aside in
a box marked 'To be respected'. His outraged disaffection, however,
I empathized with. Baghdad was a shit-hole. Rubble had bred rubble.
Green lakes of sewage spread through dark, unelectrified, rubbish-
strewn neighbourhoods. Government was only men in ministries in-
terviewing their relatives for the few new jobs. Baghdadis were so
tired of repeating the words *security, electricity, employment* that they
enunciated them dully and they fell like leaden pellets into sentences
and lives.

In the midst of this mess there was the everyday reminder of an
occupying army, faces with sunglasses for eyes, alien invaders driving
around in armour, swivelling their guns at houses, rattling their tank

treads across the tarmac. One morning I drove over a highway overpass enclosed with a chain-link fence to prevent insurgents from throwing bombs at convoys passing below. Underneath us, on the wide Abu Ghraib highway, traffic was stopped: a tank had emerged from the verge, blithely trundled across the road dragging a section of metal highway divider behind it, and come to a stop on the median strip. A pile of cars was stopped behind the curve of the highway divider, now blocking the road. A couple of drivers got out of their cars and pulled the broken divider off to the side.

Complaint, irritation, humiliation; no one even bothered to demonstrate any more. The pictures of the Abu Ghraib atrocities released all pent-up indignation. All anyone talked about were the hard-knock night raids and missing sons, missing husbands, missing fathers, missing brothers; American snipers, spies, contractors; Iraqi women taken, questioned, raped. There were a lot of stories about Iraqi girls being raped by American soldiers and plenty of cheap CDs full of porn stills showing uniformed actors ganging some dark-haired girl to prove it. 'Our women!' was the icing on the outrage, which grew by rumour and false witness. The prevailing view was that even if the particulars were fake it had probably happened somewhere.

Osama, absorbing all of this, was not so very different from many run-of-the-mill, run-down unemployed urban Iraqis – perhaps the only difference was the fact that he was fighting. Poverty and war had hemmed in his life. He longed to buy his young wife a dress, he wanted to visit the famous mosques throughout Iraq, he thought vaguely about being an ambulance driver. But in general he found it difficult to imagine a future. His brother Duraid, five years younger, felt these losses and gaps and injustices, too. 'I want to live like the world lives,' Duraid once told me. Unlike Osama, he was able to imagine his own future; he found solace in a job, in kidding about with friends, in thinking about getting enough money together to buy a car. There was not much to choose: either fight or try to get on with it.

When the Americans had first arrived, Osama said, his feelings were scattered, he didn't know what to think. He had been beaten by Ba'ath Party members for attending mosque and for neglecting to join the Ba'ath Party; he was not a supporter of Saddam Hussein's regime. But it was difficult for him to feel liberated by a foreign army. He told me his heart had soared with happiness when he'd seen pictures of the World Trade Center collapse in 2001. 'This great superpower was hurt in its heart,' he said, amazed that someone could have managed such a bold swipe. 'Those that did it were very courageous, I felt that day they gave us back a bit of our rights. America wants to control the whole world's economy. When they want to impose sanctions on a country they don't care about the UN. They want to lead the whole world and make everything according to their tune, to impose their way on the world.'

After Baghdad fell, in the interim looting, Osama and some friends from the mosque gathered the rocket-propelled grenades and other weapons left behind in abandoned barracks and police stations and buried them in caches.

'We had the idea to fight for our country, not to protect any regime, but to protect our land and our mosques and our families. We talked about fighting but we didn't yet have any idea of holding a gun; we didn't have a single bullet at home.'

They went to an abandoned Iraqi Army base and practised. Osama and his group had little or no military experience; sometimes ex-soldiers were drafted in to show them what to do.

'The most difficult thing to get used to was the noise,' said Osama. 'When you fire an RPG you have to keep your mouth open, otherwise your ears will ring for four days. Some people take a breath and shoot, others release a breath and shoot. When you're firing an RPG, just don't blink. You need to wait ten seconds and then aim. You learn how to do these things automatically, it becomes easy to put the RPG on your shoulder and brace it with your head.

Your eyes should not move from the target. You should keep your eye on the target for five or six seconds after you have pressed the trigger.

'At first I was worried and afraid. I never expected that I would have the ability to do such things. When we were first hitting the Americans I considered myself a true mujahid. I feel it has strengthened my character and given me more trust in myself, and yes, of course, pride.'

His first operation was planting what the Americans called an improvised explosive device, an IED, in August after the invasion. It exploded and flipped a Humvee.

At 8.25 on the morning of May 25, a car bomb blew up outside the Karma Hotel, on Karrada, the main road opposite the large unfinished building where the Australian troops are based. There was the usual aftermath: a crowd, American Humvees, Australian soldiers fanned out across the road, a fire engine and firemen hosing down two mangled cars into waterlogged grey metal ash. A thirteen-year-old boy who sold cigarettes from a kiosk was killed.

In a side street two Humvees parked. Some American GIs got out and began to unravel spools of razor wire, blocking the road.

'Everyone behind the wire. Move!'

A clutch of neighbourhood women wearing black abayas stood a little way off and watched them, talking among themselves.

'It will get worse than this. Because of that bastard Bush and Sharon. I hate Sharon.'

'May God not bless them, these resistance – only civilians are dying.'

'Now under Bush women go to prison and are raped; these things are normal in their country.'

'Before, Iraq was safe. It was secure. If only we would have stayed under Saddam—'

'*No, it's not true it was better then. People say what is happening now is better than under Saddam—*'

'*No, it's not better.*'

Osama's group operated along the Qanat Road, which began near the sprawling Rashid military base, now occupied by the Americans barricaded behind concrete blast blocks and observation towers. Signs written in Arabic, posted along the road, read:

ALL VEHICLES ALONG THIS ROAD ARE SUBJECT TO BE SEARCHED BY THE IRAQI POLICE OR THE COALITION FORCES. ALL PARKED VEHICLES WILL BE SEARCHED. PEDESTRIANS ARE NOT PERMITTED AFTER DARK. THIS WILL HELP TO EXPOSE ALL THE BOMBS WHICH ARE PLANTED ALONG THIS ROAD THAT ARE HARMING THE IRAQI PEOPLE. INFORM THE IRAQI POLICE OR THE COALITION FORCES ABOUT TERRORISTS OR ANY SUSPICIOUS ACTIVITY.

The road ran north through the eastern suburbs of the city to its outskirts, two wide double lanes, separated by an overgrown canal, a veld of handkerchief farm plots growing maize, piles of rubbish and some mud shacks.

One baked May afternoon, Osama and I and our friend drove down the Qanat Road listening to the American forces' Radio Freedom: the weather in Mosul, high today Baghdad 115 degrees, and how important hygiene is in the field so always wash your hands after flushing. Labourers were raking dust along the verges to tidy the rubble and the trash, Iraqi Civil Defence Corps soldiers hung their hot metal guns over their shoulders and squatted under palm trees in the shade. The undulating blacktop, laid in the Fifties, rolled past watermelon sellers, the bombed UN building, the sewage-flooded football pitches, and the double blue-domed Martyr's Monument, symbol of Saddam's reverence for his own follied dead in the Iran–Iraq war, now an American fort.

The underpasses were pocked with spattered blast marks, chunks of asphalt were bitten away with explosives. Osama's was not the only group blowing things up along this stretch. In May, IEDs went off most days, three times a week or more: bangs, bombs, RPGs. A friend of a friend of mine lived with his family in a house that faced the Qanat Road; they moved.

The day before, Osama and his friends had exploded an IED in the middle of one of the rusty iron footbridges blocked up with bales of razor wire to prevent the resistance from using them to explode IEDs. Osama pointed out the hole: a ragged metal gap, and the torn roadbed below.

Did it hit?

'Yes. Part of these bushes caught fire.' In the broken-down mess of Baghdad the hole and the scratched road surface and the bit of burnt shrub didn't amount to much.

How do you know it hit the convoy?

'We don't know,' he admitted. They could not afford to hang around to survey the damage. A week before, a mujahid from another group had been shot in the returning hail when he had fired an RPG at a midnight checkpoint.

'We can't really use an RPG on the Qanat Road,' complained Osama. 'There isn't a place you can shoot it from where you can't be seen. Mostly it's IEDs.'

The IEDs were jerry-rigged electronic appliances packed into explosives hidden in a hollowed bit of breeze block or kerbstone, the cavity covered with a piece of painted polystyrene. The signal from remote-control detonators often didn't work: maybe interference from a chain-link fence, too much distance, faulty connections somewhere – hard to tell. Groups like Osama's tried to plant the IEDs at night, when the electricity was off and everything was dark. The Americans would drive by and miss them hiding in the undergrowth. Sometimes they were spotted by the Iraqi police, sometimes they were shot at and had to run off, abandoning the device. Once, one of Osama's group was caught planting an IED by the Iraqi police and arrested. They had to pay a Kalashnikov to the custody officer to get him out of the police station.

We drove past a line of cargo trucks carrying scrap metal, past plots of kitchen garden irrigated by the canal, past a petrol queue, into a neighbourhood called Rosafa. About halfway along the road there was a small American–ICDC fort flying an Iraqi flag, surrounded by concentric rings of concrete blast-walls, the ubiquitous earth-filled Hesco baskets and tunnels of razor wire snagged with bits of plastic bags. An old Russian tank turret had been placed on the roof as artillery. On the footbridge over the road the 1st Armoured Division had put up a sign that read: ROSAFA IS FREE NOW. THANK YOU FOR YOUR VISIT. For a couple of kilometres along this stretch of the Qanat Road the Americans had put up a chain-link fence topped with three lines of barbed wire.

'So that you can't run away,' said Osama. 'You see there?' He pointed to a charred black swipe on the corner of the concrete slab wall. 'A mujahid on a motorcycle fired at a truck which rammed into it.'

Homespun, improvised, hit-and-run. I once watched a resistance propaganda video that included a twenty-minute segment of grainy night, shot as five separate hands tried to light a succession of matches to set off a mortar. One after another, matches flared and blew out in the wind. Hushed, urgent voices could be heard marshalling the mortar's aim: 'Move it, move it, just a little, just a little.' *Alhamdulillah*, finally the fire caught and flamed and lit and the rocket flashed and whooshed like a flare and hit nothing. Sometimes it was on the tip of my tongue to ask Osama: why is the resistance so crap? Anything to make a blast, a point, blow off some limbs, kill one or two Americans. The most successful operation Osama's group managed was when they blew up a Humvee and killed four Americans.

'We did not celebrate,' he said severely, 'but we felt very, very happy.'

We drove past a cigarette kiosk. Osama said the cigarette seller was a spy working for the Americans; his group had information from someone who knew, they were discussing what to do about him. There were lots of spies, the Americans paid for them, they were everywhere.

'Here,' Osama said, pointing out of the car window at a lump of nondescript concrete lying in the dust at the side of the road. A single nugget amid a city of lumps of concrete, bits of crumbled building, infrastructure rotted to rubble or pickaxed or blown up or fallen down. 'That one didn't go off, we don't know why. We want to come and get it, but we have to wait for the battery on the timer to run out before we can retrieve it.'

A hundred metres further, Osama pointed again at several mounds of sun-baked rubbish heaped by the side of the road. 'And here we planted three good successful ones. Do you see that hole?' Some sort of shadow in the verge that might have been a crater or a piece of road-kill dog blurred by. 'And there,' Osama pointed at another rubbish mound. 'We put one there but the Iraqi police saw us; our man ran off, but they got the IED.'

The road gave way on either side to palm groves and farmed plots. We drove past a shuttered amusement park with a rusty pastel-painted merry-go-round behind a faded sign that read: WITH ALL THE DELIGHTS FOR THE CHILDREN. Then there was a traffic jam and we slowed in front of an Iraqi police checkpoint. A knot of police stood in a group around two or three motorists arguing amid honking and bared forearms jabbing out of car windows. Osama reminisced about taking this road to picnics on Baghdad Island. We passed a piece of road that used to lead somewhere, a roadblock traffic jam, some barbed wire and a decapitated palm tree.

*

In the middle of a Monday afternoon, two mortars fell in a front garden in a nice upscale neighbourhood near the river bank. It was the beginning of the summer heat, a small crowd gathered, mostly kids, to look at the parked Humvees and the Americans inspecting the jagged metal holes in the iron gate and the ruptured pipe leaking a stream of water into the gutter. Boys dutifully handed bits of twisted shrapnel to the Americans, who told them there would be an investigation and those responsible would be caught and brought to justice. Then they told them to move back and make way for the wide Humvees to drive down the street. Then they told them to 'Fucking move back move back, okay?'

The family whose gate had been destroyed stood in their front garden. A shaded square of scrabbly lawn, a few roses, a hibiscus bush up against a neighbouring wall and a palm tree; an old woman with an abaya loosely draped over her head, her husband wearing his afternoon-nap pyjamas, a younger woman, two men, sons or cousins or brothers.

'What's the use of a good garden if your nerves are shattered?'

'What can we expect if we live among people who are bloodthirsty murderers? Those people who fired these mortars. Why? Ordinary people are hit, the family suffers—'

The woman in the abaya said to me: 'We were sleeping, taking a nap, and then there was shattered glass on the pillow.' I looked over and saw the windows of the front, ground-floor bedroom were broken in large sharp panes. 'Are the Americans trying to protect us? Can't they stop these people who fire the mortars?'

'They should arrest these criminals and put them on trial,' someone said.

'Our wounded nerves,' lamented the old man in his pyjamas.

'What kind of Muslims would do this?' asked the old woman again.

'Only Iraqis are being killed.'

'Only Muslims are being killed.'

'They are criminals, they are not Iraqis.'

'Al-Qaida.'

'Former regime.'

'Foreigners.'

'Those people who don't want things to settle down.'

A neighbour came around from next door carrying a pot of tea to ease the calamity. The Americans drove off, the little crowd dispersed and the afternoon settled back over itself.

At our second or third meeting Osama looked terrible. His eyes were recessed into charcoal hollows and the skin at his temples was stretched so thin I could see the veins throbbing beneath it. He had a pinched red mark on his neck, like a hickey, from bracing an RPG between his head and his shoulder; one wrist was bandaged and there was a Band-Aid stuck in the crook of his elbow. He said that he had not been sleeping or eating well and that he was tired from the operations, which were mostly at night.

'There were several this last week and they did not go well. I get headaches.' He had, in fact, his mother later told me, collapsed. In hospital the doctor had given him a vitamin drip and told him he was malnourished.

'The past week has been difficult, miserable, a failure.' Osama was ashamed and hurt, hung his head and looked off out of the window. Two helicopters were flying low, doors open, along the river bank. *'Allahu Akbar,'* said Osama, with a wry smile on his face. 'It would be very easy to hit them here because they would fall into the river. In other places they would damage houses when they crashed.'

During the week, the group had twice planted IEDs that failed to detonate and a third time had planted an IED that exploded against a Humvee but wounded no soldiers. The fourth time, Osama found himself among a group of American soldiers, trashing through the piles of roadside garbage with their carbines in search of hidden IEDs. Osama had the detonator strapped around his ankle; the IED they'd planted was a few metres away. The Americans didn't find it and Osama walked right past them. But the detonator didn't work. He was frustrated. 'And there were eight of them! We missed an opportunity.'

IEDs, RPG hit-and-runs; Osama was stuck in small-scale stuff against superpower armour. To be so much the underdog made him sad and defiant.

'You can't stand in front of an American tank, it'll just blow you up. We don't have any plans for fighting the Americans; it's out of the question to fight a tank.'

He stopped and looked grim for a moment. 'And when we hit them,' he said dully, 'it doesn't seem to make any difference. The situation cannot improve.' It was an unguarded moment, but he soon recovered from it. 'It does make a difference,' he said to counter himself, 'they are sending more soldiers.'

But you want them to leave—

'We discussed this among our group and we decided that we are happy they are staying because we can attack them more. This place will be their graveyard and their end will come at our hands. We decided among ourselves that we would take the suffering of our women and the Muslims that are killed or tortured and translate them into mortars and IEDs.' He looked determined to continue a violence that would inevitably engender the suffering of more women and Muslims, and I complained of this to him. He stuck his sullen belief out at me, proclaimed it like a banner on a wall.

'If there was no resistance it would mean that there was no religion. Our religion says that we must resist. The way to protect Islam is through jihad.'

One morning in the middle of May I watched the gravel car park of an American base a couple of hours outside Baghdad fill up with milling Iraqis and a few gatekeeping, chatting American soldiers. The Iraqis sold fruit and soda, DVDs and sometimes porn and beer (which was not permitted; the American Army in Iraq was dry). The American soldiers bummed cigarettes off the Iraqis. They swapped bits of learnt Arabic and broken English.

I saw a soldier cadge a light from an Iraqi and cheerily slap him on the back as thank you. I went over to the soldier and asked how things were going. Sergeant Tom Davis took off his helmet and showed me the wet wadding he put inside it to keep his head cool in the heat. He was waiting for a glass of tea and holding a small boy, the three-year-old motherless son of a banana seller, tickling him and swinging him upside down; the boy was giggling.

'The other gate to the base has been blown up and they hit an ammo dump with a mortar over the last month,' he told me. 'So you gotta know it's gonna happen. Just easier not to think about it.'

Osama's brother Duraid lived with his cousins nearby and sold cans of Pepsi out of a styrofoam cooler just outside the base's concrete blast-walls. He came up smiling and gave Sergeant Davis a fist-to-fist handshake. 'Hey, you are my brother, man.'

'We know just about everyone here,' said Sgt Davis, easy, smiling. I smiled back. Then I winced at the things Sgt Davis didn't know: that Duraid had a brother in the resistance and that Duraid himself had fired RPGs at American Humvees in Baghdad for the hell of it. And then I thought – a measure of solace – that here were friendly commercial relations in the car park and that maybe it was heartening to see fear and prejudice overcome face to face.

Duraid had been selling Pepsi at the base for a couple of months. If he sold Pepsi to the Americans in Baghdad, someone would shoot him for it. Here it was just a job, he was making some money. He was surprised at how nice and polite the American soldiers were – 'the Americans are good people, they treat us well' – and at the short shorts the women soldiers wore. 'Our eyes are out of our heads, with their sexy legs – we get hard-ons just looking.' Duraid was a puppy-dog teenager with a Chicago Bulls T-shirt and a baseball cap and an American accent. He liked Metallica and 50 Cent and movies with

Julia Roberts. He was curious, he was looking for nothing more than fun, he wanted to visit America.

'The way Osama thinks is different to the way I think,' he explained. 'I have girlfriends,' (he giggled a little), 'I drink, I smoke.' Osama had not had music at his wedding for religious reasons – although he had once admitted to me, laughing, that he'd liked Michael Jackson when he was younger.

After his exhaustion Osama had come to see his brother for a few days, to relax and regain some energy. The brothers played Juventus versus Inter Milan on Duraid's PlayStation. Duraid told Osama that he had been offered a translating job with the Americans, 600 dollars a month, solid work, and that he was thinking of taking it. Osama was not happy about this: he told Duraid it would be a sin, he didn't approve of his working with the Americans, and anyway it was dangerous; he was worried that the local mujahideen might learn about Duraid's job and kill him.

'I told Osama that when you respect them, they respect you back; when you hurt them, they hurt you back.' But Osama was intractable. When Duraid took the job a couple of weeks later, their relationship was strained beyond talking about it. Osama only shrugged when I mentioned it and said he knew there was nothing more he could do, his brother made his own decisions.

Their mother worried about them both. 'I don't want Osama to be fighting them and I don't want Duraid working for them,' she said. She had only learned of Osama's resistance activities when she was cleaning under his bed and found a box of RPG rockets, two Kalashnikovs and some grenades. She confronted him and he did not respond. She didn't tell his father; she knew he would only worry and then there would be two of them worrying. Osama didn't talk to any of his family. When they asked him, he said nothing. If they persisted he stood up and told them he would leave the house if they kept on about it. When Osama's wife, Aqeel, tried to pry something out of him he refused to answer, even if she turned away from him and cried about it.

'I only know his life inside this house,' Aqeel, seventeen and just pregnant, told me. We were sitting on the edge of the small double bed in the room which her parents-in-law had given up to the newly married couple. 'What he does outside, I don't know anything. When he is late sometimes I cry and then I think, *Why am I waiting? Probably he is dead somewhere.*'

Back in February, Duraid had gone out on three or four attacks with some mujahideen friends of his.

'We went to fight for fun. We'd drink and then go and do these things. It wasn't a religious thing.' The first time he went he fired an RPG at a Humvee under a highway overpass. 'It blew up and I saw a soldier come out with his arm burning. We just ran, we didn't shoot at him or anything.'

Why did you do it?

'Because of jealousy, when your heart burns for your country.'

The last time Duraid went out with a resistance group, it was an early afternoon in March, just a few days before four American contractors in Fallujah were pulled out of their burning SUV and dismembered. Qais, the emir of his group, had a plan to fire mortars at an American base in Adhamiya, the Sunni neighbourhood in Baghdad that was especially hostile to the American forces. There were five in the group; two had RPGs and everyone had a Kalashnikov. As they got to Adhamiya they saw that the Americans had surrounded the Abu Khanifa mosque with three tanks and several Humvees, ready for a raid. Qais said he was going to fire the RPG at the tank and they should all start running. He fired the RPG; it had no effect on the tank, but the gunners in the Humvees shot after them. The five of them ran like hell down a side street as the residents of Adhamiya spontaneously started shooting at the Americans. Qais was the last to turn the corner and was hit twice in the leg. They had to go back and drag him to the car and drive him to the hospital. He was there for ten days of operations; his leg was finally amputated.

Duraid spread his hands as he was telling this. 'He's sitting at home, he is still young. He is my age. My friend got hit and his leg was cut off. I was tired of bombs.' He paused, looking out the window, not at me, and said clearly in English: 'It's all useless, it's all bullshit,' and then more softly, like a defeat: 'I decided to go and work. It is much better.'

The resistance wasn't achieving anything?

'It's just going to make them stay longer. Of course if the Americans weren't being attacked their behaviour would change. But they got rid of Saddam and that was something good. We were not very happy about the war but we were hoping things would get better, I thought that we would become like the Gulf States.'

Have you told Osama you think like this?

He shook his head.

One early evening I overheard two jeans-wearing young men talking as they walked down Inner Karrada, a bustling shopping street in a good neigh-bourhood. It was a conversation that must have been repeated among families and groups of friends, relatives and colleagues all over Iraq. It began as a discussion and ended in a fight.

'We have spent our lives following Mr President. We are fed up of it,' said the one wearing a striped shirt.

'But who is your civil administrator now?' asked his more belligerent, more certain-of-himself companion. 'Who is your ruler? Who is issuing the orders? And who is running your state?'

The man in the striped shirt had no answer. 'But we have spent our lives chasing the slogans of Mr President,' he repeated, 'and those people [I think he was referring to Muqtada al-Sadr's Shi'a resistance] are doing exactly as Saddam used to do. Why can't we have a break?'

'*But you have to fight, you have to fight back against the Americans,*' *said his friend, exasperated. '*You will be killed, you will be a martyr, you will be a mujahid.*'

*His friend was unconvinced. '*Most of the Iraqis who have been killed were killed by what you call the "honourable" resistance.*'*

'*Watch it, my friend. Jihad is the right way.*'

'*Tell me, what have we got from Saddam or from the resistance? What have we got? I want to build my country. Let's use the Americans. Let's have a break and have a new life.*'

The argument increased as they passed the vegetable stalls and the man selling fresh lemon juice. They raised their arms as if to strike at each other's idiocy.

'*Jihad is the right way. Let me explain these things to you—*'

And his friend in the striped shirt nearly hit him as a crowd standing outside a kebab restaurant swallowed them up.

Once, in the car, the radio was on and Sheryl Crow was singing. Out of deference to Osama, I asked the driver to turn it off. Osama told me, laughing, no he didn't mind, really, we were the ones listening to the radio, he didn't need to impose his religion on a song.

Oh yes, I remember, I teased him, you like Michael Jackson!

He nodded. 'And I have been following his trial.'

Oh God, I said, isn't it weird?

'Yes, strange,' said Osama, 'I think the American government created this trial to distract people from the war in Iraq.'

Baghdad was full of twisted conspiracy theories. I think most Iraqis assumed all governments behaved more or less as nefariously as Saddam did – and since Western governments do try to edge and trim and manoeuvre public events such as trials or investigations or media campaigns, these conspiracy theories were often hard to dislodge in argument. Osama would just sit there and grin at my naivety. He knew very well the reality close to him, his family, his mosque and the

Qanat Road. He had no time for the nuances of democracy. I told him once that his world seemed narrow; he shrugged. It was very clear to him what he should do when he woke up in the morning. 'We only think about today, because today we might be killed. Tomorrow we think about tomorrow.'

Once, I asked him what kind of Iraq he wanted to live in and he hemmed and knotted a few sentences together trying to find an answer. I don't think he had seriously thought about it before. He asked if he could take the question away and come back with an answer next time. He wanted to represent seriously to me why he, and others, were fighting, but all conversations rounded back to emblematic words: *country, religion, family, honour, jihad.* His life's journey was already planned for him, predestined by God, its parameters sealed by the Qur'an. Detours and doubts, decisions and deliberations were all Western frippery, the distractions of infidels, blind to the truth. Sometimes when we argued he became frustrated with my inability to see what he saw so clearly and he would tell me – laughing a little, because our discussions were banter – 'You are so stubborn!'

The next time we met he sat down, we ordered tea, and he said very clearly: 'I want Islamic rule. But there would be conditions. All the other religions would be given their rights and allowed their traditions. But the Qur'an should rule in this region like it did in the time of the Prophet – the first Islamic state where Jews and Christians lived and had their rights respected.'

Okay, I said. What about freedom of speech?

'That is something very good, excellent. Everyone should have the right to say what they want openly, without pressure.'

So there can be criticism of religion, of imams and of sharia?

He paused and knit his brow and looked down at the table. These were serious matters. I pushed. Can I write an article in a newspaper saying that, for example, Islam controls women and keeps them in the home and subverts their independent rights?

He knew the answer. 'But that is not true. Islam does give its rights to women,' he said confidently.

That is what you believe, I countered, because you are certain of the truth of your beliefs. But am I allowed to express my opinion?

'Everything has its limits. I saw there was a cartoon in a newspaper in Beirut of a shoe with the words *Allahu Akbar* written on the sole. This is not respectful. This is not freedom. This is not criticism. It is insulting religion. Can I insult Christ in this way?'

I told him of course you could insult Christ any way you liked. I told him about *Piss Christ*, the Andres Serrano photograph of a crucifix drowned in urine. He looked at me and smiled and shook his head, uncomprehending, and said quietly, 'I don't understand your freedom.'

On May 31, a fat car-bomb went off on Kindi Street. Ten days earlier, a car bomb just around the corner had killed the president of the Governing Council as his convoy slowed down at the checkpoint into the Green Zone, the extremely gated community where the occupation officials and American troops were based. A couple of other journalists and I drove towards the black smoke billowing into the sky. One of them said, 'Doesn't look as big as last week's – that was at least six or seven cars burning.'

The bomb, apparently aimed at Ayad Allawi's convoy, had exploded in front of a row of shops and houses. Allawi had been named as interim transitional Prime Minister two days before. A car was left burning; the car that had exploded was scattered down the scorched asphalt. Two blocks away, the carcass was a spidery black skeleton, a soot silhouette. There were pieces of twisted metal, none larger than a thumb, and smashed rubble, a fragment of the waistband of a flayed pair of jeans, and black-pink gelatinous blobs. A boy of about fifteen was reverently picking these up and putting them in a plastic bag for burial.

A girl, perhaps thirteen years old, came out of the house with its windows blown out, directly behind the crater with its asphalt lip. She was distraught and crying and desperate. She said, 'He was standing by the car on the street, my father.' Her mother or her aunt stood behind her with a baby on her hip whose eardrums had burst and trickled blood on to its collar. The girl said, 'Take me to the hospital. I want to see my father. We are not safe in the house. Not even at home, not safe, we can't even stay in our house, our house was destroyed.' A policeman took her in his arms and gathered her into a hug and told her not to worry.

The police cleared the street, American soldiers pushed the TV cameras behind a coil of barbed wire, the burning car was extinguished, a man with blood on his calf sat on the bumper of a Humvee as an American medic bandaged him up. In the silence a woman staggered across the ruined street, screaming, 'Where is Zeid? Where is Zeid?' Someone told her, kindly, to go inside, but she sobbed, 'I can't,' and stumbled on.

A few days later I drove down Kindi Street, which by then had returned to normal. Outside the house that the thirteen-year-old girl had come out of there was a black-bannered death notice tacked to the wall.

My conversations with Osama went in circles. 'The difference is our religion,' Osama said, exasperated. He threw up his hands. 'It's not about having different opinions,' he said, 'it's about believing in something.'

You know, I told him, blowing things up is not the best way to achieve your aims. I told him I had been at the Kindi Street car bomb.

'Yes, I saw you there,' Osama told me. I was surprised.

What were you doing there?

'I was looking to see what had happened. This wasn't done by the resistance.'

I don't know and you don't know who did this, I told him.

'To some extent I know,' he said implacably. 'The people I know said it's not us. And even the place where the bomb happened; it's not a target.'

I'd heard the target was Allawi's convoy leaving the Green Zone.

'Even if it was a convoy, the resistance wouldn't put a car full of explosives in that kind of area.'

So who did it?

'I think the Americans would do such a thing. Their main aim is to give the resistance a bad reputation so that people go against the resistance.'

That's what you believe, I said, tired of me and him reflecting an *us* and *them* that I was trying, somehow, to bridge. But there's no reason to believe that. It doesn't make sense for the Americans to make Iraq even messier. It just makes them look stupid and the situation seem out of control.

'On the contrary. I feel the Americans do this in order to show people that the resistance is bad so they lose faith in it.'

As he repeated himself, I repeated myself: But there's no evidence the Americans are responsible for car bombs.

'Of course a thief would not admit to something he had done. We have come to the conclusion, we have discussed it, that it wasn't the resistance. I told you before,' he said calmly, 'there isn't anyone in the resistance who would kill an Iraqi. One time for a week we didn't attack a convoy because there wasn't any way of doing it without hurting people. We could have attacked police cars but we don't; some police are working with the Americans and some aren't, and we can't tell which is which.'

Isn't the violence destabilizing the whole country? What's the biggest problem in Iraq now?

'Security.'

Is blowing things up contributing to that security?

'We're doing it to hit Americans, not to make security.'

So you hitting Americans is more important than security?

'Yes.'

I looked down at my notebook, at the table, at the glass of orange soda. There was a *bang* from the other side of the river. I asked Osama about the wider world, about al-Qaida, Islam versus the West, suicide bombs and kidnappings.

'To be honest,' he said, 'when you use the word *terrorist*, I get angry.'

But I have not used the word *terrorist*, I reminded him.

'Al-Qaida have a big capability and work all over the world and can follow the Americans wherever they go. At the beginning our aim was to kick the Americans out of Iraq. But now it has changed. I am ready to follow the Americans wherever they go, to go to any other country and kill Americans. I mean the army only, not civilians. This is the message I want to get through to Americans. As I see it most of them support American attacks on Muslim countries. And as long as they support this American policy they will be targets themselves.'

But what about the bombs in Spain, I asked him, what's your position on the targeting of civilians?

'Yes, I supported them.'

But the majority of Spaniards were against the war.

'Really?' said Osama doubtfully. 'I didn't know that.'

And in England the majority of the people were against British troops being sent to fight the war in Iraq.

'But,' said Osama, recovering, throwing it back at me, 'the bombs in Spain changed something. People saw there was a threat, so they bought their safety. They kicked out the prime minister and brought their troops home.'

That's terrorism.

'No, it's not. You don't live here. You don't feel how we're boiling now. When each day passes and it feels like your soul is leaving your body. Killings in the street, our oil is being stolen, there's no electricity.'

I wasn't going to let go: But the electrical engineers were targeted, killed. They were Russians; they weren't even in the coalition.

And we drove ourselves around another corner: full circle again to the car bomb in Kindi Street, back to the same position, talking across a fence, separated.

'Who can tell you that the resistance did that?' Osama said.

I threw my hands in the air. Okay. Okay. I lit a cigarette. My definition of terrorism is when civilians are deliberately targeted for a political aim. What's your definition of terrorism?

Osama looked at me coyly. 'You'll be angry.'

No, tell me.

'Israel and America.'

No, tell me the definition, like it would be in a dictionary.

'Terrorism as I see it is when a person with money and power goes into a neighbourhood and starts shooting randomly. I think that is terrorism.'

And I sat back in my chair and conceded the argument.

A week after my last meeting with Osama, three American Humvees and a tank surrounded a house in Osama's neighbourhood at four in the morning. They were looking for someone called Fadhil. They knocked on a door and someone told them Fadhil lived next door. A helicopter chopped sticky Baghdad air overhead. A few minutes later, Fadhil and four others in Osama's resistance group were arrested.

Osama was the only one not there and not caught. The next morning when he heard about the raid he emptied his house of weapons as fast as he could and got ready to leave.

Will they talk? Will they give your name?

Osama was worried and frightened and his eyes darted around, looking at everything fast without focusing. 'It all depends on the beating they get.'

His mother came into the room, with tears in her eyes. 'They will come here, to this house, and Osama will not be here and they will take whoever is here. And his father doesn't know. I will have to tell his father. They will arrest all of us!'

It was clear they would have to tell the father and all would have to flee the house for a few weeks.

His mother sat on the sofa paralysed by the thing and the fear of it. She sighed something like a gasp. Osama left within the hour, first for his cousins' place out of Baghdad, and then, probably, for Syria.

AIRDS MOSS

Kathleen Jamie

If you were minded to visit Airds Moss – and I wouldn't discourage it because anywhere else and it would be in a tourist guide, and it's interesting, if you've a taste for ambivalent places – you could turn off the lorry-laden A70 a few miles west of Powharnal opencast mine and follow the B-road which links the farms on the moor's edge.

Lowland Scotland, and especially the western part of it, is not a place usually associated with unpeopled landscapes. We have the Highlands for that, and the Lowlands are often considered an unfortunate place you must drive through to reach the wild remotes. But Airds Moss is pretty much undisturbed. It's what is called 'low-altitude blanket bog', and it plateaus off at 600 feet to form a triangle between the diverging valleys of two westward-flowing rivers, the Bellow Water and the young river Ayr, from which it takes its name. It has seen human escapades, of course – a memorial at the moss's eastern edge marks a seventeenth-century Covenanters' skirmish, and there's a twentieth-century forestry plantation. Between these two interruptions, however, there was coal.

Airds Moss sits at the edge of the east Ayrshire coalfield. When coal and ironstone were discovered here, and the first pits sunk in the

1850s, the population began quickly to grow. Railways were built, whole villages grew at the moss's western fringe, generations lived and died. The coal lasted for a long century, and its villages too, but you have to look hard for them now.

I went there on a clear day in early March, leaving the A70 and crossing the Bellow Water, which means descending into a gloomy ravine and passing under a three-arched stone bridge. The bridge is just a crumbling relic now; the railway it carried is long gone. A hundred years ago it would have borne ironstone and coal to the town of Lugar, where the blast furnaces were. ⟵

After the river was crossed, the road climbed on to the wide expanse of open moor, which to me was so surprising that I pulled into the first passing place and got out of the car. I hadn't expected anything so rural – rural, but not unfrequented. My lay-by wasn't too bad, there was only a shattered windscreen still contained in its rim, but down the road other lay-bys were strewn with busted tellies and beer cans and bin bags disgorging rags.

I strolled down the road for a while, letting the silence settle in my ears. Overhead flew a party of peewits, so that was a bonus. A hundred yards over the moor stood a brick-built shed with an arched roof which made me think of a temple, rather than a leftover from another dismantled railway. But something about it, and the arched bridge I'd passed beneath, was arousing in me an old memory. Yes, I thought, of course, I have been here before. When I was wee, in a Ford Anglia, with my dad. Two or three times a year we'd come to Ayr, my parents' native place, to visit grannies. We'd travel across the moors by the same A70, down through Muirkirk and Lugar and Cumnock to arrive at the coast, there to be exclaimed over and served high teas. But my dad would always contrive to escape, to take an afternoon away 'on the skite', as my mother called it, which for him meant exploring railways. He'd leave the family and take himself into the countryside, stick his hands in his trouser pockets and saunter along railway tracks to see what locomotives were lying in what sheds and sidings. Sometimes, if I pleaded, he'd take me along too. We must have come up here in pursuit of colliery engines, steamy and black as the Earl of Hell's waistcoat, but that was nearly forty years ago. Now, the mines and their railways are no more.

The reason I stopped was, Airds Moss looked like for ever. A wide, silent for ever of pale, winter-brown moor. I hadn't expected that. There was no wind to worry the moor grass which, apart from the patch of commercial forestry, visible as a green square in the middle distance, lay as it must have done for 10,000 years. Aside from the old railways and the bings, I mean.

I spread the Ordnance Survey map on the bonnet. It showed plenty of bings hereabouts, little pocks with jagged teeth, but it called them by the more polite English word *tip*. *Bing* is a peculiarly Scots word. From the lay-by here, I could count four eruptions out on the moor, marking where coal and ironstone pits had been. They were dark heaps slowly being colonized by grass and scrubby hawthorn, and each was served by a track from the road but the tracks had been blocked with huge boulders and the track-ends were full of dumped rubbish. But at the foot of one range of bings was a small shining loch. A nameless loch, according to the map, so maybe it wasn't very old, but it was holding a fair number of birds. I got out the binoculars and was leaning against the car looking at a party of whooper swans when, to my surprise, a male hen harrier glided into view. He was hunting low over the marsh and I followed him until, with a single wing-beat, he vanished behind the bings. Now that was a turn-up for the books. Hen harriers and busted tellies; a liminal place, the edge of the moor.

My great-great-grandmother on my mother's side was a girl called Maggie Rowan and I have a soft spot for her, based on nothing but her sylvan name, though I bet she was a tough cookie. She first turns up in 1881 as a sixteen-year-old mill-girl in nearby Catrine, one of the eight children of a labourer. In 1890 she married a local coal miner, James Stirling, himself a miner's son, and promptly produced John, my great-grandfather.

Though they did their courting hereabouts, on the edge of Airds Moss, both Maggie and Jim were Irish – we were all migrants once – brought over as children when their parents joined the droves of Irish workers piling into Scotland. They were sinking pits quickly then, populations were growing fast, but still more labour was needed and in 1870 the mine owners, Bairds & Co, advertised in the Irish papers. Some migrants were Catholic and famine-driven, some were Protestants with ancestral links to Ayrshire, and over they sailed, bringing their families and sectarianism with them.

My mother is ambivalent about her forebears, and certainly doesn't volunteer much. In her view the past is probably best forgotten, and ours is not the kind of family that tells, or even reads, stories. A Presbyterian distrust of the idle fancy, I suppose. My father has never, to my knowledge, been to a theatre or even read a novel. My mother reads thrillers but is not much interested in the shapings and workings of fiction. The last time the subject of her family came up, she just said, 'Ach, they were all miners,' and reached again for the TV remote. Her tone, as ever, was poised exactly between contempt and pride.

But I had names, and Ordnance Survey maps which give less detail with every new edition, and copied from Dale Love's informative *History of Auchinleck* a 1900 sketch map which showed this area as a populous warren of miners' rows – their mean little terraced houses – and railways, pitheads, stables and schools. The present maps show no more now than a square mile of moor edge with a few stalwart farms. When I told my dad I was thinking of going off on the skite to see what I could find of the old mining places, he warned me there might be nothing at all. He hasn't been up this way himself for a long time, there being no railways now, but I wanted to come anyway, because there's no such thing as 'nothing'. (He meant opencast mining. 'Nothing' as in 'blown to smithereens'.)

So the hen harrier and the quiet moor had left me feeling wrong-footed. Having read census returns and local history, my head was full of miners' rows and dark mines and Victorian squalor, and on the way I'd passed with trepidation the big opencast mines round Muirkirk, so I hadn't imagined sunlit moors and distant hills, the warmth in the spring sun. I drove on. Half a mile further, a farmer was leaning over a gate contemplating some sheep. The animals' field had been cleaved by a narrow, steep-sided cutting, as though a massive axe had fallen there. It could almost have been Neolithic, an ancient and mysterious earthworks. Then the road took a sudden dog-leg round a farm, and this was one of my way-signs, a jumping-off point, if possible, for the hike I wanted to make up on to the Moss.

The mining settlement to which Maggie Rowan had come as a bride was called Darnconner, and it appeared on the most recent map as a farm, the furthermost from the road, well up on to the moor. There were two or three possible approaches shown, but the map was ten years old, and as I turned the corner I was still steeling myself for an industrial-apocalyptic vision.

And there it was, to an extent. At the roadside, wide metal gates were lying open, and the remains of a sign which had once read DANGER NO ENTRY hung on a pole. Beyond the gates a rutted track led into an arena of rubble and rain-flooded craters, and heaps, like sand dunes, of some sort of mineral which was a curious duck-egg green, certainly not coal. (Later I was told it was fireclay.) Beyond this site, a couple of fields' length away, any access on to the moor was blocked by a long dark rampart of spoil, maybe thirty foot high, steep as the curtain wall of a medieval castle. I pulled into the site access and walked a few yards through the gates. It was orderly enough; bulldozed avenues, organized heaps of green stuff, old mangled cars stored in a pile of their own. The whole site was fenced off from the surrounding farmland by wire, nothing that couldn't be climbed, but it was hardly inviting and I didn't fancy floundering through the mud-filled ruts. Anyway, in the direction of Darnconner, like a monstrous mouldy loaf, rose the daddy of the old coal bings.

I scanned the site with binoculars, but it was eerily quiet. No rumbling diggers or men in hard hats – or so it seemed, but right on cue a yellow Caterpillar digger chuntered into view with its bucket raised. Back and forth it went, back and forth. I couldn't fathom what it was doing, and didn't like to watch, because at the gates a yellow sign, itself with an aggressive picture of binoculars, informed me that I, too, was being watched, and so the whole thing began to feel sinister, what with the moor, the stranger's car in the lay-by, the trash in the ditch, the lumbering machine. It might be the gateway to my ancestral homeland, but I didn't fancy it, and retreated to the car for another look at the maps, and plan B. —

Pretty sure now that Darnconner hadn't been obliterated, merely obscured by bings, I drove a couple more miles on the narrow road, making a series of right turns to follow the moor's edge as it curved north-west. Then, just before the road entered a forbidding pine plantation, a more promising farm track set off on to the moor. I left the car, determined this time to walk regardless of obstructions and my own unease. It wasn't my patch, and the trash in the ditches felt like the territorial markers of a foreign tribe. Frankly, there was something not quite right about this landscape. Indians behind the bluff, that sort of feeling. But my papers were in order. Like a guarantee of safe passage or letters of introduction, I'd shoved into my pocket the family history I'd written out, the three generations of miners and miners' wives, and all their many children. I took that, the old sketch map and a camera and set off along a pitted track. It passed a couple of houses, but no one was about. Green and wavy like a distant sea, the fireclay site was half a mile ahead, sheep grazed the rough grass at the foot of more bings, a pair of thrushes hopped about on the railbed that ran from them. The sun shone, and somewhere nearby a curlew uttered its lovely, evocative call, and I began to relax.

But just for a minute. All at once, over the moor came an eldritch sound: *I'm forever blowing bubbles*, as though played on a vast heavenly xylophone. I stopped, looked around, but the sheep were grazing heedlessly, the thrushes hopped, the moor and the bings were as before. *Pretty bubbles in the air. I'm forever blowing bubbles* ... Then it stopped. I heard it twice more that day, drifting over the countryside.

The track was potholed, but the holes had been repaired so it must have been in use; and it was muddy ('glaur' is the local word for this clinging mud). Where it met the fireclay site, access to the site was blocked by a large boulder and the track did an abrupt left turn and continued slightly uphill, flanked by bings and the fireclay dump on one side, and on the other by a long, ominous embankment. However, I could see buildings at the top of the track and they appeared almost dreamlike. It was hardly Manderley, but it was unsettling to approach an old house through an unnatural landscape of ramparts and bings. And it was the long embankment to my left, screening something from the track, where the strange atmosphere was coming from, where things were not quite right. I squeezed through the fence, climbed the bank and there was what my father had warned me of. All the land between this farm and the next had been gouged out. Opencast. A dirty great hole. But there were no machines, no workings, no noise. It too had been abandoned and was flooded with sullen green water which looked almost ashamed of itself, as if it couldn't help but gather there. It was like a loch, there were even a few ducks. The banks on the far side fell and rose, almost as nature intended, but they were old bings. 'Ye banks and braes,' I thought, 'how can ye bloom sae fresh and fair?' But 'I'm Forever Blowing Bubbles' had installed itself in my head instead.

The farm looked like a proper farm, a single-storey L shape with a steading and a tractor parked there. It was older than any of this intrusion, so had once enjoyed the sun and a southward view, but the big bing had put paid to that. In its yard two white geese came about me, hissing, and an elderly dog shambled up and began licking my hand. A light was on within the farmhouse; a car was parked outside. The farm was not without neighbours; behind fancy railings were two tidy red sandstone houses with decorative ridge tiles, out of place among the farm and bings, more like middle-class townhouses than the homes of miners or farmhands.

The geese kept a wary eye, the dog licked my hand. So far as I could see, the track continued through the farmyard, turned right beyond some stored caravans, and ended out on the open moor. It was out there, according to the old map, that the considerable Darnconner settlement had been, where all the folks rolled into my pocket had lived out their lives.

To read the census returns of 1881, 1891 and 1901 is to read, obviously, lists of names. Miners had big families and, like a dim torch shone into the gloomy interiors, the census illuminates for a moment the faces inside the cramped houses. I suppose the census enumerator must have walked this very track, knocking on door after vanished door and entering with a patient hand the names of all those people he found. In 1891, at No. 41 Darnconner were James and Agnes, my great-great-great-grandparents, with three grown-up children, and a grandson, too. Three generations in a room and kitchen, not to mention the lodger. Maybe they took in the lodger when their son Jim had married Maggie and established his own house a couple of doors along. Their names are noted in the same handwriting, along with their baby son's. Another baby was born a couple of years later but she died. By 1901, however, when the census man again came knocking, they'd filled the house with five children more. In the census, the adult men are 'coal miner', 'pitheadman', 'general labourer'; the women are 'miner's wife'. The census man had to note how many windows each dwelling had, and for every household he has drawn a single pen line – one.

My own knock was answered by a heavy-faced man in green farmer's overalls. He spoke a robust Ayrshire Scots, and though he was quite elderly, he retained some of his youthful stature. Aye, he said, this was the right place, and aye, he recognized the family name, there had been folk of that name here until the end, that is, until after the Second World War, when the last pits had closed and the opencast came. The old man had been born here, so he'd seen a lot of change. Twenty-six pits there had been up here, at one time or another. As one was worked out, another would be sunk, it was like that.

The old farmer offered to show me where the rows had been, so he took a stick and came out into the yard and, with the old dog following and the geese at a watchful distance, we walked together round the back of the farm, pausing to look at the two sandstone townhouses, both with mature trees growing around them. One he said had been the manse, though the church is long demolished, and the other had been the schoolteacher's house. There were a number of caravans parked up around the steading, a whole row of them covered in tarpaulins and backed against a brick wall under some sycamore trees. Maybe storing caravans for winter was a way for the farmer to make a few bob. I mean, folk would hardly come here for their holidays.

I say that, but as soon as we were behind the farm where neither the fireclay nor the opencast site could be seen, I felt the same astonishment at the sight of the open moor of dun-coloured grasses and moss, warming into spring under a huge blue sky. It looked as though we would walk out on to the moor, but at the gate the farmer stopped and with his stick, pointed to two shrubs growing side by side a short distance out on the Moss.

'See thon twa trees?' he said.

I nodded.

'That's whaur the raws were.'

'That's it?' I said.

'That's it. And see thon brick wa?' – This time he turned to point behind us, he meant the wall the caravans were parked against.

'Well, that's a' that's left o' them.'

'Do you mind if I have a look?'

'Not at a'. There's been a few folk, ower the years, come out to see the place.'

By 1913 the miners were growing militant. In that year two union men, Thomas McKerrell and James Brown, made a tour of all the miners' settlements in Ayrshire and compiled a trenchant and sardonic report on the housing conditions they found. They went to nearly sixty places but, being stuck up on the wet moor, Darnconner was among the worst. My great-great-grandparents, Maggie and Jim, their children, Jim's mother and siblings and cousins were among the tenants the union men found here, nigh on 400 of them, living among 'stinking refuse strewn about' and the 'glaur' that, because of the want of pavements, lay inches deep at the doors. Keeping clean amid glaur and ash and coal dust would have been the womens' bane, but the mine owners had provided 'not a single washhouse for all these residents'. They had boilers for washing, but 'whoever erected them forgot to build a house over them, and the women have to do their washing in the open air'. As for latrines, that was a joke. A mere eleven closets had been provided and 'none had a door, so owing to the want of privacy they cannot be used by females or grown up persons. The floors of the closets are littered with human excrement.'

As the farmer and the old dog made their way back to their house, I stood between two caravans looking at the brick wall that had been the back wall of a row of houses, each not much bigger than the caravans stalled here now. 'The coal houses are so dilapidated several tenants keep their coals beneath their beds.' You have to wonder, with yourself and your husband, your five or six children, and coal beneath the bed, where in God's name do you put the lodger?

The sunshine had enticed gnats from their hiding places and they danced in throngs above the tussocks of moor grass. I jumped clump to clump, trying to avoid the mossy hollows, across the place where most of the miners' rows had been, till I reached an old railbed which, being made of clinker and raised a little, was drier underfoot than the surrounding moor, and I walked along it a way. A spur off the railbed led to the inevitable bing, which supported enough scant grass to allow a couple of sheep to graze and they went bounding off as I climbed on to its summit. My foot slipped and released a few flakes of coal slag, so I put them in my pocket, with a notion to take them home to my mother. The little elevation, twenty-five feet or so, afforded a view of the whole hushed and windless moor and its plantations. Impossible to imagine that folk didn't come out here for a walk on a summer's evening. I was trying to imagine the arrival of the union men, perhaps by train, and how news of their visit would have spread. They might have met Maggie Rowan, millgirl turned miner's wife, leaning against her door-jamb in a pinny and telling them just what she thought of the excrement and glaur she struggled against. She was forty-seven then, but I doubt she was able to speak because she was already ill, and died just three weeks after. Her husband managed on for a few more years until his miner's lungs got the better of him, and he died here too.

Airds Moss tilted away cast and south, to where the Bellow Burn ran, and a mute parade of lorries travelled the distant A70. I could see Powharnal Opencast as long black terraces cut at the hill's foot. My dad says they're thinking of reopening one of the disused railways to serve it. That's how it's done now, opencast. The old pits here were just that, pits sunk 180 feet down into the ground. When one was exhausted, it would be abandoned, another would be sunk a quarter-mile away. Above the opencast mine the land rose solemnly into distant, rounded hills, pale after the winter, some still with snow on their north-facing slopes. Up on the hilltops, turning slowly and with no hint of irony, were wind turbines.

The union men had recommended only one thing: a closure order. I don't suppose they had bulldozers in 1913, but that's what they meant. Away with the mean, damp, cramped houses and the ashpits and middens and doorless, unprivate privies. Away with the disease, excrement and glaur. Decent workers' houses provided at fair rent by the council, not the mine owners, that's what they were agitating for.

I doubt they would believe the place a century on; I was having trouble believing it myself. The mines themselves away, and the miners too, leaving no trace bar the grassed-over bings and old railbeds. Where the 'horrible place of Darnconner' had been, with its hundreds of homes, I could see, if I squinted, tiny filaments of cobweb wafting from the moor grass. Where there had been pitheads, clanking trains, and all those reeking chimneys, there was nothing but a sweep of obliviating moor, and a twittering lark. Just two small bare trees marked the place. Hazels, I think, not rowans.

During the First World War my great-grandfather John Stirling bade farewell to his recently widowed father and his grandmother and sisters and headed off with the Royal Artillery. He was twenty-five and already a widower himself. He left spoil-heaps, trenches and glaur, so if he actually got to the front perhaps it wasn't as alien to him as it was to lads from parishes of ploughing matches and harvest home. John had a better war than many; he returned intact and with a new wife and a child, my grandmother. If he brought them up here on to the moors, to the filthy rows, it was only for a short while. These mines were in decline anyway. Belatedly, after the next war, the union men had their wish, the miners' rows were cleared, and the last tenants rehoused in new council schemes in Auchinleck. Then the

Coal Board dispensed with the niceties of sending men below ground in cages, and stripped the earth back, dumped the clay aside, gouged out the coal, and left the hole behind.

I scrambled down off the bing and followed the railbed just a bit further and discovered that the land on the north-west of the moor is being restored. The slow remedial work of nature, a thread of moss here, a crumb of windblown earth there, is being hastened by human intervention. The old railbeds had become paths, new gates were installed, friendly signs announced a forest, which was a tad premature but around yet more old bings many trees had indeed been planted, protected by plastic tubes. The tubes stuck up from the earth as if venting something below ground. There must be tunnels down there still, 180 feet down in the utter dark. The same tree-planting treatment is proposed, if I understood the farmer right, for the fireclay site – to spread a depth of sewage sludge over it and so bring the soil's fertility up, then plant willows – the unlovely term is 'biomass' – which can in turn be cropped as fuel for power stations. Some query the wisdom of using sewage sludge, for fears of pollution and run-off. When the union men described Darnconner as 'a sea of human excrement', they spoke truer than they knew.

John went to work at Garallan pit, near Cumnock, where his wife Isabel bore another six children. My mother remembers her grandfather coming home and setting his carbide lamp on the mantelpiece. Over six foot, tall for a miner. He died, too breathless to walk, not long before I was born.

The farmer was waiting for me in the yard, but I didn't know what to say, I couldn't decide if it was an appalling place to live or not too bad, considering.

I hazarded, 'Some place to live – funny to think of all those folk here . . .' but he made a non-committal sort of sound.

'When you read about the housing . . .' I said.

'Aye, the housing . . . But mind you, when the last were sent down to Auchinleck, some of the auld anes didnae want to go. And there's been a few have wanted their ashes scattered here, whaur the auld raws were.'

I was thinking, as I walked back down to the car, that if I had a gift for the reconstructed landscapes of fiction I could write an epic novel with an embossed cover, a saga-of-three-generations of miners, migration, poverty, sectarianism, moors and marriage, glaur and war, militancy and the black lung. I could call it *The Cry of the Curlew*. Or maybe *Blowing Bubbles*, because when I reached the car that weird dislocated tune was wafting through the air again. It must have been an ice-cream van touring the housing schemes of Auchinleck. But I couldn't write that stuff. It's too sure of itself. Too . . . unequivocal.

A child's scooter was lying on the roadside verge but it was hard to tell if it was waiting for the school bus to deliver its owner home, or whether it, too, had just been dumped. I suppose you can understand it, in a way, why folk go to all the effort to cart their knackered sofas and tellies away up here – some old memory of the moor as the place of tips, abandoned workings, closure orders and all that's best forgot. My mother's attitude. I'd taken a few photographs of Darnconner to show her, because I knew she'd be interested despite herself. I'm a poor photographer, though, and the photos won't show much of her forebears' short lives and toil; just a farmhouse and some bings, and a stretch of empty moor.

SRI LANKA: DECEMBER 28, 2004

John Borneman

The morning after Christmas in Unawatune, a village on the south-western tip of Sri Lanka. We got up around 7.20, went swimming at the beach across from our hotel, returned to our room, showered, and by eight we were one of two couples enjoying breakfast in our hotel's dining room, a small, solid concrete structure with three open sides and a corrugated tin roof on the beach side of the narrow road that runs through the village. Our hotel, the Neptune, was on the other side of the road. By nine we had finished our meal and our final pot of tea and were preparing to leave and go snorkelling, when Parvis, my partner, said, 'The beach has disappeared.' The water was nearly at the level of the dining room, which stood about eight feet above the beach and twenty feet from the water. We stood up and went to the edge to look. The water was lapping at the chairs put out for sunbathing. They began to float and risked being swept into the sea. I said, 'The chairs are disappearing. That's too bad.'

A waiter in the restaurant tried to help a young girl wearing a fashionable black bathing-suit climb over the wall from the beach, as the water seemed to be engulfing her. But she let go of his hand and tried to climb the stairs instead. She was halfway up when the rising water swept the stairs away, too, and the man helped her up out of the water. She laughed and ran out of the restaurant. Everyone else laughed along with her. A wave splashed over the wall and got us a bit wet. By then all the tables in the restaurant were full of tourists, and everyone laughed, again, amused at this unexpected wave. Within seconds, however, the water had risen above the three-foot restaurant wall; dishes, teapots, silverware fell off the tables, which began to float and overturn. The water was dark, not the clear blue in which we earlier swam. It poured over the top of the wall and small waves lapped at everything inside the room. The Sri Lankan waiters stood as dumbfounded as their customers. In an orderly fashion, without a word being exchanged, everyone rose to leave. No rush here in paradise, which is where I told my friends I was going: a sunny spot in a lazy, friendly beach town on the south Sri Lankan coast.

It is all happening too fast to recognize what is happening. I am helpless as I realize that the waves are going to cover us; the water is becoming a rising wall, not a wave, and simply overtaking us. We, like the others, are not able to escape. I ask myself, is this a tidal wave? Parvis is in front of me and seems to be waiting for others to clear out, not in any particular hurry, unfailingly polite as always. I rush towards the exit and say, 'Let's get out, Parvis, don't wait.' But he is thinking, he tells me later, don't panic, take your turn. Seconds later, I am one of the first to begin down the steps to the street, towards the hotel, but an aggressive push by the gushing water on my legs and lower back sweeps me off my feet, and I take a ride down the steps on my ass as if on a water slide. With my left hand I am holding high our guidebook, *Lonely Planet Sri Lanka*, with all the addresses of places we are going to visit. This is only our fourth day out of seventeen planned in Sri Lanka, and, I think, there goes our itinerary. The water grabs the book from my hand. I sense a middle-aged woman, also sliding on her ass, close behind me. I land on my feet about two yards away, but tables and chairs follow me, threatening to knock me down, so I walk, crawl, stumble quickly towards the wall in front of me, which is part of our hotel. To the left side of the entrance I see two windows above the water, which is rising about a foot every ten seconds. A Sri Lankan girl wraps her arms around my neck. She is light, and I drag her, or she floats behind me, toward the window sill, and a Sri Lankan boy hooks his arm in mine as I begin to climb the wall. Or are we simply floating up the wall?

The window sill provides no purchase, no place to grab on to. I am afraid of falling back into the water, which is not only coming straight at me now but has also formed a river through the village street, a swift river that begins to roar and threatens to carry me to my left towards the other end of the village. I suddenly find my hands are able to grasp on to the wooden lattice work between the upper window panes and I grip it, as do the girl and boy next to me, who are screaming hysterically, their dark, round eyes betraying a deathly fear, and a plea for my help. I am silent, though; Parvis later describes me as 'bewildered'. I think, just hold on.

The water had broken the windowpanes, enabling us to resist its pull. But it is still rising, and within less than a minute we are submerged. I hold my breath. The water goes down, and then re-submerges us. This pattern repeats. The boy and girl scream loudly every time the water subsides. After our second submersion, the boy suggests we go through the open window into the building, but I notice the low ceiling and think, better to ride the water outside, we might get trapped under the roof. So we climb as high as we can up the wall. Nothing goes through my mind but to hold on, to focus on the immediate task, to stay calm, to relax – no prayer, no thoughts of others, or of what to do next.

I do, however, take note of the absurdity of the moment, as the water waxes and wanes, comes up, goes down. I keep thinking, it won't stay up for ever, it has to retreat, and we will keep rising to the top. But its intensity increases, threatening to pull us into the river and downstream, and it gets louder, competing in my ear with the screams of the boy and girl. My glasses get caught in the girl's long hair, close to a ribbon that holds her hair in place but is coming loose, and as she turns now and then and struggles to climb the wall, to stay above the water, my glasses nearly come off. I think, if I lose them, I can't see! 'My glasses are caught in your hair,' I tell her, but she is in no state to understand. Perhaps she doesn't speak English. Eventually I tear them free from her hair. We endure this for what seems an eternity but is more likely less than ten minutes.

Just as quickly as the water arrived, it begins to go back, steadily. It reveals the boy's leg, and he sees a huge gash above his thigh. He whimpers, then stops; his mouth remains open for a long time, silently screaming. The girl looks at his wound, and then looks at me uncomprehendingly. When the water recedes below the window sill, I jump down. The water now stands slightly above my waist. The boy and girl make garbled noises, grunts, whines, pleading that I should take them with me. I say, just stay calm, and motion, wait, wait, the water is going down, I'll get help. I wade back towards the restaurant, which has collapsed, and I find a concrete slab under the water to stand on, and I survey the scene. Could I make it to our room on the second floor? I notice electric wires in the water. I think, electrocution! The street is empty. Everything is quiet. Risk it, I say to myself. As I move, a young Sri Lankan man emerges from the hotel; he approaches and extends his hand. I say, 'No, I am okay, get the two people on the window sill.'

Then I hear Parvis calling in a panic-stricken voice, 'John, John, John.' I turn the corner and he holds out his arms and rushes towards me. We embrace. 'I thought I lost you,' he says, 'I have been calling for minutes, didn't you hear?' 'No,' I say. We wade through the water on the fully devastated ground floor. The street is still a river, now shallow instead of ten feet deep, littered with furniture, instruments, the head of a Buddha statue, odd pieces of things. We go upstairs to our room. It is untouched. The bathing suit I had put out on the balcony is now dry. The sun continued shining through this whole thing, whatever it was. Why, I think, do I expect the sun to coordinate its activity with the ocean?

We look out on the balcony, where another couple are standing. Parvis tells them they can stay as long as they like. We think out loud: Should we leave or stay? I sit on the bed to take stock of what happened to me, to us. Parvis gets out his camera. 'There's always a second wave,' he says, and he begins to yell to people as they appear in the street/river below us, 'Get out. Get out. A second wave. Leave.' They don't seem to respond, they look dazed. 'You wouldn't believe this,' he says to me, as he takes pictures. 'Look at this, come and look at this.' I join him. 'Look at the water,' he says. It had receded to about a kilometre away from the former beachfront. Furniture, house parts, trees, tuk-tuks, cars, clothes, everything human filled the exposed ocean bed.

We discuss what to take with us. Parvis says one computer. I say, 'Oh no, both.' We gather our documents, passports, money, leave all our clothes, and go downstairs, planning to go inland. The people on the street appear to be mindlessly wading through the water, though then I realize they are looking for the missing.

Parvis goes back upstairs for some reason and finds the young boy who had shared the window sill with me. He is resting on a bed. Some tourists had bandaged the opening in his thigh. I wait for Parvis, get anxious and impatient – the second wave! I yell for him, he answers the first time, yes, then gets angry at me, and refuses to answer. I go upstairs and find him: he has offered to help carry the young boy, who is in shock and cannot walk, and holding on tightly to a blanket and a pillow. Parvis has given his computer to someone else. I retrieve it. As they carry the boy downstairs, the water tugs at the end of his blanket. He drops it, and then his pillow, saying nothing. Local people are urging everyone to leave; there is higher ground behind the hotel.

We begin climbing the mountain, including some large, slippery rocks. We take off our shoes or sandals to scale them.

Halfway up the mountain, women are wailing under an open-sided hut. Men are gathered around a woman lying on her back under a blanket. I realize she is dead. There must be more, I think. Further up, a Japanese nurse is treating people's wounds with nothing but a bit of cotton and alcohol. I have scraped knees, several deep cuts on the left foot, with glass embedded in my soles, and a few other scratches. Parvis seems to have nothing, though later he discovers a cut on a toe that becomes infected.

Further up the hill, everyone had a different and unique story they wanted to tell. I sat at the nursing station and listened. I would have liked to take pictures, but it seemed obscene to photograph people in that state. Some were seriously wounded, others, like me, merely cut and bruised. A young man borrowed a notepad and a pen from me to make a list of the missing: a Czech girl, a Polish boy, Japanese, Australian, Brit – and that was the start of his efforts. He said that nine tourists and twelve Sri Lankans from our village had been confirmed dead. The dark-haired girl in the black bathing-suit showed up, totally in control. She was from Singapore and in Sri Lanka with her boyfriend, who had sustained a few deep cuts and scratches across his chest. 'You're the one who climbed out of the water in our restaurant,' I said. 'Yes,' she laughed. As she was being pulled out of the water, the concrete wall of the restaurant was scratching her legs, so she let go, to use the stairs, which then got swept away. 'I was laughing as it collapsed,' she said, 'because I thought, damn, there went my cigarettes!'

We European and Australian and Asian tourists gathered in the villages on the top of the hill, and local people served us tea. The second wave came, and the third, but Unawatune had been evacuated. Some watched the second wave from the hillside. We had water, and a couple of boxes of cookies, but we had no other food.

Local phone lines were not working. I ran into a couple of Australians and Brits with cellphones, but their networks only allowed them to call home, which they did, and were told by people at home watching CNN, that a 'tsunami' – I'd never heard the word before – had hit, that thousands of people were dead. A few villagers came by and offered individuals beds or floors in their huts to sleep on, but most of us planned to sleep out in the open. Only mosquitoes to fear.

Just before dark, the men from the village returned from their search for the missing. One of them, a middle-aged man, came up to me. He had found the body of his closest friend, who, he said, greeted him endearingly every morning on his way to work. He would miss that. He offered Parvis and me his bed for the night. Anything to avoid the hard ground, I thought. He repeated his offer – I am an honest man, he asserted, a carpenter, and my house is on the way to the bus route.

Parvis felt bad about leaving. He wanted to share the fate of the others. I thought: no food, no communication, no sign of rescue; we're only a burden; let's make our way inland. We spent the night at the carpenter's house. It was late, and there were only candles, no electricity, so we declined his offer of food and only drank tea with him. He gave us his explanation for the tsunami: the culture of the beach, the drugs, the tourists, the sex – the wave was revenge for these pleasures. The last time something like this had happened was 2,000 years ago, he said, as recorded in some mythical texts. I did not sleep a wink that night (though Parvis did fine), it was either a mosquito that got under our net, or the hardness of the bed.

The next morning, we climbed down a steep mountain passage with our luggage and walked along the beach road to Galle amid massive destruction: debris everywhere, upturned buses, uprooted railroad tracks. Eventually we got a bus to Colombo.

When I switched on my computer, nearly a hundred emails awaited me. My friends and students in Syria, where I was teaching in Aleppo as a Fulbright professor, made anxious enquiries. 'I am really concerned about you and happy new year *alsalam alikom* bye,' wrote Abedasalam, a young waiter who had just been fired from his job at a restaurant I often went to. 'I and rami ask god to you the full health and coming back quickly,' wrote Husam, a clerk who worked down the street from my apartment in the al-Medina souk. When I replied 'bruised but alive' to them and other Syrian and American friends, many wrote back to express relief and joy that their prayers had been answered.

I am not a believer, and the experience of the tsunami only confirmed my agnosticism. It was an arbitrary, capricious event – nature calling. It had nothing to do with my being human, and in that respect was infinitely humbling. To my Syrian friends I wrote, 'But God sent this tsunami, he tried to kill me.'

NIGHTWALKING

Robert Macfarlane

Moonrise woke me at one that morning. The blizzard had blown over, the cloud cover had thinned away, so when I opened my eyes there was the moon, fat and unexpected above the mountains. Just a little off full, with the shape of a hangnail missing to black on the right side, and the stars swarming around it.

I scrambled up and did a little dance on the snowfield, partly to get warm, and partly because if I looked backwards over my shoulder while I jigged, I could see my moon-shadow dancing behind me on the snow. It was that bright.

That moonlight had made quite an effort to reach me. It had left the sun at around 186,000 miles per second, then proceeded through space for eight minutes, or 93 million miles, then bounced off the moon's surface and proceeded through space for another 1.3 seconds, or 240,000 miles, before pushing through troposphere, stratosphere and atmosphere, and arriving with me: trillions of lunar photons pelting my face and the snow about me, giving me an eyeful of silver, and helping my moon-shadow to dance.

Snow perpetuates the effect of moonlight, which means that on a clear night in winter mountains you can see for a distance of up to thirty miles. I know this because I saw that far that night, and because I have seen that far on several previous occasions. Several, but not many, because you require the following circumstances in unison: a full moon, a hard frost, a clear sky – and a willingness to get frozen to your core.

The previous day, the weather forecast had spoken of a 'snow-bomb' – the remnant of a polar low, dragged south by other fronts – which would hit north-west England, before quickly giving way to a high. When the snow-bomb landed, temperatures over high ground were expected to drop to fifteen degrees below zero Celsius, and the wind would gust at speeds of up to fifty miles per hour.

It seemed too much to hope that I would be rewarded with such conditions. But I drove north the next morning on the chance that the forecast would hold true. I passed through snow and sleet, and reached the mountains by the afternoon. The path to them switch-backed up through old oak woods from the lake shore.

Snow lay between the trees. Black snow-clouds were starting to hood the earth from the east. An hour up the mountain, I crested a rise into a hanging valley, and the lake below became invisible. I had left early spring and walked back into winter. All I could see were white mountains. Sunlight fell like bronze on distant snowfields. The wind was satisfactorily cold, and already so strong that I had to lean into it at a ten-degree vaudeville tilt.

Beyond the hanging valley, the path was thick with hard snow. The small rocks on the path were grouted with ice. By the time I reached the ridge, the blizzard had reached me. Visibility was no more than a few metres. The white land had folded into the white sky. It was harder to stand up in the wind. I cast about for sheltered, flat ground. There was none.

Then I found a small tarn, roughly circular, perhaps ten yards across, pooled between two small crags, and frozen solid. The ice in the tarn was the milky grey-white colour of cataracts and noduled in texture. I padded out to its centre and tested the ice's strength. It did not even creak beneath my weight. I wondered where the fish were. The tarn was, if not a good place to wait out the storm, at least the best place on offer. I liked the thought of sleeping there, too: it would be like falling asleep on a silver shield, or a giant clock face.

'Noctambulism' is usually taken to mean sleepwalking. This is inaccurate: it smudges the word into 'somnambulism'. 'Noctambulism' means walking at night, and you are therefore etymologically permitted to do it asleep or awake, just as, etymologically, you can somnambulate at high noon. I recommend awake for noctambulism, and night for somnambulism, but those are just my preferences.

Generally, people noctambulize because they are seeking melancholy. Thus Kafka, a regular noctambulizer, who wrote in his diary of feeling like a ghost among men. 'Walked in the streets for two hours weightless, boneless, bodiless, and thought of what I have been through while writing this afternoon,' he noted of a winter night.

There is another reason for being out at night, however, and that is the mix of strangeness and wildness which the dark confers on a place. Sailors talk of the eerie beauty of seeing a familiar country from the sea: it turns the landscape inside out. Something similar happens at night, except the landscape is turned back to front.

Night, though, is a diminishing resource. Among the many resources which modernity is exhausting is darkness. Look at a satellite image of Europe taken on a cloudless night. The continent gleams. Italy is a sequinned boot. Spain is trimmed with coastal light, and its interior sparkles like a rink. Offshore, Britain burns brightest and most densely of all.

This excess of light pollutes night with what is known as skyglow. Artificial light, inefficiently directed, escapes upwards before being scattered by small particles in the air, such as water droplets and dust, into a generalized photonic haze. The stars cannot compete, and are invisible. Energy worth billions of pounds is wasted. Migrating birds collide with lighted buildings. The leaf-fall and flowering patterns of trees – reflexes which are controlled by perceptions of day-length – are disrupted. Glow-worm numbers are dwindling because their pilot lights, the means by which they attract mates, are no longer bright enough to be visible. Towns tint their skies orange: from a distance it seems as though something is on fire over the horizon.

Up on the ridge, the blizzard thrashed for two hours. I lay low, got cold. I watched red reeds in the tarn's frozen water flicker in the wind. Hail fell in different shapes: first like pills, then like tiny jagged icebergs, then in a long shower of rugged spheres. It clustered in dents in the tarn ice.

Lying on the tarn, I remembered August Strindberg's experiments with night photography in the 1890s. Strindberg had become convinced that photography, despite its relentless reliance on surface for its effects, might in fact see through exteriors to reveal the essences of people and objects. First, he tried to photograph the human soul with a large and lensless camera which he built himself. He failed. Next, he tried to photograph snow crystals, hoping to reveal the central monadic form of the universe: the repeating structure which, at all scales, determined the world's appearance. He failed. Finally, he tried to photograph the stars. On cold nights, he laid large photographic plates, primed with developing fluid, out on the earth, hoping they would take slow pictures of the stars' movement.

He failed. But the resulting plates carried exquisite evidence of the stars: dots of white and silver light, constellated into strange astral patterns. Strindberg named the plates 'celestographs', and he sent them and an account of their making to the French astronomer, Camille Flammarion. Flammarion did not reply. It is likely that the astral patterns were caused either by dew or dust settling on the plates, creating a nebula of micro-oxidations.

On the tarn, slowly over half an hour, the hail turned to snow, which had the texture of salt, and fell on to the ice with a soft granular hiss. Then the snow stopped altogether.

After moonrise had woken me that morning, and after I had danced, I looked around. I was in a metal world. The unflawed slopes of snow on the mountains across the valley were fields of iron. The deeper moon-shadows had a tinge of blue to them; otherwise, there was no colour. Ice gleamed like tin in the moonlight. Everything was neuter greys, black and sharp silver-white. The hailstones which had fallen on me earlier lay about like shot or ball-bearings, millions of them, drifted up against each rock or nested in snow-hollows. My face felt burned by the cold. The air smelled of minerals and frost.

Looking south, the mountain ridge was visible, curving gently round for two miles. It was as narrow as a pavement at times, at others wide as a road, with three craggy butte summits in its course. To east and west, the steep-sided valleys, unreachable by the moonlight, were in such deep black shadow that the mountains seemed footless in the world.

I began walking the monochrome ridge. These were the only sounds I could hear: the swish of my breathing, the crunch my foot made when it broke through a crust of hard snow, the wood-like groans of plate ice cracking and sinking as I stepped down on it. Once, stopping on a crag-top, I watched two stars fall in near-parallel down the long black slope of the firmament.

When the ground became steep, I moved from rock to rock. On the thinner sections I walked out to the east, so I could look along the cornice line, which was fine and delicate, and proceeded in a supple phosphorous curve along the ridge-edge, as though it had been engineered.

At one point, several small clouds drifted through the sky. When one of them passed over the moon, the world's filter changed. First my hands were silver and the ground was black. Then my hands were black and the ground was silver. So we switched, as I walked, from negative to positive to negative, as the moon zoetroped the passing clouds.

In 1979 three scientists, Lamb, Baylor and Yau, performed what is agreed to be among the most beautiful experiments in the field of optics. They used a suction electrode to record the membrane current of pieces of toad retina with high rod-cell density. They then fired single photons at the retinal pieces. The membrane current showed pronounced fluctuations, proving that a rod cell could be tripped into action by the impact of a single photon.

The human eye possesses two types of photo-receptive cells: rods and cones. The cone cells cluster in the fovea, the central area of the retina. Further out from the fovea, the density of cone cells diminishes, and rod cells come to predominate. Cone cells are responsible for our acute vision, and for colour perception. But they only work well under bright light conditions. When light levels drop, the eye switches to rod cells. It takes rod cells up to two hours to adapt most fully to the dark. Once the body detects diminished light levels, it begins generating a photosensitive chemical called rhodopsin, which builds up in the rod cells in a process known as dark adaptation. So it is that at night we become more optically sensitive. Night sight, though it lacks the sharpness of day sight, is a heightened form of vision. I have found that on very clear nights it is possible to sit and read a book.

Rod cells work with great efficiency in low light-levels. However, they do not perceive colour: only white, black and the greyscale between. Greyscale is their approximation of colour: 'ghosting in' is what optic scientists call the effect of rod-cell perception. It is for this reason that the world is drained of colour by moonlight, and it is also for this reason that night is the natural home of the melancholic.

The brightest of all nightscapes is to be found when a fat moon shines on a landscape of winter mountains. Such a landscape offers the maximum reflection, being white, planar, tilted and polished. The only difficulty for the night-walker comes when you move into the moon-shadow of a big outcrop, or through a valley, where moon-shadow falls from all sides and the valley floor receives almost no light at all. The steep-sidedness of the valley is exaggerated: you have the powerful sensation of being at the bottom of a deep gorge, and you long to reach the silver tide-line of the moonlight again.

After two hours, I reached the flat-topped final summit of the ridge. I cleared some space among the rocks, and slept. The cold woke me just before dawn, and I was grateful to it. I cut a snow-seat facing east, and sat watching as the dawn broke, polar and silent, and then colour returned to the world.

The first sign of it was a pale blue band, like a strip of steel, tight across the eastern horizon. The band began to glow a dull orange. As the light came, a new country shaped itself out of the darkness. The hills stood clear. Webs of long, wisped cirrus clouds, in a loose cross-hatched network, became visible in the sky. Then the sun rose, elliptical at first, red as a snooker ball, astonishing in its colour.

Within half an hour the sky was a steady tall blue. I stood up, feeling the early sunlight warm my cheeks and fingers, and began to make my way down. As I got lower, the land began to free itself from the cold. I could hear the gurgle and chuckle of meltwater moving. Yellow-green tussocks of grass showed through the snow. I found a waterfall which was only part frozen. Its turbulence was surprising and swift after the frozen night-world. I stood for a while watching it, then drank from the stone cistern it had carved out beneath it and snapped off an icicle to eat as I walked.

The shoreline forest, as I came back through it, was dense with dawn birdsong. I felt tired, but did not want to sleep. Near the head of the lake, just downstream of a small stone-and-timber bridge, where the river widened, there was a deep pool, glassy and clear, with a bank of turf next to it.

I sat on the turf for a while and watched light crimp on the water and flex on the stones which cobbled the streambed. I undressed and waded into the water. It felt like cold iron rings were being slid up my legs. Dipping down, I sat in the water up to my neck, huffing quietly with the cold. The current gently pushed at my back. I listened to the whistles and calls of a shepherd, and saw sheep streaming across the tilted green fields on the lake's far shore. In an eddy pool a few yards downstream, between two dark boulders, the curved rims of sunken plates of ice showed themselves above the surface. The sun was now full in the eastern sky, and in the west was the ghost of the moon, so that they lay opposed to each other above the white mountains, the sun burning orange and the moon its cold replica.

THE PARIS INTIFADA

Andrew Hussey

One cold evening in late November last year I left my flat in southern Paris, took the *métro* to Saint-Denis, a suburb to the north of the city, and then a bus to an outlying council estate, or *cité*, called Villiers-le-Bel. The journey took little more than an hour but marked a sharp transition between two worlds: the calm centre of the city and the troubled banlieue. 'Banlieue' is often mistranslated into English as 'suburb' but this conveys nothing of the fear and contempt that many middle-class French people invest in the word. It first became widely used in the late nineteenth and early twentieth centuries to describe the areas outside Paris, where city-dwellers came and settled and built houses with gardens on the English model. One of the paradoxes of life in the banlieue is that it was originally about hope and human dignity.

To understand the banlieue you should think of central Paris as an oval-shaped haven or fortress, ringed by motorways – the *boulevards périphériques* (or *le périph*) – that mark the frontier between the city and the suburbs or banlieue. To live in the centre of Paris (commonly described in language unchanged from the medieval period as *intra muros*, within the city walls) is to be privileged: even if you are not particularly well off you still have access to all the pleasures and amenities of a great metropolis. By contrast, the banlieue lies 'out there', on the other side of *le périph*. The area is *extra muros* – outside the city walls. Transport systems here are limited and confusing. Maps make no sense. No one goes there unless he or she has to. It's not uncommon for contemporary Parisians to talk about *la banlieue* in terms that make it seem as unknowable and terrifying as the forests that surrounded Paris in the Middle Ages.

The banlieue is made up of a population of more than a million immigrants, mostly but not exclusively from North and sub-Saharan Africa. To this extent, the banlieue is the very opposite of the bucolic *sub*-urban fantasy of the English imagination: indeed for most French people these days it means a very urban form of decay, a place of racial tensions and of deadly if not random violence.

In November 2005 the tensions and violence in the banlieue threatened for one spectacular moment to bring down the French government when, provoked by a series of confrontations between immigrant youth and the police in the Parisian banlieue of Clichy-sous-Bois, riots broke out in major cities across France. They were fuelled at least in part by the belligerence of Nicolas Sarkozy, then Minister of the Interior, who said that he would clean the streets of *racaille* ('scum'). Since then the troubles in the suburbs have been sporadic but have never gone away. The day before I set off for Villiers-le-Bel, two teenagers of Arab origin had been killed at La Tolinette, one of the toughest parts of this tough neighbourhood, after their moped crashed into a police checkpoint. They had been on their way to do some rough motocross riding in an outlying field. No one in the area believed that this was an accident but rather a *bavure* – the kind of police cock-up that regularly ended with an innocent person dying or being injured. Within an hour gangs of youths closed their hoods, covered their faces with scarves and went on to the streets to hurl petrol bombs and stones at the police. A

McDonald's and a library were burned down. Streetlights were smashed or taken out so that the only light came from the flames of burning cars. The mayor of Villiers-le-Bel, Didier Vaillant, had tried to negotiate with the gangs but retreated under a hail of stones. A car dealership was set alight. By daybreak, as many as seventy policemen had been injured. President Sarkozy, in Beijing, was alerted to the fact that a small but significant part of French territory was beyond control.

By the time I arrived in the banlieue the next day, the scene was set for another confrontation. 'See, they treat us like fucking niggers,' said Ikram, a young man of Moroccan origin who lived nearby. He pointed at the police lines that were blocking all access to certain areas. Ikram didn't actually use the word 'nigger'. He used *bougnole*, a racist French term to describe Arabs that dates back to the Algerian War of Independence, 1954–62, when the French military used torture and terror against Algerian insurgents. The term *bavure* also comes from the same period. (The most infamous *bavure* was the so-called Battle of Paris, in October 1961, when a skirmish on the Pont de Neuilly between demonstrating Algerians and police led to a riot that ended with more than a hundred dead North Africans. Their bodies were thrown into the Seine by the police, under the orders of police chief Maurice Papon. Papon had previously been involved in the deportation of Jews during the German occupation of the early 1940s but was not accused of his crimes until the 1990s.)

As it was getting dark – at around five p.m. – the mood and atmosphere changed in Villiers-le-Bel. Drinkers in the café where I was sitting smoked harder. Civilians – that is to say non-rioters – were hurriedly leaving the scene and then, quite without warning, the area was entirely made up of the police and their opponents. I watched as the gangs moved in predatory packs around the road, the car parks and the shops. I had heard on many occasions their stated aim of shooting a policeman. The rumour was that this time the gangs were armed, with cheap hunting rifles and air pistols. But the only weapons I saw belonged to the police.

Later, on returning to the centre of the city and my flat, and then watching on television the surprisingly dispassionate coverage of what was going on in the banlieue, I reflected that Paris had become hardened to levels of violence that, in any other major European capital, would have threatened the survival of the government. The French were used to violence, to mini-riots and clashes between police and disaffected youth. Even in my own neighbourhood, the quiet district of Pernety, armed police regularly sealed off parts of the *cité* adjacent to the RER train lines running into central Paris (the RER is the fast commuter train that connects the banlieue with the city). Across the city, the Gare du Nord was a regular site for battles with police. It was there that an unnamed Algerian had recently been shot during another police *bavure* in the *métro*.

This past winter I set out to learn more about the banlieue. I started by visiting the area around Bagneux, to the south of the city. This was far from being the worst neighbourhood of the banlieue: Courneuve and Sarcelles to the north are much more run down and dangerous. These districts were portrayed in the 1995 film *La Haine*, in which a black, an Arab and a Jew, all from the banlieue, form an alliance against society. I found the film unconvincing, because I suspect that a Jew could never be friends with blacks and Arabs in this part of the city. Also, although I know plenty of Jews in Paris, I don't know a single Jew who lives in the banlieue. At one time the Jewish community flourished in the suburbs and there are still synagogues in Bagnolet and Montreuil that date from the 1930s. *La Haine* is an enjoyable thriller but no more true to Parisian life than *Amélie*, the fairy tale set in Paris that became an international hit in 2001.

Much more realistic, to my mind, were the intrigue and shocking violence of Michel Haneke's film *Caché* (2005). This is a story of murderous revenge in which a middle-class French intellectual is disturbed by memories from a deeply repressed and violent past. His fears are related both to his mistreatment of an Algerian child adopted by his parents and his complicity as a Frenchman in crimes committed by the French state against Algerians. *Caché* is set in the southern suburbs of Paris, not too far from Bagneux, the centre of which is much like any small French town. There is a church, a small market, cafés and green spaces. The architecture is not uniformly 1960s brutalism: there are cobbled streets and small, cottage-like houses.

The original meaning of 'banlieue' dates back to the eleventh century, when the term *bannileuga* was used to denote an area beyond the legal jurisdiction of the city, where the poor lived. In the late fifteenth century, the poet and bandit François Villon described how Parisians feared and despised the *coquillards*, the army deserters and thieves who lived on the wrong side of the city wall. As the city grew larger through the eighteenth and nineteenth centuries, the original crumbling walls of the Old City, now marking the city limits, became known as *les fortifs* or the 'zone'. This was marginal territory, with its own folklore and customs, a world of vagabonds, ragpickers, drunks and whores. This was also the fertile ground that later produced street singers such as Frehel and Edith Piaf, who dreamed and sang of *le Grand Paris* or *Paname* (slang for Paris), of the rich city centre only a few miles away from where they lived but as distant and alien as America.

In the 1920s and 1930s, as France began to industrialize rapidly, the population of the banlieue swelled with immigrants, mainly from Italy and Spain. The *banlieue rouge* ('red suburbs'), usually led by a Communist council, were key driving forces in the Front Populaire ('the Popular Front'), the working-class movement that swept to power in May 1936. The first truly left-wing government in France since the days of the Commune of 1871 (when a rag-bag of anarchists and workers' groups held the city between March and May), its success changed France for ever with the introduction of paid holidays, a working week of forty hours and the sense that, for the first time, the workers were in control.

During the *trente glorieuses*, the period of rapid economic growth that occurred between the 1950s and 1970s, other major towns across France adopted the Parisian model of building estates far outside the centre. The first new developments in the banlieue were sources of pride to the Parisian, Lyonnais and Marseillais working class who were often grateful to be evacuated there from their slums in the central city. Once, long ago, the banlieue was the future.

I remarked on this to Kevin, a rangy black lad of twenty who, with his mate Ludovic (roughly the same age), was showing photographer Nick Danziger and me around the area. Both of them were obsessed with football, especially with the English Premier League. They were impressed that I had met and interviewed French footballers Lilian Thuram, who is black, and Zinedine Zidane, who is from an Algerian family. 'I can't imagine this as anyone's future,' Kevin said, gesturing at the car parks and boarded-up shops. 'All anybody wants to do here is to escape.'

Kevin himself is a footballer of average ability; he had a trial with Northampton Town in England. 'I hate France sometimes,' he told me. 'And, at other times, I just stop thinking about it. But the real thing is that here, when you are born into an area and you are black or Arab, then you will never leave that area. Except maybe through football and even that is shit in France.'

I asked him about his English name. 'I like England. And like everyone here, I don't feel French, so why should I pretend?'

Ludovic, who at least has a more conventionally Gallic name but is originally from Mauritius, joined in. 'They don't like us in Paris, so we don't have to pretend to be like them.' By 'them' he means white French natives, *Gaulois* or *fils de Clovis*, in the language of the banlieue.

It is this Anglophilia, transmitted via the universal tongues of rap music and football, which explains why so many kids in the banlieue are called Steeve, Marky, Jenyfer, Britney or even Kevin. They don't always get the spelling right, but the sentiment is straightforward: *we are not like other French people; we refuse to be like them.*

As we walked and talked we soon entered a dark labyrinth of grey crumbling concrete. This was 'Darfour City', a series of rectangular blocks of mostly boarded-up flats where the local drug dealers gathered. This was what the police called a *quartier orange*, largely a no-go area for the police themselves as well as for ordinary citizens. DARFOUR CITY was scrawled across a door at the entrance to a block of flats. As we wandered deeper into the estate, there was more graffiti, in fractured English: FUCK DA POLICE; MIGHTY GHETTO. Halfway down the street we were hailed by a pack of lads, all black except for one white. They were all smoking spliffs.

These were the local dealers, a gang of mates who, according to Kevin, could get you anything you wanted. They delighted in selling dope and coke at wildly inflated prices to wealthy Parisians. They were pleased to hear that I was English. 'We hate the French press,' said Charles, who is thin and tall and of Congolese origin. 'They just think we're animals.'

They looked at me with suspicion. 'No one comes here who isn't afraid of us,' said another of the gang, Majid. 'That's how it should be. That's how we want it.'

Then the gang tired of me and my questions; I understood it was time to go.

In January 2006 a twenty-three-year-old mobile-phone salesman named Ilan Halimi was kidnapped in central Paris and driven out to Darfour City in Bagneux. Halimi, who was Jewish, had been invited out for a drink by a young Iranian woman named Yalda, whom he had met while selling phones. It turned out that it was her mission to trap him and lure him away from safety. Yalda later described how

Ilan had been seized by thugs in balaclavas and bundled into a car: 'He screamed for two minutes with a high-pitched voice like a girl.'

Three weeks later, Ilan was found naked and tied to a tree near the RER station of Sainte-Genevieve-des-Bois. He died on the way to hospital. His body had been mutilated and burned. Since being kidnapped, he had been imprisoned in a flat in Bagneux, starved and tortured. Residents of the block had heard his screams and the laughter of those torturing him, but had done nothing. Fifteen youths from the Bagneux district were arrested. They were members of a gang called the Barbarians, a loose coalition of hard cases, dealers and their girls who shared a hatred of 'rich Jews'. The alleged leader of the Barbarians, Youssef Fofana, went on the run to the Ivory Coast to escape arrest. His trial began in Paris in February 2008.

Theories about motives for the crime were initially confused. Was it a bungled kidnap? A *Clockwork Orange*-style act of pure sadism? Or was it the work of hate-fuelled anti-Semitism? The police were, at first, reluctant to say that the crime was motivated by anti-Semitism. But Yalda, who turned out to be a member of the Barbarians, said in her testimony that she had been specifically told to entrap Jews by the gang. Her confession was widely reported, as was the fact that she called Fofana 'Osama', in homage to Bin Laden.

At the same time, out in the banlieue itself, the murder took on a skewed new meaning: the word was that what had begun as a heist and kidnap to extort a ransom from 'rich Jews' had become a form of revenge for crimes in Iraq and, in particular, the scenes from Abu Ghraib. Bizarrely, in the view of some, this made the torturers martyrs, soldiers in what is being called the Long War against the white Western powers. An ever-present slogan in the banlieue is *'Nique la France!'* (Fuck France!). The kids of Bagneux accordingly gloried in their own 'intifada'. They openly identified with the Palestinians, whom they saw as prisoners in their own land, like the dispossessed of the banlieue.

One afternoon I visited the rue des Rosiers, the Jewish quarter at the heart of the Marais. This is a little Tel Aviv in central Paris, a place where French-Israeli waitresses, dressed in combat fatigues, serve up beer and schwarma. It was from here, during the Occupation, that French Jews began the final journey to the death camps of Eastern Europe or, closer at hand, to the the the Vél d'Hiv, the sports stadium to the south of Paris where thousands died because of squalid conditions. The cries of the dying in the stadium, like those of Ilan, were ignored by their Parisian neighbours.

In a coffee shop near the rue des Rosiers, a place owned by Moroccan Jews, I spoke to Myriam Berrebi, herself a Tunisian Jew, about the killing of Ilan. 'I have never known such terror and anger in this neighbourhood,' she said, 'not since the shootings at Jo Goldenberg's Deli.'

She was referring to the massacre by Arab gunmen in 1982 of six diners at Goldenberg's Deli, just across the street from where we were sitting. 'But, you know,' she continued, 'there were other echoes too – especially of the Nazi period, when Jews died and everybody pretended everything was all right.'

After the murder of Ilan, to the anger of many Parisian Jews, the Chirac government dissembled about 'social problems' in the banlieue. Only Nicolas Sarkozy, then an ambitious Minister of the Interior and whose mother was a Sephardic Jew, denounced the murder of Ilan as 'an anti-Semitic crime'.

With Sarkozy's intervention the terms of the debate were changed. Was the killing of Ilan the isolated act of individuals, or was it a political murder in the largest sense: an act that expressed a collective hatred? Did it belong to individuals, or the whole community?

Good stuff happens in bad places. I said this to Hervé Mbuenguen as we sat in his flat in Vache Noire, in what is meant to be a less impoverished neighbourhood of Bagneux. 'That is a very quaint idea,' he replied. 'Nowadays the banlieue only means one thing: trouble.'

Hervé's family is originally from Cameroon but he has lived in the
banlieue all his life. He is educated and articulate, a graduate of the
elite Ecole Normale Supérieure, and makes a living as a computer
engineer. 'If you live here, if you speak with an accent *banlieusard,* you
are condemned as an outsider in Paris and in fact all French cities. It
is in fact a double exile – you are already an outsider because you are
black or Arab. But then you are an outsider because you are *banlieusard.'*

Yet he has chosen to live here. 'The banlieue is my home. I cannot
feel comfortable anywhere else.'

Hervé's block of flats was rotten; the walls of the lift-shaft were
falling apart from the inside. But his apartment was tidy and
organized. This was a place where a full, hard-working life was being
lived. His flat is the headquarters of Grioo, a website devoted to the
African diaspora in France (Grioo is in fact a mild corruption of the
West African term *griot,* meaning 'storyteller'). With Hervé, I was
trying to talk through the idea that, in spite of the murders and the
riots, good work is going on in the banlieue. The success of the Grioo
website is testament to that. The only taboo subject between us was
that of Jews in the banlieue. I had asked, innocently, why there were
so few, if any, Jews left.

'They cannot live here,' Hervé said.

Hervé is not an anti-Semite but his remark reflected a shameful
reality about the prevalence of anti-Semitism in the suburbs, a reality
that makes even open-minded people such as him feel awkward.
Through several weeks of my travels in Bagneux, I chatted casually to
hip-hop kids, footballers, football fans and self-proclaimed *casseurs*
('wreckers' or 'rioters'). I met and talked to them in cafés, at bus
stops, in shops and sports centres. It was mostly entertaining and
enlightening; there is a lot of serious laughter and benign mischief
going on in the banlieue. But the more time I spent there, the more,
like a secret code being revealed, I began to pick up on the casual

references to synagogues, Israelis and Jews. These references would be refracted through the slang of the banlieue. So phrases such as *sale juif*, *sale yid*, *sale feuj*, *youpin*, *youtre* (this last term dates from the 1940s and so, with its echoes of the Nazi deportations, contains a special poison), all racist epithets, were being widely used but also framed by irony. Yet for all I heard about the crimes of the Jews, it was hard to find anyone who had met a Jewish person. 'We don't need to meet Jews,' I was told by Gregory, a would-be rapper and Muslim from La Chapelle. 'We know what they're like.'

But that was the problem: nobody knew what 'they' were like. It seemed to me that hating Jews – like supporting Arsenal or listening to the rap band NTM – had become a defining motif of identity in the banlieue.

Hatred of the Jews: this was one of the oldest traditions in Paris, dating back, like the very notion of the banlieue, to the medieval period. In *Portrait of the anti-Semite*, written in the wake of the German occupation of Paris, and searching for an explanation for his compatriots' complicity in anti-Semitic crimes, Jean-Paul Sartre describes the typical French anti-Semite as driven by his own sense of 'inauthenticity'. By this he means a sense of existential and psychological unreality which at once challenges and undermines the anti-Semite's identity as a middle-class Frenchman. Unconvinced of his own true place in society, the anti-Semite nonetheless finds comfort in the reality of his Jew-hatred.

Anti-Semitism in France is a phenomenon of the political Left as well as of the Right, of the underclass as well as of the ruling elite. This in part explains, if it does not justify, the writings of Louis-Ferdinand Céline, the great chronicler of Parisian working-class life in the twentieth century. Céline hated Sartre. In response to Sartre's accusation that he had been paid by the Nazis to write anti-Jewish propaganda, Céline retorted with fury that he did not need to be paid to feel hatred for Jews: his hatred was authentic enough. Rather, it was his identity as a petit-bourgeois, a member of a class forged in the late nineteenth century and already sinking into history, that felt most unreal. Céline describes the banlieue to the north of city as a kind of inferno. His description of the imagined banlieue called Rancy in his 1932 novel *Journey to the End of the Night* is as dank and polluted as the Wigan described by George Orwell in *The Road to Wigan Pier*. But Céline's banlieue is infected by a particular kind of metaphysical misery:

> The sky in Rancy is a smoky soup that bathes the plain all the way down to Levallois. Cast-off buildings bogged down in black muck. From a distance, big ones and little ones look like the fat stakes that rise out of the filthy beach at the seaside. And inside it's us!

Céline was a pessimist, obsessed by disease and filth. He saw no hope for the poor of the banlieue. In the end, he blamed nearly everything on the Jews. 'War in the name of the bourgeoisie was shitty enough,' he wrote in one of his pamphlets, 'but now war for the Jews! ... half-negroid, half-Asiatic, mongrel pastiches of the human race whose only aim is to destroy France!'

In recent years, Céline has become an inspiration of rappers in the banlieue, who admire his use of stylized slang and street language. The rapper Abd al Malik has devoted a song on his latest album to Céline. 'Céline revolutionized literature because he was very close to real people, like us rappers today,' he said in an interview on his blog. 'That's generally a good thing, but there's a danger about being so close to the people; you can start to embrace all the things that are wrong with society.'

Today the literary heir to Céline as the chronicler of the Parisian underclass is novelist Michel Houellebecq. His vision of the banlieue is of a failed utopia, a district that has now reverted to wilderness.

Houellebecq gives voice to this view in the novel *Platform* as the businessman Jean-Yves Espitalier muses on the rape of a female colleague by Arab and black youths on a 'dangerous railway line' between Paris and the banlieue.

> As he was stepping out of his office, Jean-Yves looked out over the chaotic landscape of houses, shopping centres, tower blocks and motorway interchanges. Far away, on the horizon, a layer of pollution lent the sunset strange tints of mauve and green. 'It's strange,' he said, 'here we are inside the company like well-fed beasts of burden. And outside are the predators, the savage world.

*

One afternoon I visited Jean-Claude Tchicaya, a black official in the *mairie*, the local town administration. I had read an interview with him in which he had spoken of knowing the murderers of Ilan Halimi. Tchicaya was dressed in a smart suit with a black leather *gilet* draped over his back. In his office, amid old copies of *Jeune-Afrique* and *Libération*, there were portraits of Martin Luther King and Nelson Mandela. Wasn't it a contradiction to admire these 'heroes of peace' when the reality of the struggle for racial equality had also involved so much death and conflict?

'Struggle doesn't just mean violence,' Tchicaya said. 'It also means dignity.'

I asked him how he knew the murderers of Halimi.

'This is not my milieu,' he said, 'but everyone in Bagneux knows everyone.'

Then I asked him if he knew the Tribu Ka, a group of black militants, resident in Bagneux, who openly declared that they hated Jews and had issued messages in support of the Barbarians who had killed Ilan Halimi. Tchicaya was becoming agitated. 'Look,' he said, 'all extreme situations create extremists. It's the pattern of history. But I don't want to know about those people.'

Out on the street, the Tribu Ka is in fact a hard-core political movement of black supremacists led by Kémi Seba, whose real name is Stellio Capo Robert Chichi. He was born in Strasbourg in 1981 into a first-generation immigrant family from Benin. Kémi was a clever, restless and angry young man who, at the age of eighteen, began his apprenticeship in radical politics with Nation of Islam's Parisian chapter, based in Belleville, the traditionally working-class district in the north-east of the city. Founded by Elijah Muhammad in the 1930s and now led by Louis Farrakhan, Nation of Islam has only a tangential relationship with 'authentic' Islam. It preaches that the black races are descendants of the Tribe of Shabazz, the lost tribe of Asia.

Nation of Islam gave Kémi a cause and a philosophy, but he was determined to lead his own political group. He travelled to Egypt in his twenties, and there he began to construct his own worldview, a mix of Islam, black power and revolutionary politics. Kémites are the chosen race of God, or Allah, and will lead the black race out of slavery to their rightful position as masters of the world. The non-violent methods of Martin Luther King (a betrayer of the black race, according to Kémi) and Gandhi (an enemy of Muslims and agent of the British Crown) are denounced as ineffectual.

Even when Kémi was imprisoned for five months, in 2007, for inciting racial hatred, he placed his faith in Allah and called himself a martyr. During his time in the jail of Bois d'Arcy, to the west of Versailles, until his release at the end of last year, Kémi's blog was regularly updated on his website and his supporters spoke of his being *embastillé*, locked up in the Bastille.

The Tribu Ka are regarded as the real masters of Bagneux. 'Those guys are mad fuckers,' I was told by Kevin, my guide through the suburbs.

Kémi has a variety of modes of dress, ranging from Afro-centric gear to suits in the style of Afro-American intellectuals of the Black Panther generation. Tribu Ka are having a discernible impact on France: if you are hassled by tough black kids in the shopping centre at Les Halles in central Paris, they will often be wearing the Tribu Ka's colours of black, red and yellow, or the insignia GKS (Génération

Kémi Seba). This happens less than half a mile away from the rue des Rosiers where, in May 2006, the Tribu Ka marched, chanting anti-Semitic slogans, and launched 'a declaration of war against Jews' while attacking anyone in their path with baseball bats. Two months later, they launched a raid to 'take back African treasures' from the new museum of colonial history at Quai Branly.

Tribu Ka are now banned on the orders of President Sarkozy, but they are set to return to the political front line with Génération Kémi Seba. This new group is effectively the Tribu Ka, reinvented and well organized, but with a new media-friendly profile; support is professed on their website by rappers such as ragga star Princess Erika, and Orosko Racim of Ghetto Fabulous Gang. One of Kémi's defenders is the mainstream black comedian Dieudonné, who was once as mild and inoffensive, and as popular, as the black British comic Lenny Henry. Now, Dieudonné has become widely known for his virulent anti-Semitism.

Kémi's website is still publishing his speeches on the end of the white and Jewish races. He remains an accomplished public speaker and a master of double-talk. His interviews and speeches on YouTube are models of chilling self-righteousness, and he is seldom seen without two menacing guards at his side. For several weeks I tried to arrange a meeting with him. I was told by an intermediary that 'Kémi will speak soon. But he doesn't want to speak to the white press you represent. His time will come later. This will be when the white press is no more.'

I was then told that they knew who I was and it might be wise to leave them alone. Or stay out of Bagneux.

'I understand Kémi,' I was told by a friend, a young black woman. She has a degree, a good job in publishing and a white boyfriend who is a lawyer. 'Only if you are black or Arab in France can you understand the contempt people feel for you, and the hate and desire for revenge that this inspires in you. Kémi is nasty but I understand his appeal. He is about war and violence. What angry young man in the banlieue doesn't feel the same at some point? It's the same for the Taliban as the youth in the banlieue: they are fighting to let us know that they exist and that they hate society as it is. They feel that the Jews rule the world, and from one point of view it can look that way. They see Iraq and Gaza and Rwanda and Kenya and the Jews of Paris or New York who have profited from their pain. To them, it all makes sense.'

It would naturally be foolish to describe everyone in the banlieue as an anti-Semite. But there is a prevailing anti-Semitic, and indeed anti-European, mentality there, the anguish and prejudice of the truly lost. From the most moderate voices to the extremists of Tribu Ka, anti-Semitism is a binding cultural force, a singular bigotry in which genuine and complex historical grievances and pan-Arab sympathies cohere in disfigured form. What makes the events there so troubling is that they don't conform to any previously established pattern of revolt. French historians have written of *le passage à l'acte*, of the moment when a society passes into revolutionary violence, which is precipitated by a confluence of negative forces: bad government, poverty and hunger. But what is happening in the banlieue is different – which may explain why French intellectuals have been so notably silent on the subject. What is happening there is perhaps best understood in the language of psychoanalysis, because the violence seems more and more to be an expression of post-colonial trauma, the kind of 'motherless rage' that Frantz Fanon diagnosed so acutely as the defining condition of post-independence Algeria.

France may be in Europe but many of its fears and nightmares began during the brutal Algerian War of Independence. It was during this conflict that many horrors of our new century – asymmetric war against Muslim terror groups, the systematic use of torture in the name of democracy – were first deployed. France may be unique among Western European nations in refusing to recognize its colonial crimes: deeply embedded in the psyche of political parties of the Left and Right is the idea that the French colonial empire performed a mission *civilatrice*, a 'civilising mission', imposing universal republican values on the 'uncivilized' world. This 'mission' was less about capital and commodity than an explicitly political task of exporting 'Frenchness'. The loss of Algeria was, following this logic, less like losing a dependent colony than the sudden death of a family member. The bereavement continues to affect both colonizer and colonized.

France is far from coming to terms with the repressed memories of its colonial past. Like the dead Algerians who were thrown into the Seine in 1961, and whose bloated corpses shocked ordinary Parisians when they were found in the days after the massacre on the Pont de Neuilly, these memories are once more resurfacing to provoke new and fresh anxieties.

Back in the banlieue the rioters, wreckers, even the killers of Ilan Halimi, are not looking for reform or revolution. They are looking for revenge. Their rage is often expressed symbolically: the appropriation of the language of the Intifada, which, at its origin, was a spontaneous and legitimate uprising against oppression; the speaking of Arabic slang, the waving of the Algerian flag and the provocative wearing of the veil. These are all acts directed at subverting the French Republic. For many Parisians, the banlieue represents 'otherness' – the otherness of exclusion, of the repressed, of the fearful and despised. Until this ceases to be the case, the unacknowledged civil war between Paris and its disturbed suburbs will go on. The positions and tactics of the immigrants of the banlieue – their identification with Palestine, their hatred of France – reveal the struggle to be part of the Long War every bit as much as those caught up in the conflicts in Iraq and Afghanistan.

In the nineteenth century, Charles Baudelaire wrote of Paris being haunted by its past, by 'ghosts in daylight'. In the early twenty-first century, the ghosts of colonial and anti-colonial assassins, from Algeria to Beirut, from Congo to Rwanda, continue to be visible in the daylight of the banlieue. It may be that what France needs is not hardheaded political solutions or even psychiatry, but an exorcist.

KASHMIR'S FOREVER WAR

Basharat Peer

On an early December morning in 2009, I was on a flight home to Kashmir. It doesn't matter how many times I come back, the frequency of arrival never diminishes the joy of homecoming – even when home is the beautiful, troubled, war-torn city of Srinagar. Frozen crusts of snow on mountain peaks brought the first intimation of the valley. Silhouettes of village houses and barren walnut trees appeared amid a sea of fog. On the chilly tarmac, my breath formed rings of smoke.

The sense of siege outside the airport was familiar. Olive-green military trucks with machine guns on their turrets, barbed wire circling the bunkers and checkposts. Solemn-faced soldiers in overcoats patrolled with assault rifles at the ready, subdued by the bitter chill of Kashmiri winter. The streets were quiet, the naked rain-washed brick houses lining them seemed shrunken. Men and women walked quietly on the pavements, their pale faces reddened by the cold draughts.

In Kashmir, winter is a season of reflection, a time of reprieve. The guns fall silent and for a while one can forget the long war that has been raging since 1990. In the fragile peace that nature had imposed, I slipped into a routine of household chores: buying a new gas heater for Grandfather; picking up a suit from Father's tailor; lazy lunches of a lamb ribcage delicacy with reporter friends; teaching young cousins to make home videos on my computer. Yet I opened the morning papers with a sense of dread, a fear of seeing a headline printed in red, the colour in which they prefer to announce yet another death – the continuing cost of our troubled recent history.

Political discontent has simmered in the Indian-controlled sector of Kashmir since partition in 1947, when Hari Singh, the Hindu maharaja of the Muslim-majority state, joined India after a raid by tribals from Pakistan. The agreement of accession that Singh signed with India in October 1947 gave Kashmir much autonomy; India controlled only defence, foreign affairs and telecommunications. But, in later years, India began to erode Kashmir's autonomy by imprisoning popularly elected leaders and appointing quiescent puppet administrators who helped extend Indian jurisdiction. India and Pakistan have fought three wars over Kashmir since then. In 1987, the government in Indian-controlled Kashmir rigged a local election, after which Kashmiris lost the little faith they had in India and began a secessionist armed uprising with support from Pakistan. The Indian military presence rose to half a million and by the mid-Nineties Islamist militants from Pakistan began to dominate the rebellion. The costs of war have been high: around 70,000 people have been killed since 1990; another 10,000 have gone missing after being arrested. Although there has been a decline in violence in the past few years and the number of active militants has reduced to around five hundred, more than half a million Indian troops remain in Kashmir, making it the most militarized place in the world. India and Pakistan have come dangerously close to war several times – once after the terrorist attacks on the Indian parliament in 2001, and more recently after the attacks on Mumbai in November 2008.

And the attacks continue. A few weeks after I left Kashmir again, on the cold afternoon of 7 January, two young men walked through a crowd of shoppers in the Lal Chowk area in Srinagar. They passed bookshops, garment stores, hotels, and walked towards the Palladium Cinema, which once screened Bollywood movies and Hollywood hits such as *Saturday Night Fever*, and was now, like most theatres in Kashmir, occupied by Indian troops. As they neared the Palladium, the two men took out the Kalashnikovs they had been hiding and fired several shots in the air. One threw a grenade at a paramilitary bunker. Passers-by rushed into shops for safety; shopkeepers downed the shutters. Hundreds of armed policemen and soldiers drove from the military and police camps nearby, surrounded the hotel and began firing. The hotel caught fire.

The fighting continued for twenty-seven hours before the two militants were killed. The police announced that the militants were from the Pakistan-based terrorist group Lashkar-e-Taiba (the Army of the Pure), which had also been responsible for the November 2008 attacks on Mumbai. One of them was from Pakistan. Although most of the Kashmiri guerrillas who had started the war are either dead or have laid down their arms, the second militant, Manzoor Bhat, was a twenty-year-old from a village near the northern Kashmir town of Sopore. I was curious about what had led Bhat to join one of the most dangerous Islamist militant groups, many of whose members are from Pakistan.

I left my parents' house on a calm May morning of no news and began driving out of the city to Bhat's home. The village of Seer Jagir is a palette of apple trees and rice paddies, brown wood and brick houses. Old men smoked hookahs and chatted by shop fronts in the village market. Schoolboys in white-and-grey uniforms waited for the local bus. Everyone knew where Manzoor, the martyr, lived. On the outskirts of the village an old man and a boy sat by a cowshed. The sombre-faced boy in a blue *pheran* was Bhat's brother. He led me past the cowshed to an austere, double-storeyed house. His mother, Hafiza, a wiry woman in her late forties, joined us a few minutes later. She wore a floral suit and a loosely tied headscarf. 'I was feeding the cows,' she said in apology. Hafiza and her husband, Rasul Bhat, had three sons: an older one who worked in a car garage; the youngest son, the student who sat with us; and Manzoor, the dead militant. Though the Bhats lived amid a great expanse of fertile fields and orchards, they owned only a small patch of land, which produced barely enough rice to feed the family. Bhat gave up his studies after ninth grade and began work as an apprentice to a house painter. He learned fast and had in the past few years painted most of the houses in the neighbouring villages. 'He made around 8–9,000 rupees [US$200] a month,' Hafiza told me. 'He bought the spices, the rice, the oil, the soap. He ran the house.' She fell silent, her eyes fixed on a framed picture of Manzoor: a round, ruddy face, shiny black eyes and a trimmed beard. I was struck by the younger brother muttering something, repeating his words like a chant. 'He bought me clothes and shoes. He bought me clothes and shoes.'

On 1 September 2008, Bhat left home in the morning, ostensibly for work. He stopped in the courtyard and greeted his mother as usual. It was the first day of Ramadan. He didn't return in the evening. Hafiza and Rasul assumed their son had stayed with a friend. They got another friend of his to call the phone Bhat had recently purchased; it was switched off. They tried again the next morning; the phone was still off. 'We feared he might have been arrested by the military,' Hafiza said. Rasul went to a police station and filed a report about his missing son. Then he went to several military and paramilitary camps in the area, seeking information. A police officer told him that his son had joined the militants.

And here we have a familiar story. Two weeks before Bhat signed up, he had joined a pro-freedom march from the nearby town of Sopore towards the militarized Line of Control, the de facto border.

The protests were provoked by a land dispute with the government and quickly morphed into a call for independence.

On 11 August, Bhat and his fellow protesters marched on the Jhelum Valley road which had connected Kashmir with the cities of Rawalpindi and Lahore prior to partition, before the Line of Control stopped all movement of people and goods between the two parts of Kashmir. When the protesters – riding on buses, trucks and tractors – reached the village of Chahal, fifteen miles from the Line of Control, Indian troops opened fire. Manzoor saw unarmed fellow protesters being hit by bullets and falling on the mountainous road. Four were killed at Chahal, including a sixty-year-old separatist leader, Sheikh Abdul Aziz. In the months that followed, the scene in Chahal was repeated as hundreds of thousands of Kashmiris responded, marching in peaceful protests. They were often met with gunfire. By early September 2008, an estimated sixty protesters had been killed, and up to six hundred reported bullet injuries. Kashmir was silent and seething, crouching like a wildcat. Indian paramilitaries and police were everywhere, armed with automatic rifles and tear-gas guns.

Many of the injured from across Kashmir had been brought to the SMHS Hospital in central Srinagar. The hospital complex is surrounded by pharmacies and old buildings with rusted tin roofs. The surgical casualty ward has a strong phenyl smell, the cries of the sick and the wails of relatives echoing against its concrete walls. Here I met Dr Arshad Bhat (no relation to Manzoor), a thin, lanky man in his late twenties. The night before Manzoor Bhat, the would-be militant, saw protesters being shot near the Line of Control, Dr Bhat slept uneasily on a tiny hospital bed in the doctors' room. The next morning he walked into the surgical emergency room with five other surgeons at nine-thirty. He and his colleagues were expecting an influx of wounded protesters. Within two hours, streams of them, hit by police fire, were pouring in. He summoned every team of surgeons in the hospital; some thirty doctors arrived and by the end of the day they had treated a few hundred people with grave bullet wounds. 'We might have saved more,' he told me, his voice full of regret, 'if they had not tear-gassed the operating theatre.'

Several young men I interviewed pointed to the killings during the protests of 1990 to explain their decision to join militant groups. Yasin Malik, then a wiry twenty-year-old from Srinagar, worked for the opposition during the rigged 1987 election campaign. After the election, many opposition activists, including Malik, were jailed and tortured. Malik and his friends decided to take up arms against Indian rule and cross over to Pakistan for training after their release. By the winter of 1990, Malik was leading the Jammu and Kashmir Liberation Front (JKLF), a guerrilla group that became the focus of overwhelming popular support.

'Self-determination is our birthright!' – all of Kashmir was on the streets shouting it. In those heady days, an independent Kashmir seemed eminently possible. But India deployed several hundred thousand troops to crush the rebellion; military and paramilitary camps and torture chambers sprang up across the region. Indian soldiers opened fire on pro-independence protesters so frequently that the latter lost count of the casualties. Before long, thousands of young Kashmiris were crossing into Pakistan-administered Kashmir for arms training, returning as militants carrying Kalashnikovs and rocket launchers supplied by Pakistan's Inter-Services Intelligence Agency (ISI). Assassinations of pro-India Muslim politicians and prominent figures from the small pro-India Hindu minority followed, leading to the exodus of more than a hundred thousand Hindus to India.

Pakistan was wary of the JKLF's popularity, its demand for an independent Kashmir, and chose to support several pro-Pakistan militant groups who attacked and killed Malik's men. Indian troops killed many more. Malik spent a few years in prison in the early

Nineties; his body still carries the torture marks as reminders. In prison, he read works by Gandhi and Mandela. On his release in 1994, he abandoned violent politics, turned the JKLF into a peaceful political organization and joined a separatist coalition called the Hurriyat (Freedom) Conference, which pushed for a negotiated settlement of the Kashmir dispute.

By the time Malik came out of prison, however, a pro-Pakistan militant group called Hizbul Mujahideen dominated the fight against India. Its leader was Syed Salahuddin, a Kashmiri politician turned militant who had been a candidate for Kashmir's assembly in the 1987 elections. By the late Nineties, most of Hizbul Mujahideen's Kashmiri fighters had either been killed in battles with Indian forces or arrested, or had spent time in Indian prisons and returned to civilian life, like Malik's men. Pakistan's ISI began backing jihadi groups like Lashkar-e-Taiba, which had no roots in Kashmir politics and were motivated by the idea of a pan-Islamist jihad. Hafiz Muhammad Saeed, a Lahore-based former university professor and veteran of the Afghan jihad, heads the Lashkar-e-Taiba. Most of Saeed's recruits came from the poverty-stricken areas of Pakistan's Punjab province. The jihadis from Pakistan introduced suicide bombings and took the war to major Indian cities – most dramatically with their attack on the Indian parliament in 2001, which brought India and Pakistan to the brink of full-scale confrontation.

Yet by late 2003, after vigorous American and British diplomatic intervention, a peace process between India and Pakistan was under way. The insurgency began to wane. Pakistan reduced its support to insurgent groups and India's long campaign of counter-insurgency appeared to be a success. However, Kashmir remains heavily militarized, and the abuse of civilians by Indian security forces continues, fuelling more rage and attracting recruits for Islamist radicals like Saeed.

*

The dead speak in Kashmir, often more forcefully than the living. Khurram Parvez, a thirty-two-year-old activist, is part of a Srinagar-based human rights advocacy group, the Jammu and Kashmir Coalition of Civil Society (JKCCS), which produced a report in 2009 exposing hundreds of unidentified graves in the Kashmiri countryside. We met in a garden cafe in Srinagar. Parvez, a tall, robust man with intense black eyes, walks with a slight limp. In the autumn of 2002, he was monitoring local elections in a village near the Line of Control. As he drove out of the village with a convoy of military trucks ahead of him, a group of militants hiding nearby detonated an improvised explosive device which blew up under his car. The driver and his friend and colleague, a young woman, Aasiya Jeelani, died in the attack. Parvez lost his right leg. Several months later, with the help of a German-made prosthetic, he began to walk again and returned to work. 'I couldn't give up,' he said softly. His engagement with the pursuit of justice in Kashmir has been personal from the beginning. His grandfather, a sixty-four-year-old trader, was one of the protesters killed by the Indian paramilitaries on the Gawkadal Bridge in January 1990. For months, Parvez had thought of taking up arms in revenge, but was persuaded to stay in school by his family. They lived on Gupkar Road, where the Indian security forces ran some of the most notorious detention and torture centres in Kashmir. Almost every other day, he saw desperate parents walking to the gates of the detention centres in his neighbourhood, looking for their missing sons.

Parvez's cousin and mentor, the lawyer Parvez Imroz, co-founded the Association of Parents of Disappeared Persons, along with a Srinagar housewife Parveena Ahangar, whose son, Javed, had been missing since early 1990, when he was seventeen, after being taken from their home in a night raid by the Indian Army. Ahangar and Imroz campaigned for information about the whereabouts of 10,000 people who had disappeared in Kashmir after being taken into custody by Indian troops and police. Parvez joined them full-time after graduating from college; by late 2005, when a devastating earthquake struck Kashmir's border areas, he was a veteran of civil rights activism. 'We were doing relief work in the earthquake-hit areas when we began hearing about mass graves of unidentified people,' he told me. His group placed several advertisements in Kashmiri papers requesting that people contact them with any information they had about the unidentified graves. Parvez, Imroz and a few other activists travelled widely, documenting this information. Their report, 'Buried Evidence', startled Kashmir.

At Kupwara in northern Kashmir, miles of lush green paddy fields spread out from the fringes of the run-down, cluttered town square. A short walk from the market, Shabir, a young shopkeeper, and I climbed up to a small plateau of walnut trees, willows and vegetable gardens, which was also one of the biggest graveyards described in the report Parvez's group had produced. Unmarked graves covered with wild grass stretched ahead of us in neat rows. Shabir and others from the neighbourhood had placed a tiny white plaque on each grave, with a number and the date of burial. The number on the latest grave read: 241. 'The police would bring the bodies and say they were militants killed in encounters or on the border,' Shabir told me. 'A lot of the faces would be disfigured. Some were mere teenagers, some older.' I had heard similar accounts on visits to other such sites in the area. 'We have no way of knowing who these people really are,' Shabir continued. Parvez had sent a copy of the report to the head of the Kashmir government. Nothing happened.

Civilians continue to be killed and described as terrorists. In April, a spokesman for the Indian Army announced that the troops had killed the 'oldest militant' operating in Kashmir. Aged seventy, Habibullah Khan was from the village of Devar on the slopes of a mountain range by the border in the Lolab Valley, an hour and a half from Kupwara town.

Khan had had a tiny patch of land, not enough to feed his entire family. He and his three sons worked as labourers and sold timber they gathered in the forest to make ends meet. In the early Nineties, one of Khan's sons crossed the border into Pakistan and stayed there. In the summer of 1999, his oldest son, Ahmedullah, left to fetch wood in the forest; Indian troops patrolling there suspected he was a militant and shot him.

By 2003, Khan couldn't work any more because of ill health. In desperation, he took to begging in the nearby town of Sogam. 'I couldn't stop him,' his remaining son, Raj Muhammad, told me. On the morning of 11 April, Khan left for Sogam, where he would normally spend the day in the market, outside a mosque, returning in the evening with whatever generous strangers had given him. He never returned home.

On the fifth day of his father's absence, having made enquiries in the neighbouring villages, Raj Muhammad travelled to Kupwara. He heard talk about the army killing of a seventy-year-old militant in the forests of Handwara District, a couple of hours from his village. In a press release, the Indian Army claimed that they had shot him in a joint operation with the police and that an AK-47 rifle, four magazines and sixty-seven bullets were recovered.

Raj Muhammad went to the police station closest to the shooting. 'A police officer we met showed me a picture of the dead man on his cellphone screen,' he said. 'It was my father.' He was granted permission to exhume his father's body from the graveyard where he had been buried as an unidentified militant.

Two decades of insurgency and counter-insurgency have resulted in the creation of a state of affairs that provides incentives to troops and policemen to show 'kills'. Those involved in counter-insurgency in Kashmir receive fast-track promotions, as well as monetary and other rewards for getting results. In February, the Indian government awarded one of the highest civilian honours, the Padma Shri, to

Ghulam Muhammad Mir, a notorious counter-insurgent who worked with the Indian troops in central Kashmir and has several murder and extortion charges still pending against him. One of India's top bureaucrats, Home Secretary G. K. Pillai, told a television channel, 'Mir had done yeoman's service for the national cause.'

Two highly controversial Indian laws, the Armed Forces Special Powers Act and the Disturbed Areas Act, which have been in operation for twenty years, give the troops stationed in Kashmir the power to shoot any person they suspect of being a threat, and guarantee impunity from prosecution. To bring a soldier before a civilian court, India's Home Ministry has to remove his immunity and grant the Kashmir government permission to prosecute him. More than 400 such cases are still waiting for that permission.

All this has taken its toll. Srinagar used to be a city of elegant latticed houses, mosques and temples on the banks of the river. Srinagar was people strolling on the wooden bridges and wandering into old bazaars or stepping with a prayer into a Sufi shrine with papier-mâché interiors. Now it is a city of bunkers, a medieval city dying in a modern war. One of the most prominent landmarks of war is the sprawling Martyrs' Graveyard in north-western Srinagar; several hundred Kashmiris killed in the early days of the conflict are buried here. Among them is a well-known politician and head cleric of Srinagar grand mosque, Moulvi Mohammed Farooq, who was assassinated by pro-Pakistan militants on 21 May 1990. More than sixty mourners were killed when Indian paramilitaries fired upon his funeral procession. The cleric's eighteen-year-old son, Omar Farooq, left school to inherit his father's mantle. He is now one of the best-known Kashmiri separatists, heading the Hurriyat (Freedom) Conference coalition.

A few days before the twentieth anniversary of his father's assassination, I walked past the Martyrs' Graveyard to an old wooden mosque nearby, where Farooq was holding a meeting with his supporters. In an elegant brown lambskin cap and delicately embroidered beige gown, he deftly mixed his roles as a modern politician and the head cleric in Kashmir's Sufi tradition, leading his followers in a sing-song voice humming Kashmiri and Persian devotional songs and then moving effortlessly to the question of Kashmiri politics. He spoke of the memory of the thousands who had died in the battles for Kashmir, including his father. He spoke of preventing further deaths. And then the old Kashmiri slogans for independence followed. 'Kashmir is for Kashmiris!' Farooq shouted. 'We will decide our destiny!' the people replied. He was about to lead a march through the city. Outside, excited young supporters were revving up their motorbikes and raising flags on cars.

Over the years, Farooq has engaged with both India and Pakistan and sought to rally the Kashmiris towards a peaceful agreement, often at a high personal price. In 2004, after failed peace talks with India, pro-Pakistan militants assassinated his uncle. Farooq had become cautious but participated when the Indian and Pakistani governments started secret talks to find a way to resolve the Kashmiri crisis. 'I met both Pervez Musharraf and Manmohan Singh and argued for de-militarizing Kashmir. Musharraf was sympathetic to Kashmiri concerns and Manmohan Singh said most things were possible except redrawing the borders,' Farooq told me. India and Pakistan agreed to withdraw their troops from the region gradually, as violence declined. It would be a great leap for the two countries, who had been stuck with their competing, aggressive nationalisms for around sixty years. This framework for the resolution of the dispute was due to be announced in 2007. In the spring of that year, Farooq was preparing a campaign in Kashmir to build public support for the deal. 'It was supposed to be an interim arrangement for the next five or ten years and then the people of Kashmir, India and Pakistan could make a call and move towards a final arrangement,' Farooq said.

However, things fell apart as Musharraf lost power and Pakistan was bogged down in a series of bombings by the Taliban and the takeover of the Swat Valley in the North West Frontier Province. In November 2008, while India was struggling to curb the biggest wave of pro-independence protests since 1990, a group of terrorists from Lashkar-e-Taiba attacked Mumbai. The peace process came to an abrupt end. In the two years that followed, hundreds of lives were lost in Kashmir and the tales of repression and protest drowned any hope of any settlement.

Since then, Kashmir's youngest generation has started a Palestinian-style intifada against Indian rule. Young Kashmiris, who are coming of age with war, cable television, mobile phones and the Internet and are exposed to political images from other conflicts, see echoes of the Israeli occupation of Hebron and Gaza in India's military control of Kashmir. Palestinian stone-throwers become their inspiration. The nucleus of the intifada is the vast square and maze of lanes around Srinagar's grand mosque, an elegant structure of fine brick and filigreed wooden columns which rises like a trapezium to meet its pagoda-like roof. Two summers ago, when the stone-pelting battles between Kashmiri teenagers and Indian paramilitaries and police were nascent, I spent a few days hanging out around the grand mosque. One Friday afternoon, after the faithful had left, and the shops had closed for prayers and remained closed, fearing *kani jung*, or the 'war of stones', I stood behind an arched gate. Paramilitaries and policemen carrying assault rifles, tear-gas guns and bulletproof shields, stood in a semicircle staring down at the growing crowd of teenagers and young men in their early twenties, wearing jeans, stylish T-shirts, trainers and Palestinian scarves and masks, armed with lumps of brick and stones.

A sudden volley of bricks tore through the nervous silence and struck an armoured car that charged at the boys, firing a burst of shells. Pungent tear gas filled the square; the stone-throwers scampered for cover. The soldiers made a ferocious charge, waving batons and raising a roar. The stone-throwers had melted into the houses, alleys and nooks they knew by heart. Soon a barrage of rocks came flying from balconies and narrow lanes, sending the soldiers retreating to their earlier positions. Stones, tear gas, stones, tear gas. And so it went on. I stood there watching the clashes, until the sun was about to set and the police officer in charge called it a day. A celebratory roar rose from the rebellious crowd. In a brief moment of reprieve I had asked a police officer what he made of the stone-throwers. 'It is a blood sport; it gives them a big kick,' he said calmly. 'When they push the police back, they feel like they have pushed India out of Kashmir.'

These clashes have grown increasingly violent. Hundreds have been injured. Many have died, including bystanders. The police launched a serious crackdown earlier in the summer and arrested around three hundred stone-throwers between the ages of fifteen and eighteen. But the news of death is frequent in Kashmir and so are occasions of protest. Another generation of young Kashmiris is being consumed by war.

I met up with some of this new generation in a college not far from the grand mosque. Wary of police informers, they refused to talk in the college cafeteria and led me instead to an empty classroom. They sat on wooden chairs, in a semicircle facing me, textbooks jutting out of their bags. As we made small talk, a wisp of a boy with curly gelled hair, wearing a white linen shirt, blue denims and black Converse trainers, played with his mobile phone. 'He is the commander of our group,' one of them said, half joking. The boy smiled. 'You can write about us, but don't use our real names. We will be arrested if we are identified.' His voice was measured, grave. I agreed. 'Call me Shahbaaz,' he said. Shahbaaz – the falcon. The boys laughed.

A friend of Shahbaaz's passed me his phone. 'That's him in a protest after Wamiq was killed.' I had read about Wamiq Farooq, a fourteen-year-old student who was killed when troops fired at a crowd of boys after a clash in January. I looked at the picture on the phone: a masked boy lunging at a bulletproof police car with a stone in his right hand. The memory hardened Shahbaaz's face. 'I was very sad and very angry the day they killed Wamiq. If I had a gun that day, I would have ...'

Shahbaaz was born in the autumn of 1988, a year before the war began, in downtown Srinagar in a middle-class home. His father, a bureaucrat, worked for the local government. In 1991, one of his uncles who had joined a militant group was killed by the military. He did not remember the uncle. His first memory of the war is coming back from school when he was in fourth grade and seeing a big protest pass by his house. The military fired. A boy from his neighbourhood was hit by bullets and died outside his door. 'That was the first time I saw someone being killed,' Shahbaaz said slowly. He remembered feeling angrier after an incident in the autumn of 2000, when he was preparing for his eighth-grade examinations at his maternal grand-father's house. Protesters fired at the paramilitary and killed a soldier and angry troops began house-to-house searches, barging into Shahbaaz's family home. 'A soldier pushed my aunt around and asked where she had hidden the militants. Another soldier began beating my grandfather and asking him questions.' His aunt and grandfather repeatedly told them that nobody had come into their house. A soldier grabbed Shahbaaz by the neck and put a dagger to his throat. 'Tell me where the militants are or I will kill him!' the soldier shouted. After a while, the soldiers left. Shahbaaz stood there shaking in fear and anger. 'I still remember the cold edge of that dagger,' he said, lighting a cigarette.

We left the classroom after a while and walked to Nohata Chowk, the square where Shahbaaz and his friends often clash with the soldiers. Every street corner was a reminder of a battle. 'Here I was hit by a tear-gas shell,' Shahbaaz said, pointing to a communal tap. 'Here I was almost arrested,' said one of his friends, pointing towards an alleyway. We passed the square near the grand mosque and Shahbaaz signalled at a crumbling, empty house by the road.

'This used to be a BSF [Border Security Force] paramilitary camp,' he said. 'Two of my friends were taken there and tortured.' We crossed a small roundabout and the boys stopped and pointed at the plaque on a electricity pole: MARTYR MUNTAZIR SQUARE. DATE OF MARTYRDOM: 7 JULY 2007.

We walked through a labyrinth of lanes and reached an old bridge over the river Jhelum. Shahbaaz talked to me about a boy named Muntazir. 'I was with him when he was shot,' he said. 'We weren't close friends but that day we shared a cigarette before the fighting began.' He didn't remember what had led them to come out on the streets that day. Shahbaaz, Muntazir and a few others were leading the attack on a group of paramilitaries outside the grand mosque. The paramilitaries ran for cover and the boys followed them. Then police came out of an alley and fired. 'Muntazir was hit in the abdomen and shoulder and fell on the street,' Shahbaaz said. 'Two of us picked him up and ran back towards the rest of the boys. The police fired tear-gas shells. The other boy was hit and fell.' Shahbaaz carried Muntazir to the alley where their friends waited. 'I saw some boys run towards us and they took Muntazir. He was bleeding intensely, dying. I fainted.'

We sat on a *ghat* by the banks of the river Jhelum under the bridge. Beautiful old houses with ornate balconies and shingle roofs towered over the river. A lonely-looking soldier stared out of the box-like hole in a bunker on the bridge. Shahbaaz suddenly stopped talking and turned to his friends. 'Look at that!' They rose from the steps we were sitting on and walked closer to the bank. A brown stray dog was struggling to swim his way across the river. The boys debated his chances and stood there until the dog reached the bank. I stood behind them, watching, and hoped they wouldn't end up as plaques in a town square.

I asked about their fears. They could be killed, or arrested and put in a prison for a year or two, which would block most possibilities in the future. 'We too have dreams of a good life. I want to be a computer scientist, but we can't look away when we live under Indian occupation. We aren't fighting for money or personal gain. We are fighting for Kashmir,' Shahbaaz said, looking directly at me. He insisted he was aware of the price he and his friends could pay. 'I was arrested last year. They beat me so hard in the police station that bones in both my legs fractured. I wore plaster and couldn't walk for a few months.' One of his friends, Daniyal, who had sat quietly all this while, spoke up. 'I was arrested after a clash with the CRPF [Central Reserve Police Force]. They took me into a bunker and . . .' He stopped mid-sentence, rolled up the sleeves of his shirt and held out his bare arms. He had been burned with heated iron rods; each arm had four lines of scarred flesh running across it.

Shahbaaz invited me to his house, a short walk away. A car was parked outside the double-storeyed building. We sat in his carpeted room while he switched on his computer and began clicking through a series of videos on the desktop. He played a video from the early Nineties, showing the wreckage of the north Kashmir town of Sopore after its main market had been burned down by Indian soldiers; he played a video of a funeral with relatives crying over the body of a young man shot by the soldiers, and then he played a video of Kashmiri protesters being fired on in Chahal village in August 2008 (the protest that Manzoor Bhat, the house painter turned militant, had been part of). 'How can we forget this?' Shahbaaz said, his eyes on the screen. 'But do you think stone-throwing will make India leave Kashmir?' I asked. 'It makes a difference. We show them that we are not completely helpless,' he replied. Then he lit a cigarette, took a long puff and said, 'We are not using guns. When Kashmiris used guns, the

Indians called us terrorists. Yes, the gun was from Pakistan, but the stones are our own. That is our only weapon against the occupation.' He wanted to show me something else and played a documentary about the life and death of Faris Oudeh, the fifteen-year-old Palestinian boy who was immortalized by an Associated Press photograph taken a few days before his death: a diminutive youth in a baggy sweater, slinging a stone at an Israeli tank some ten metres away. 'He was hit in his neck by an Israeli sniper when he bent to pick up a stone,' Shahbaaz said. 'His friends couldn't get to him, he was so close to the Israeli tank.' As he spoke, Shahbaaz's voice was low and full of passion.

I returned to New York a week later. My thoughts would often drift back to Shahbaaz, as every other day Indian paramilitary and police fired at young boys like him. Each death brought out more protesters and the uniforms would shoot to kill. In the month of June, seventeen boys were killed by Indian troops and Kashmir was under curfew again. A friend wrote in a newspaper article, 'The ages of the boys killed in the past few days read like the scores of a batsman in very bad form ... 17, 16, 15, 13, 9 ...' In Srinagar, the troops attacked the funeral of a young protester. Photojournalists, several of whom were beaten, captured the moment. On a stretcher in the middle of a street is a young man killed by the troops as they went about crushing the protests. Behind his fallen corpse, angry soldiers and policemen assault the pall-bearers and mourners with guns and batons. The mourners run for safety, except for a man in his late fifties: the father trying to save his son's corpse from desecration, spreading himself over the boy, his arms stretched in a protective arc.

I called Shahbaaz several times from New York, but I couldn't reach him. His phone was always switched off.

ARCTIC

Lavinia Greenlaw

There is a place in Lapland called Arctic Circle. You can step across a painted line and receive a certificate, although the actual circle, around 66 degrees latitude North, is unfixed. It wavers over the north like a lasso and slips according to the tilt of the earth on its axis.

Midwinter

The feeling of slippage is immediate. The nights are at least twenty hours long and the world is snow. While my mind gives up trying to keep time, my body clings to any familiar sign of it. The sky pales for three or four hours, although a constant black haze remains over the pole. A small sun inches into view and rolls along the horizon, and the sky takes on a faint wash of yellow and blue. I feel as if I've caught a glimpse of an actual day happening somewhere else. As the sun tips away again, I can't keep my eyes open.

The Arctic Highway runs north from Rovaniemi along a river, only now there is no river, just fields of snow. There is no road, either, and the few cars that come this way follow its compacted grey trace past signs that cannot be read because they, too, have been wiped out. This is fairy-tale snow, hanging in glittering swags from trees which double over under its weight. It emphasizes telegraph wires and heaps up cosily against windows. Snow scatters light and flattens perspective. It is absence and substance at the same time, a perfect form of equilibrium. There is nothing to read in it, just a fundamental continuity that makes every place familiar. I am near the edge of the compass. From the pole, whichever way you head is south.

What does minus fifty mean? That the ink in a pen freezes, that water thrown from a cup turns to ice before it hits the ground, that your lungs might bleed. Even now when buildings are heated and sealed and streets can be as brightly lit as a film set there is an inheritance of cold and darkness.

In a hospital in Lapland I meet a Finnish psychiatrist who is an expert in Arctic Personality Disorder. He says that darkness is less of a problem than the cold; it makes the body hoard blood around the heart, depriving the brain. He explains that the Arctic personality is characterized by *sisu* – adaptability and perseverance. Such people have a tendency to be greedy, stingy and ruthless. They hoard information, are suspicious of strangers and are 'sexually specialized'. His other interest is suicide, and he remarks that women have started to kill themselves in the same way as men. They used to take an overdose or drown themselves, 'so as not to leave a mess', but now they are as likely to use a gun.

This darkness doesn't trouble me. I came to the Arctic having lost my imagination and soon feel restored, not because there is nothing to see but because this is such a fundamental way of seeing. Even when it is cloudy, you can catch sight in the sky of wild streaks, sheets and pillars of gaseous colour. The aurora borealis or Northern Lights are a form of elemental disturbance (electron showers stirring up hydrogen and nitrogen) and the rawness of their colours, like the rawness of that small sunset, suggests a time when light was first occurring. The Finns call the Northern Lights *revontulet* or 'foxfire', after a mythical fox who swept snow into the air with its tail, igniting it. If you talk to the Northern Lights, they will come down and grab you. If you don't wear a hat, they will clutch at your hair.

Not being able to see did not trouble me as I am so short-sighted. My understanding of light begins with fractured auras and haloes, leaky shifting colours and granulated shapes which might or might not become clear. There is a moment, though, when this world becomes very clear indeed, a winter twilight called, in Finnish, *sininen hetki* or the 'blue moment'. It is as if blue light rises out of the snow and, because everything is covered in snow, everything turns blue, so the world is full of its own space and silence and not empty at all.

Midsummer

A night in the port of Bodø in northern Norway, where every building, from the fishery to the church, is compact, functional and low. The town looks as if it has been constructed from a kit and could be packed up and driven off in a single day.

Even softened by cloud, the light is insidious. I am waiting for something to happen, for the sky to break, but nothing will happen and all night people circle the harbour square or ride back and forth in cars and on motorbikes, just passing the time. I lie down for three hours and, once or twice, dip into sleep.

The next day the ferry sails for five hours towards a dark line that breaks down into islands. Their cliffs are so sheer that they veer away from themselves and each island sits in black shadow, giving the impression that it is hovering on the sea. Everything is unanchored. There are too many islands, too much water and too much light.

Vaerøy is one of the Lofoten Islands. Here, the sun does not rise for a month in winter; nor does it set for two months in midsummer. The beach is little more than a ledge of blanched sand; the sea is so thickened by cold and light that it might be glass. For now it is calm, but whatever washes up has been pounded and scoured: heaps of stones worn into huge, beautiful eggs shot through with quartz, a sheep's vertebrae, eye socket and jaw as smooth as paper, translucent shells of crabs, sea urchins and limpets, fraying husks of seaweed.

This is bird land. Their eggs are hidden beneath my feet among the egg-shaped stones. There are no trees so they make do with ground cover: rock, gorse and grass. Oystercatchers run past screaming, warning or distracting. Redshanks blurt from fence posts, their nests scattered among whatever grass they can find. Masses of gulls and terns explode out of the cliffs. Crows mob the oystercatchers, after their fledglings. Cormorants wheel and dive. Auks come onto land to breed. They nest on high ledges and lay eggs which have evolved into a tear shape so that they won't roll.

Midsummer is the feast of John the Baptist. Tonight the trolls come out to make mischief and the witches go to meet the devil on the mountain top. By late afternoon, the sun begins to make its way from stage left. People appear along the coast building fires. They share the traditional midsummer feast of dark beer, salami and semolina, but this is no raucous affair. The light is so bright that the flames are invisible. There are no leaping shadows. People gather round long enough to make sure that their unwanted furniture and tyres have properly caught light, and then they go home, long before midnight.

I wait on the beach as the sun makes its way to the centre of the view. At midnight exactly it starts to sink down on to the sea, so smoothly that it looks like a ball about to bounce. And then it does bounce, off the horizon. It is immediately rising again. I feel thrown into reverse. For all my years in the city, in London, my nights manipulated by tungsten, neon and sodium, halogen and sixty-watt bulbs, traffic lights, street lights and security lights, my body insists that this is wrong.

It is wrong to be able to see so far and so clearly that the earth curves, wrong to have a fifty-foot shadow, wrong to be sleepless and wrong to be so happy. Light meets every thought and glance. I have no imagination here.

CONTRIBUTORS

Decca Aitkenhead, b. 1971, is an author and journalist who writes for the *Guardian*. She has previously worked for the London *Evening Standard*, the *Independent*, the *Observer* and the *Sunday Telegraph*. Her first book, *The Promised Land: Travels in Search of the Perfect E.*, about global club culture, was published by Fourth Estate in 2002.

John Borneman, b. 1952, is Professor of Anthropology at Princeton University. He has been guest professor in Sweden, Norway, and France, Germany and Syria, and done ethnographic fieldwork in Germany, Central Europe, Lebanon and Syria. His books include *Settling Accounts: Violence, Justice, and Accountability in Postsocialist Europe* (1997), *Syrian Episodes: Sons, Fathers, and an Anthropologist in Aleppo* (2007), and *Political Crime and the Memory of Loss: Events of Closure, Rites of Repetition, and Accountability* (2011).

James Buchan, b. 1954, is the author of seven novels, including *A Parish of Rich Women* (1984), which won the Whitbread Book of the Year Award and the Betty Trask Award, and *Heart's Journey in Winter*, which won the *Guardian* Fiction Prize in 1995. His non-fiction books include *Adam Smith and the Pursuit of Liberty* (2006). His most recent novel, *The Gate of Air* (2008), was nominated for the 2009 Ondaatje

Prize. He is a former correspondent for the *Financial Times* and contributes regularly to the *London Review of Books* and the *Guardian*.

Bruce Chatwin (1940–89) was a novelist and travel writer. His works include *In Patagonia, The Songlines,* and a collection of essays, *What Am I Doing Here?* In 1982 his novel *On the Black Hill* won the James Tait Black Memorial Prize and was later adapted for a film, as was his first novel *The Viceroy of Ouidah* (as *Cobra Verde*). His last novel, *Utz* (1988), was shortlisted for the Booker Prize. A special travel issue, *Granta 26,* 1989, was dedicated to him after his death.

Pierre Clastres (1934–77) was a French anthropologist and ethnographer. His book *The Chronicle of the Guayaki Indians* (1972) was the result of his experiences of living with the Paraguayan tribe from 1963 to 1964. He is credited with having helped overturn anthropological orthodoxy in the 1970s, his most famous work being *Society Against the State*, published in 1974.

Lavinia Greenlaw, b. 1962, is a poet and novelist. Her 2003 collection, *Minsk*, was shortlisted for the T. S. Eliot, Forward and Whitbread poetry prizes. Her latest book of poems is *The Casual Perfect* (2011). She has published two novels, *Mary George of Allnorthover* (2001) and *An Irresponsible Age* (2006) and two non-fiction books: *The Importance of Music to Girls* (2007) and *Questions of Travel: William Morris and Iceland* (2011). A sound work, *Audio Obscura*, was commissioned by Artangel and the Manchester International Festival in 2011. She is Professor of Creative Writing at the University of East Anglia

James Hamilton-Paterson, b. 1941, is a travel writer, novelist and poet. He left the United Kingdom twenty-seven years ago and since then has lived mainly in Italy and the Philippines. His first book, *Gerontius* (1989), won the Whitbread First Novel Award (now the Costa); his novels since have included *Griefwork* (1994), *Ghosts of Manila* (1994) and *Loving Monsters* (2001). His non-fiction books include *Three Miles Down* (1990), *America's Boy* (1998) and *Empire of the Clouds* (2010).

Andrew Hussey, b. 1963, is Dean of the University of London Institute in Paris and a regular contributor to the *Guardian* and the *New Statesman*. He is the author of *The Game of War: The Life and Death of Guy Debord* (2001), and *Paris: The Secret History* (2006). In 2009, he wrote and presented a documentary, *France on a Plate*, for BBC Four, which explored the relationship between food and the health of French democracy. He was awarded an OBE in the 2011 New Years Honours list for services to cultural relations between the United Kingdom and France.

Ian Jack, b. 1945, was the editor of *Granta* magazine from 1995 to 2007 and previously the editor of the *Independent on Sunday*. His contributions to *Granta*, beginning in 1987, include pieces on the killing of three IRA members in Gibraltar, the *Titanic*, the Hatfield rail disaster and the singer Kathleen Ferrier. He has published three books, most recently an essay collection, *The Country Formerly Known as Great Britain* (2009), and an anthology of his writing on India is forthcoming from Penguin India. A Fellow of the Royal Society of Literature, he writes regularly for the *Guardian*.

Kathleen Jamie, b. 1962, is a poet and travel writer. Her poetry collections include *The Tree House* (2004), which won the Forward prize and the Scottish Book of the Year Award, and *Jizzen* (1999), which won the Geoffey Faber Memorial Award. Her travel book about Northern Pakistan, *Among Muslims*, was published in 2002, and her book of essays, *Findings* (2005), was shortlisted for the Ondaatje Prize and the Scottish Arts Council Book of the Year Award. She is part-time Reader in Creative Writing at St Andrews University.

Ryszard Kapuściński (1945–2007) was a Polish historian and journalist who spent much of his life in Africa. His books include *Another Day of Life* (1976) about the war in Angola, where he was the only foreign journalist at the time; *The Emperor* (1978), about the downfall of Haile Selassie in Ethiopia; *Shah of Shahs* (1982), about the revolution in Iran; and *Imperium* (1993), about his relationship with the Soviet Union. *Travels with Herodotus* was published in 2007 shortly before his death.

Thomas Keneally, b. 1935, has published over thirty novels, non-fiction titles, dramas and screenplays. His most famous book, *Schindler's Ark*, won the Booker Prize in 1982 and was later adapted for the award-winning film, *Schindler's List*. Keneally was made an Officer of the Order of Australia in 1983, and in 1997 was named one of 100 Living Treasures by the National Trust of Australia. His latest novel, *The People's Train*, was published in 2009, and a history, *Australians: Volume 1: Origins to Eureka*, in 2010.

Robert Macfarlane, b. 1976, is a British travel writer and literary critic. His first book, *Mountains of the Mind: A History of a Fascination*, won the *Sunday Times* Young Writer of the Year award in 2003 and the *Guardian* First Book Award. His second book, *The Wild Places* (2007), won the Boardman-Tasker Prize for Mountain Literature, and was adapted in 2010 for an episode of the BBC's 'Natural World' series, which Macfarlane presented. *The Old Ways* – the last in his trilogy of books about landscape, travel and imagination – will be published in 2012. He is a Fellow of Emmanuel College, Cambridge.

Albino Ochero-Okello, b. 1956, studied at Makerere University in Kampala before becoming a member of the Uganda People's Congress (UPC) Party in 1979. After the disputed elections of 1980, Uganda's descent into civil war and the overthrow of the military junta in 1986, it became impossible for him to remain in Uganda. In 1988 he fled to the UK and sought political asylum. 'Arrival', first published in Granta 65 in 1999, is the fourth chapter of his unpublished life-story *Lost in London As a Refugee and the Refugee Life*. He is now a caseworker for the British Red Cross.

Andrew O'Hagan, b. 1968, was selected as one of *Granta's* 20 Best of Young British Novelists in 2003. His first book was *The Missing* (1995), which will be adapted by the National Theatre of Scotland in 2011. His first novel, *Our Fathers* (1999), was shortlisted for the Booker Prize and the Whitbread First Novel Award. In 2001 he was named as a UNICEF Goodwill Ambassador and has travelled to Sudan, Mozambique, Malawi and India in aid of its projects. His 2006 novel *Be Near Me* won the Los Angeles Fiction Award. His most recent novel is *The Life and Opinions of Maf the Dog, and of His Friend Marilyn Monroe* (2010). He was made a fellow of the Royal Society of Literature in 2010.

Redmond O'Hanlon, b. 1947, is a travel writer known for his exploration of remote locations. His books include *Into the Heart of Borneo* (1984), *In Trouble Again* (1988), *Congo Basin* (1996) and *Trawler* (2005). He was the natural history editor of the *Times Literary Supplement* for fifteen years and contributed to the 1982 Centennial Commemoration of Charles Darwin. His most recent book, with Rudy Rotthier, is *The Fetish Room: The Education of a Naturalist* (2011). He is a Fellow of the Royal Geographical Society and Royal Society of Literature.

Basharat Peer, b. 1977, is a Kashmiri author and political commentator. He studied political science at Aligarh Muslim University in Uttar Pradesh followed by a master's degree in journalism at Columbia University. He worked as an editor at *Foreign Affairs*, New York, and is a former fellow of the Open Society Foundations. He contributes to the *Guardian, Foreign Affairs,* the *Financial Times, n+1, The Nation, New Statesman,* and *The Caravan,* among other publications. His memoir, <u>*Curfewed Night,*</u> about growing up with the war in Kashmir, was long-listed for the *Guardian* First Book Award in 2010.

<u>**Jonathan Raban**</u>, b. 1942, is a British travel writer, essayist and novelist. His books include *Foreign Land* (1985), *Hunting Mister Heartbreak* (1991), *Bad Land* (1996), *Surveillance* (2006) and, most recently, *Driving Home: An American Scrapbook* (2010). His awards include the Thomas Cook Travel Book Award (twice), the Royal Society of Literature's Heinemann Award, the PEN USA Creative Nonfiction Award, the National Book Critics Circle Award and an honorary doctorate from the University of Hull. He lives in Seattle.

W. G. Sebald (1944–2001) was a German writer and academic. He settled in England in 1970 and joined the University of East Anglia, where he was appointed to a chair in European Literature in 1987 and was founding director of the British Centre for Literary Translation in 1989. *Die Ausgewanderten* (1993, translated as *The Emigrants* in 1996) received eight awards, including the Berlin Literature Prize and a Nesta Fellowship. It was followed by *The Rings of Saturn* (tr. 1998), *Vertigo* (tr. 1999) and *Austerlitz* (tr. 2001). Sebald died in a car crash near Norwich in 2001. *On the Natural History of Destruction,* a collection of essays, was published posthumously in 2003.

Wendell Steavenson, b. 1970, is a journalist and former *Time* correspondent whose work has been published in the *New Yorker, Prospect* and the *Daily Telegraph.* Her first book, *Stories I Stole,* written after two years in post-Soviet Georgia, was shortlisted for the *Guardian* First Book Award in 2002. She has lived and worked in Ethiopia, Iran, Iraq and Lebanon. She drew on her own experiences to write the screenplay for *The Situation* (2006), the first film to address the American occupation of Iraq. Her second book, *The Weight of a Mustard Seed*, was published in January 2009. She is currently based in Egypt from where she reports for the *New Yorker*.

Rory Stewart, b. 1973, is a British writer, academic and politician. In 2010, he left his position as Ryan Family Professor of Human Rights at Harvard University and Director of the John F. Kennedy School of Government Carr Centre for Human Rights Policy when he was elected as Conservative Member of Parliament for Penrith and the Borders. Prior to this, he had served in the British Army, and then with the British Diplomatic Service in Jakarta and Montenegro. Stewart's first book, *The Places in Between*, tells the story of his solo walk across Afghanistan in 2002. Appointed coalition Deputy Governor of two Iraqi provinces in 2003, his second book, *Occupational Hazards: My Year Governing in Iraq*, outlines his experiences there. He established the Turquoise Mountain Foundation to help regenerate Afghanistan's traditional crafts, and remains Executive Chairman.

Paul Theroux, b. 1941, is a travel writer and novelist. In 1963 he worked as a Peace Corps teacher in Malawi and then as a lecturer at Makerere University in Uganda. In the late Sixties he taught English at the University of Singapore before moving to England in 1972. His non-fiction books include *The Great Railway Bazaar* (1975), *The Old Patagonian Express* (1979), *The Pillars of Hercules* (1995), *Sir Vidia's Shadow* (1998) and *Ghost Train to the Eastern Star* (2008). His novels include *The Mosquito Coast* (1981), *My Secret History* (1989) and *A Dead Hand: A Crime in Calcutta* (2009). He divides his time between Cape Cod and the Hawaiian Islands, where he is a professional beekeeper.

Colin Thubron, b. 1939, is a travel writer and novelist. His first books were about the Middle East and Cyprus before, in 1981, he embarked on a journey by car into the Soviet Union, which resulted in *Among the Russians* (1983). His classic travel books followed, among them: *Behind the Wall: A Journey through China* (1987, winner of the Hawthornden Prize and the Thomas Cook Travel Award), *The Lost Heart of Asia* (1994), *In Siberia* (1999, Prix Bouvier), *Shadow of the Silk Road* (2006) and *To a Mountain in Tibet* (2011). He was awarded a CBE in 2008 and became President of the Royal Society of Literature in 2010.

PERMISSIONS